Two Decades of *The ALAN Review*

Two Decades of *The ALAN Review*

Edited by

Patricia P. Kelly
Virginia Polytechnic Institute and State University

Robert C. Small Jr.
Radford University

National Council of Teachers of English
1111 West Kenyon Road, Urbana, Illinois 61801-1096

Prepress Services: Precision Graphics
Staff Editor: Tom Tiller
Interior Design: Doug Burnett
Cover Design: Precision Graphics
Permissions: Kim Black

NCTE Stock Number: 55448-3050

Library of Congress Cataloging-in-Publication Data

Two decades of The ALAN Review / edited by Patricia P. Kelly, Robert C. Small, Jr.
p. cm.
Includes bibliographical references and index.
ISBN 0-8141-5544-8 (pbk.)
1. Young adult literature, American—History and criticism.
2. Young adults—United States—Books and reading. I. Kelly, Patricia P. II. Small, Robert C.
PS490.T88 1999
810.9'9283—dc21 98-55147
CIP

Contents

Introduction
Patricia P. Kelly and Robert C. Small Jr. xi

I. The Authors

Robert Cormier

1. The Pleasures and Pains of Writing a Sequel
Robert Cormier
12.2 Winter 1985, 1–3 3

2. A Telephone Interview with Robert Cormier
Judith Bugniazet
12.2 Winter 1985, 14–18 8

3. Cormier and the Pessimistic View
W. Geiger Ellis
12.2 Winter 1985, 10–12, 52 15

Sue Ellen Bridgers

4. Stories My Grandmother Told Me: Part One
Sue Ellen Bridgers
13.1 Fall 1985, 44–47 23

5. Stories My Grandmother Told Me: Part Two
Sue Ellen Bridgers
13.2 Winter 1986, 53–55, 61 29

6. Responding to the Magic: Sue Ellen Bridgers Talks about Writing
Anthony L. Manna and Sue Misheff
13.2 Winter 1986, 56–61 35

7. Southern Literature for Young Adults: The Novels of Sue Ellen Bridgers
Pamela Sissi Carroll
18.1 Fall 1990, 10–13 45

Paul Zindel

8. Of Fiction and Madness
Paul Zindel
14.1 Fall 1986, 1–8 55

9. The Effect of Gamma Rays on the Man-and-the-Writer Zindel: *The Pigman* Plus Twenty Years and Counting
Mike Angelotti
16.3 Spring 1989, 21–25, 43 67

10. Welcome Back, Zindel
John A. Davis
9.1 Fall 1981, 2–4, 10 79

11. Something Wonderful, Something Beautiful: Adolescent Relationships through the Eyes of Paul Zindel
Kim Hansen
18.2 Winter 1991, 41–43 86

Bette Greene

12. What Does It Feel Like to Be Human?
Bette Greene
11.1 Fall 1983, 1–2, 47–48 95

13. America's Designated Victims: Our Creative Young
Bette Greene
21.2 Winter 1994, 2–4 101

14. Understanding Adolescent Homophobia: An Interview with Bette Greene
Lynne Alvine
21.2 Winter 1994, 5–9 105

Richard Peck

15. Some Thoughts on Adolescent Literature
Richard Peck
3.1 September–October 1975, 4–7 115

16. Ten Questions to Ask about a Novel
Richard Peck
5.3 Spring 1978, 1, 7 120

17. Social Protest in Young Adult Fiction
Hugh Agee
6.2 Winter 1979, 4, 10 122

Hadley Irwin

18. Collaborative Writing for Young Adults
Hadley Irwin
20.1 Fall 1992, 2–7 129

19. Hadley Irwin: A White Writer of Colored Ethnic Fiction
Charles C. Irby
13.3 Spring 1986, 21–24, 50 145

Virginia Hamilton

20. Here's How It Goes: A Tale-Teller's Tale
Virginia Hamilton
6.3 Spring 1979, 1, 8 155

21. The Spirit Spins: A Writer's Resolution
Virginia Hamilton
15.1 Fall 1987, 1–4 158

22. Gothic and Grotesque Effects in Virginia Hamilton's Fiction
Anita Moss
19.2 Winter 1992, 16–20 168

Sandy Asher

23. Best Friends: Talking with Young Readers through My Books
Sandy Asher
17.1 Fall 1989, 1–4 181

24. The Problem with Realism
Sandy Asher
12.3 Spring 1985, 1–3 188

25. Sandy Asher Discusses Writing, Reading, and Teaching
Genny Cramer
15.1 Fall 1987, 44–46, 54 193

II. About Young Adult Literature

26. Twenty Years of YA Books: The Publisher's View
Laurel Barnard, Jean Feiwel, and Marilyn Kriney
15.3 Spring 1988, 48–51 201

27. Rural Youth: The Forgotten Minority
Lin Buswell
11.2 Winter 1984, 12–14 211

28. The Hispanic in Young Adult Literature
Patricia Tarry-Stevens
17.2 Winter 1990, 31–32, 3 217

29. Why the Success of the Teen Romance Depresses Me
Alleen Pace Nilsen
9.2 Winter 1982, 12–14, 39 222

30. Adult Midlife Crisis in Adolescent Novels
Richard F. Abrahamson
8.2 Winter 1981, 29–30, 38 229

31. The Image of Working Blacks in YA Novels
Margaret Bristow
13.1 Fall 1985, 38–40, 55 236

32. Christianity in American Adolescent Realistic Fiction from 1945 to 1981
Julia H. Nixon and Robert C. Small Jr.
12.3 Spring 1985, 9–12, 53 242

33. Touchstones in Nigerian Youth Literature
Osayimwense Osa
15.3 Spring 1988, 56–58 250

34. The Image of the Teacher in Adolescent Fiction
Mary Ann Rygiel
8.2 Fall 1981, 12–15 256

35. The South in Recent Young Adult Novels
Robert C. Small Jr.
13.2 Winter 1986, 62–66 263

36. Appalachian Literature and the Adolescent Reader
Carolyn L. Mathews
11.1 Fall 1983, 11–12, 47–48 270

37. The Search for Identity: A Theme Common to Adolescent and Native American Literature
Raymond D. Kemp Jr.
16.2 Winter 1989, 10, 13 281

38. Before "Teaching" a Novel: Some Considerations
Patricia P. Kelly
11.2 Winter 1984, 36–37, 48 — 285

39. Derek's Story: The Complex History of One Adolescent Reader
Margaret Mackey
20.3 Spring 1993, 39–42 — 289

40. Familiarity with Reference
Donald J. Kenney
19.1 Fall 1991, 48–54 — 297

41. Shift Out of First: Third-Person Narration Has Advantages
Elizabeth C. Schuhmann
9.2 Winter 1982, 40–42, 48 — 314

III. Something about ALAN and *The ALAN Review*

42. A Brief History of ALAN
Ted Hipple — 323

43. The Beginnings of *The ALAN Review*
Alleen Pace Nilsen — 330

44. The *ALAN Newsletter* and *The ALAN Review,* 1978–1984
W. Geiger Ellis — 334

45. Editing *The ALAN Review,* 1984–1990: The Coming-of-Age Years
Arthea J. S. (Charlie) Reed — 338

46. Four Years, Ten Issues, and 560 Pages: The Brief but Happy Life of an *ALAN Review* Co-editor
Leila Christenbury — 344

Index — 351

Editors — 359

Introduction

Patricia P. Kelly
Virginia Polytechnic Institute and State University

Robert C. Small Jr.
Radford University

Since its beginning more than twenty years ago as the *ALAN Newsletter,* the journal now called *The ALAN Review,* has published articles by most of the leading authors of fiction, nonfiction, poetry, and other works of literature for young adults. Its parent organization, the Assembly on Literature for Adolescents of the National Council of Teachers of English, has grown from a gathering of a few interested individuals at NCTE meetings to an organization of more than two thousand members including elementary, middle, and high school teachers; school and public librarians; authors and publishers of works for young adult readers; and college and university English education specialists.

The annual meeting of ALAN at the NCTE Annual Convention draws a large and enthusiastic crowd for the two-day program at which prominent authors share their ideas about writing for young readers, the value of literature, censorship, and other topics on their minds and those of their listeners. In addition, publishers discuss their industry, trends in book selections, and other matters such as censorship problems; and teachers and librarians discuss teenage literary interests, book selection, and the teaching of YA literature. Those who attend the ALAN Workshop carry away with them a tote bag full of books by the authors speaking at the Convention, materials about the books and their authors, and copies of *The ALAN Review* and other journals dealing with books for young readers. Over the years, many of the presentations at the ALAN Workshops have appeared as articles in *The ALAN Review.*

As the current editors of *The ALAN Review* looked back across the first two decades of the journal, they realized both what a wealth of material related to books for young readers those volumes contained and how much of that material was not easily available. Thus was born the concept for this book.

Selecting the articles for inclusion turned out to be a major problem because the book was to be one volume of reasonable size. Rereading the twenty volumes of the *ALAN Newsletter* and *The ALAN Review* was a captivating experience; deciding what to include and, worse, what to leave out was a painful one. What we finally looked for were three categories of articles, three that seemed to encompass most of what was published during those twenty years: articles by and about individual authors and their works, articles about YA literature in general, and former editors' memoirs of the history of *The ALAN Review.*

Articles by and about Individual Authors

Nearly every issue of the journal during those first two decades contained one, usually more than one, article by an author of books for young adults. Robert Cormier appeared several times, as did Sue Ellen Bridgers, Sandy Asher, Richard Peck, and most of the other prominent authors of YA literature. In addition, many of these authors responded to interviews that were published in *The ALAN Review.* Paul Zindel was interviewed, as were Bette Green and Hadley Irwin. And, of course, the issues were filled with articles about these authors' books, themes, styles, characters, etc. This section of *Two Decades of* The ALAN Review is organized around individual authors who, for the most part, have written for *The ALAN Review,* have been interviewed for the journal, and have been the subjects of one or more of its critical articles. In a few cases, although we found a rich variety of material about an author, *The ALAN Review* during its first twenty years had not published an interview with that author or had not published critical material. However, given the amount of attention that author received both at large and in the journal, we decided to include him or her. On the other hand, where there was not extensive and multidimensional material available, we had to leave out many exciting articles by and about some authors of YA literature.

A different volume might have included only articles by authors of YA literature. Indeed, we toyed with creating a volume just by and about authors, followed by a second volume of articles about YA literature, and a third about censorship and YA literature. Saner heads prevailed, as the cliché goes, but perhaps other volumes will follow this one.

Articles about YA Literature

The majority of articles published in *The ALAN Review* during its first two decades were, as one might expect, discussions of YA literature: what it is about, how it is written, what it says to its readers. Those of us who read it, enjoy it, think about it, select it for libraries, recommend it to students, include it in our middle and high school classes, and teach about it in colleges and universities naturally are intrigued to share what we discover about literature for young adults. Given the increasing richness of YA literature during the first two decades of *The ALAN Review,* there was much to discover, much to share. We looked at how teachers are treated in YA novels; we lamented the rise of the teenage romance novel. We considered the techniques of writing—for example, the use of the first-person versus the third-person point of view; and we looked at a teenager who could read fluently but who rarely chose to read at all.

Throughout the two decades, brilliant, insightful, and provocative articles appeared in every issue, looking at what YA literature was, wasn't, should be, could be. Writers explored science fiction; adventure; social protest; both straight and gay sexuality; race relations; and family relations as they appeared in the literature for young readers. As books for teenage readers dealt increasingly with profound human and social issues in the lives of their young protagonists, such articles found more that was important to explore; and as the authors of YA literature insisted on using more complex and varied approaches to their works, critics prepared more analyses of the art of YA literature.

From this rich collection of thoughtful, analytical material, we have chosen a representative sample. We looked for variety in order to represent the range of what was published. We looked for articles that took a different and interesting slant on YA literature. We also looked for articles that, somehow, for us, spoke to what was going on in the heart of the subject. Then we looked for articles that would give the book a broad, balanced look at books and authors from many ethnic and racial groups. Finally, we threw in a few of our favorites.

The History of *The ALAN Review*

In the third section of this book, Ted Hipple has pulled together a history of ALAN, from the meetings that led to its creation onward to the present, so that we have a record of the people and ideas that gave birth to and have guided the organization throughout its more than two decades plus of activity. Further, the editors of the journal during its first two decades—from the *ALAN Newsletter* created by Alleen Pace Nilsen, to its transformation into *The ALAN Review* under Guy Ellis, and through its growth and development with Charlie Reed and Leila Christenbury—have reflected on what the journal and YA literature were like during those years.

Part I The Authors

Section 1
Robert Cormier

The Pleasures and Pains of Writing a Sequel

Robert Cormier

Photo by James Patrick Langlands, courtesy of BDD/Random House Children's Books

Blame Tubs Casper.

And, literally, hundreds of young readers.

Blame them for always asking: Did Jerry Renault live or die at the end of *The Chocolate War?* What about Archie Costello? Did he ever draw the black marble? Was he ever defeated?

Tubs Casper was a special case. The students are almost angry about Tubs Casper. Why did you get us interested in him, they ask, and then drop him completely? Did he keep the money from the chocolate sale to buy that girl the bracelet? Did she really like him or was she only pretending?

These questions, and many others from students, both in letters and during my travels to schools across the country, kept the characters in *The Chocolate War* alive in my mind and heart long after the novel had been published.

The characters in my novels are always vividly real to me as I write—I cry when they cry—but once the novels are finished they reside in a sort of limbo, tucked away in a corner of my mind, their fates sealed. For instance, I know that Miro, the young terrorist in *After the First Death,* did not live long after escaping to Boston. He died very soon, either from police or military bullets, or at the hands of his fellow terrorists, appalled that he had not chosen to die sacrificially on that railroad bridge. (Few people inquire about Miro's future, though.)

But Archie Costello and Jerry Renault and Tubs Casper, and, yes, Brother Leon are different. They haven't been allowed to remain dormant in my mind simply because of those unending questions.

Until the moment when I thought: I wonder what *did* happen to them.

And I began to write what eventually became *Beyond the Chocolate War.*

Reprinted from *The ALAN Review* 12.2, Winter 1985, pages 1–3, by permission of the author.

I am not, ordinarily, sympathetic to sequels. And never thought that someday I would write one. I knew all the hazards, in particular the immediate, inevitable comparison with the original.

There is another factor.

My writing usually is sparked by emotions so strong that they affect my comings and goings, until I sit at the typewriter, using those emotions to create characters and action.

In the case of *The Chocolate War,* my son's refusal to sell the chocolates at his school's annual sale touched off the emotions that led to the novel. But that sale was held more than a decade ago. The emotions have long been used up, are now only dim echoes from the past. (My son, Peter, is now a husband, and father of a two-year-old-child).

Thus, I approached the writing of the sequel with a degree of tentativeness, telling myself that I was not *really* engaged in doing a sequel but merely exploring the possibilities of what might have happened to those characters at a later time.

I was curious but not emotionally involved.

I knew that my knowledge and craft and experience could carry me through the mechanics of writing and plotting. Yet, I felt uneasy as I wrote.

Obie saved me, however.

And also saved the day.

I had always had a special feeling for Obie. He was such a poignant character, the way a stooge is always poignant. In *The Chocolate War,* Obie had been overcome by sadness when he pondered his years at Trinity, all of the things he had not accomplished, serving only as secretary of The Vigils, something he could not even tell his parents about.

Secretly, I had identified more with Obie than with anyone else in the novel. I also felt I had not done him justice as a character. Obie, caught in the worlds of Trinity and The Vigils. I thought of all the times I had been a stooge to my fears and apprehensions, serving them instead of my strengths. All the touchdowns I had never scored. All the sins of omission as well as commission. I discovered some notes I had scribbled during the writing of *The Chocolate War.* One scrawled jotting caught my attention: What if Obie had been in love? I had not answered that question, left it dangling in my mind. Perhaps the time had come to answer it.

Obie brought me back to the original mood and feeling of the novel, seizing my imagination, freshening my emotions. Forsaking formal plotting, I began to write about Obie and a girl called Laurie Gundarson, all the sweetness and doubts and torments of young love, and the effect of their relationship on others at Trinity.

Without Obie and his involvement with Laurie, the sequel to *The Chocolate War* might have stumbled to a halt after only a handful of pages. Writing about him created sparks that brought other characters to life. I realized that the world of Trinity High again had gripped me, haunting my days and nights.

I returned to Page One at this point, certain that I was on the right track. As I began to write in earnest, I encountered the countless problems of writing a sequel. As well as the pleasures.

The first problem is this: Writing the sequel so that it can be read independently of the original novel. Obviously, references must be made to that first novel but these must be introduced in the natural course of events.

I chose the most obvious and simplest device in solving this problem, introducing a character who, in effect, would be the surrogate for the new reader. The necessary information would be funneled through this character.

In this case the newcomer is a boy named Ray Bannister, whose family has moved, at mid-term, to the city of Monument in Central Massachusetts after his father received a promotion from his firm.

Ray is miserable in Monument, far from the beautiful resort town of his childhood. He is attending Trinity High School, a school with weird undertones where students are not only distant but, in most cases, downright unfriendly.

Gradually Ray Bannister learns more about Trinity and so does the new reader.

More than that, Ray Bannister becomes not only a guide to the reader, but a vital character in the events that bring the novel to its climax.

Here's where serendipity—that sweet finding of things unlooked for—once more played a role in my writings.

And what began as a device became a delight.

Which brings us to Tubs Casper.

Let me explain about Tubs.

There are certain characters who exist in novels for specific purposes. They are created in an instant, have their brief moment on the page and then are quickly forgotten. They are, in brief, devices.

Such was Tubs Casper.

In the chapter in *The Chocolate War* dealing with the actual sale of the chocolates, it was necessary to show how the sale was going. The operative word here is *show.* Not simply tell. In order to be effective, the sale had to be dramatized. As a result, John Sulkey ran eagerly and enthusiastically through the streets of Monument visiting the customers who had been his regulars through the years. Paul Consalvo was merely going through the motions, having terrible luck, tired of yet another school sale. And Tubs Casper was madly selling the chocolates but holding back his returns to the school, "borrowing" the money to buy a birthday present for Rita, the girl with whom he was desperately in love.

Tubs Casper and John Sulkey and Paul Consalvo faithfully played their roles, did what was required of them, and then left the scene, not important in themselves.

But in the case of Tubs Casper, young readers felt otherwise.

The image of Tubs running through the neighborhood on his "short fat legs" and later agonizing as his beloved Rita brushed against him stayed in the minds of countless teenagers.

They were upset by the fact that Tubs appeared only in that single brief scene. They wanted to know more about Tubs and his love for Rita.

And, after a while, so did I.

In the sequel, Tubs Casper returns to the scene. We learn what happened to him and Rita. How Tubs also becomes involved with The Vigils. How . . . but let me not be carried away.

The special pleasure of writing a sequel is taking a minor character like Tubs Casper in the original novel and allowing him to develop. This also happened to David Caroni, who made only brief appearances in *The Chocolate War.* He was another character who seemed to cry out for fuller development. In the sequel, he plays a major role.

It may have been Chekhov who said that, if a rifle is observed on the mantel in the first act of a play, it must be fired before the curtain falls at the end of the play.

I have always been conscious of introducing "rifles" during the course of writing novels and short stories, sometimes directly, sometimes indirectly. Rather than rifles, I like to think of them as quiet time bombs ticking away, waiting to explode at unexpected moments.

(The package that Ada Farmer carried with him on his bike ride in *I Am the Cheese* is such a time bomb. Interestingly enough, I did not know the contents of the package when I began the novel but let my old friend, serendipity, take matters in hand.)

In *Beyond the Chocolate War,* the time bomb is planted in the first sentence of the novel.

But first, let's consider Ray Bannister, who is the reader's guide through the intricacies of the plot.

In the loneliness that pervades his first weeks in Monument and at Trinity, Ray entertains himself by fooling around with his magic tricks. His father had been an amateur magician in his younger days. He had recently given Ray a box of basic tricks, hoping they might assuage the boy's loneliness. Ray is surprised to find that he has a natural talent for manipulating cards, his fingers surprisingly adept at the now-you-see-them, now-you-don't maneuvers with the cups and balls.

Unpacking old boxes in the cellar, Ray discovers some of the more sophisticated effects and illusions performed by his father. They challenge Ray's ingenuity as a budding magician and his skill at building things. (Ray had built his own beloved skiff back on Cape Cod.) One particular illusion draws Ray's attention. Using the remnants of the effect found in the packing case and applying his talents, Ray embarks on his project, carefully constructing the effect, forgetting those solitary hours, the emptiness and frustration of his life in a new town, at a new school. He is delighted with the finished project.

Evoking that old Chekhovian rule, the first sentence of the sequel to *The Chocolate War* is:

> Ray Bannister began to build the guillotine the day Jerry Renault returned to Monument.

The blade, of course, must fall.

But the guillotine is merely an illusion, an effect, isn't it?

Or is it more than that?

The pleasures of writing a sequel are far far greater than the pains.

A Telephone Interview with Robert Cormier

Judith Bugniazet

I was so nervous! This was my first interview, and it was with my favorite author. I had a small group of students, as excited as I was, grouped around the new speakerphone I had managed to talk my department into buying. It started out well; Robert put me at ease right away. Then, halfway through the third question, the speakerphone became so full of static that we couldn't hear anything. All the students left, but as they did they commented that the phone call had made their day. I called Robert back and we continued the interview. He was so easy to talk to. The interview was over far too soon.

Q: First, how do you pronounce your name? Is it Cormier with the A ending like the French pronunciation, or do you pronounce the R?

A: It's actually supposed to be pronounced with the A ending, and it's pronounced that way in the South, but in the area that I live in, they pronounce the R and I consider that the correct pronunciation.

Q: You have such a positive relationship with your children, as discussed in *Eight Plus One.* Why are the relationships with the parents in your books so weak, among those that are present at all?

A: The short stories were almost autobiographical, and I was consciously writing about the relationships with families. In the novels, I was doing something entirely different. The only character in any of the novels that's related to me is probably Adam (*I Am the Cheese*). Adam pretty much represented me as a boy, wanting to be a writer and being bothered by bullies. Adam's relationship with his father was only strange because of circumstances.

Jerry and his father, or the absence of fathers and mothers in most of the stories, was because I wanted the young people to be judged by themselves. Particularly in *The Chocolate War,* I kept all the parents away except Jerry's father because I wanted people to judge the characters by what they did, not because Archie, maybe, came from a broken home. That was a conscious choice in *The Chocolate War.*

Reprinted from *The ALAN Review* 12.2, Winter 1985, pages 14–18.

Q: Why are your books concerned with such depressing subjects? Do you see this type of book as a catharsis for young adults?

A: *After the First Death* was occasioned by the violence and hijacking and by my influence as a newspaperman. They don't reflect any particular personal philosophy of mine. I try to write contemporary novels about what's going on. As far as the young adult audience goes, I'm not trying to have great role models for kids. I don't think of my audience as that; I think of my audience as really intelligent readers who, I hope, are interested in what I'm writing. Those readers happen to be, for the most part, in their teens, but I'm hoping there are also people in their thirties or forties or fifties.

Q: Your books are a catharsis for me. I can't read them without crying. Do you get many boys that say things like that to you? I think your books are particularly powerful for boys.

A: Boys won't admit to me that they cried, but when I go out to speak to them, or in their letters, they will say things like, "That's exactly the way we feel." But I do go into a few schools and do talk one to one with a few boys. The things that upset some adults are not the things that upset kids. They're very sophisticated, today's youth, but they're still kids. They have questions about things, like masturbation, and one boy told me that when he read about that in *The Chocolate War,* and it was so casually referred to, it helped him because he had been worried about what was wrong with him. It made him feel that he wasn't strange. Boys don't break down and cry, but I've had letters from people saying that the books upset them.

Q: I don't feel that upsetting them is particularly bad, because I always feel better after reading your books.

A: I guess it is a catharsis, particularly for young adults, but I write to affect people. Everything is to affect the reader. And, at any particular moment in the book, I want the reader to be angry or upset or even happy or laughing. Amy, in *I Am the Cheese,* was introduced for comic relief. I'm always trying to affect the reader because I'm hoping that ultimately the book, as a whole, becomes a catharsis and causes some kind of emotional response, so that's my aim.

Q: I see a lot of hope in your books rather than depression, but this is something we argued about in class. What do you think?

A: Well, maybe it's what the individual reader brings to the books, but I thought I had this element in my books all the time. Adam's out there pumping on his bike. I said it all in *The Bumblebee Flies Anyway* when I had Barney say, "The bad thing is to do nothing." I thought *Bumblebee* had moments of triumph. Even the downbeat pattern in *The Chocolate War,* there's a time when Jerry was defeated yet nobody came to his rescue. What kind of a book is it when people have to come to the rescue of others to survive? There are those elements in the books that are sometimes overlooked.

Q: You have a theme of death running through your books, more untimely and tragic death, rather than natural death. Why, and what is the connection? Is death a fear, or did you lose someone you loved in an untimely, tragic way?

A: I think that maybe because I was a writer in my personal life I've always been aware of my own mortality. I had a death in my family, a death I can barely remember and yet can remember well. My brother died when he was three and I was five. I can still remember the little white coffin in the front parlor. My mother later said that he and I were very close. I used to watch over him like the big brother that I was. Then, when my father died when I was in my mid-thirties, that was really traumatic because he and I were like friends more than father and son, and that was devastating to me. I've always been aware of my mortality because having been a writer at an early age leads to introspection and introspection leads to those kinds of thoughts. My awareness of the briefness of life has always been very much a part of my everyday life. Almost every day I'm just glad to be here. It can end so briefly, so you take advantage of every day you have. I can't understand people who say they're bored because life is so precious that, to me, that's almost a sin.

Q: Brother Leon sounds like he may be related to the dark riders in the Tolkien trilogy. He seems to be surrounded by dark and he hisses. Was there an influence here?

A: That was chance because I'm really not into Tolkien's work at all.

Q: Who did influence your writing?

A: Well, way back, Ernest Hemingway and William Saroyan stylistically influenced me because they wrote very simple prose, and, I think, when everybody starts out writing they have a tendency to be fancy, or think they have to write ornate phrases. The first one who ever influenced me was Thomas Wolfe and, of course, his mountain kind of prose. He inspired me because he came from a small town, Asheville, and he longed to be a writer. I discovered him when I was thirteen, and while he was my inspiration, that somebody else in the world felt the way that I did, trying to write like Thomas Wolfe was very self-defeating for me. It wasn't until later, when I discovered Hemingway and Saroyan that I saw that you could write simply. Later in life, the greatest influence in my life, as a writer, and the writer I admire most is Graham Greene. He, to me, is the ultimate writer. His similes and metaphors. And, he always has a second level and almost always has a religious theme running through his books. His writing is so beautiful. I don't consciously try to imitate him because I couldn't. I think, by now, I've developed my own style, but his is the major influence of my adult years and I read and reread his books. They're virtually textbooks for me on what great writing should be, and that's what I aim for. I aim. I don't often hit the target, but I aim for his kind of quality.

Q: Your son's experience prompted you to write *The Chocolate War.* Was the experience as bad for him as it was for Jerry?

A: No. In fact, Peter wasn't particularly introverted; he was an extroverted kid; he was on the football team. And, I think if he hadn't been this way, and able to handle it all, I don't think we'd have allowed him to do it. So, really, nothing happened to him. In fact, it became a kind of a joke that this kid, Cormier, isn't selling the chocolates. They really did have the roll calls. It affected me, to the point that I wrote the book about it, especially those first few days.

Q: This quote stood out, for me, in *The Chocolate War:* ". . . and he did see that life was rotten, that there were no heroes, really, and that you couldn't trust anyone, not even yourself." Do you believe this yourself or do you say this as a warning to watch out for your own naiveté?

A: For that particular moment and in that particular case, that was the message from Jerry, but it doesn't, in any sense, represent my overall lifelong philosophy. It doesn't apply for a later book, it's just that particular circumstance.

Q: In one of my classes, we had an argument about *I Am the Cheese* and the ending. Some of the students thought everything that had happened was in Adam's mind and that he was institutionalized because he was disturbed. I argued that what had happened to him was real, and that he now had no other choice than to suppress the information he knew in order to save his own life. Can you comment on this?

A: Oh yes, it wasn't all fantasy. The fantasy part was the trip on the bike around the grounds of the institution, but everything that happened was real: his father being an investigative reporter, Amy Hertz was real, the mother was real. The only fantasy was the trip. I think he's still up for his sixth or seventh questioning right now, and is still going around the institution on his bike and maybe something will happen that he does survive and is not terminated.

Q: Do you get phone calls from listing your number in *I Am the Cheese?*

A: Oh, all the time. In fact, it's strange, but after all this time I seem to be getting more mail and the phone calls continue. Last week one was from Virginia Beach. They come in clusters. I might go a couple of weeks without any and then in a week I'll get five or six calls, and they're from all over the country. I tell them right away that they're calling long distance. They play the scenario too. They'll call up and they'll ask for Amy, and I'll say, "Well, Amy's not here, but her father is," and then there's a big pause because a real person is calling a fictional character and a fictional character, who's really a real person, answers. Sometimes there's a big pause and they'll say, "Oh, my God!"

Q: Do you tell them who you are?

A: Yes, and then we talk about it. Once one called and my daughter answered. They asked for Amy and she said, "Speaking," and this kid said, "Well, Adam's been trying to reach you all day so I won't try to keep you on the phone too long." In all these calls there's never been a crank call, an obscene call or a put down call; they're all very good.

Q: In *After the First Death,* I felt that one of the things you were saying was that innocence can be evil. I agree, but how did you come to that conclusion?

A: That's one of the things I wanted to explore. I was really trying to explore extremism. Even patriotism, carried to extremes, can be evil, as in the person of the General, and also innocent. I resort to that belief when I read about bombs being left indiscriminately by terrorists in post offices, where they could go off at any time and probably injure a child and a mother, and I thought, "What kind of a mentality could do that?" My conclusion was that it could only be done out of a great innocence. People are so caught up in a cause that they're doing these things innocently. They're not realizing how important one particular life is, even though it's not within the cause they uphold. Certainly that was one of the big themes in *After the First Death.* Miro was the epitome of the innocent monster.

Q: Artkin was Miro's father wasn't he?

A: Yes. I left it ambiguous, but why should Artkin rescue these two boys and put them through all this special training if he wasn't their father, but I waited for the last moment to spring it so that it would be the one thing that would really spell Kate's doom.

Q: Can you comment on the parental manipulation of children, as in *After the First Death?* How far should parents be allowed to go in the manipulation of their children?

A: I think that as parents we manipulate our children, we hope for the right reasons, but bringing up children is really one little manipulation after another. We manipulate them into toilet training, and into good manners, but then there comes a time when you have to give them choices, too. It comes earlier for some kids than others. My wife and I, at an early age, have given our children freedom of choice. One thing that irked me as a kid was that nobody ever consulted me about anything—"You're going to the dentist next Thursday"—and they never consulted me ahead of time. I tried to avoid that in my kids and tried to give them a choice. Even knowing they had to go sooner or later, but at their own time when they're psychologically ready for it. That's a theme that runs through my books, this feeling that each person, no matter his or her age, should have their own dignity.

Q: In a review that I read of *The Chocolate War,* the reviewer accused you of destroying innocence. Can you comment on this?

A: When you review, you try to be kind, but in order to do an honest job you might have to say things that sometimes upset the author. The overall scenes are positive, I think, but then again it's what the person brings to a book. Sometimes the reviewers just think differently than I do on things, and that's life. You don't expect everybody to be in agreement with everything you do. When a book comes out you feel very vulnerable and naked because you know people are going to read the book, and sometimes they're just indifferent, or they agree, or they like it or don't like it. That's part of the profession.

Q: You mentioned in the letter you wrote to me that *The Bumblebee Flies Anyway* was different in impact than your other books. How is it different?

A: The impact is different, to me, in that people are taking it differently from the other books. I haven't had as much response from that book as I have from the others because it's just now going into paperback and getting into the schools. An example of the response I have had: A woman wrote to me from Maine last week and said that she cried all the way through it. It really affected her very personally. I spoke last night to a group here at a local college and they had been studying my work and when we came to *The Bumblebee Flies Anyway,* there was an entirely different approach to the novel. They all took it personally. We had two young high school kids commit suicide two weeks ago here in Leominster, and they were very affected by the suicidal tendencies in the book. Even in the writing of the book, after I finished it, I set it on the shelf for months and didn't send it in because I thought it was more than downbeat, and I didn't know if I wanted to publish that kind of thing at that particular moment. Then later, I did.

Q: Did you have to write, then stop, and then write some more and stop? I had to take breaks in reading it.

A: Yes. It was a very difficult, emotional book to write and I didn't feel comfortable writing it and yet as I got near the end, I felt there was a note of triumph in it. What bothered me about it in writing it was I wasn't sure I'd be able to reach that point. The Cassie character was very bothersome for me. I wrote about fifty more pages about her and finally left them out because it took us away from the complexities of the story.

Q: You develop your characters so well, and you use a lot of psychological force. Do you do a lot of research to develop your characters or do you draw them out of yourself?

A: They're really drawn out of myself, but I think what they are are composites of people that I've known through the years. As a writer, I'm always storing up things and observations. I have a pretty good memory for emotional things. People that affect me emotionally through the years. While I'd like to say that the characters are creations that come out of me, they really are composites. I don't think they're recognizable to anybody. I've never had anybody from this area claim they're one of the characters in the books. People see themselves in its good light; they never see themselves as the bad guys, so I don't have to worry too much about the villains.

Q: Have you thought of writing adult books again, or will you stay with writing for young adults?

A: The adolescent years have really fascinated me all this time. Right now I just finished a sequel to *The Chocolate War* and I've had a couple of ideas and one of the ideas has an adult as the protagonist, although there would be young people in the book. I'm putting down notes and sketching things. As I get into it, sometimes the novels fall apart and I have other ideas. I'm not pointed to writing young adult novels; I've just been writing novels with teenagers as the main characters, and that may change some time. I have started several novels over the years, and after awhile the characters don't seem to come to life enough, or the plot just runs itself out so that that's one reason I never announce ahead of time what I'm working on, except in the case of the sequel, and once it was well launched I let people know. Even the sequel, I began writing very tentatively.

Q: When will it be out?

A: March.

Cormier and the Pessimistic View

W. Geiger Ellis

Oh yes, Cormier really writes well, but I couldn't use The Chocolate War *(or substitute another Cormier title) with my students. It is just too depressing. There would be some parents who would complain about his dark view of life. I really don't think it is good for kids to concentrate on such a negative portrayal of humanity.*

This kind of reaction to Robert Cormier's novels is widespread. I regard such reactions with more than a little suspicion that the holders of this view lack a sound critical understanding of Cormier's work, and they lack faith in individual young people. This second shortcoming becomes ironic when the first fault is overcome.

A consideration of the man and his work should be done with a view of their socioliterary context. Literature for adolescents has come a long way in recent years. Up through the 1950s and into the '60s, most books so identified were didactic and formulaic, presenting characters who were static (except the teenaged protagonist could be counted on by the book's end to make an abrupt change toward what was accepted as adult behavior) and moved through predictable plots and reasonably safe settings.

Then came the social revolution often simply referred to as "the '60s," with its call for something called "relevance" and its focus on various social ills. As the resultant changes in values and behavior worked their way through society, the field of adolescent literature underwent corresponding changes in both quality and content.

For one thing, the writing has shown a much fuller range of literary quality. Notice that I do not simply say that the writing is better these days, for we have plenty of potboilers, cheap commercial efforts to exploit an identifiable market, and some outright trash, masquerading as "realism."

What I am noting here about the current state of adolescent literature is that with increased productivity in the field, there has been an attendant increase in the number of books at each of several levels of literary merit. The most encouraging aspect of that increase, of

Reprinted from *The ALAN Review* 12.2, Winter 1985, pages 10–12, 52, by permission of the author.

course, is the greater number of fine books. Ken Donelson noted this trend in an article in *Media & Methods* when he wrote, "The '70s more than fulfilled our hopes for mature, well-written adolescent literature; in the midst of the inevitable gunk . . ." (44–45).

While the range of literary quality has been filling out, so too has the content or subject matter been expanding. Books that bear the YA label are not so easily defined as once was so, for these books (or their authors) have pushed beyond the narrow social restrictions once imposed on life and literature, especially for young people.

These books embrace all of life and the imagination. In short, they are more like adult books, which also have undergone some changes themselves over the years. This shift was characterized by Lois Duncan when she told of writing her first novel that included a scene in which a boy of nineteen drank a beer:

> The publisher I submitted it to returned it promptly, saying "This is unmarketable. School librarians would never purchase a book in which a young person imbibed alcohol." I changed the beer to a Coke and resubmitted the manuscript. Not only was it accepted for publication, but it went into paperback, was serialized in a magazine, and received a national award. My career was launched, and I had learned a dramatic lesson in the process: To achieve success in life you play by the established rules.
>
> Today those rules are gone. . . . There are books about alcoholism, drug use, premarital sex, childbirth, physical handicaps, social and racial problems, divorce, mental illness, and homosexuality. Judy Blume's eleven year old menstruates. Richard Peck's seventeen year old gets raped. Fran Arrick's fourteen year old becomes a prostitute. The doors of life have been thrown wide, and the writer of youth books today has an entire world . . . to draw upon and to utilize. . . . (1)

This, then, was the tenor of adolescent literature in 1974 when Jerry Renault dared to disturb the universe of Brother Leon, Archie, and the others in *The Chocolate War.* Three years later in *I Am the Cheese* Adam was struggling for psychological survival in a world seemingly controlled by Mr. Grey. In 1979 Kate Forester of *After the First Death* reached for new strengths, not only for her own survival but for that of the children for whom she felt responsible. Now in the eleventh year after *The Chocolate War,* Barney Snow and his friends in *The Bumblebee Flies Anyway* are taking their places beside Cormier's earlier characters in the fight to gain individual control of individual destinies.

If you have not yet read *Bumblebee,* I can assure you that this novel is consistent with Cormier's other work by focusing on the struggle between individuals and an institution. Institutions are dehumanizing, but humans do not succumb easily or necessarily. While the larger theme is unchanged, he has forced us to think in yet another area, for the battle we see in *Bumblebee* involves the medical establishment. Yet it would be a disservice to suggest that this novel is an exposé of the world of medicos. Like its predecessors, it explores the boundaries of the human spirit together with the possibilities within these boundaries.

In noting these things about this recent novel, I am, of course, commenting on the other three novels as well. Consistently, the central theme has been the struggle between individuals and institutions. In *The Chocolate War* the institution is a combination of church and the educational establishment; in *I Am the Cheese* it is a combination of government and a psycho-medical institution; in *After the First Death* it is a military/political combination; and *The Bumblebee Flies Anyway* presents the medical establishment as it dabbles chemically and psychologically with individuals.

In each instance the institution holds overall control of the arena within which the characters move. It sets the boundaries, both physical and psychological, and most of the people are behaving in acceptable patterns acceptable to the institutions because the patterns do not disturb the universe. But Cormier, again in each instance, focuses our attention on individuals. In doing so, he causes us to see, through these individuals, that the boundaries and the controls need not be accepted passively. They can be challenged; indeed, they *must* be challenged.

Jerry clearly bucks the system by making decisions for himself so that he can gain control of his life. Adam is constantly trying to gain such control. In his mind he is courageously traveling beyond the constraining boundaries of his institution, and in reality he is fighting to grasp the reality that he glimpses. Kate relentlessly schemes against her captors and takes actions whenever possible. Barney Snow undertakes a surreptitious project that carries him across the imposed boundaries.

So here are these characters, this body of work, set in the existing milieu of adolescent literature in which realism had been the dominant mode. Not one of Cormier's characters is concerned with "alcoholism, drug use (except where imposed by institutions), premarital sex, childbirth, physical handicaps, social and racial problems, divorce, mental illness (except where imposed by institutions), and homosexuality" (Duncan 1). His focus has not been on menstruation, rape, or prostitution.

Cormier's characters stepped boldly and independently into the world of adolescent literature where most characters finally got their first bra, reached a decision about having intercourse, chose to have an abortion or a baby, kicked a drug habit or adjusted to a single parent home. While surely Jerry, Adam, Kate and Barney will sometime in their lives have to confront similar concerns, it took the good sense of their creator to have a larger view and see the much greater problems that young people face.

Cormier clearly has been out of step with the mainstream of adolescent literature, as out of step as his protagonists are with their environments. It is by hearing a different drummer that a person may become an individual. Through his novels Cormier sounds an alarm much as Walter Van Tilburg Clark did in *The Ox-Bow Incident*. An assessment of Clark by Walter Prescott Webb seems to fit Robert Cormier as well:

> He is not consciously trying to be either heroic or profound, but rather to see how much he can understand in order that he may make others understand what he sees. His refusal to pander, to join the parade of popular . . . writers, is something for which he probably deserves little credit. He is bound by his own limitations, one of which seems to be a built in integrity that forbids him to do what he does not himself respect. Considering his background, one could say that he must have a New England conscience standing guard over his impulses. To such a man fame and fortune come as incidentals, not as a result of a calculated chase. (220)

While different in important ways from his contemporaries, in one respect, a most important one, Robert Cormier is a part of the movement of adolescent literature, for he not only contributes to the expanding number of fine books, but he is a leader in their creation. As Alleen Pace Nilsen has written, "Cormier is one of a relatively small number of contemporary authors for young readers who makes use of the full range of techniques available to skilled literary artists" (3). Cormier was an unquestioned part of Ken Donelson's listing in *Media & Methods* of outstanding books from the past decade. Cormier's books explore the boundaries of literary expression for his audience rather than safely following the pack.

His approach sharply differs from that expressed by Lois Duncan. Remember her words: "My career was launched, and I had learned a dramatic lesson in the process: To achieve success in life you play by the established rules." Perhaps Duncan is right if success is described in limited terms, but the scope of an individual's success depends upon the scope of that person's perception. There is a difference between confronting the inevitable difficulties of maturation and confronting the larger issues of humanity.

One of the major issues confronting humanity today is the survival of freedom and individual human rights. While super patriots are busy enhancing their political standing by rattling sabres, shouting "the Russians are coming" and wrapping themselves in our flag, a real threat is gnawing at our innards. It is as has been said, "The enemy is met, and it is us."

Walter Van Tilburg Clark, speaking of *The Ox-Bow Incident,* said:

> . . . it was a kind of American Naziism that I was talking about. I had the parallel in mind, all right, but what I was most afraid of was not the German Nazis, . . . but that ever present element in any society which can always be led to act the same way, to use authoritarian methods to oppose authoritarian methods.
>
> What I wanted to say was, "It can happen here. It has happened here, in minor but sufficiently indicative ways, a great many times." (224)

Such an insinuating evil was amply noted by Dwight Eisenhower when he warned Americans of the "growing military-industrial complex." That institutional threat to freedom is but one part of the ubiquitous threat posed by the variety of establishments which permeate and control our lives, ever subduing rather than preserving individual freedom. As Clark sent a warning to his readers forty years earlier, so Cormier sounds an alarm today. He has given us carefully crafted, inspiring novels that give readers a feel for the struggle between these two forces, the individual and dehumanizing institutions, which are ostensibly good but have an insidious nature. School, church, hospital, government—surely these are people-serving, individual-enhancing institutions. Look more closely, as Cormier guides us, for unsettling views are waiting. These negative portrayals of established institutions are bound to be unpopular in some circles and will make some individuals uncomfortable, especially when they themselves are a part of and subject to such institutions. Specifically, many teachers feel that they dare not disturb the universe, and as Cormier has made perfectly clear, there is danger in doing so.

It is no more difficult to understand why a teacher would choose not to assign a Cormier novel to a class than it is to understand why Jerry Renault would choose to go along with the crowd. As Lois Duncan pointed out, "To achieve success in life you play by the established rules." Make no mistake about it, "established rules" means the rules of the established institutions. But the question remains for the thoughtful individual: What kind of success do I want? And that is certainly a worthy question for young people to consider.

It may be pointed out that the evil is not conquered in Cormier's novels. His heroes are more tragic than not. It may be suggested that their flaw is an unwillingness to "play by the established rules." They share this trait with Phineas in *A Separate Peace,* who was too pure, too individualistic to survive, rather than being like Gene, who was willing to make accommodations. I can say only that had Cormier's protagonists annihilated their institutional adversaries, the novels would have been absurd.

The fact is that the evil has not been overcome. It is still with us and must be fought with all the wit and courage that individuals can summon, just as happens in the novels. Rather than saying that the struggle is hopeless, it might be better to say that it is formidable. Besides, adolescents have an innate sense of immortality, and they perennially carry the seeds of the idealism which is the lifeblood of humanity. No one is better suited for recognizing and taking up the challenge.

I hope that idealism is not only tolerated but encouraged in our schools. Idealism is not for the young alone, nor is it predestined for defeat. Remember the accomplishments of an individual like Dr. Martin Luther King, Jr. If ever an individual faced overwhelming odds, Dr. King did in those early years of the 1950s. He did not always have the hundreds of thousands behind him, but still he recognized a just cause and was its champion. Yes, he was shot down, but his dreams and his accomplishments live. Another Nobel Prize winner, the Hindu poet Tagore said, "We do not raise our hands to the void for things beyond hope." In the works of Robert Cormier, I see a writer of hope, not despair.

Is Robert Cormier a pessimist? Hardly so. Nearly fifty years ago, Bernard DeVoto said of Mark Twain, "Pessimism is only the name that men of weak nerves give to wisdom." Cormier is a writer of hope who may heighten the awareness of those who are subject to the forces he depicts and inspire his readers with ennobling portrayals of human beings as individuals.

References

DeVoto, Bernard. "Mark Twain: The Ink of History." Address given at the University of Missouri. December 1935.

Donelson, Ken. "Spanning the Decades: Books from the '70s that Will Endure into the '80s," *Media & Methods* V16.7 (March 1980): 44–45.

Duncan, Lois. "Breaking the Rules." *The ALAN Review* V7.3 (Spring 1980): 1+ .

Nilsen, Alleen Pace. "The Poetry of Naming in Young Adult Books." *The ALAN Review* V7.3 (Spring 1980): 3.

Webb, Walter Prescott. "Afterword." *The Ox-Bow Incident* by Walter Van Tilburg Clark. New York: New American Library, 1960.

Part I The Authors

Section 2
Sue Ellen Bridgers

Stories My Grandmother Told Me: Part One

Sue Ellen Bridgers

In the late afternoon, after she'd spent the early morning in the field, then cooked dinner, tended the plants in her greenhouse and prepared the Bible lesson for the nightly class her children attended at her knee, she would walk down the road to her sister-in-law's house, knitting as she went.

She walked briskly, watching her work, those quick hands clicking the needles as she purled a sweater for a winter's child. She never watched the road. She knew the way.

Around her waist there was a bulge—not another pregnancy—but her apron full of quilting pieces, the ends pulled up securely into the waistband to contain the squares. When she reached Bett's house, she would sit on the porch and piece awhile, stitch squares side by side, catching the corners until she had a big square. Then another. And another.

While she pieced, they would talk. They would be women together, looking out across the fields that belonged to them, where they had buried their babies, where older children now labored in the summer heat, where with every season the face of the land changed—and yet, was always the same.

Oh, to have been privy to those words spoken in the quiet of late afternoon, to have hung on those silences that hovered between them like smoke! There is no conversation of kings, no exchange between poets I would rather hear than the ordinary talk of those women who discovered themselves and each other with words and who, therefore, shared a common language.

No matter what they talked of, I know it was rooted—as they were themselves—in the land: the quest for it that brought their families across the Atlantic, the struggle to find it that brought them up the coast from Savannah into eastern North Carolina. The determination to keep it that put them in the fields next to their parents,

Reprinted from *The ALAN Review* 13.1, Fall 1985, pages 44–47, by permission of the author.

their brothers and sisters, their husbands, and finally their sons and daughters.

They knew about the land. My great grandmother Bett, on whose porch they sat, saw sharp deep rectangles dug into that earth to bury six of her seven daughters. She washed that black soil—the blackest that has ever been—from clothes against a washboard, days of hands in stinging lye—washing clean, cotton she had spun herself, woven at her loom, sewn by hand with invisible, invincible stitches, miles of stitches, days on end of cotton picked.

The land held the cotton, received seed, blossomed pink, split open their furry bolls. She could remember when there had been slaves to pick the cotton. She could see them in the commissary her mother ran, exchanging hours for sugar, a slab of pork, cornmeal. She saw the soldiers, too, blue coats as raggedy as any hired man's and she hid behind her mother's skirts when what she wanted to do was to scoop up the land, all of it, acre upon acre, into her tiny hand and hold it safe. The greatest threat was not that they would lose the slaves but that they would lose the land.

The land mattered to them because it was a place. It was tangible. They couldn't take it with them, but they could leave it behind. It was permanence beyond themselves, the discernible boundaries of their family history, a map with their names upon it.

Here there stand twin chimneys, crumbling, brick turning to chalk, set within a grove of ancient oaks that once shaded a roof. Once a swing hung there and beneath it a black hollow of earth, scooped out of the grass by the brushing and skidding of bare feet as children pushed themselves off into the branches, listening as they did to the slight whistle of wind, the satiny rustle of leaves, the laughter below.

I can see my grandmother there, her auburn head almost level with the balcony veranda, as she swung high, fearlessly in her cotton shift, making for herself a breeze in the still afternoon air. Her mother and her aunt talked on the porch. Their voices rose to her now and then, or else fell into her breeze—she could never tell which. She heard the tail end of a story or else the beginning of one. It didn't matter, because the stories went round and round, embellished as they went like the ball of yarn her mother wound. Somewhere at the center there had to be a beginning of the thread and there would be an end, too, tucked almost invisibly into the ball against its raveling. But they didn't consider a story ever ended because there would always be the past to reach in to the future. There would always be this place, and they would always own it.

The past, a history, is captured in a place; and a thing named is a thing possessed. They knew that from the Bible—God did not create the darkness, but He called the light Day and the darkness Night.

By naming, He took possession, and so it is with the naming of places. My great grandparents drew three letters from my great grandfather's name and added "town" to it, and so the place had a name, Renston, an identity separate from every other crossroads and post office in North Carolina. It could be recalled, evoked, discussed, disparaged by name. It was home.

And so the land, the place, the home became one. It was where you started from. It was your connection to birth because you had been born as much out of the soil as from your mother's womb. Such fertile ground to bring cotton and tobacco and beans and corn and babies out! And you knew you would go back to it.

My grandmother was a young girl when her older sisters, all married and with babies of their own, began to die. One by one they hacked blood, grew thin, milk dried up, hair limp, foreheads clammy with tuberculosis. Who could have known it was catching, spread on spoons and linens?

A girl of twelve, my grandmother stood in the doorway to watch her mother hold a dying daughter in her trembling arms and to hear a clear, dauntless voice rise above the labored, rasping breath, to sing: "There's a land that is fairer than day, and by faith we can see it afar. . . . In the sweet by and by, we shall meet on that beautiful shore."

She had buried babies, too. There would always be miscarriages, stillborns, little ones to wrap a final time. The night Lucy Belle died, my grandmother held the lantern while her mother lined the tiny coffin with the finest material she had in the store—material set aside for a wedding or else a funeral.

In the darkness she pressed the soft carded cotton to the bottom and sides of the pine box her husband had made, measured and cut the cloth, making a bed, bringing all her skill to those quick sure hands that would have trembled had she let them know the dreadful task they were about—it was my grandmother who cried, robbed of her baby sister, a toddler who days ago trailed behind her begging to be carried, to go to the store for a chunk of rock candy, to hear the piano played and thump at it herself. My grandmother leaned toward the coffin, casting her feeble, shaky lantern light, and closed her wet eyes to the sight of it. Who could look, except a mother who measured the cloth, knowing the unmeasurable nature of grief and resigned to it. Dust you are and to dust you shall return. She knew it to be true, and so she loved the earth even as it swallowed up her children.

These women and their land were the subject of much of my writing seventeen years ago. The pages have long since found the dustbin—the voice was a strained one, interrupted by the demands of my own babies, desperate for home because as a young married woman I left North Carolina for South Dakota. The old houses there were homesteads, or so it seemed to me, not homeplaces. The homeplace I am speaking of is a white house, most likely two story with a veranda or at least a porch, a kitchen stuck to the back so that to enter it one has to cross the side porch where the pump drips and a communal cup hangs beside a small square of glass.

Here farmboys washed up for dinner and made awkward attempts at their jaws with papa's straight edge razor. Here girls pressed talc spiced with lavender to their throats and shoulders. Here they flattened their mouths for a stain from a wet red cloth and pinched their cheeks until they stung. All before the fragile reflecting glass. Here at the back and side of the house was a community of enterprise—the smokehouse, the washhouse, the chickenhouse, a playhouse for the children, a pen for the dogs, a shed for the buggy. Here the chickens and geese could run loose in the yard and a goat nib bled at the grass through the front-yard fence. The dust rose and settled its sooty gray color on the wall. But at the front there was green—the lawn—grass cultivated with the pains and care due a fragile crop, a brick walk, rockers on the sparkling porch.

Come in. The hall is cool, but with sunlight at the back like an airy, fragrant tunnel. Come into the parlor, the dining room. See the screen door through which food miraculously appears as mother brings platters in on her arms for Sunday dinner or company supper. There is the stairway where children huddle in the dark listening to the talk below, scaring themselves with their own twitching and the shadow of the lamp on the landing. Above and below are bedrooms, and also the spare room for the loom and the desk at which my great grandmother keeps the accounts. Further below the cool cellar where sweet potatoes, Irish potatoes, cabbages, and apples breathe the dirt and endure.

This is a homeplace. It is set in a field as if it is a rare and wonderful plant cultivated by a woman's care and formed to her design. The prophet Joel said that "your young men shall see visions," but it was a young woman who saw this house in her mind and then set about to have it, to give her children not just "a" roof but this roof, and these roots. Her vision was to make a home in the wilderness. To keep the country, but to bring rarefied air into this one place, beneath these trees that washed her with its breezes and encircled her in winter like a stark tower wall. All over eastern North Carolina you can see this vision enacted. Or you can see a clump of trees in a field and know that once a homeplace stood there as proud as the woman who cared for it.

Stella Willis saw a house like this one—remodeled, of course, and thank God for it, because a house can have another life and still retain the old one. It was the house where my father had been born, where his family had lived for generations, and although the land itself was home to him, the house was always the focus of his memory. A house is a place you can go "into" and that entering is a special event because you are suddenly surrounded by what a family holds dear, the symbols of their life. Here you find what they made by hand and bought with money. And all of it came from the land.

Even Stella's little house, a tenant house half painted, was a miracle to her. When she stepped alone into it, she sensed "it was an empty, dusty world of filtered light waiting for her to clean it up and fill it with her whole life. . . . Now she had a place to store the secret Stella and draw her longings out slowly, carefully, one by one, and keep them safe." And so she thinks that "she would never desert this place, never let it slip away as her daddy had. They could all vanish, and she would stay, because already what counted for her was here, in side walls that didn't move. . . ."

"Walls that don't move, a place to store"—that was what a house meant to this migrant girl.

A house, especially an old house, a homeplace, owns us as much as we own it, maybe more so. Bleached boards hold memories. Crackled china catches light and holds it. Photographs on the mantel reflect our own faces. The timber of the house also provides the timbre—it creaks and squawks under foot, swells its window sashes and door jambs in summer, relaxes its hold in winter to let the cold in. The rafters make music, too, holding the roof steady in the wind. A summer storm blows up. Rain pellets the tin roof, a clattering music, and in the hallway downstairs, the bowl of crepe myrtle branches trembles as thunder spreads the sky open and a streak of lightning, like the one that killed Mae Willis, makes a hot, jagged path to ground.

Everything comes back to the earth. And so near every homeplace there must be a cemetery, set in a cornfield so that in summer it is invisible—the earth is breaking open to give out life, not to receive it—but in the winter, the narrow crosses and shallow etched stones stand above the frozen plowed-up fields, a reminder of pneumonia, killing colds, long nights of waiting through chills and fevers, the helpless biding of time.

And so Mae Willis, a migrant mother unable to accept a stationary life—a woman who had never had a homeplace or a sense of self—a powerless, disconnected woman—was laid to rest in the place from which she most wanted to flee. Her daughter Stella understood that because she knew the difference between them. Everything her mother rejected, Stella wanted and so she stayed in the tenant house, her own little homeplace set beside the real one, refusing to give up what belonged to her. The experience of ownership was new, a symbol of all the possibilities of her life.

"None of us ever owned anything," she said as she grasped at this new understanding, "until we came back to Daddy's home and Newton gave us that little house. But, somehow, I felt like it had always been ours. That land out there belonged to us no matter what anyone said. Daddy was born to it, and I was born to Daddy so the land and the house were mine. They truly belonged to me and I belonged to them, like I had known the house and the land long before and had somehow forgotten about them for a while."

Here is that connection to the land, the house, the identified place. In fiction, the writer pins down a place, identifies and defines it, gives the reader directions to it. For James Herriott, it is Yorkshire; for Eudora Welty, Mississippi; for Wilma Dykeman, it is western North Carolina and east Tennessee. For me, it is North Carolina.

That is not because what we know best is easiest to write about. To the contrary, the knowing makes it hard. That terrain that touches us deepest, that moves us most, is the most difficult to capture, but the most necessary. This is the map of my memory, the place I want to understand well and to illuminate completely. I want to show you my vision. I want to see it for myself.

Stories My Grandmother Told Me: Part Two

Sue Ellen Bridgers

Time and place are joined to each other in a blood tie. The vital signs for a novel pulse there, at the "where" and "when." Once identified, they lack only the "who" because surely the "what" that follows will come naturally, the progression of events in time and place directed by a cast of characters to whom things will happen. "And so," the writer scribbles, frequently with invisible ink—and goes ahead.

The longer I work with the characters who people my books, the less sure I am of where they come from and why. There are some like Maggie Grover in *Home Before Dark* who take on a life apart from my intention and thereby change the course of the story, and some like Mae Willis who are so unsure and desperate that they let me control their destinies. There is Hazard Whitaker in *All Together Now* who proposed to Pansy quite spontaneously and against my better judgment. There is Jane Flanagan who assumed with ease and validity the role I gave her. I give up trying to approach these people in an objective fashion. I will leave that to scholars and reviewers whose hapless job it is to study creative-after-the-fact.

Of course I wouldn't deny the technical aspects of fiction writing, for writing is more work than inspiration and more practiced than spontaneous. It's important to me that I know what I'm doing while I'm doing it, but generally I don't know it in a way that can be recounted later. Recalling what I am thinking while I'm writing would be as impossible as recalling the actual words spoken between my great-grandmother and her sister-in-law on that front porch in 1898.

And yet, I know what they were saying, not because I heard it then, but because I can imagine it now. Their voices come to me over the snap and rhythmic fall of beans into a tin pan, over the squeak of

Reprinted from *The ALAN Review* 13.2, Winter 1986, pages 53–55, 61, by permission of the author.

a chair and the swish of feet under the swing. They speak of a wedding, a dress cut from Aunt Clarsy's new pattern ordered by mail. They talk of the new teacher who is coming to board for the winter, the new books they will send for. Aunt Clarsy recounts in half whispers the gossip from town because she has recently been there. They worry over a summer cough that doesn't go away, that common dreadful sign of impending doom. They speak without guile, or pretense or conceit, binding the common wounds of their difficult lives with a language that is sincere and supportive.

I could put words in their mouths, punctuated with the scene around them—fading light through the trees, a lamp suddenly lit in the parlor, the soft throaty warble as one of the girls sits down at the piano to accompany herself. I could give them words and you would not object because fiction would make the words real. You would be willing to be there with them. Together, you and I would make it happen, whether it did or not.

What is real and what is not? What is truth and where is it separate from fiction? Eudora Welty says that "human life is fiction's only theme." And so there is a place beyond the physical location, the land, the home. There is the heart.

When I began writing my second book which became *All Together Now,* I knew the place and it was not a country homeplace like the one Stella had loved, but a town homeplace—a big house on a shady street with more rooms than it needed—a room for a granddaughter, a room for a traveling man. It was the kind of house my great grandfather built at the turn of the century for families of comfortable means in eastern North Carolina towns. It was a grandmother's house. It had a side porch off the kitchen with red geraniums in clay pots on the ledge, a front porch with a swing, a dining room of inherited china and bulky, substantial furniture with a place for everyone at the table.

If *Home Before Dark* is about the land, then *All Together Now* is about the heart. And it is a grandmother's heart. Readers are apt to tell me what they think of Casey and Dwayne, and of course, I hear about Pansy and Hazard because their affairs seem most poignant and were intended to be. And yet it is Jane Flanagan, the grandmother, who holds the story together. She is the reason for Casey's coming and for Hazard's, too. She is Ben's wife, Taylor's mother, Pansy's friend. She provides the sustenance of their lives and it is not just meals, clean clothes and dustless surfaces, but also comfort and courage and a stillness at the center of things. It was she who laid on hands during Casey's illness. It was she who sat patiently on Pansy's porch waiting until her friend could break the silence that "shattered around them like tiny shards of glass they must be careful not to tread on." It was she who, years ago, took the summer sheers off her living room windows so her son could wrap them on the wings of a dream. She was like the women on the porch in 1898, but brought into 1950. Although she saw the world getting larger while her life stayed the same, she was proud of who she was. Beyond her identity as wife, mother, grandmother, she knew another one—a personal private sense of her womanhood itself. Like her ancestors she could say by heart the *Magnificat,* and the last chapter of Proverbs. She knew the story of Deborah, and of Jael's defeat of Sisera, and that the resurrected Christ first appeared to women. She believed that the hand that rocked the cradle ruled the world. Her world was small until she lost brothers in one war and sons in another. While the starred flag hung in the shadow of her window, she planted a victory garden. She never failed to vote. She survived the Depression, supported the Red Cross and joined the Mother's March for the March of Dimes. Her faith in her own power was so unquestionable that she never even identified it as power. She was admired for her community service, her patience, her thriftiness, her cooking, her cunning, her grace. In 1950, this woman, herself in her fifties, was content in little towns and rural communities all across this country.

She is not so happy today. Young women around her are making choices that didn't exist when she was younger. They are questioning the validity of the "stay at home" life she accepted, of volunteerism, of commitments that now seem more supportive than active. It is not enough to stuff envelopes—now she must make speeches. She buys frozen vegetables and jars of preserves in the supermarket because she is too busy to "put up" anymore. She makes use of every household convenience available to her and is not nostalgic about the limitations of the good ole days. She is on political advisory committees, the pulpit committee, the boards of directors of hospitals, homes for troubled children, banks and colleges. She's back in college herself. Her granddaughters have no intention of "coming out" or of marrying young, but they share expenses and apartments with their boyfriends. This grandmother has a job now outside the home or else there is something she "does."

In *Notes for Another Life,* the grandmother is a music teacher and a tennis player who cleans house because it is a necessary chore. She has taken in her grandchildren and also her son who is mentally ill and unable to function outside her care. She tries to understand her daughter-in-law who lives a life separate from her husband and children. She struggles to accept the fact that, just as she didn't make her son ill, she cannot make him well.

When this grandmother was young, she did not have options available to her daughter-in-law or her granddaughter. Perhaps she didn't even want them. Or perhaps she has regrets. Still she has accepted another woman's pursuit of a consuming, dynamic career and is supportive of her granddaughter's intention to become a concert pianist. But even with all the changes in the world that reflect on her life and values, this woman is still related to the women on the porch. The blood tie to place and family is still intact.

Because I feel this attachment keenly I write about life in families. I find that the lives that interest me most are not isolated ones but those involved daily in the complicated footwork of family living. People related by blood share, whether they want to or not, a past and prospect of a future as real and as important as their present. I believe that a nurturing figure, whether it be mother, father, grandparents or some other adult, is essential to family life but I realize, looking back on my accumulated efforts as a writer, that I do not have many successful mothers. Forced to face this subject, I have tread on the troubled waters of my own psyche to discover that for me, motherlessness provides the ultimate, the all consuming conflict. No matter what the relationship is, close or distant, strained or loving, mothers are still our source. They are perhaps the most unique and certainly the most complex attachment we will ever have.

Surely Casey's summer would have happened with her mother there. Surely Stella could have found a place to be without her mother's death. I admit that Kevin and Wren could have had plenty of trouble dealing with their father's illness even if their mother had been available to them. But for me, the absence of these mothers makes every word more poignant, every step more stumbling, every question more difficult to answer.

So there is a personal reason for these motherless situations, but at the same time, I believe I write about people as I find them. Technically the characters always come first and then the kind of people they are dictates what they do, just as you and I are products of heredity and environment.

Every writer faces the dilemma of whether to write about life as it is or life as it should be. I have never found much to say about the best of all possible worlds because fiction is based on conflict, not perfection. If Kevin and Wren were perfectly adjusted to their mother's absence and their father's illness, there would be no story to tell about them. In the world as it should be, there would be no mental illness and the decisions Karen Jackson had to make would be non-existent. She would be free to do whatever was best for her, unhampered by misunderstandings or disapproval. But that isn't how the world is, although I believe that in *Notes for Another Life,* three women are working toward their individual best possible worlds, each in their own way and with their own set of values and commitments. Bliss, the grandmother, is making the best of what life has given her. Karen, the mother, has changed her life drastically, taking action to save herself. The daughter, Wren, who is reaching maturity in the 80s, has the possibility of everything: faithful inspired commitments to other people, work she loves to do, a sustaining sense of self-worth that is not based on nurturing someone else. What these three women share over three generations of experiences is the hard knowledge that love is not always enough. They are each living with loss, but they are surviving.

I celebrate their opportunities and their achievements. I approach them longing to understand, never to prosecute or defend. They are part of a widening circle of family that I embrace every day: men and women, both blood relations and close friends, who take us in, lending their security to our panic, their hopefulness to our despair, offering their acceptance of us which is not unlike that of a mother who, knowing our dark places, loves us anyway.

In the making of a book there are the essentials I have spoken of: time, place, the human element of character. But also commitment on the part of the writer to create this work she has envisioned, a world which contains the essentials in particular rather than general terms: a particular place, a certain time, human beings who are both singular and familiar. The writer must have an intention of some sort, a base of action. I see family life as the core of my writing. I have a personal past, a family history that, while providing me with fertile creative ground, also provides me with awesome responsibility. These people who remind me of the child in me, also remind me of the continuum. They show me that I am a link between the past and the future. In the present, I can explore a way of life that is the expectation of some and the memory of others.

We are all caught in our culture, searching for sense in the confusion, and no one is more trapped than the teenager. Faced with the problems of daily life—the tremendous freedom they have, the problems of ecology and economy, the real and oppressive fear of nuclear holocaust—they have more need for interdependence than ever before. They need to share their mutual concerns with adults. They need concrete goals. They need to know we are with them and that they have ideas and visions and love to share that we adults are in true need of. They need books that reflect both the confusion and the calm, books that speak to the basic human need for companionship, books that portray family life in such a way that young people see the possibility of commitments to it that can sustain rather than destroy them.

I hope that the characters in my books portray such a commitment. I believe they are responsive to the collective well-being as well as to their individual goals and accomplishments. They face their days knowing how often the rain will fall, how frail we all are and yet how resilient.

My great-grandmother Bett and my Aunt Clarsy knew that. They came together in the late afternoon on one porch or the other. They came loving each other, hearing in the silence between them as much as in the words they spoke, a history, a past woven into the present so that who could separate either of them from the future. They came knowing the world was changing. Already in cities electric lamps brightened the evening sky. There was a telephone in the house and a sewing machine that bore stitches quicker than the eye could see. There was money now to send the children to college and colleges to send them to. They knew their daughters and their sons—those survivors—would be different from them, would know more about the world away from Renston, would be better educated, lose fewer children, find better ways to preserve the land and harvest its yield. Between them, as always, there was common cause and therefore, common language. And so I know what they spoke of and so do you. It was of the earth and of life and death and always—of love. It was women's talk, the fabric of fiction. I can hear it now.

Responding to the Magic: Sue Ellen Bridgers Talks about Writing

Anthony L. Manna

Sue Misheff

For Sue Ellen Bridgers the key to writing fiction is the ability to become receptive to the stories that reveal themselves to her. From somewhere within the child or adolescent inside her, a scene comes in to view, a character emerges and she knows that a story is forming. Long before the story appears on paper she becomes personally acquainted with her characters, endowing each of them with distinct traits and a unique voice. She not only must know their names, ages and physical characteristics; she must also become personally involved in their problems and relationships and how they fit into the world of the story. Kevin, Wren, Dwayne, Casey, Karen, Bliss and, most recently, Sara Will—these are a few of the younger and older characters who, like intimate friends and family members, have made themselves known to her through an almost magical communication. As she points out in the following interview, when her characters begin to speak, her challenge is to learn to listen to them.

Bridgers's skill in creating characters who live and breathe and who change and are changed by the world around them has won her continual acclaim by critics as one of the foremost contemporary writers of fiction. *Horn Book* praised her ability "to explore the innermost thoughts of her characters within the confines of a few pages" (April 1977) in *Home Before Dark,* and to create characters who are "remarkably individualized" (April 1979) in *All Together Now.* Publishers Weekly has described Bridgers as an author who "knows how

Reprinted from *The ALAN Review* 13.2, Winter 1986, pages 56–61, by permission of the authors.

to write and how to make readers care about people in a story. . . ." (March 5, 1979).

In *Sara Will,* her most recent work, she continues to explore topics and themes found in each of her four novels: the tensions that develop in complex human relationships, the conflict between dependence and independence, resistance to personal change, and cultural stability and discontinuity. According to *Booklist, Sara Will* is "a beautifully written, ultimately heartwarming gem of a novel, with vital, memorable characterizations" (January 1, 1985).

Bridgers was born and raised in rural North Carolina where she continues to live and write. She is currently working on a novel, tentatively titled *Permanent Connections,* about a young man named Rob Dickson who matures outside the security of his family. The following interview between Sue Ellen Bridgers and Anthony L. Manna took place in Detroit where she was the keynote speaker at the 1984 meeting of ALAN.—*Sue Misheff*

ALM: When did you first develop an interest in writing?

SEB: In the first grade, when I realized that the alphabet I was learning had the same letters as the ones in the books my mother read to me. Now that I had the tools, I started immediately, within just a few weeks, to put words together into little poems and phrases. I was that interested in writing and language already, but of course I had years of having other things take precedence over writing.

ALM: Were you encouraged to write at home and at school?

SEB: I was given lots of opportunities to write creatively at school. Although the kinds of things my teachers did were not particularly innovative, they sure helped. Sometimes they would give us the first three sentences of a story and tell us to complete it, or now and then they would assign a poem. Class assignments made writing more valid in a way because when you got a grade it was like getting paid. I'm sure the rest of the class despised me because my English teachers would often include a writing assignment for my sake since they knew I was interested. I've always been appreciative of the fact that they provided these opportunities. This just wasn't the standard thing to do in a small country school in the South. Then I got lots of poems published when I was in high school. You see, one of the newspapers in Raleigh, North Carolina, published a poem every day so the editors were always looking for poems. When I was about thirteen or so I started sending my poems to them. It was very good for me to have this kind of success every few weeks. I was writing at home too. In fact, with the very first money I ever earned I bought a used typewriter, and, if my mother heard my typewriter clicking away, she would tell my friends that I was busy when they called or visited. All of this gave me the right and the encouragement to keep writing. It was as though people were saying that writing was important. But, you see, even in college when I was publishing poems and short stories in the school's literary magazine, I wasn't thinking about becoming a professional writer. I didn't think I could make a living at it. Every writer I knew, and I knew very few, was teaching. Maybe, just maybe, I might publish something, but that would be a diversion from teaching or some other job. Naturally, I wanted to be published. The writer who doesn't want to be published is not a writer. In the end there has to be somebody out there with whom you're communicating. Up to a certain point you can communicate with yourself, but after a short time that just doesn't suffice.

ALM: You have said that your mother encouraged you to become a writer. Was she an important influence?

SEB: Well, what she did on one occasion made such an impression on me that I can tell you what stoplight the car was sitting at when she said it to me. I was about twelve when it happened. I was talking about my career goals and how I wanted to be a nurse when she said, "Why are you bothering yourself with all that? You know you're going to be a writer."

ALM: How did she know that?

SEB: Because she knew I had a strong interest in it. Maybe she also knew that if I got that kind of support from somebody as important as she was in my life, it would make a big difference. She was always very supportive of anything creative her children wanted to do. She never considered writing a frivolous activity or a waste of time. My grandmother influenced me too. She was a great storyteller. As a matter of fact, the oral tradition was very, very important in my family. A child's ability to listen to a story was valued. Also, I was read to a lot.

ALM: You've created a wide range of multidimensional women in your books. There's Mae in *Home Before Dark* who has such a hard time connecting with people and there's Karen in *Notes for Another Life,* who leaves her family to pursue a career. Where does your mother fit into that range?

SEB: My mother's not in that range. I was very concerned about that when people started questioning me about the role of mothers in my books. I've done a lot of thinking about it and I've come up with a very simple theory. You see, my attachment to my mother is so strong that one of the worst things I can imagine is the loss of her. Therefore, writing about people who don't have a mother makes everything about their lives more moving to me and more powerful. It seems to me that the problems many of my characters have are so much harder to deal with because of that absence. Some of my readers assume just the opposite. They assume that I had an estranged relationship with my mother, that she was an absent parent and that I'm writing about my own childhood. Actually, I'm writing about my fear of her absence. That fear is an undercurrent in most of my work. Actually, my children think that Bliss, the grandmother in *Notes for Another Life,* is very much like my mother. Of all my older female characters she probably does have more of my mother's qualities, but I didn't think of that consciously while writing.

ALM: Have any writers influenced you?

SEB: I guess the first writers who influenced me are the ones who influence many teenagers. Hemingway and Steinbeck, for instance. You know, there was no young adult literature as such when I was an adolescent, so I moved from Nancy Drew and stuff like that to *A Farewell to Arms* and *Jane Eyre.* Books like these showed me what a good story was like and how you could take a small incident and make a good story out of it. Of course, I didn't understand a lot of what I read, but I did see examples of good style. I guess I have been very influenced by Hemingway since those short sentences and the general terseness of his style has always appealed to me. It's important to me that there not be anything in a book of mine that is not essential. I feel most books are too wordy and so I do a lot of editing by skipping stuff. I would rather read a small, finely written book than one that's overwritten. That's why I tend to read writers such as Eudora Welty, Reynolds Price, Anne Tyler and other southern writers. Unfortunately, I don't write like any of these people.

ALM: Earlier, you mentioned that for a while other things took precedence over writing. Was there a time when you didn't write?

SEB: After I got married I had three children in five years. That was a very difficult time for me emotionally since I saw myself giving up everything but my role in the family. I had a lot of difficulty with that. It was only when my son, my youngest child, was three or four years old that I started writing again. I wrote secretly though because I didn't want anyone to know I was doing it. Luckily, the first things I sent out were bought by little literary magazines in North Carolina.

ALM: Once again, your audience was saying that they liked your stories.

SEB: Now I can look back on all those traumatic times when I was feeling useless, when I felt I had lost myself somehow in the domestic role, and realize that it was a very useful period. I learned so much about life when I was a young mother. Before that time I had been in a sheltered academic world, and now I was living in the real world with little money and a husband in the Air Force and then in law school. All those early experiences mattered because they helped to shape my sense of life and people. Yet, I've never been able to write about what's happening to me on a daily basis or about people my own age because it seems that the people who make themselves known to me as characters are invariably older or younger. I've never directly used my own life as material for my fiction. In a way, I guess you could say that I escape out of my life and into another place and time when I write.

ALM: Your characters are so complex. How do you develop them? Where do they come from?

SEB: I see all of them visually in some way. I see the opening scene, but where it comes from I don't know. I still haven't been able to figure out what's happening in my life that makes the character or the plot appear. It's just a heightened awareness that triggers some memory. For instance, I saw *Sara Will* coming down the road. I saw what she looked like and knew where she was coming from. I thought a long time about who she was. It's almost as though she was a long way from me, and over a period of months she got closer and closer until I knew her intimately. By that time she had a sister and they were in a situation. Then these other people came along. When I'm writing I don't think about a theme as such. Instead, I think about who these people are and what happens to them. Theme develops from there. When I got around to Eva, the teenager in *Sara Will,* I thought there was a possibility that the book would be about how she would live with other people, but Sara herself remained too strong. She dominated the book and I let her. When a character says to you, "Here I am," I have to go with that or else I would be giving myself more stress than I need. For instance, a new character by the name of Rob Dickson is presently coming into being. Although I've not had enough of a period of sensitivity to explore him fully, he has told me so far that he's seventeen and that he's living away from his family. I'm struggling a little with him now, but I do know that I need to take him out of his own environment and put him into a place where he'll change and grow and find himself. At this point, he has revealed that much to me.

ALM: Is that kind of sensitivity to your characters something you have developed? Have you become better at it?

SEB: I don't know if I'm getting any better at being responsive. It's such a spontaneous thing. At first, there was so much mystery attached to it that I tried not to tamper with it because it was going real well. Now, I have to think about it more; it seems to me that it is getting harder to work spontaneously; that it is getting more difficult to find the key about the character that I latch onto. But this might mean an improvement in my work. I hope that the work is getting a depth that it may not have had to such a degree before. It's like the difference between Stella in *Home Before Dark* and Kevin in *Notes for Another Life.* With Stella the complications are up front and immediately exposed. There's a lot more going on in Kevin's life; he was harder to get at because he's a much more complicated person and I was dealing with parts of his life that were hidden and complex.

ALM: Your characters are so fully developed it seems as though there are no minor characters in your books.

SEB: I hope not. They're all so important to me that when I'm writing I try to give each of them as much time and attention as they deserve. That's sometimes as difficult for me as it is for my readers. It's hard to get into so many minds at one time. Every time I do that I have to change gears and so does the reader. Remember that dinner scene in *All Together Now* when most of the characters are around the table? There are about six people in that scene. It was so intriguing to think about what's going on inside and outside their heads that I couldn't help moving from one character to another.

ALM: Does the small-town rural way of life you grew up in figure into your work?

SEB: Oh, yes. When I was growing up I had a watchful eye. I listened to what people said and I figured out that there was a lot going on there. I was always looking for the undercurrent of why people were behaving the way they did. You see, the rural way of life is not necessarily a simple way of life. Although the setting of my books is rural and big adventurous things don't happen, the internal lives of people there can be very complicated. What they decide to do about their lives is just as important at the moment as when some powerful person is going through a big emotional upheaval. For rural people to be considered simple is really pejorative. One of the biggest problems facing the South right now is that the rural way of life as it used to be is not there anymore. For instance, no one's making money growing tobacco. And that's a real dilemma for me, someone who is so opposed to smoking, yet who comes from that way of life. Life in the rural South is very different now. It's hard to survive. I think that's where the statement, "We're all that's left of the Willises," comes from in *Home Before Dark.*

ALM: In *Something about the Author* you said about yourself: "I am also interested in family relationships, especially the tradition of southern women's two faces of gentility and power as portrayed in the domestic setting." What did you mean by that?

SEB: I am drawing on a great deal of heritage that implied that women have power but are not given the opportunity to use it effectively. That's what I was feeling during the early years of my marriage. I knew that I had something to say, but I didn't think I had any expression for it. When I was growing up I was constantly exposed to a sacrificial attitude in domestic settings, not only in my own family but in the rural southern town where I grew up. When I was young, I saw a variation of this theme in almost every home I visited where women were putting their lives aside in order to do what was expected of them as wives and mothers and daughters. I looked at my grandmother in that way. She was a very intense woman, but she was burdened with so many responsibilities that she could never get free. She was probably the writer in the family. She was certainly a wonderful storyteller. If only she had had the courage to step out and do what she could have done. I can remember as a child how I would watch her and wonder, "Why is she responding like that?" "What's happening with her now?" Of course, nobody gave me any answers because people's internal lives were supposed to be secret. You just didn't tell a child these things. And I don't know how accurate I am now as I relive some of this past and work pieces of it into my stories. After all, I am looking at it from a child's perspective because my emotional link with this kind of living is still a child's perception of it in lots of ways. I'm concerned about this because, on the one hand, I want to be a grown-up person. I have this fear that if I get rid of too much of the child within me that I'm going to be in trouble as a writer. Someone once told me that creative people ought to find their ailment and take real good care of it because if you get rid of it you might lose whatever it is that makes you work. I think I have to keep that child perspective alive because that's where some very important memories are locked.

ALM: Family ties are given a lot of attention in your books. What does the idea of family mean to you as a writer?

SEB: I guess the reason family is strong in my work is that I feel so tightly connected to other people. I see my relationships to other people as family relationships; even my friends are my extended family. And I also see family life as the place where we're most apt to be terribly, terribly hurt, because people know so much and can use it against us. There are so many opportunities to either support or to crush someone. I just think you get a full range of what life can be in this little unit of three or four people, and so why not use that as the method or the metaphor for writing stories.

ALM: Who's your favorite character among the characters you've created?

SEB: Right now it's Sara Will, but ask me that question next year and I would probably say it's the character I'm working on at the time. I especially like Karen in *Notes for Another Life* because I've worried about her so much. I didn't want her to be misinterpreted; so I tried very hard to make her true to herself, to do what was necessary for herself so that she could make a life despite how people felt about her leaving her family. I didn't want to think about whether she was right or wrong in leaving. I was determined not to judge her. I wanted instead to accept her, to accept the fact that she said to me, "This is what I have to do. This is my survival." It was as if a friend had said that to me. The kind of support I would give a friend, I had to give Karen while I was imagining people around her reacting to her decision. I would simply have to say, "She did what she had to do." I found it intriguing that one reviewer thought I disliked Karen and that I was upholding Bliss as the epitome of womanhood. I never intended to be judgmental. I just wanted to present the facts of a life.

ALM: Do you have a routine as a writer?

SEB: My work habits have changed as my children have grown up. When I first started writing seriously, about the time I was working on *Home Before Dark,* and the children were in school, I would start writing in the morning and I would still be pecking away until the school bus dropped the children off. I was awfully hostile to my children when they got home. I'm so slow at figuring things out that it took months before I realized that a quick transition from writer to mother was more than I could take. So I changed my routine and stopped working at about noon in order to give myself some time before I took on the family role again. Now that the children are away, I'm free to write whenever I want. I only write when I'm writing though. I mean, I may have a period of a year between books when I don't write anything. That's my thinking period. That's when my room is filling up. I jot some things down of course, but I don't approach the typewriter with it until the characters are fully revealed to me, until I feel comfortable with their ability to tell me their story and my ability to be receptive to it. Basically, I may know how their story starts and how it's going to end, but the trail in the middle is still unknown to me. In order for them to tell me about the middle I have to know them fairly well or else they don't know what to tell me and I don't know what to hear.

ALM: It's as though you're opening yourself up to the story.

SEB: It's making yourself responsive to a life that is being revealed to you by some magical means. That's the strange part which I really don't understand. I always worry the whole time that nothing is happening in the story. My husband says I sound like a broken record because I'll say, "I've got 200 pages and nothing is happening." The only time I wasn't concerned with that was when I was writing *All Together Now* where some major event was happening in every chapter. I wrote that book chapter by chapter, finishing each chapter before I went on to the next. I knew that some active event was happening in each chapter.

ALM: Do you rewrite a lot?

SEB: No, I don't, because I've written most of the book in my head before I ever get to the typewriter. I'm probably into the second draft by the time I begin typing. I do rewrite some, but I don't have messy manuscripts. If anything, I might add to rather than take away, because in an effort to write tightly I sometimes don't write enough. You know, frequently you can record what someone's thinking in one sentence; you don't have to write three pages to do that most of the time. When I find myself slipping into three or four pages to cover a description of someone's thoughts, I assume I don't know what I'm talking about. But maybe I think everybody's attention span is as short as mine.

ALM: How do you feel about being labeled a young adult author?

SEB: I was really surprised that *Home Before Dark* was marketed as a young adult novel. I didn't know anything about young adult novels so when I sent the manuscript to Knopf who accepted it in the juvenile department, I was surprised. But then I immediately thought, "Who better to have read this book than teenagers?" I knew nothing about the market, about the longevity that a YA novel can enjoy. My first thought was, "How great that kids are going to be offered this book." Of course, I was very gratified that adults were offered it as well. It was published in *Redbook* and *Reader's Digest* condensed books. I got a lot of mail from older people who said the book made them feel nostalgic. They got some very warm feelings from the rural atmosphere. However, when I write I really try not to think about specific readers. I just can't afford to restrict myself in any way because I would wind up trying to please my audience rather than myself. I have to write the novel that is being revealed to me.

ALM: What advice do you have for teachers of writing?

SEB: I think it's very important for children to be given lots of opportunities to express their emotions about things and to talk and write about their personal experiences. One of my friends who teaches remedial reading thinks the reason many of her students are nonreaders is that they have never considered their emotional lives valid. Because they are not taught to value their emotional lives, they don't know how to respond to a character in a book who has strong feelings. This affects writing too. When kids learn that their emotional lives don't count, then it becomes almost impossible for them to write down a story about somebody else and what's happening in that character's emotional life. We need to nurture students' feelings so that they don't pull the shade down on their emotional lives. Writing can flow from there.

ALM: Do you have any advice for aspiring writers?

SEB: Read a lot! Writers need to know something about everything. I know now that I overlooked some important areas in my education like the study of biology and the natural world. I need to know all of that. I would advise other writers to learn as much about everything as they possibly can.

Southern Literature for Young Adults: The Novels of Sue Ellen Bridgers

Pamela Sissi Carroll

Since the Southern Renaissance emerged as a literary phenomenon during the early 1920s, critics and scholars of Southern literature have labored to identify the particular combination of qualities that distinguish it from the broader spectrum of American literature. The most obvious feature is extratextual: Writers of Southern fiction are Southerners, either by birth or by experience, usually both. They are influenced by the society, history, culture, and land of the region. A second obvious feature is closely related to the first: Southern writers tend to rely on the geography of their own origins for the settings of their literature. Even when fictionalized, as in Faulkner's Yoknapatawpha County and Welty's Morgana, the towns and communities of the region's literature are identifiably Southern.

Comparison of the theories of critics and scholars such as Louis Rubin, Lewis Simpson, Allen Tate, Robert Heilman, Gordon Weaver, and Lewis Lawson allows for the drawing of a composite of the textual features that contribute to the distinct flavor of Southern literature. The features identified below are necessarily general in scope. Like those suggested by Louis Rubin, they are "by no means exclusively or peculiarly" typical of Southern fiction, but are "common themes, common attitudes, common preoccupations" to which Southern writers "keep returning again and again" (1953, 13). They are

1. attention to place, entailing evocation of a particular geographical location, and the values of its people;
2. emphasis on memory, particularly the influence of the past on the present—a memory especially cognizant of the military and

Reprinted from *The ALAN Review* 18.1, Fall 1990, pages 10–13, by permission of the author.

cultural defeats of the Civil War, the shame of slavery, and disenfranchisement of blacks;

3. concern with the clash of traditional values against modernity, pitting the agrarian lifestyle against industrial and technological intrusions and forcing questions about the strength and integrity of religious, community, and family institutions and producing loneliness and alienation for Southerners who have lost a sense of neighborhood;
4. use of language, reflecting the oral history of the lyric, vernacular Southern voice.

These features of Southern literature intersect with the qualities of fine young adult literature in each of Sue Ellen Bridgers's five novels. The reader is treated to the unique regional self-consciousness—the flavor—of Southern literature when he or she tastes the fiction of Sue Ellen Bridgers.

In *Home Before Dark,* attention to place is the strongest element of Southern literature that is present. The novel exhibits what Rubin refers to as the tendency of contemporary Southern fiction to presuppose "a strong identity with place, a partnership in its life, a sense of intense involvement in a fixed, defined society" (1961, 24). The homeplace becomes the central symbol in *Home Before Dark.* With it, Bridgers achieves the creation of what Gordon Weaver refers to when he contends that place is "not only a significant atmosphere establishing tone and mood, not only a subtle and pervasive ambience permeating the sensibilities of characters, [but is also] often a primary agent of action, a dramatic catalyst in and of itself" (Bridgers 1985, xxi).

After traveling for years in search of part-time work, James Earl Willis decides to return home and settle on his family's North Carolina tobacco farm. He brings his wife and three children to the place where he had grown up, determined that they will not have to live in the back of an old station wagon any longer. For James Earl, "the land itself was home" (4). For his wife, Mae, the homeplace was threatening; it tugged her husband and children away from her. However, for their daughter Stella Mae, even a shabby tenant house on the farm property offered a strong sense of belonging: "For she knew, as surely as her mother had known the road was home, that this shotgun frame was where her life was. She wouldn't leave it" (122). Stella Mae views place in a way that reflects what Lucinda MacKethan refers to as the way "man, seeking his own identity, 'attaches' himself because it offers a concrete mechanism through which he can order and hold onto the beliefs that give meaning to his life" (182).

In *All Together Now,* an emphasis on memory—a family's and a community's—is the strongest element of contemporary Southern literature that is present. Lewis Lawson speaks for modern critics who have learned that

> much of the historical matter of Southern fiction was neither retrogressive escapism nor chauvinism, but rather a readily available method for apprehending the present. The past existed not merely for its own sake, but because it provided the metaphors through which the present could be described and understood. Shared history could provide ready reference points for private experiences. (16)

Through memory Jane Flannagan is able to communicate with her twelve-year-old granddaughter, Casey, across the generation that separates them. By spending the summer with her grandparents while her mother works and her father fights in the Korean War, Casey steps into the childhood world of her father and begins to know him better through the memories shared by his parents, brother, and boyhood friends.

One such friend is Dwayne Pickens, a thirty-seven-year-old mentally retarded man for whom time is frozen. He stars in imaginary baseball games with Casey as his outfielder, much as he played years earlier with David, her father. While the world grows up, Dwayne remains virtually unchanged. Another friend is Hazard Whitaker, who sees Casey's father in her: "You favor him, you know. Got those eyes and that mouth. Gimme a smile. Yeah, there it is. Just like David" (20). Casey's uncle, Taylor, shows her a wooden plane that her father made and hid in the woods, a plane that lay abandoned for years. Taylor describes it as his older brother's "visionary, awkward, beautiful attempt at making a dream come true" (173). These words, ironically, could also be used in reference to Casey's effort to hide her gender from Dwayne so that he would accept her companionship.

Casey's grandparents, Jane and Ben, care for her as though she were their own child, their David. And they let her go at the end of the summer, aware that when she returns she will be a young lady instead of a child, much as they must have let David go to return as a man. These and other memories that connect Casey with her father demonstrate what Rubin finds as a tendency in Southern literature to promote "a belief and conviction . . . that human beings exist or have existed in a condition of becoming as well as being" (1953, 292).

Memory is not restricted in Southern fiction to the personal experiences of families. The consciousness of a region must include its heritage. In *All Together Now,* Bridgers briefly shifts attention away from Casey's story to delve into the small Southern town's injustices and prejudices. In a town meeting scene, the concerns of black women about the quality of their sewage service are voiced, yet no one really listens. The mayor and council members smile condescendingly and quickly move to consideration of another issue. Bridgers's attention to the race issue, though brief, is an example of what Lawson finds typical of contemporary Southern writers:

> [A]s [the Southerner] loses his preoccupation with himself as a victim of history, he seems to be turning his eyes outward to see for the first time the man with whom he has always shared the South—the black. And he is seeing him with greater clarity. . . . (17)

Notes for Another Life, like much of Southern fiction written since the 1920s, deals directly with what Lawson identifies as the disappearance of "the once emphatic sense of family, social, and religious integrity" and the subsequent "disintegration of self" (15). The tormented relationships that Tom and Karen Jackson have with each other and with their adolescent children, Kevin and Wren, are the novel's strongest indictments of the troubled modern family.

Tom Jackson is chronically and severely depressed; he spends most of his time in a mental hospital, withdrawn when not catatonic. Karen runs away from the "isolation of a silent marriage" (19) to a job in far away Atlanta and leaves Bill and Bliss Jackson, the grandparents of her children, with the responsibility of raising them.

In the context of disintegrated family values, Kevin and Wren suffer alienation; neither can effectively communicate through the emotional obstructions of Tom's illness or Karen's selfishness. However, through Bill and Bliss's care, the brother and sister experience the love and stability of a more constant generation. Bill and Bliss provide a buffer of resistance against the encroachment of a fragmented, cold modernity. Wren, Bliss, and eventually Kevin sing familiar songs as they ride together to visit Tom; that simple act is a strong adhesive and tonic for the teenagers and their grandmother. Bill and Bliss are respected members of their church and their community. Through them, Bridgers suggests that what Spivey asserts about the South is still possible: "community really does mean "'common unity'" (6). Her guarded optimism provides evidence, too, of what Spivey finds characteristic of contemporary Southern writers: "They have refused to be rootless and have therefore achieved visions of the possibility of cultural revival" (11). They are writers who, "even when they are most at war with the South, maintained a belief in certain cultural values that they absorbed from their native region" (15).

Sara Will is identifiably Southern in its themes and setting, yet the use of language is probably the novel's most dominant feature. Language becomes an important means by which Southern distinctions are illuminated. Bridgers treats the dialects of the Appalachian characters in *Sara Will* with respect, not ridicule. Each speaker makes subtle contributions to the sound of the Southern voice with which the novel resonates. Particularly effective in *Sara Will* is Bridgers's use of three elements of Southern language: (1) names and phrases that ring true to the Southern ear, (2) the tradition of storytelling, and (3) reliance on concrete details drawn from the natural world.

The double first names of the older leading characters, Sara Will Burney and Swanee Hope Burney Calhoun, have an undeniably Southern flavor. With the younger generations' names, Michael, Eva, and Rachel, the Southern distinctions fade. As in *All Together Now,* the flavor of the Southern voice is strongest in conversations that take place in the kitchen or dining room. Following are examples:

> Sara forked a bit of egg into her mouth, tasting the dull flat flavor. (10)

> "Do you think you could eat a poached egg?" she asked.
> "I think I could worry it down." (274)

The "penchant for storytelling" identified by Core in *Southern Fiction Today* is a characteristic that even Eva, from the younger generation, exhibits (52). When asked about Uncle Fate's disfigured arm, she delivers a complete account of Fate's accident, an account that includes facts that a car fell on his arm and "'mashed it flat'" and that Fate's "'cussing and hollering'" were enough to convince doctors to "'see how long they could let it go'" (17) instead of performing immediate amputation. Eva's enthusiastic rendering is an embellishment of the oral accounts she had heard her family pass on.

Bridgers uses concrete details to convey information about abstract concepts in *Sara Will.* In the opening chapter, differences that fuel antagonism between the sisters throughout the novel are clearly presented:

> [Swanee Hope] hardly ever moved except to make a marble cake or dust or sweep the porch. She liked to cook sweet things: puddings smooth with patience, and angel cakes folded slowly, rotating bowl easing its circle against her curving rubber spatula.
>
> Sara Will hadn't the patience for it or the desire. . . . She'd take her blackberries plain or mixed with a little sugar and poured over a hot sweet biscuit she didn't need a mixer to make. (8–9)

Bridgers's use of concrete imagery is most powerful when it includes elements of the natural world. Sara Will's long-sought but elusive contentment, an abstract concept, is beautifully described as an essence that finally "poured over her like warm water, as sunlight penetrated the leafy vault of her woods, making every bud visible, every leaf transparent and singular" (305)

In *Sara Will,* Bridgers achieves the kind of fiction described by Weaver as quintessentially Southern:

> The reader will "hear" the language he already knows if he knows the Deep South, a vernacular that includes elegant refinement no less than earthy imagery, rhythmic, blunt and crude, strewn with

> metaphors from an elevated, literary tradition as often as those taken directly from vulgar experience. It is a language spoken nowhere else in the world, however much it has been diluted by its popular imitation. (xii)

With *Permanent Connections,* Bridgers temporarily travels beyond her characteristic boundaries. Her fifth novel opens in a New Jersey setting that is the home of the adolescent male protagonist. Nevertheless, *Permanent Connections* certainly qualifies as an example of Southern literature. As in her previous novels, in *Permanent Connections* Bridgers uses family relationships as a unifying element, a source of both conflict and comfort. It is on the warp of family that the features that characterize Southern literature are interwoven in a symmetrical pattern. After spending several months in Tyler Springs, North Carolina, the childhood home of his father, Rob Dickson begins to understand and appreciate his relatives from the rural South. Rob, who brings suspicious, modern, urban values to Tyler Mills, suffers alienation, yet he benefits from the situation. He grows from feeling self-disdain toward gaining self-respect; he learns to value his position as the Dickson family's male heir.

Bridgers uses memories, and the sound of voices that share them, as tools for making distinctions not only according to region but also according to the different generations of the Dickson family. The voices reflect what Rubin refers to as Southern writers' concern "with the sensuous properties of language and its imaginative use" (1961, 12). Rubin refines the description by referring to Southern writers' use of the voice as "an uninhibited reliance upon the full resources of language and the old-fashioned moral absolutes that lay behind such language" (1969, 412). Implied is a strong connection between memory, traditional values, and language.

Bridgers uses no specific dialect markers to render the speech of the adolescent outsider, Rob Dickson, and few in the speech of his father, Davis. The taste of dialect that once may have connected them to Tyler Mills has faded during their years in New Jersey. However, in the speech of Davis's brother and sister, Fairlee and Coralee, and of Grandpa, Bridgers takes advantage of the "full resources" of her Southern characters' language. Fairlee reminisces about his sister when he explains to Rob: "She's always had a hankering for rings and bracelets and earbobs and the like" (86).

The most obviously Southern voice in *Permanent Connections* is Grandpa's. The oratorical tradition identified by Core, as well as the "moral absolutes" noted by Rubin, are as obvious as the Appalachian dialect with which Grandpa reprimands Rob and accuses his son, Davis, of indifference to Southern and family values:

> "Well, you went and got yourself in a heap of trouble anyhow," Grandpa complained. "Ain't ever been a Dickson in court, unless

> you're talking about the land dispute my pa had back before the Depression, and by God, he was on the side of the right. The judge said so. No Dickson never got hauled in by the scruff of his neck. Nary one of us got ourself arrested." (207)

> "Davis don't care nothing about where he come from. This here family was in the war, boy, and got hurt by it. My grandpappy lost everything he had, his good eye included. His brother Jessie got hit in the mouth, bullet took his tongue right out so's he couldn't even yell out his pain. He couldn't never tell what it was like at Shiloh 'cause he couldn't write moron just his name. Spent the rest of his life dumb. But he tried to protect what belonged to him. That's what it was all about, boy! Protecting yourself. Protecting the people from the government." (156)

The Southern flavor of Bridgers's novels depends on her delicate, carefully measured spice of spoken words. Her gifted use of language falls within the tradition that Southern writer and critic Allen Tate describes:

> The Southerner always talks to somebody else, and this somebody else, after varying intervals, is given his turn; but the conversation is always among rhetoricians; that is to say, the typical Southerner is not going anywhere; it is not about anything. *It is about the people who are talking,* even if they never refer to themselves, which they usually don't, since conversation is only an expression of manners, the purpose of which is to make everybody happy. This may be the reason why Northerners and other uninitiated persons find the alternating, or contrapuntal, conversations of Southerners fatiguing. Educated Northerners like their conversations to be about ideas. (584)

Literary analysis of Bridgers' novels not only reveals the merit of her fiction. It also suggests that the genre of young adult literature has matured enough to allow for specialization; that is, Bridgers should not only be respected as a writer of young adult literature but also as a writer of fine Southern literature.

Works Cited

Bridgers, Sue Ellen. *All Together Now.* New York: Knopf, 1979.

———. *Home Before Dark.* New York: Knopf, 1976.

———. *Notes for Another Life.* New York: Knopf, 1981.

———. *Sara Will.* New York: Harper, 1985.

———. *Permanent Connections.* New York: Harper/Keypoint, 1987.

Core, George, ed. *Southern Fiction Today: Renascence and Beyond.* Athens: U of Georgia P, 1969.

Lawson, Louis A. *Another Generation: Southern Fiction Since World War II.* University: UP of Mississippi, 1984.

Manna, Anthony L., and Sue Misheff, "Responding to the Magic: Sue Ellen Bridgers Talks about Writing." *The ALAN Review* 13.2(Winter, 1986): 56–61.

MacKethan, Lucinda H. *The Dream of Arcady: Place and Time in Southern Literature.* Baton Rouge: Louisiana State UP, 1980.

Rubin, Louis D., Jr. "Second Thoughts on the Old Gray Mare: The Continuing Relevance of Southern Literary Issues." *Southern Fiction Today: Renascence and Beyond.* Ed. George Core. Athens: University of Georgia Press, 1969.

———. "Southern Literature: The Historical Image." *Modern Southern Literature in Its Cultural Setting.* Ed. Louis D. Rubin, Jr., and Robert D. Jacobs. Garden City: Doubleday, 1961.

Rubin, Louis D., Jr., and Robert D. Jacobs, eds. *Southern Renascence: The Literature of the Modern South.* Baltimore: Johns Hopkins Press, 1953.

Spivey, T. R. *Revival: Southern Writers in the Modern City.* Gainesville: UP of Florida, 1986.

Tate, Alan. "A Southern Mode of the Imagination." *Essays of Four Decades.* Boston: Swallow, 1968.

Part I The Authors

Section 3
Paul Zindel

8 Of Fiction and Madness

Paul Zindel

Courtesy of HarperCollins

It's a great honor for me to be here with you. With my friends from Bantam and Harper & Row—all the other fine publishers and honored guests. On your seventy-fifth birthday! And I'm very happy—not jealous or envious of my colleague Sue Ellen Bridgers to whom you've given special recognition this morning. I'm not always forgotten. Your students send me fan mail. I hate authors who read letters from fans at conventions. I usually don't do it because it's such a bore and cop-out. I did receive one special letter recently I'd like to share though:

> June 14, 1985
>
> Dear Mr. Zindel,
>
> I thought I should let you know your writing is a lot of senseless junk. I've read most of it and if I ever catch my kid reading it I'd cream her. They should put rough loonies like you in jail.
>
> Yours Truly,
>
> Dick Doyle
>
> P.S. My real name is Louise Walker and I think your senseless junk is the best senseless junk I've ever read. I particularly like *The Undertaker's Gone Bananas* and I love *The Effect of Gamma Rays on Man-in-the-Moon Marigolds.* My mom was in it, and when I get older I want to be in it, too. I'm 14 right now. My favorite things to do are read, draw, act, write, laugh and disturb my teachers. When I'm a writer, I hope I can write as well as you.
>
> With Love,
>
> Louise

I really wanted to bring you something special today. I thought perhaps at least a lesson plan. At least a mildly subconscious reminder of the staggeringly impressive timelessness of the human behavior of storytelling. I thought that would make you especially alert during

Reprinted from *The ALAN Review* 14.1, Fall 1986, pages 1–8, by permission of the author.

your conferences and discussions-to-come during this historic meeting in this particular city. But I wanted you to also know about my new book *Harry and Hortense at Hormone High.* My own book is all I could possibly be something of an expert on. And what's worse—I'm anecdotal. My fiction comes out of my life, and I imagined you'd be sleepy this early in the morning. I decided I'd better stick to my painful autobiographical experiences which for some reason always make my ALAN friends laugh. At least I'll know you're awake between all the munching of toast, bacon, and Diet Center Wasa Crackers.

The bottom line this morning, however, is that I'm a little schizo because I've had to reawaken the energies and neurotic flights which led me to write *Harry and Hortense.* First I had a premise: Our greatest need is to find meaning in our lives. This was a personal need for several reasons. I was in my own male menopause or climacteric. Adolescents seem to be in perpetual menopause. My symptoms were that I was depressed and burning out. UCLA had sent for me to examine my brain figuratively. I told them I was finished with autobiographical bellyaching. I told them I wanted to write about greater vistas, of heroes and heroines. Themes of staggering importance. The graduate students and the professor of this special artistic brain-examination class told me that whatever I write should be based on what came before. There's no truthful escape from the artistic and personal past. But whatever I write I should be certain I can bring a level of Beauty to it. Beauty in the classic sense.

A second depression symptom was I was eating huge quantities of Baskin & Robbins' World Class chocolate ice cream and pizzas with extra cheese. This culminated in my being attacked by a gypsy woman outside the Vatican last summer. For some reason she picked me out of a crowd, ran up to me and pinched my left breast fiercely. I took that as a definite omen I was getting too fat.

In order to work out my problem in fiction I decided to use Harry and Hortense as my depressed teenage protagonists. I let Harry tell the story and he starts the book by telling us:

> Hortense and I were so depressed last term we used to get together every Saturday night to split a can of diet cola and talk about how mean most of the kids and teachers were to each other in our high school. But that was all before we met Jason Rohr, the most dynamic and exciting teenage schizophrenic we've ever known.

Harry tells us he wants to be a writer, that he's basically good-looking but not in the usual sense: "I'm tall, which doesn't mean anything since a lot of famous historical people were dwarfs and they did O.K." He works with Hortense as co-theater critic on The *Bird's Eye Gazette.* When I was a student at Port Richmond High School on Staten Island I worked on *The Crow's Nest.* My faculty advisor was Miss Conlan, an English teacher I've mentioned in other novels.

Hortense is described as wanting to be a psychologist. I based her on my wife Bonnie, so I had to make her character very charming—about five-foot-two, with very black straight hair which she wears in bangs:

> "She's very distinctive and told me her hair style is called the China doll style. And she has a very slightly cute nose and wears make up that makes her eyes look like Elizabeth Taylor's as Cleopatra."

The incident in reality which incited me to write *Harry and Hortense at Hormone High* was an experience that happened when I went to a horrible play in Los Angeles. Some actress I knew from my brief six-month excursion into acting lessons was in it. I quit the acting school because the middle-aged lady who ran it liked to wear very big boots and do too many improvisation exercises in which we in the class had to pretend to be prisoners in a detention camp—and she'd send her young lover of the moment in to portray a persecuting storm trooper.

At the intermission of the play I was in a line to buy a glass of wine and a few other local actors recognized me and started chatting, when I noticed, about forty feet from me in the lobby, a Ryan O'Neal-ish looking guy, about twenty-nine, staring at me with a warm and open smile. Backstage after the show I was congratulating the actress I knew in the cast, and I was surprised to turn around and find the Ryan O'Neal guy (who I'll just call Ryan for Reality) coming up to me and introducing himself. He had a normal looking girlfriend with him—nothing like one who turned up later in the chain of events to come. He knew I was a writer and wanted to know what I was working on. I told him I was planning to write a story about a hero. My first real hero. His eyes exploded. He told me he was an actor and desperately needed to find a writer because he knew the story of an incredible hero. We exchanged phone numbers and set up a meeting.

At this point when I tell an audience about these experiences I use one of two bird calls my children bought when we were in Paris last summer. One device makes a "TWEET" like a sweet little canary, and the other makes a "HONK" like a loud duck. Because the Reality of Fiction of writing this book was so intertwined I decided to clue the audience with a "TWEET" if I was talking about the Fictional areas from my book, and I sounded a "HONK" every time I was back into the Reality of my adventures. These devices were amusing and helpful to the audience as far as I could tell.

TWEET!—In my novel this young guy became the highly pivotal character of Jason Rohr, and Harry and Hortense meet him at the high school's spring production of *South Pacific:*

> Anyway, suddenly there was this mysterious-looking boy with a big black dog outside on the entrance steps to the school. We had never seen him before. He was just standing there staring at us, and feeding his pet. He looked sixteen, six feet tall, and very dynamic, as though he was a star on a major soap opera.

In my fiction I had to start hinting at all the tension and adventures to come regarding Jason. Someone is mysteriously putting up bizarre notices on the school bulletin board.

> Attention students and teachers! I am very sad and in great despair. I noticed last week that only twenty-three parents and three teachers showed up for the PTA meeting. The Principal and Dean of Boys didn't even go. I also noticed there were no guards at four of the street entrances. Several Agents of the Devil were able to just walk in off the street and steal school supplies and a typewriter. But don't give up hope. Watch for more of my bulletins. And lift your sights to the heavens.
>
> Yours Truly,
>
> ICARUS, a god

Icarus, of course, is from mythology—the son of Daedalus who flew too close to the sun and the wax melted on his feathered wings and he fell to his death.

I needed to think about my characters' motivations at this point in writing. Who wanted what? What were the driving forces? The best characters are always the ones who want to get something so badly they will destroy or be destroyed to get it. I suspected I was using Harry and Hortense as my own needs. Jason was the Ryan O'Neal-ish guy from reality—someone who wanted to save the world. The school of the novel was a microcosm. Harry tells us during the course of his writing the novel that in this "exposé" he'll have to call his real high school *Hormone High* or everyone would know which teenage loony bin it is, and the Board of Education would come after him and Hortense and make them eat three consecutive Mongolian chop sueys in the school cafeteria.

HONK!—I wanted this school to contain every madness of kids today. The schlemiels, the addicts to rock, alcohol, drugs, the truants, dropouts. A condensation of every article written about whacky kids in *Psychology Today* and *Atlantic Monthly* during the last ten years. Of course, I know a lot of teachers from my teaching days and they fed me some of the more current events from reality at their schools. For example, a teenage couple on their lunch hour had their bodies sensuously linked on a lawn across the street from Tottenville High School. The cops brought the kids into the school and they still refused to stop their passion. Also, a junior high girl student in Elizabeth, New Jersey, spanked her home economics teacher with a yard stick all the way to the principal's office to make a student's arrest because the student didn't care for the amount of homework being assigned. When I was teaching, my own students threw an apple at a movie screen in the Franklin Institute.

TWEET!—So Hormone High is a fictional school, housing the pupil wildness of everywhere. I put in a few good kids and teachers, too, just to balance things.

I also wanted an antagonist who was a worthy antagonist. I picked Dean Niboff, the Dean of Boys. Harry says:

> "Dean Wiboff's face was a fear something. He was a short man, about 55, with a booming voice, and looked just like one of those judges from a movie who condemns someone to die in a gas chamber. He also had jowls like Winston Churchill."

But I created a lot of other supernumerary villains: (1) June Peckernaw, a brazen snippy tart of a cheerleader, (2) Rocky Funiceli, the football star who usually ends up playing the sailor in the spring production of *South Pacific,* wearing a grass skirt and a pair of half coconuts for the "Honey Bun" number, (3) most of the lunchroom mob of students; (4) a couple of big, muscle-ridden gym teachers (even though most gym teachers I've known are small), (5) Principal Greenburg, a psychotic principal I once had, (6) a 300-pound school psychologist (Why are so many school psychologists in need of Dexatrim?).

I also had to consider what the Quest or Mission was for my heroes and villains. I began to see that forming when I had my hero Jason Rohr tack another message on the school bulletin board:

> Aristotle knew how to create a meaningful curriculum! Dean Niboff and Principal Greenburg hide in their offices and we know they don't care about us. Aristotle would never have let them into his academy at the court of Phillip the Great of Macedon. He would have tied them naked to the roof and left them for the vultures. Aristotle was a great teacher! He taught his students things they needed to know, like how to protect them from the Barbarians. He taught them the secrets of Homer and mythology, where the keys to happiness and godliness lie. No, everyone isn't o.k.! Aristotle and Socrates knew it. We're in hot water. Shape up or ship out, Dean Wiboff and Principal Greenburg. I will give you one week to change your ways or you'd have to answer to me and to the spirit of Aristotle.
>
> Signed,
>
> ICARUS, a god

Harry and Hortense visit Jason at this dump of a house on Wild Avenue in Travis, Staten Island. They don't know he thinks he's Icarus yet, but they meet his Aunt Mo' who has thirty Great Danes in kennels in the backyard: "She must have been a hundred years old, and she walked by means of moving one leg and then doing a little pole vault on a cane. . . ."

HONK!—Well, the large number of dogs comes from my reality when I was eleven and Lassie was hot. My mother wanted to get rich quick so she bought one male and one female collie and started breeding them. We ended up with twenty-six; the only one sold was to the Empire Theater who had a Lassie Contest and a deaf and mute boy with grateful eyes was the winner. Mo' was basically an old lady dog breeder I met in California who had extraterrestrial experiences in Guatemala.

TWEET!—Harry and Hortense visit Jason's room and notice he doesn't refrigerate his butter and papaya juice. He tells them the ancient Greeks never refrigerated anything:

> "You said you had a story about a hero you wanted us to write," they remind Jason.
>
> "Oh, yes. I need you to write about a hero greater than any astronaut, president, greater than Alexander the Great or anyone you could possibly think of!"
>
> "Who?"
>
> "Me. I am the one. Do you understand what I'm saying?" he asks them.
>
> "Oh, yes, We understand all right. . . ."

HONK!—The reality of Wild Avenue when I was growing up was mysterious. I was in the fifth grade and living in Travis. Kids trapped muskrats. Boys went skinny dipping and paid girls like Rosemary Fleiser twenty-five cents to get a glimpse of her charms. One family had a teenage son with a huge head. Milton, my best pal, and I got trapped in a blackberry thicket and we were bombarded by dragon flies. In fact, you can read about this area in the *1986 Ripley's Believe It or Not Calendar* ironically for my birthdate—May 15. It tells us that the site of the world's biggest garbage dump is here on Staten Island and receives over 10,000 tons of garbage a day.

Now, the Ryan O'Neal-ish character in reality told me a story about a hero which must be written. He thought he was the reincarnation of Alexander the Great. His steady girlfriend looked like Marilyn Monroe. She was a model—but she wore unironed puffy short dresses that made her look like Bo Peep with cleavage. She and Ryan were both in commercials at that time. He played a lifeguard where Taco Chips magically flew through the air. She was in something like a Cranapple ad where she spun around on roller skates in short-shorts. They both had a brilliant understanding of the psychology of their relationship which was often quite fiery; and they spent most of their days researching Alexander the Great in the archives of UCLA and attending lectures at the Jungian and Philosophic Institutes in California. Wednesdays they went to Unemployment to pick up their checks.

In fiction and real life I had to ask where the adventure was taking me—and Harry and Hortense. I had to start guessing ahead. Catch glimpses of the future and my own subconscious to imagine the "plants" I'd have to seed in order to build my story into something as meaningful and important as possible. In fiction I sensed wings from Icarus. Flight. A death. And a victory.

I had Mo' show Harry and Hortense a flying device she mentions Jason is working on:

> In an old barn we were amazed to see a hang glider of some sort sitting in the center of the dirt floor. A lawn mower gizmo was mounted on it. The glider looked more like a junky homemade sort of thing that one really wouldn't want to do any serious sky gliding in. . . .
>
> "Jason's always loved flying, you know," Aunt Mo' said.

HONK!—I was forgetting about being depressed, and becoming quite absorbed in the mystery of Jason's madness itself. One night Ryan broke down crying in front of me and told me that when he was five years old he witnessed his mother being hacked to death by a maniac lover. Harry and Hortense discover a similar background on Jason when they sneak a look into the school's record room—and I had also come across a case of the same ilk when I was a chemistry teacher. Everyone was coming down hard on a student, but I took the time to really check out his records and found a similar murder. With Ryan I had agreed to become part of his pseudocommunity. The pseudocommunity he had built around him—that of a brilliant and very likeable schizophrenic. He knew every detail of Alexander the Great's life. He knew more than scholars from the universities who were astounded when he'd talk to them after their lectures—and they'd invite him to address their classes. He taught me details about the life of Greek, Roman, and Persian cultures in the several centuries before the birth of Christ. He was brilliant in the areas of mythology and the origins of consciousness. He was spectacular and generous with his knowledge and wisdom, and there were many events which could be interpreted as confirmation that he was indeed Alexander the Great reborn. He was aware of the survival of a society by a reexamination of the power of archetypes. Ryan had magnificently developed an entire magical existence for himself. I traced it back to the fact that when he was five—and still in the childhood trauma of witnessing the murder of his mother—he was given a book. The power of a book. This book was on the life of Alexander the Great. His need and pain were so great, his child's mind became the book. It was a rather classic case, I suppose, but I've always felt I could understand many of the mad in this world. None of us is so distant from madness. A Dr. William Dement once said, "Dreaming permits each and everyone of us to be safely insane every night of the week."

Scholars who have analyzed my work say in every book I knock off an animal: in *Marigolds,* a rabbit; in *Pardon Me, You're Stepping On My Eyeball,* a raccoon. In *Harry and Hortense at Hormone High* I was determined not to kill the Great Dane. I only had him slightly poisoned by the vicious cheerleader and football star—but he recovers.

In my writing I had to ask myself constantly if there was a convincing inevitability of the situation I had bitten off?

TWEET!—Jason's madness causes so much trouble at the school that Dean Niboff and the authorities really have to do something about him. Jason takes over the P.A. system at one point and declares for the entire school to hear:

> "Attention! Attention! All students and teachers! You, too, Dean Riboff. I just want to talk to you about some important things. Hello. Can you hear me? This is Icarus. I know you haven't wanted to believe that I am really a god, but I am. I am a special god who has sometimes been called Jason Rohr, but I know if you listen to me today, you won't laugh at me or treat me the way you did on other occasions. What you don't understand is that although I am a god, I am just a boy, too. And you shouldn't be frightened of me. I've been sent here to help you all. This time I'm not leaving until I really get things straight with you all!"
>
> "What do you mean, they took him away?" Hortense gets to ask Jason's Aunt Mo'.
>
> "They put him back in the sanitarium again."
>
> "What sanitarium?"
>
> "The one on the top of the hill—Sea Vista, or something. That's where they always end up putting him away."

HONK!—In reality Sea Vista was really Sea View Hospital on Staten Island. When I was in the fifth grade it was an old age home and my class went there to jitterbug on the stage for the old folks. When I was fifteen it was learned I had TB and I was sent away to a sanitorium for a rest cure at Lake Kushaqua in New York State—while ironically the miracle cure was being developed by a doctor at Sea View, which had been partially converted for veteran TB patients.

After the drug existed Sea View turned into Staten Island's "poorhouse" and my aunt became a dietitian there. I used to visit her and watch hundreds of the old folks line up and gallop madly for seats in the dining room every meal time. They'd hit each other with crutches and all sorts of things just to create some excitement for themselves.

In the fiction of my story I had Jason escape from the sanitarium—but Harry and Hortense realize they've got to level with him. From the plotting point of view, I knew I had to find a renewal and reinforcement for the homestretch of my story. I had to really look at all my emotion and action to this point in the novel in order to at least glimpse the ending. I had Jason hide for a while at a construction site. Dynamite is soon missing from the area. I got the idea to incorporate dynamite into the story (as a threat to the school) from a high school clerk who works in Sacramento. She gave me a list of what all the crazy kids do in her school, including asking her to hold hollow apples in which they've stashed their day's supply of pot. She told me there was no way to save her school and that the only sensible thing to do was blow the whole thing up and start all over again. That would be the only way to create a school that could handle and create the values and course of study kids really need today. The system was too corrupted to repair. She was drunk when she told me this, but I found the idea exciting.

Dynamite—The Sense of an Inevitability. And this led me to sensing an incipient conversion—the loosening of some knot in the minds of Harry and Hortense. This had to be an action rendered plausible, a change due to a new fact or motive—or possibly some hitherto untried appeal to reason and emotion. Hortense writes a letter to Jason in which she has to try to tell him the truth.

To bring reality to the mad is a difficult assignment. Madness doesn't usually change easily nor that much—which is what I found out with Ryan, as well as with Jason. I made a decision to lead him closer and closer to realize he wasn't Alexander the Great or any time-warp manifestation of him. When you hold up such mirrors you risk violence.

Now a storyteller's chief difficulty is to find a final crisis with an ending which satisfies at once his artistic conscience and the requirements of dramatic effect. The difficulty becomes the greatest as we approach reality.

TWEET!

> It didn't suddenly end, but what happened was the huge mob of students stood gaping up toward the roof of the school and all we could hear was what sounded like a small engine starting up. It was the sound of a leaf blower or lawnmower. Nearly a couple of thousand kids and teachers and other people had collected by now, and there

> was only the sound of this little engine which seemed to be coming from the very top of the roof. And then we began to see it. . . .

So there is this crowd. Barriers. Cops. A final note tacked up by Jason—this time on the front door of the school. The note says:

> NO SCHOOL TODAY! I HAVE A LOT OF DYNAMITE! . . . AND I'M GOING TO BLOW IT UP!!!
>
> SINCERELY,
>
> ICARUS!!!

Jason flies from the roof of the school in his lawnmower-powered contraption. Dynamite blows up the record room. I couldn't bring myself, even in fiction, to blow up a whole school. I like schools far too much. Jason soars. The kids run after him. He's escaping by flight over a river toward Bayonne, New Jersey. There's a wind drift. The Bayonne Bridge from my childhood. A memory from reality of a near crash my wife and I had once in a helicopter flying under the Golden Gate. Terror buttons from past and present were being pressed in me in order to feel Jason's death as he falls.

Aristotle suggested that after the climax of a story the author should allow about a half-hour for the audience to listen to the surviving characters, to just sit around and chat about what became of it all.

Harry writes:

> Jason Rohr had the most unusual wake and funeral of any kid who ever passed away while attending Hormone High, and certainly the most unusual of any kid Hortense and I had ever heard of anywhere. Over seventeen hundred showed up to pay their respects during the three day wake at Pagliggini's Funeral Parlor.

In reality, during my first year teaching, a freshman boy in my homeroom class died from a brain tumor. The funeral parlor was on the next block from the school. The principal had teachers led their classes over to the funeral home to pay their last respects. The boy looked very much like my own eleven-year-old son David does now. His head was bandaged in the coffin. That was the wake I gave Jason Rohr in my novel:

> But there were only six of us and a dog at the actual burial in Wood Knoll Cemetery. The funeral director, a minister, Hortense and Me, Aunt Mo', the mother of the kid with the big head, and Jason's dog at the freshly dug grave.

This came from the Reality of my own mother's funeral seventeen years before. She was to be buried on top of her father in the same grave. The morning of the funeral the existing gravestone fell into the open grave, canceling the burial for that day. The next day there was just a few of us going back to the cemetery. The grave-diggers and I had to carry the coffin to the grave. Three or four of us were handling a weight meant for six or eight or a machine. I almost died carrying the coffin. I was ready to hire a passerby to help—anything. It was terrible. And it was lonely.

But in my book it was now time for Harry and Hortense to have their moral peripety—that sudden dissipation of some illusion or defeat of some imposture. They had to have a crumbling of some castle in the air. Harry writes:

> "I mean, there's something about what happened to Jason I don't understand. Something that makes me not want to believe in anything anymore."
>
> "What do you think is missing?" Hortense asks him.
>
> "The BOON."
>
> "The what?"
>
> "The boon. A boon is like a prize, I told her. It's something the hero wins and brings back so the rest of the world can be better."

Finally Harry has to ask:

> "What would have happened to Jason if he hadn't read about the myth of Daedalus—if he hadn't become Icarus?" [OR IN THE CASE OF REALITY, WHAT WOULD HAVE BECOME OF RYAN IF HE HADN'T READ THAT BOOK ON ALEXANDER THE GREAT!]
>
> "Then he might have been no one at all," Hortense answers.

And this is often the truth with many who are what we call "insane." Chesterton said, "Do not free a camel of the burden of his hump. You may be freeing him from being a camel."

At this point in my speech I brought forth some strange hair appendages which I affixed to my ears—and donned a partial grotesque face mask. Anything for drama!

And isn't there something in all of this that happens to many of us. To many of the young we teach. All start with the profound need to be loved. The profound fear of being worthless. A staggering love of life. And a terrifying fear of dying. By the time we meet them in high school, the kids have already begun to wear their experiences—the good and the bad—like pieces of what usually becomes a permanent costume.

At this point I removed my grotesque mask, etc.

And you and I have the same job, don't we? The storyteller and the teacher. We have to lead the kids to divest pieces of their forming madnesses, to let them see and be as much of Life as they deserve. Often, we help them see by means of . . . books.

But now for the victory! The change from gloom to exhilaration in my novel.

The ending for *Harry and Hortense* came to me in a very strange way. I was flying back from L.A.—a 747 window seat—heading for a landing at JFK. For the first time in a hundred such flights I was on a plane making its approach directly over Staten Island. I was right over my mother's grave—a thousand feet in the air—but I could look down and make out the cemetery, and I saw my characters and began to cry. That's my acid test—that I've made a genuine investment of emotion in any book. As I cry I'm really quite happy because it signals me I've tapped into something truthful to me. I could see Harry and Hortense below. Harry was looking up at the plane. He caught a glimpse of himself in the future. Of himself and Hortense, he writes . . . imagining he's now in a plane passing over Jason's graveyard:

> We were in the future looking down at our old hometown, flying over Jason's old, old grave and the graves of our parents and our teachers—and even Dean Wiboff. There in the future I knew it was Hortense and I flying somewhere because we had heard a call to an important adventure—and accepted! Hortense and I were like Jason. Because of him we would go forth with amulets against the dragon forces. Hortense and I would always hear the call to adventure and we would go!!!!!

The Boon; the Insight

They realize it is up to them to become the next heroes. The reversal. That was the gift of Jason's madness and life. My book, like most books, should be a crucible for the emotions of the young readers. It should allow them a container in which to examine their own secrets and imaginations. It should be a place to invite their souls. As Emily Dickinson said, a book should not only provide them with facts, but the phosphorescence of learning.

Though my premise had been to find meaning in my own life—it's clear you and NCTE already have great meaning. You've lasted seventy-five years. I've lasted twelve books, thanks to you. It's also certain each of you is not afraid to go forth on a journey. No matter what your own personal problems may be, you've managed to put on clothes, shoes, socks, propelled your bodies—many from great distances—to be here this morning. Also, your presence at the Conference proves you are generative. You're here to refresh and discuss and discover boons that you will bring home to your schools, colleagues, and students, to give them amulets against the dragon forces. Good morning to you, and I wish you a vital Conference.

The Effect of Gamma Rays on the Man-and-the-Writer Zindel: *The Pigman* Plus Twenty Years and Counting

Mike Angelotti

The response to The Pigman *was different. Many of my nonreaders took the book home and finished its 200 pages in two days. Then, shyly at first, students walked by my desk saying, "I really love* The Pigman. *This is the kind of novel we should be reading."*

—*Else Weinstein, "High School Teacher"*

Q: What place has young adult literature in the schools?
A: Young adult literature has a firm place in the schools. In a sense it is like a young person choosing a friend, a friend his own age, a friend who talks to him in a way he can understand, a friend who talks to him about living, loving, and surviving in a world that he finds himself. It prepares the very foundation of loving books. It shows a student that reading can be exciting and can give information and help and provide a mythology that is usable at a time when he needs it. Leading the right student to the right book is the secret—the greatest secret of demonstrating how important a book can be. Reading is not a useless snobbery. Reading is not a premature drudgery. Reading the right book allows the student to cry out—come, beast, mystery, come.

The following is, I think, a unique interview piece—no, more like a Vulcan mind meld—with Paul Zindel. Although he may be known best to most of the ALAN membership for *The Pigman* and other YA novels, and for his Pulitzer Prize-winning play, *The Effect of Gamma Rays on Man-in-the-Moon Marigolds,* some may not be aware that he is known also in other circles for screenwriting such films as *Up the Sand Box, Mame, Maria's Lovers,* and *Runaway Train;*

Reprinted from *The ALAN Review* 16.3, Spring 1989, pages 21–25, 43, by permission of the authors.

and such teleplays as *Alice in Wonderland, Babes in Toyland,* and *Let Me Hear You Whisper.* In addition to *Marigolds,* he has written other stage plays such as *And Miss Reardon Drinks a Little, Ladies at the Alamo,* and, most recently, *Amulets Against the Dragon Forces,* which will open at the Circle Repertory in New York this spring. A comprehensive listing of Zindel's works and a bibliography of related articles may be found in *Presenting Paul Zindel* (1988) by Jack Jacob Forman (Twayne's United States Authors Series, Young Adult Authors, Twayne Publishers, Boston). Two facts noted by Forman in that biography clearly demonstrate Zindel's remarkable success in the YA field: one, "the hardcover edition of every young adult novel that Zindel has ever written is still in print," and, two, "in December, 1987, Zindel concluded an agreement with Bantam Publishers which guarantees that all of his young adult novels. . . will be in paperback until the year 2003" (93). Included is his forthcoming *A Begonia for Miss Applebaum* (1989).

The compelling question is why? Why so much success to Paul Zindel in the YA field for so long? Else Weinstein, who made the opening quote to this piece in a November 6, 1988, *New York Times* "Education Life" article entitled "High School Teacher" (Section 4A: 16), answers that question in, perhaps, the most telling way when she describes the reactions of her students to *The Pigman:*

> My student Ghita wrote: "Teachers all over the world should give their students such books to read. It makes them understand about responsibility, about growing up, and not always thinking about themselves. It also shows how to deal with death. I am glad you gave us this book to read."
>
> Janice wrote: "This book is both happy and sad. What I most enjoyed was when John and Lorraine first went to Mr. Pignati's house. They had such a good time. The saddest part was when Mr. Pignati lost trust in them because of the party. He had lost his wife, and now he also lost his friends. He was all alone at the end."
>
> Brenda wrote: "This book has taught me to spend more time with my grandparents. For old people are often lonely like the Pigman. You could be the cause of them living a little longer, and being happy, even if it is just for a limited time."

People who read somehow develop a clearer sense of human values and larger souls than those who never learn to appreciate literature. *The Pigman* changed my students' perceptions and made them aware of death, compassion, and taking responsibility for their own actions. Chris even argued with the author about Mr. Pignati's death, a sign that it disturbed him greatly. Finally, after many years of schooling, my students experienced the real meaning of literature.

The purpose of this piece, however, is neither to review Zindel's works nor extol his virtues, but to get at the gut of Zindel, the writer and the person. I will leave you to judge how successful our collaboration was in meeting that intent. In that you may find the form of this "interview" unusual, you should know some things about how it was developed and edited. First, the substance, flow, and letter of Zindel's musings are faithful transcriptions (with my punctuations) of the first part of an audiotape. Zindel responded to written questions (included in the text) *spontaneously* (he decided he would not read the questions ahead of time to create the best conditions for spontaneity). The questions were clustered to provoke depth, to get inside Paul Zindel. After listening to the tape, I decided that the best interests of the ALAN readership would be served by presenting Zindel's more or less stream-of-consciousness responses to the question clusters *as* they were delivered. The second part of the tape focused more explicitly on "writing process." That segment, hopefully, will appear in another publication in the near future.

For me, the experiencing of the tape was an extraordinary event for two reasons: one, and most significantly, I learned something about human beings and writing literature; and, two, I was surprised and gratified to discover the depth, the truth, of Paul Zindel—the man, the novelist, the playwright, the screenwriter—at this moment of his life. It is no secret that even as he has strength, he has weakness as a writer. But the important point to me is that he is aware of both and determined to be better. Whether he can deliver on that is another question. I think he can. I hope he can.

And so, the interview.

As we talk, we are in the twentieth-anniversary year of *The Pigman.* It would seem that this interview should be something special, something appropriately commemorative, maybe a more reflective piece on your life as a writer than the usual interview probing the writing of this or that work, although we'll certainly do some of that. Let's begin with you and *The Pigman.*

Q. The book is considered a young adult classic by most YA professionals and by its continued readership. How do you account for its capacity to touch so many generations of readers? So much has changed for them since the sixties.

A: Well, I think there are two main reasons I can think of. Number one is I did commit a great portion of my own emotional truth to it. Emotional truth tends to pretty much age fairly well, and so there is something about the book that does bring many people to tears towards the end of it. I think it is probably rooted in the fact that when the Pigman dies, in some way it touches people, children, of all ages in their own "lack of innocence," not lack of it, but loss of it. So, I think that often all through life human beings come across certain moments of growth, and when we remember them from the point-of-view of nostalgia or experience the insight for the first time, there's a weeping. We tend to not like to move on. There is some sadness because we are saying goodbye to a part of ourselves, and that reminds me of some of the more emotional farewells—almost as when a ship is sailing. I've seen some farewells around the world in which the tears and the emotions of the event are not covered by inhibition.

Then the other reason why it hasn't dated, I think, is a conscious choice. I knew from teaching over a period of ten years that the kids changed their slang every few years. It is like them changing the color and shape and textures of their hair. They have a slang that gets to be unique for them and is something that seems only to fit properly on them. I didn't imitate that aspect of their language. There were certain elements that they did use that I think were timeless, for example, the use of bathos, or the use of hyperbole by taking some very common word and then juxtaposing it with something very lofty or by taking some very lofty concept or word and then juxtaposing it with something very common. This tends to give the illusion of slang, but there was really very little in *The Pigman* that was intended to copy the way young people spoke in the sixties. And I think that has allowed it some longevity.

At the tail end of that question you say that so much has changed for the readership since the sixties. And yet, again, I never picked themes nor qualities that do change. My books always, and certainly in the case of *The Pigman,* are linked to timeless elements about the human being, which is what I have always been interested in. I am never very interested in something that is terribly trendy or a disguise of any type. I think my purpose has always been to look into the heart and soul of the human being in order to discover what truth I might find there—ironically, for myself probably more than anyone else.

Q. What about you? What has been the significance, the value, of the writing of *The Pigman* and of its remarkable success as a YA novel to you as a writer and as a human being. Do you think much about such an early work? Or maybe you can't escape it (re: the "Star Trek" actors. To the public, Leonard Nimoy *is* Mr. Spock and William Shatner *is* Captain Kirk—no matter how brilliantly they may play other characters). Are you The Pigman?

A: Then, in the next question you say what about me, what has been the significance, the value of writing *The Pigman* and its remarkable success as a YA novel to you as an early writer and as a human being? Well, it was a winning on one front of my creative urge in life.

It was actually the transitional book by which I went from chemistry teacher to writer. So it was the book that actually in its first year from a practical point-of-view matched my teaching salary so that I felt I had the chance to be a writer. Aside from that sheer monetary point-of-view—allowing me to exist—it reinforced the applause I received from writing in general, which was something I had contracted very early on in high school when I had first written a small piece in the high school newspaper and had received some praise for it from the other kids and from the teachers. So, *The Pigman* was very important. The reviews for it were very important. They fed me as a writer and as a human being. For almost twenty years I didn't think about *The Pigman.*

When you ask—"Do I think much about such an early work?,"—I didn't. And I was never amazed that I didn't because I think fairly early on I began to learn that the writing process was really problem solving, and when anyone would talk to me about my work, I would always only remember and talk enthusiastically about what I was working on at that moment because whatever I am working on at that particular moment, as with many writers, is the most important and the most vital and the most alive because it is the current problem solving, the immediate trying to come to terms with some aspect of being human and some aspect of being on earth, or in space as that may be. But, I didn't look back. And, in fact, I hadn't reread the book until we were approaching the twentieth year. And I did that for a number of reasons. There was another work that had been successful just after *The Pigman.* It came within two years and it had preexisted *The Pigman.* That was the play, *The Effect of Gamma Rays on Man-in-the-Moon Marigolds.* And, there was, of course, even a greater applause from it receiving the Pulitzer Prize. So I had the good fortune of a writer hitting in two different mediums and receiving all the energy that comes from that type of success, which I don't consider staggering, but it is certainly sufficient for any writer to give him a chance to make writing a career. The reason I went back to reread *The Pigman* just a year or two ago was exactly the same reason I went back to see *Marigolds* in two productions, one in Toronto and one down in Houston, where the play had its first performance in 1964 or 1965. What I was doing was going back to look at another writer who no longer really existed. I was going back to look at me at a younger age. I was going back to look and see what all the praise was based on, and I went back looking for a renewed energy, as I was beginning to feel a change coming into my writing. I wanted to know what was so special about what I had done then, and what was so *unspecial* about many of the things I had done in between, and what I needed to be very special for the work that lies ahead of me.

I was amazed when I read *The Pigman.* I hadn't realized how much energy had gone into that book. I hadn't realized what a wealth of images and emotions and audacity that arrived into that book, since I had freshly written it actually while I was a teacher on a Ford Foundation Grant. I came fresh from the classroom. I came bearing a tremendous quantity of reality and a tremendous quantity of emotion, not only in myself but in all of the kids I was teaching.

I would be in a classroom, and I knew some of the good kids, but the ones that were having problems were fascinating to me. I would find a kid that seemed to be brewing like a volcano in the class, and I would go down and check out the records to find out why was this kid tougher, hardened, difficult to speak to, and I would find astounding facts, such as in one case the boy had witnessed his father murdering his mother. Those were the extreme cases. But there were others where kids had told me that a pregnancy had been involved and abortion was going to have to be performed; and kids who were running away from their homes to friends' houses, and just a whole massive amount of problems, reality—actually, kids who were doing things that were so far beyond any kind of decision I could make at their age. My life was not exactly a dream as a teenager, but there was nothing in me that could put me into the kinds of situations these kids got into. So their emotional "angst" was quite contagious, and I wanted to tell other people and kids about that. I wanted to tell them about the things that amazed me. And when I looked back at *The Pigman,* I could see that that was a kind of book I could only write once. It is like the first play; it's like what *Marigolds* was, which becomes the family play. It's the first novel with *The Pigman.* It's when you *can* for the first time—you may have had several misconceived attempts on sophomore drawing boards before that—but it's the first time when somehow you just feel the energy to inform the world about something you think it should know, tell the world about a couple of microcosms that you may have stumbled into—that I stumbled into. And, at that time, with both the play and the book, I had no idea that I was doing problem solving for myself, but in reexamining them it became quite clear.

I remember one girl who sent me an interpretation of *The Pigman.* She had just drawn a cartoon. It showed a boat sailing away from land, and I think she placed two children standing on the land, and they were watching a boat called "Innocence" sail away. Every week I get a lot of mail, but once a week there is a special letter; it comes from somebody who is able to say much better than I what they feel, but it seems to be the same. Last week's letter was from a woman who was sixty years old, and her daughter was a teacher who asked her to read *The Pigman,* and she wrote me saying that she cried a great deal at the end. She said, "To me it points up the absurdity of pigeonholing anyone, thinking you know what is going on inside of them. It must be very hurtful to be a child in an adult's world and even more difficult to maintain a close relationship with a child inside one's self. I don't want to leave my childhood behind," she continues to say, "maybe others are caught in this kind of limbo too, and, therefore, we never quite come to grips with what life might be all about. Does anyone really know? We enjoy, we hurt, we think we learn, we would like to love. But it is all so difficult isn't it?" The story really says a hell-of-a-lot about those things, doesn't it? I think I believe those letters. And I think they say it clearer than I do.

So, getting back to why I started all this. I went back to the earlier work to see myself as the earlier writer, and I learned from myself.

You asked a question, or maybe I can't escape it, regarding the "Star Trek" actors. "To the public Leonard Nimoy *is* Mr. Spock and William Shatner *is* Captain Kirk, no matter how brilliantly they may play other characters. Are you the Pigman?" Well, no. Fortunately. Again, there was one group of people that I would meet who would think that I was the Pigman. Then, there's another group of people that I meet who know nothing about my young adult novels and only know about my plays, such as *Marigolds,* so to them I am *Marigolds.* And then, there is still another group of people I see in California who know nothing about either of those and only see me as my last movie. The interesting thing about working in the three fields for twenty years is that they are slowly coming together. There are more and more people who are beginning to know that I wrote The Pigman, and that I wrote Marigolds and have a new play coming out, and that I have written movies. So, I would say I certainly haven't been pigeonholed. And I haven't pigeonholed myself, which is probably the important point. It must be very sad to take on a single persona to the public and to have them not allow you to do anything else. I often have mentioned in regard to this a quote from Noel Coward who said, "Every time out, pop up out of a different hole." I think it has allowed me to remain less of a caricature of myself and to return, when I have the courage from time to time, to writing honestly, which I say is the basic thrust of my life at the moment.

Q: Moving away from *The Pigman,* there seems to be a lot of zany Paul Zindel out there in articles about you and in your own speech making. But your books suggest that a serious commitment to the betterment of humankind underpins the sometimes crazy names and unbelievable situations of your characters. What about the Paul Zindel inside? What is he like?

A: In general in that question, it seems to me you have tapped upon something I guess I would call "the camouflage." Particularly, it is interesting you mention the speech making. I had fairly stopped speech making over the last few years because I couldn't stand to listen to myself. I think that I had never found a way to be comfortable making a speech. I found it becoming more and more of a strain. It seemed like I needed almost stand-up comic response from an audience. And, yet, making a speech is, again, something totally different than all the other media.

I am glad that my books suggest that a more serious commitment underpins the crazy names and unbelievable situations of my characters. That's because most of them do. When they don't, it means that I was on some sort of literary vacation, or maybe I was in the middle of some sort of transition in my own life that prevented me from writing more honestly during a particular book or play or movie, here or there.

I guess the success of the books is that almost everyone, a good number of kids and teachers and librarians, has been able to see the seriousness under the zaniness. And it is interesting because lately I have been learning and beginning to believe a theory that the major plot of a creative work is never the story that carries the emotional truth of a book, or a play for that matter; that, ironically, it's usually a subplot; that the subplot carries the emotional truth. So, there is really nothing wrong with selecting an exaggerated reality as the first level of a plot, and then, in the story "B" level, having the emotional truth come through. I think that is almost the way humans manage to exist in a daily life. We go through life, which seems to me, quite mad and unpredictable and unbelievable. It is only the slower, more subtle experiences that weave their way beneath that zaniness of reality that end up carrying the true important message of why we are alive.

So, the Paul Zindel inside, I think, is sort of the subplot. It is my subplot of humanity. So, the events that happen to me in everyday life I find, I really don't have to exaggerate them very much for them to be humorous or startling or shocking; they just simply are. I think that life is now, and probably always has been, a *tremendous* shock and, ironically enough, I do think that some people have much better defenses, such as rationalization and sublimation and all those processes which I thought were undesirable. I thought that we should always be looking starkly at reality and recounting it intact. I now realize that the mind is given to many paths to ease the startling and often painful passage through reality. The serious commitment to humankind actually, like anything, I think has to start with the person. So, I do have a very serious commitment to the betterment of myself. I would use the words "survival of myself." The interesting thing about any sort of creative work is I do think the best creative work comes from an artist who is desperately motivated to find survival for himself; a problem solving for himself, and then if he does it for himself, then comes the magnificent, startling benefit that since humans are basically the same, the boon, that is, what the hero finds in the story, then becomes a prize for everyone who is able to understand it or need it at that particular time. And the creative work comes along.

I am pausing on the question again about what Paul Zindel is like inside; and inside he is constantly problem solving. I would say I glimpse and feel the problem, and what is terrific is that even though you begin to think you know what problem you are solving out for yourself—why you are researching, and why your desk is covered with books and staplers and papers and word processors and typewriters and paper weights, and why you're running about madly in the world drinking in all sorts of images and focusing in on all sorts of research and libraries and looking at everything that has ever been done before on one particular theme. The big surprise is that all the reasons one thinks as a creative person, why I think I am running around doing these things to tell a story, that before I have finished telling the story, I find out the reason I did all those things was for something else: that the problem I thought I was solving—the story I thought I was telling, the story in which I wanted the protagonist to solve a particular problem—that the true problem was something that was completely unknown to me. It's what comes as a surprise at the end of all storytelling, because even when you are telling the story to yourself, which is the first person the writer does tell the story to, when you find out what the surprise epiphany is, when you find out what the surprise answer is, what the shocking climax is, there comes that moment of insight, which I think was best expressed in one book by some man who tried to equate all of the biology of a human being to a creative functioning. I never remember who he is, and I have never been able to track him down, but he used a metaphor of the way insight comes about: It's like light beams that pass through your eye, and as they enter the lens, the lens focuses the image on the back of the retina, upside down; it's the brain that then is able to switch the image so that it is right side up. And, a process very much like that occurs for the writer as he is nearing the close of his story. It can't be predicted; the image cannot be seen in advance. If it is, it is contrived and usually unemotional and usually what might be called "melodrama."

I think that is what is going on inside of me. Always collecting, building, writing, plotting, doing everything necessary to finally equip me to glimpse something that makes life worthwhile for me, and then, hopefully, in turn, it makes life a little more understandable to others. You know what Zindel is inside? He's a good guy. And he's sort of just like everybody else. (Long pause) God forbid the world should know that.

Q: (Now I am going to the next question). Let me play off of a character in one of your more recent novels, *Harry and Hortense at Hormone High.* According to Hortense, Jason is a schizophrenic. He probably fits the bill. Aside from your work in young adult literature, you are Pulitzer Prize-winning playwright and a premier screenwriter. Do you ever have attacks of professional schizophrenia? (Huh, that's a good one). How do you deal with your fiction writing and drama writing passions professionally? Personally? Does the drive for another *Pigman* ever clash with the drive for another *Man-in-the-Moon Marigolds?*

A: Well, that's terrific. I hadn't preread these questions and I like this one a great deal because I think it very much points (chuckle) points to sort of where I am now. In this area there is something very interesting that happened to me. I was invited by a professor of a graduate class in English at UCLA. They wanted me to come in for a three-hour class to dissect my creative brain. They had read everything that was available that I had written before, and they spent the three hours discussing those things which . . . well, I had an expectation going to that class. This was about three years ago. I knew there was a transition coming into me, and I knew that I had drives that were going to send me beyond *The Pigman* and beyond *Man-in-the-Moon Marigolds.* Interestingly enough, at that point I didn't feel I was receiving any interesting information from the class or the professor for over two-and-a-half hours of them discussing my brain. But, they asked me a question in that last half-hour which lead to something I found very interesting. They asked me what I would be writing next, which is the future—what do I think my brain should be doing with the future? And I told them about an expectation that I would be writing on larger canvasses, that I would be moving away from my Staten Island background, from my autobiographical and semiautobiographical and direct experiences on that island, into more powerful, vast, creative sojourns, excursions, and adventures; that what I was going to write in the future would be magnificent. I asked them, "Did they have any ideas how I was going to accomplish this?" The professor and the class were very helpful at that point because they told me something which I have found to be true. The professor said that it would be deceptive of me to think that suddenly a day will come when I will write completely different elements from those that were in *The Pigman* or in *Marigolds* or anything I have ever done before; that actually there is a certain wisdom for a creative person to look at the work which he has done before and to move on, certainly, but to realize that whatever comes ahead will always have its basis in what went before. And as I thought about that, I realized that I am not trying to escape from myself any longer; that I am lucky, or probably the word would be I am realistic, and kindly realistic, kindly to myself; that anything I write in the future that is original will have roots that can be traced back to other work. The professor also mentioned one other thing; he said, when you choose your story, when you choose to tell or write your next creative work, you really should make sure you do pick adventures to which you can bring a sense of beauty. Beauty in the classical sense—beauty in the literary sense, I imagine he was speaking of. And, what that also told me is there is a part of me that is able to be almost cruelly realistic, there's a part of me that is able to describe with almost a ferocity, to describe life with a ferocity. The irony of that type of one-dimensional look at any world is that it is deceptive; it's limited; it is, as I have mentioned, one-dimensional. The beauty is the hardest part for me, and it's the hardest part for me to know about myself because within the beauty are all the light and brightest colors of being human—the colors of compassion, warmth, need, love. All those elements are ones that are not easy for me to express. And, that pretty much leads us into the heart of the matter. Paul Zindel, me, I am a person who is able to put on a great display of fireworks to dazzle and shock and surprise, and, at times, even light up the sky, but those displays never move people. Those are displays for which I am least rewarded or applauded because what, fortunately, most of the human race wants is to see and to feel the part of life that is good. So, the battle of good and evil goes on still in probably all creative work. We don't care to see anything in total blackness and we don't care to see anything that's totally shining. Neither of those reflect what life is, and neither of those lead us to the human condition where there is a combination. And, only by heading into the darkness with some sense of beauty can you come out at the other end with a story that's useful for yourself, for myself, and for mankind.

The drive for another *Pigman* at this point doesn't clash with the drive for another *Man-in-the-Moon Marigolds* because I have already written my other *Pigman.* That is called *A Begonia for Miss Applebaum* (Harper, 1989). The amazing thing about (chuckle) *A Begonia for Miss Applebaum,* to me, is that it is not the *Pigman.* What it has in it is other qualities—some of the same qualities—and, yet, other richer, more interesting and compassionate qualities. It's a book, for me, that has begun to move me towards where I have to go. So, I am not haunted by *The Pigman.* I am grateful for *The Pigman* and quite excited by the future. Also, as we talk now, my drive for another *Man-in-the-Moon Marigolds* has been accomplished. It is a play called *Amulets Against the Dragon Forces,* and it will open at Circle Repertory here in New York in the spring of '89. It matters only in that it helps to have written *The Pigman* and *Marigolds* because these other two pieces I could never have written had I not been the person who wrote *The Pigman* and *Marigolds* twenty years ago. I am renewed with creative vision and I am moving forward. My career goes on, which means my life goes on, which also makes me feel as though I am going to live some time because I still have new works on the drawing board. I see a future for myself. (Laughter) Yeah, I think I am going to do all right as a writer.

10 Welcome Back, Zindel

John A. Davis

Some years ago one of the more popular TV situation comedies was a show called "Welcome Back, Kotter." It chronicled the antics of a group of unruly, undisciplined, unmotivated but lovable Brooklyn high school students and the efforts of Mr. Kotter, a social science teacher, to ease their way into adulthood. I would occasionally ask my adolescent literature classes to view one or two of the episodes when we were discussing stereotypes in adolescent fiction, or when the portrait of the teacher became too Machiavellian; for week after week Kotter reassured his adolescents through their identity crises, their confrontations with adult authority, their reluctant acceptance of adult responsibility.

I have most recently been reminded of the show as I read the two adolescent novels published by Paul Zindel in 1980: *The Pigman's Legacy* and *A Star for the Latecomer,* the latter written in collaboration with his wife, Bonnie. What called to mind the Kotter show, and particularly the show's theme song which welcomes Kotter back to where his talents are truly needed, is that in these two novels Zindel seems to have also come back where he is needed after something of a departure in *Pardon Me, You're Stepping on My Eyeball* (1976) and *Confessions of a Teenage Baboon* (1977). This is not to say that these novels were not written for an adolescent audience, or that they were not read by the thousands of Zindel admirers, or that they failed to show an acute understanding of the adolescent experience. It is to say that Zindel's 1980 novels seem more akin to the vintage Zindel of *The Pigman* (1968), *My Darling, My Hamburger* (1969), and *I Never Loved Your Mind* (1970), an avuncular Zindel always nearby, always compassionate, always understanding, and above all, always reassuring his charges that although adolescence was a time of turmoil and stress, they could meet it.

Pardon Me, You're Stepping on My Eyeball and *Confessions of a Teenage Baboon* seem hybrid Zindel. Marsh Mellow and Edna Shinglebox of *Pardon Me* and Chris Boyd of *Confessions* appear to be condemned to a legion of the damned, with Zindel standing at the gates of Hell watching his progeny enter with no reassuring word or quip

Reprinted from *The ALAN Review* 9.1, Fall 1981, pages 2–4, 10.

to alleviate their misery. The hybrid Zindel of these two books is a grafting of a Zindel who could balance the trials of his adolescents with humor, irony, and optimism—as he did in his other novels—to a Zindel who seems possessed of a Dostoevskian mood of gloom and despair.

Before attempting to demonstrate what I have suggested above, let me remove *The Undertaker's Gone Bananas* (1978) from the discussion. This book was advertised as Zindel's first murder mystery and so it was. It is fast paced and roundly humorous but reveals only tangentially the character and persona of the adolescent. The usual concerns of Zindel's adolescents are subordinate to a Hardy Boys concern to unmask a killer. I read it as a deliberate departure by the author from his earlier novels where the adolescents were victims of their own frustrations; here Zindel used the macabre figure of a murderous undertaker to hound his adolescents. Perhaps the book was an exercise in restorative therapy, a kind of literary purgative for the agony of his two previous novels.

Certainly *Confessions* and *Pardon Me* show marked kinship to all of Zindel's novels. A survey of his twelve-year migration over the adolescent landscape will reveal the unique Zindel features found in all his novels. He unfailingly has pursued similar themes throughout. He has cast his dramas with like characters: the lost, lonely, becalmed, frightened, and frustrated adolescents. He peoples his books with dishonest parents or authority figures whom few of his adolescent characters hope to emulate. He accentuates the natural loneliness of the adolescent by the cruelty and indifference of ruthless parents and peers. He breaks the family bonds by death, divorce, or desertion. And in all, humor and irony intrude.

Zindel has a favorite storehouse of themes which he fictionally depicts from a Pandora's Box of adolescent anxieties, fears, dreams, and failures. One of the more persistent themes was elaborated initially in *The Pigman* where John Conlan and Lorraine Jensen recoil in horror at the prospect of reaching adulthood and acquiring its inevitable accretion of hypocrisy, deceit, and self-delusion as palliatives. John muses, "Maybe I would rather be dead than to turn into the kind of grown-up people I know." Maggie Tobin in *My Darling, My Hamburger* sees the penalties as well as the inevitability of having to accept an adult role in a somewhat philosophical vein at the book's end and accepts the necessity of change, not necessarily as desirable but as a factor in achieving one's adult integrity. In *I Never Loved Your Mind,* a kind of tongue-in-cheek Baedeker for the adolescent lured by the Hippie life, Dewey Daniels refuses to follow Yvette Goethals to her Taos commune and its promise of eternal adolescence, but only because he sees some peripheral good in the adult world where one might sometime need an appendectomy.

In *Confessions of a Teenage Baboon* and *Pardon Me, You're Stepping on My Eyeball* Chris Boyd and Marsh Mellow respectively hold tenaciously to their childhood by pursuing the spectral figure of a dead father as an anchor to a non-existent, dream-created childhood. Chris carries with him in his peregrinations with his nurse-mother the one solid, romantic relic left by his father, a Chesterfield coat. Marsh, in his wish-fulfillment fantasies, creates a romantic lifescript worthy of Harlequin Romances in which he and his father are loved by all the exotic beauties of the world.

In *A Star for the Latecomer* Brooke Hillary passively views an adult life planned for her by a mother determined to make a star. Brooke herself prefers a love and marriage scenario, but for the most part is willing to accept her mother's equally romantic notion of a life of first nights and public admiration. The John and Lorraine of *The Pigman's Legacy,* although still students of Franklin High, are less inclined to view maturation with the horror shown in *The Pigman,* but they still cling to the child's romantic notion that life can be a mysterious and exciting adventure when they seclude Colonel Glenville from the talons of the IRS and arrange his deathbed marriage to Dolly Racinski.

Another premier theme in the Zindel canon is the adolescents' burden of accumulated guilt and its destructive aftermath. John and Lorraine appropriate the guilt for Mr. Pignati's death at the end of *The Pigman* and recognize that their part in his death has exacted a death of a part of their being, their innocence; it is, they feel, a terrible price to pay. In *The Pigman's Legacy* John and Lorraine assume responsibility for the Pigman's reincarnation, Colonel Glenville, because of a desire to atone for Mr. Pignati's death. But once again the two are partners in an act potentially as destructive as the wild party they threw at Mr. Pignati's home when John gambles away the modest nest egg Colonel Glenville entrusted to him. Once again the two adolescents have acquired a burden of guilt for their immature behavior.

In none of the other Zindel novels does the burden of guilt assume the proportions and generate the psychotic effects it has on Marsh Mellow. When his drunken father is run over by a bus, Marsh feels himself responsible, a crime of omission for not stopping his father's reckless drinking. This feeling of his culpability in his father's death has preyed on Marsh until he finally constructs a delusion in which his father is not dead but a prisoner of nebulous officials who are trying to silence his effort to reveal their collective perfidy. All of this Marsh fleshes out in his daily intercourse with Edna Shinglebox, in forged letters and in ambitious plans for his father's rescue, even though the urn containing his father's ashes rests all the while under Marsh's bed. The potential for a similar overwhelming accumulation of guilt is present in *A Star for the Latecomer* where Brooke watches her mother die of cancer without Brooke having made that one triumphant step toward stardom that her mother so longed for. However, the anguish Brooke feels for having failed her mother vanishes in the girl's realization that her mother's dreams for her were the somewhat selfish dreams of a frustrated woman and were not her own dreams.

As identical themes reappear in Zindel's novels so too do characters who might very well be the consequence of incestuous inbreeding in the writer's ink. Aside from the tormented adolescents burdened by feelings of guilt, inadequacy, and rejection, the most familiar figure in his works is the anguished parent, generally the mother, who is incapable of showing love or affection for the child because some real or imagined inadequacy or rejection has warped her life. The mothers of Lorraine and Chris have been deserted by their husbands and vent their life-hatred on their defenseless children. Marsh's mother, in those rare moments of sobriety, demeans and humiliates Marsh with charges that he is either a sex fiend or a drug addict or both, implying that this acorn did not fall far from the tree. That Zindel has not abandoned the lament of the deleterious effect of the possessive, frustrated mother is noticed in *A Star for the Latecomer.* Here Brooke's mother, whose life as a wife and mother was ultimately unsatisfactory, drives her daughter, with a callous obsession, to be a star, to be famous.

I mentioned earlier that irony is a prevalent feature in all of Zindel's novels, but nowhere is it more apparent than in a kind of archetypal scene of physical or psychical destruction that climaxes each novel. The incident, begun in adolescent innocence, ends as a kind of Götterdämmerung of adolescence, where the fragile fabric clothing the adolescents' lives is shredded. It is as though Zindel feels the need to dramatize his compassion for the adolescents by some symbolic representation of the death of adolescence and innocence, with flamboyant and theatrical proportions.

In *The Pigman* this scene is the boisterous party thrown by John and Lorraine. The destruction of Mr. Pignati's treasured collection of pigs and his wife's wedding dress also demolishes the sanctuary John and Lorraine had built against life. In *My Darling, My Hamburger* Liz undergoes her abortion on the night of the senior prom, a grim contrast, and among the other casualties are Maggie's romantic naiveté and the adolescent quietude of Liz, Sean, Dennis, and Maggie. Zindel chooses a hippie commune, "Love Land," in *I Never Loved Your Mind* for a violent free-for-all among the "flower people" to inform Dewey of the fakery of the life Yvette has chosen and his ineptitude for such a farcical existence.

In *Pardon Me, You're Stepping on My Eyeball* Zindel produced a classic model for an adolescent Armageddon. A teenage party degenerates into an orgy of sex, drinking, drugs, and vandalism, where the guests are rewarded for their folly by the awesome destruction of the hostess' beautiful home by fire. In this fire Marsh's pet raccoon, which has served him as a kind of lifeline to his humanity, burns to death. Another party, again unreal in its cast and consequences, serves as the catalyst to shatter Chris's fragile equilibrium in the world in *Confessions of a Teenage Baboon.* Lloyd Dipardi's drunken brawl with his adolescent faithful occurs as his mother dies in an adjoining room and terminates when Lloyd commits suicide, forcing Chris to a realization that there is and always will be a dark side to life.

The climactic scenes in Zindel's last two novels follow the Zindel guidelines but have more of the optimistic overtones underlying the conclusions to *The Pigman, My Darling, My Hamburger,* and *I Never Loved Your Mind.* In *A Star for the Latecomer* Brooke has her mother's coffin opened at the funeral home so she can place her dancing shoes in the coffin and whisper to her mother, "I may not be what you want me to be, but I do hope, whatever I choose, that you'll be proud of me." Only after the painful, agonizing death of her mother is Brooke free. Zindel's flair for the dramatic setting in which his adolescents apprehend the death of their innocence is apparent in *The Pigman's Legacy.* Here in a gaudy Atlantic City casino, amid all the pathetic dreams of miraculous wealth, John compulsively gambles away Colonel Glenville's money, to realize once again that he had trespassed into the adult world of lies, deceit, and delusion.

What is it then that caused *Confessions of a Teenage Baboon* and *Pardon Me, You're Stepping on My Eyeball* to stand out so starkly and ominously from the rest of Zindel's novels? It was not an alteration in the thematic insistence that adolescence is hell, no matter how it is viewed nostalgically over a distance of years. Nor was it the appearance of a new cast, for Chris, Marsh, and Edna, although more somber, less resilient, and quicker to despair, are the same troubled adolescents as John and Lorraine and Dewey and Brooke. It was not a different structural design since the two novels build to the same moment of truth, a disastrous and dramatic incident, which signals the end of childhood innocence and the acceptance, hereafter, of the responsibility for one's behavior. Nor were compassion and sympathy for the ineffectual and harassed adolescents absent in these novels; Zindel seems to love his various literary offspring equally.

The answer, I believe, can come only from the author himself. In the biographical data that has surfaced about Zindel since the success of *The Pigman* and his Pulitzer Prize-winning play, *The Effects of Gamma Rays on Man-in-the Moon Marigolds,* there is evidence of a troubled and unhappy childhood, of agony and anger over the separation of his parents. One can only speculate that the Zindel who wrote *Confessions* and *Pardon Me* was deliberately purging some personal demons, demons that forbade even a modest relief to the miseries of Marsh or Edna or Chris. He allowed them no momentary interlude of adolescent happiness or rapture such as John and Lorraine enjoyed in Mr. Pignati's home, or as Brooke enjoyed with Brandon on their picnic, or as Dewey experienced as the lovely Yvette vacuumed the living room in the nude. Instead March, Edna, and Chris suffer a continuous anxiety, endure misfortune and humiliation without hope of relief, even with a sometimes psychotic acceptance of the inevitability of despair. In only one other adolescent novelist have I noticed this propensity for making the adolescent the total victim, Robert Cormier in *The Chocolate War* and *I Am the Cheese.*

Marsh, Edna, and Chris are victimized relentlessly throughout by an unrelieved anxiety; Marsh is unable to free himself of the guilt of his father's death; Edna is constantly reminded at home and at school that she is the "Super-Loser"; Chris suffers the endless indignity of squatting in the homes of strangers who are sick or dying. The chances for relief from these pressures are defeated constantly by the characters themselves or those around them, or merely by an unlucky throw of fate's dice. Marsh, who has lied to himself to keep his father alive, perpetuates the lies to maintain the one contact with reality he has found, his tenuous friendship with Edna. Edna, who has come to accept her mother's appraisal of her as "a sad sack," "in the forest of romance a desert," is unwilling to jeopardize the relative safety of anonymity and views high school as "just one more place [she] won't have to face the world." Chris's reclusive and hapless life of passively following his mother from case to case is mocked by the scorn and derision of the cruel but well-intentioned Lloyd Dipardi and the innocent promiscuity of Rosemary. These anxieties mercilessly hound the three to the novels' conclusions.

The unrelieved tensions weighing on each character are compounded by the squalid, sterile, or hostile environments in which the three characters forever move. Marsh's home is a pigsty; his high school life includes daily attendance in a group-therapy experience class peopled by the school's misfits, including Edna; his mother drinks herself senseless each night; he frequents the "kooky" bars his father has raised him in. Edna's home life is palled by her parents' loveless marriage; her natural sexual anxieties are magnified by her mother's intention to make her into a likely candidate for a conventional middle-class marriage with no concern as to how the transformation is achieved—she suggests Edna engage in a little "hanky-panky" on her dates and do a little research to learn where the erogenous zones are located; her despair in dealing with Marsh takes her to the foul-smelling, roach-infested shack of a charlatan palmist named Miss Aimee. Chris passes his adolescent years living in an attic or cubicle in the homes where his mother is nursing; his school life is equally lonely and he is derided by his classmates as a mother's boy; he is in constant contact with the sick and dying; his meager childhood possessions, which fit into one small, cheap cardboard suitcase, contain only one treasure, his dead father's Chesterfield coat. The succession of scenes depicting Marsh's, Edna's, and Chris' trails reminds me of nothing so much as Hogarth's pen-and-ink sketches of the miseries of London life.

Even the redoubtable Zindel humor has taken on a black cast in these two novels. Although there is always an undercurrent of pathos in Zindel's humor, the humorous episodes in *Confessions* and *Pardon Me* do nothing so much as reinforce the misery of the moment. Witness the scene in the office of the guidance counselor where Edna's mother is tripping over herself in her haste to catalogue Edna's failures as Edna listens in total despair; or friendless Marsh's frantic recital of all the friends he has made among the freaks of the circus and of the women who just cannot resist him—an exotic dancer in a topless bar, a curvaceous daughter of a congressman, hookers; or Chris's mother's wholesale thievery from the Dipardi's while she refuses to allow Chris to use Lloyd Dipardi's toilet and instead presents him with an empty milk carton.

But with *The Pigman's Legacy* and *A Star for the Latecomer* the Zindel of the earliest novels is back, back where he is needed. The latter-day Lorraine and John leave the dead Colonel's room where Dolly now performs the mourning rites to walk past the hospital's nursery where the promise of life is most obvious, a promise which prompts a declaration of love for Lorraine by John. Brooke survives her mother's agonizing death with a regret that she was unable to fulfill her mother's dreams but with no sense of personal guilt. The reassurance Zindel offered his earlier adolescents is back, and though adolescent readers of Zindel will never be led to the false notion that the quality of adolescence is unbounded joy, with the rerouted Zindel they will not see in it only the blackness suggested by *Confessions of a Teenage Baboon* and *Pardon Me, You're Stepping on My Eyeball.*

And this, I believe, is good. Adolescence is not a time to demolish thoroughly those faint lingering childhood myths of the world's perfection; it is a time to call the adolescents' attention to some of the fraying edges of the myth, to some of the imperfections of the warp and woof of the fabric, but not a time to destroy the myth's whole cloth. If adolescents are permitted to let the myths dissolve slowly, I feel there is far more likelihood they will attempt to reweave the myth as best they can throughout their lives. Welcome back, Zindel.

Something Wonderful, Something Beautiful: Adolescent Relationships through the Eyes of Paul Zindel

Kim Hansen

Adolescence is a period of adjusting to the reality that one is growing up. Still a child in many ways and yearning to be an adult, the adolescent is confronted with many new ideas and experiences. One of the most worrisome of these new experiences is forming interpersonal relationships. Adolescents turn to their peers early on for support in forming a self-image and a feeling of self-worth. Soon, this support extends to more mature relationships with members of the opposite sex.

In early adolescent relationships, teens form Platonic male/female relationships, friendships. As teens grow up, the attraction becomes stronger than friendship. Adolescents become occupied with trying to meet and make an impression on members of the opposite sex. Once the art of attraction is mastered, teenagers begin to think in terms of pairing off. During this state, individuals decide what they are looking for in a partner—what they find attractive and what they find unattractive. As emotional growth increases, relationships become longer-lasting and more intense, and adolescents begin to explore their sexuality. The culmination of this growth is usually finding a suitable partner and developing a give-and-take relationship.

For the adolescent, this transition from immaturity to adulthood is confusing, frightening, and often painful. The transition is marked with problems including "all those perplexities and conflicts which young people may encounter in making satisfactory adjustments in

Reprinted from *The ALAN Review* 18.2, Winter 1991, pages 41–43.

boy-and-girl relationships" (Butterfield, 1). It is hard to know what to do in a world that keeps changing its demands; a little insight could be helpful. Author Paul Zindel is one possible source of this insight. In many of his novels, he presents teenaged characters who are very real and easy for an adolescent reader to identify with. These characters have many questions about love, sex, and life in general. Zindel covers the confusion of these issues with empathy and understanding, and he helps sort through the questions and concerns of teenagers. His novels trace the process of maturing into a young adult with clarity and insight.

Finding a Friend

The first level of the adolescent relationship is friendship. It is the easiest relationship because it is familiar and there is little pressure to be mature. *The Pigman* focuses on two high school sophomores, Lorraine and John, who share a close Platonic friendship. The experience that they both have with a lonely, elderly widower, Mr. Pignati, helps them both to grow emotionally. One result of this growth is the realization by John and Lorraine that their friendship could develop into something more.

Before meeting Mr. Pignati, whom they nickname "The Pigman," the friendship between the two teenagers is based on mutual understanding, something they both feel they are lacking at home. John refers to his parents as "The Bore" and "The Old Lady" and lies constantly to attract attention. Lorraine's unhappiness stems from her mother's distrust of men. She tries to shelter Lorraine, and she limits Lorraine's chances of learning about relationships. According to Lorraine, "She always warns me about getting into cars and things like that. . . . Beware of men is what she's really saying. They have dirty minds, and they're only after one thing" (*The Pigman* 97).

John and Lorraine use their acquaintance with Mr. Pignati to escape their homes. The older man shows them how to have fun; in their company he acts young again. The three visit the zoo, shop, and roller-skate together. Though he is using the teenagers to help himself feel young, Mr. Pignati also teaches them about life and love lessons that come with the wisdom of age. By talking about his deceased wife, he teaches John and Lorraine how good a meaningful relationship can be: "We loved each other. We didn't need anyone else. She did everything for me. We were each other's life" (*The Pigman* 102).

Perhaps it is the image of a good relationship that Mr. Pignati presents that helps John and Lorraine evaluate their own relationship. The older man's heart attack gives the two teenagers an opportunity to be alone in a house that is not their parents' houses, and they begin to model a relationship that is more serious than friendship. They "play house," cleaning and cooking together, and even dressing up in grown-up clothes and pretending to be romantically involved. As the scenario progresses, things become more serious. John tells the reader: "She started laughing again right in my arms, but I stopped it by putting my lips on hers. It was the first time we had ever kissed. When I moved my lips away from hers, we just looked at each other, and somehow we were not acting any more" (*The Pigman* 119).

A kiss is a small beginning toward a mature male/female relationship. It is the first sign that members of the opposite sex can be more than friends. Lorraine reflects: "I think when we looked at each other in the candlelight, it was the first time I was glad to be alive. I didn't know exactly why. . . . [I]t was as if I was being told about something, something wonderful, something beautiful waiting just for me. All I had to do was wait long enough" (*The Pigman* 123).

This new awareness of each other as more than friends leads to tension that did not exist before. As adolescents, both John and Lorraine are uncertain and confused, not just about their feelings for each other, but about life in general. Their new view of each other alters how they act around each other because there are no set guidelines for a relationship that is other than friendship. They are in new territory, and they are unsure of what to do or to expect. Lorraine notices the changes in John first:

> I don't know whether he had just started thinking about our relationship—that I might be something more than his straight man . . . But suddenly we had become slightly awkward in front of each other. . . . I knew I had been in love with him for months. I also knew he liked me a lot but only as a friend . . . now suddenly he was wearing shaving lotion, combing his hair, and fighting with me. . . . (*The Pigman* 125)

Mr. Pignati's death at the end of the novel also ends John and Lorraine's narration—their testimony of what they learned from the Pigman. However, even as Mr. Pignati stops living, he teaches these two adolescents about life. He helps them to see new possibilities for themselves and their futures. A new stage of maturity has been reached.

For adolescents, the transition from child to adult brings fears about their maturity. The confusion leaves the teenager wondering who he or she is and what he or she believes in. The realization that an intimate relationship may be desirable brings new questions: Am I attractive? How do I meet someone? What do I say once I have?

Pairing Off

The next stage in adolescent relationships is that of pairing off. This level of maturity often includes the issue of sexual intercourse: "The sexual behavior of many young adolescents is not typically an expression of a basic sexual need as much as an attempt, through sexuality, to meet a more all-encompassing need" (Josselyn 104). According to one view, this need is not physical; it is emotional: "In young people the ultimate goal of sexual gratification is finding an appropriate identity for oneself" (Lambert 113).

Zindel's *My Darling, My Hamburger* explores this stage in the development of adolescent relationships. The story focuses on seniors in high school, particularly a couple named Sean and Liz. The novel opens at the stage of their relationship where the decision whether or not to have sexual intercourse is discussed: "They had gone to a picnic on the first date. . . . He remembered feeling like a creature from outer space who after a million years of banishment from his home planet had at last found another exile" (*My Darling, My Hamburger* 16). Sean finds that his feelings for Liz have grown to the point where he feels ready to have sexual intercourse. He sees these feelings as completely natural. His rationale concludes, "Nature starts doing things. The hormones start rolling and all those testicles start producing and all the rest of it—like breathing. You don't go around asking for it. It happens (*My Darling, My Hamburger* 38).

For Liz, the issue is not that simple. She does not feel ready to have sex, and she sees Sean's impatience with her as rejection. Liz tries to communicate her feelings in a letter to Sean: "We don't have any fun now when we go out. We used to enjoy the evening and think about kissing at the end of it. Now I can tell by looking at you . . . You think about what's going to happen at the end of the evening before it gets started" (*My Darling, My Hamburger* 44). Sean never reads the letter; his father takes it before he sees it, and Liz and Sean's relationship dissolves.

Liz tries to hide the hurt of this rejection by dating an older boy named Rod Gittens, who has a reputation for using girls. Liz is trying to prove that she is desirable without having to go all the way, but the idea backfires. Rod is more insistent than Sean, and he has no respect for Liz as a person. At the school dance Liz is with Rod, trying to create a scene and make the school believe she is mature. However, she cannot follow through, and Rod's forcefulness frightens her: "A few minutes before, she had been in possession of the situation. All she had needed to do was flutter her eyelashes, and she had her way. But now she wanted him to stop and he wouldn't" (*My Darling, My Hamburger* 62).

This encounter with Rod shows Liz how important Sean, who at least respected her wishes, is to her. This realization gives her the emotional courage to be what Sean wants her to be. Her fear of sex is replaced by her desire to have a relationship that is based on more than sex. She sees her relationship with Sean as just such a relationship: "She was no longer frightened about building the world in which she wanted to live. The start had already been made" (*My Darling, My Hamburger* 67–68).

Sean and Liz have reached the level where they can have a mature relationship; however, they are not yet mature enough to be responsible for their actions. Liz becomes pregnant. Suddenly, the two teenagers are forced to make very grown-up decisions. Liz feels she is ready to take on the role of wife and mother and Sean initially agrees to marry her. However, in time he realizes that he is not ready for the commitment or the responsibility, and he begins to resent Liz: "He hadn't dated that many girls. By going with Liz, he had cut himself off from a lot of others. . . . What the hell was he supposed to do? Stop his life?' (*My Darling, My Hamburger* 97). Sean is unwilling to take responsibility for his act; he is not mature enough to follow through on his intentions.

As a result, Liz terminates the pregnancy. Sean's rejection teaches Liz a painful lesson, and her idealistic adolescent notions give way to something more grim but more realistic. Both teens face the fact that although they want to act and be treated like adults they are still not ready for all of the responsibility that adulthood brings. They are not yet free to choose the life they want to lead.

Gaining Freedom of Choice

With maturity comes the freedom to make one's own decisions. Adolescents must reach this stage before the complete transition into adulthood is made. *I Never Loved Your Mind* is a novel about two people who have begun to make these important decisions for themselves. Dewey Daniels, who is almost eighteen, has decided to drop out of high school and get a job. Although he lives with his parents, the reader gets the impression that he is independent and can make his own choices. He is at the stage in development where sex, and lots of it, is a central focus. It is a period of exploring the possibilities so that a decision about a lifetime partner can be made.

While working in a hospital as an inhalation therapist, Dewey meets Yvette Goethals, an eighteen-year-old dropout who lives on her own. Dewey's pursuit of Yvette begins with only sexual intentions, and he tries to impress her from the very beginning. However, he still has not outgrown his adolescent awkwardness, and his initial conversations do not go over well: "I knew what I'd said was dumb, but somehow I couldn't stop it from coming out" (*I Never Loved Your Mind* 13). Yvette, who is more mature as most females are at this age, does not open up to Dewey, but his persistence keeps her intrigued.

Yvette criticizes Dewey regularly, but her criticism only makes him think of her more, though it also adds to his uncertainty: "I kept thinking of Yvette Goethals, and there were two feelings going on at the same time. One minute I felt warm and titillated contemplating her body. Next I'd hear her enunciating 'leering cannibalistic virgin,' and I'd feel asthmatic" (*I Never Loved Your Mind* 33).

Determined to succeed with Yvette, Dewey begins a full-blown courtship that includes flowers, candy, and the Burpee seeds that Yvette informs him she prefers in bulk. Every instance of contact with Yvette at the hospital is like a triumph to Dewey, and even the most mundane comment excites him. Yvette has only to tell Dewey to hook up oxygen for a new patient and, "That mealy-mouthed confrontation had produced such palpitations in my pancreas that I walked into room 400 in a daze" (*I Never Loved Your Mind* 36).

Slowly, the ice around Yvette melts, and Dewey actually gets a date with her. In short time, Dewey is invited over, and they have sexual intercourse. For Dewey, it is love: "I was so much in love it made any other girl I'd ever known seem, in retrospect, to be a dehydrated Bartlett pear" (*I Never Loved Your Mind* 91).

Soon after this Yvette begins to pull away from Dewey. She is mature enough to know what she is doing with her life, and Dewey is a setback to the plans. She tells him, "We're too different, Dewey. . . . There too many things you have to learn" (*I Never Loved Your Mind* 97). Dewey cannot accept this rejection, and he denies that she should feel this way: "That rhapsodic recline in the crimson bedroom was something very beautiful to me . . . Maybe for her it was like blowing her nose. But I had begun to see so many lovely things about her that I just couldn't believe it" (*I Never Loved Your Mind* 99).

Dewey continues to pursue Yvette, tracking her down at the Love Land commune she has moved to, and she finally has to tell him why she does not want to be involved with him any further. For her, the drawback is the difference in their maturity: "Dewey, you don't seem to realize that I'm not all hung-up and twisted, with nothing but sex on my brain. There're a lot more important things in this world, and there just isn't enough time for me to teach you about them" (*I Never Loved Your Mind* 115). Dewey feels hurt because he has finally reached the stage where he wants a serious adult relationship, but she will not give him the time to develop it.

Yvette's plans include leaving town soon to see the world, and, by leaving, she teaches Dewey a lesson: He begins to look forward and make plans for the rest of his life. Yvette has brought Dewey to the brink of adulthood. He tells the reader, "I don't know what I'm going to do. It's not going to be that Love Land crap. And I'm not going to give civilization a kick in the behind. . . . But I'm going to do something, and I have a strange feeling it's going to be phantasmagorically different" (*I Never Loved Your Mind* 135).

Conclusion

Perhaps the ultimate goal of maturing is not finding the right relationship. Perhaps it is just finding the courage to make one's own decisions about life. Certainly, human relationships have an impact on the happiness of humans, and the issue is a central focus during the years of adolescence. Writers like Zindel provide a base of understanding for teenagers who are confused about relationships. Though male/female relationships are not his only topic of adolescent life, it is usually present, as it is in the mind of any adolescent reader. Zindel explores the full range of adolescence in his novels, and he captures the irony, confusion, and ecstasy that comes with growing up. He presents characters that talk directly to the reader, not hiding his didacticism, but presenting it openly, hoping to help the reader understand. In this way, the reader can find a friend in Zindel's novels, someone with the same experiences and questions. Zindel breaks the isolation of adolescence and helps his readers to see that the problems that they feel are their own, are really universal.

References

Butterfield, Oliver M. *Love Problems of Adolescence.* New York: Columbia U Bureau of Publications, 1939.

Josselyn, Irene M. *Adolescence.* New York: Harper, 1971.

Kiell, Norman. *The Adolescent through Fiction.* New York: International U Press, 1970.

Lambert, Geraldine B., Barbara F. Rothschild, Richard Atland, and Laurence B. Green. *Adolescence: Transition from Childhood to Maturity.* Boston: Brooks/Cole, 1972.

Zindel, Paul. *Confessions of a Teenage Baboon.* New York: Harper, 1978.

———. *I Never Loved Your Mind.* New York: Harper, 1979.

———. *My Darling My Hamburger.* New York: Harper, 1978.

———. *The Pigman.* New York: Dell, 1978.

Part I The Authors

Section 4
Bette Greene

12 What Does It Feel Like to Be Human?

Bette Greene

Courtesy of BDD/Random House Children's Books

One of the fun things about being a writer is being invited to schools, universities, and professional meetings. There is a recurrent theme that I've heard expressed in California and Massachusetts and a lot of places in between, though, that isn't at all fun to hear. Students are complaining that they're made to read "boring" books while teachers and librarians are complaining that students aren't usually reading the books that their professional organizations have proclaimed the best.

I'm not exactly a disinterested party to these discussions, as I believe that exciting writers turn students on to reading while dull writers, no matter how many hearts that they may have in the right places, turn students away from books.

One teacher from Greenville, Mississippi, said flatly that her students "wouldn't willingly touch most award books." I asked the teacher what her own personal opinion was about these books in question. Right off, she said that "The writing was usually very good and there were some good moral points in them."

I asked, "Did all or any of these books create an experience for you? Did they make you feel anything?" She fingered a gold cross at her neck before answering. "No, not all that much."

> All good books are alike in that they are truer than if they had really happened and after you are finished reading one you will feel like all that happened to you: the good and the bad, the ecstasy, the remorse and sorrow, the people and the places and how the weather was. If you can give that to the people, then you are a writer.
>
> —Ernest Hemingway, 1932

When readers, teachers, librarians, professors, and critics demand more of us writers—demand that our books have to be "truer than if they had really happened"—then there'll be a lot more of what Hemingway calls "good books" and fewer of those nicely written Sunday school lessons. Now, there's nothing wrong with

Reprinted from *The ALAN Review* 11.1, Fall 1983, pages 1–2, 47–48, by permission of the author.

nicely written Sunday school lessons, but they have no business disguising themselves as books.

"It is with noble sentiments," Andre Gide once wrote, "that bad literature gets written." If we can fill our reading lists and libraries with a lot more of those "good books," the real plus just may be that those kids who really don't like to read will be found . . . READING!

Hemingway's right-on-target definition makes enormous demands on us basically lazy folks who are known as writers. And the demands are actually twofold. The first is pure craft: the ability to use the language with precision and charm. Now that is difficult enough. I know because I've personally been arranging and rearranging words for thirty years.

The main way I struggle is by writing and rewriting sentences in longhand on clipboards until I like those sentences well enough to commit them, at least temporarily, to my typewriter. Eventually, when I have gone through enough yellow legal pads to supply the entire first year class of Harvard Law School, I find that I have actually produced a first-draft, typed manuscript.

Without reading it, I drop this typed manuscript into a file folder which is labeled: First Draft—Untitled Novel and try for a few days to forget all about it. Although I don't actually succeed in forgetting it, I do, however, repeatedly tell myself that it's only a first draft and it's probably not all that bad. At least not as bad as I think.

Days later and well fortified with coffee, I finally sit down to read and discover that no—no, I wasn't wrong. It's what I thought: depressingly awful. I struggle to find something good to say (total rejection doesn't produce good books), and I do find something good to say: As a typist I'm not half bad. Additionally, the plot more or less functions and the writing is obviously professional. So why is it bad and why am I hating it?

I hate it because I know that my characters are stillborn. They do not live because I as author had neither the energy nor the courage to look below and beyond the surface and therefore to write from that wellspring within which is the deepest, the purest, and the most real. Again, it's Hemingway, or to be more exact, one of his characters, a writer, in "Death in the Afternoon" who expresses it best:

> I was trying to write then and I found the greatest difficulty, aside from knowing truly what you really felt, rather than what you were suppose to feel, and had been taught to feel, was to put down what really happened in action; what the actual things were which produced the emotion you experienced . . . the real thing, the sequence of motion and fact which made the emotion and which would be as valid in a year or in ten years, or with luck and if you stated it purely enough, always.

Why should it be surprising that we writers have trouble with being real? Didn't we all grow up learning the same lessons? Hearing the same advice: "Little boys don't cry . . . Nobody loves a sourpuss . . . Stiff upper lip . . . Laugh and the world laughs with you . . . But cry and you cry alone. When you're smiling . . . when you're smiling, the whole world smiles with you. . . ."

Do you sometimes get the impression that we're all being programmed to express certain things while at the same time withholding other things? Who, or rather what, is this ubiquitous force teaching us how we as people ought to feel rather than really do feel? The important thing is that we all do learn, quickly learn, that if we can't be strong we can, at the very least, be silent. Keep your sunny side up . . . or shades of the great cop-out!

Being real is a major problem for everybody, but for the novelist, the poet—for every artist—it's both a major personal problem and a major occupational one because nobody can ever become more dimensional as an artist than they already are as a human being. So we who call the arts home are obligated, not only to grow and develop our talents, but also to relearn. Or to be more accurate, we must work like hell to unlearn. Because how long has it been since we've been as comfortable with all those things that we really feel? And when and how did we replace the really-feel with the only pretend-to-feel?

If it's the artist's job (and I'm convinced that it is) to examine life, the only little grain of life that we know, then we cannot be concerned with posturing like heroes or playing like clowns, but only with being real. Because if we are not real, then how will we know—how can we ever express what it means and how it feels to be human?

This "realness" is necessary in any good book, fiction, fantasy, or nonfiction. When, for example, President Nixon was preparing to leave office, the agent, Irving "Swifty" Lazar, was contacted. How much, he was asked, would the president's memoirs be worth? Now Mr. Lazar, who came by his nickname honestly, shot back, "Oh, somewhere between ten dollars and a million dollars."

The agent's answer may have sounded flip, but he wasn't wrong, because if Mr. Nixon's book turned out to be a soft-focused account of why and how he became a hero-in-his-own-time, then there would be pitifully few readers. Pat, Tricia, Julie, for sure, but even David Eisenhower would have to be counted as a maybe.

But if the man from Whittier could look at himself with unflinching honesty and write about his unique experiences from that perspective, then multitudes would clamor to read . . . and to learn. What drives a person to power? What does it really feel like to have power that the Pharaohs would have envied?

A few hundred years before Christ, the philosopher Plato said, "The life that is unexamined is not worth living." I know for certain that it's not worth writing about because in books, as in life, it's not actions that are so important as the examined responses to those actions. For twenty-five years, a few men and women have soared through interplanetary and interstellar space. They have had adventures that the rest of us can't even conceive of having, and yet where are their books? The books that only they could write? The books that can make us feel that, yes, it's happening to us, too?

A sizable group of people who have been pronounced dead (sometimes for minutes) have been miraculously restored to life. Many of these people admit to having had "other world" experiences. How many of us would even wait for the soft-cover edition in our quest to learn what it's really like to be dead? And yet where are their books? You know, the ones that can make us feel as though it is happening to us, too?

Thoreau, on the other hand, never claimed extraordinary adventures; never traveled more than ten miles from Walden Pond, and yet he was always reaching within for truths universal. So external adventures (read here as a strong story line) in tandem with a heightened internal awareness—now you have just entered the climate conducive to good writing.

What literary or professional goodie will be waiting for us if we actually stop running from our own personal monsters long enough to commit them to paper? Remember what happened to Count Dracula? In the last minutes of the reel, it occurs to the hero that if a cross is waved in front of the vampire, he miraculously loses power. Well, in some metaphysical way which I'm not sure I understand, real writing power is like that too. Or, as my ninth-grade science teacher once explained, "Matter is never used up. It only reverts to another form."

So the power doesn't disappear; it's only transformed. Transformed from the vampire to the cross. From the writer's personal monsters to his manuscripts. So if we can somehow . . . somewhere find the courage to confront our own lives, then truths can be grudgingly extracted because we will have staked our claim to the mother lode.

When I was about twelve years old, I spent some long afternoons thinking about Judy Garland. Wondering how I could be so moved by a voice that as a musical instrument was strictly run-of-the-glee-club.

And at a recent world's fair, the longest lines were reserved, not for a gleaming piece of space-age technology, but for Michelangelo's ageless Pietá. Judy Garland and Michelangelo in the same breath? Well, why not? Didn't they both soar beyond the purely technical aspects of their crafts because they both intuitively understood that art to be art must—absolutely, positively must—be rooted deep within their own experiences?

Last March, I was traveling through a remote Kenyan village in a Land Rover. Villagers in crimson robes crowded four or five deep around something or somebody. I asked my native guide what was going on and he explained that it was only a storyteller.

I shook my head no. "I've seen storytellers in Africa before. They don't draw that kind of a crowd."

Suddenly the guide's face caught fire. "He's Kabenni!"

"Kabenni?"

"The greatest storyteller in all the land! The greatest storyteller in any land!"

"But . . ." I said, trying to frame a question amid all that enthusiasm. "You say he's the greatest, but how do I know that he is? What makes him better than all the rest?"

The guide placed both his index fingers at the side of his eyes before suddenly thrusting both fingers forward. "All our story tellers tell us what they see." Then the guide slowly tapped his heart. "But only Kabenni can tell us what nobody can ever see."

A few weeks later, I'm back at my desk in a converted attic room in an old house in Brookline, Massachusetts. The dust of Kenya has been washed from my chinos, and now I reopen that dreaded manila file folder. The one that's so neatly labeled: First Draft—Untitled Novel. This time I'll do it, I tell myself. I'll explore as deep as a Texas oil rig, deep enough to force life and breath into every single one of my characters. My pep talk doesn't really impress me very much, probably because I remember sitting through at least a quarter of a million of these "cheering" talks before.

I speak directly to the manila folder:

> Enough dawdling! Start the second draft already. Other writers have faced the same challenge and done it. Shakespeare, Carson McCullers, Arthur Miller and, undoubtedly, Kabenni to name just a few. It's simple, really, all you really have to do is to write about all those things that make you want to burst out into song . . . or into tears. So why can't you do it, too? You may be chicken, but you know—now you know where all the good writing is hiding.

I shake my head. "Don't tell me it's simple. It's not simple! To strike at this good writing, a writer would need all the instincts of a kamakazi pilot. The writer must have the courage to see. The courage to explore. No more hedging bets or equivocating."

I picture four people. A teacher, a librarian, a critic, and a student in a green sweater. They're all looking at me and none kindly. Now they all speak, all in one voice: "Look, nobody begged you to be a writer. That was all your own idea, remember? So quit your bellyaching and don't think we're going to buy your book cause we're not. Not unless you do what you're paid to do. So get to it! Go crashing against your own personal subterranean devils, and with luck and persistence, the explosion will be like a bicentennial fourth of July.

"Well, even if you don't actually succeed in lighting up the Western sky, then, at the very least, you will have illuminated your pages with living, breathing people who though painfully struggling towards new insights will offer vitality and truth to your work."

"Guess maybe you're right," I tell them as I break open a new ream of white paper, slide a sheet into my typewriter and begin to type: Page 1 Untitled Novel—2nd draft.

13 America's Designated Victims: Our Creative Young

Bette Greene

After my novel *The Drowning of Stephan Jones* (inspired by a true crime, the drowning of a gay man by a teenager on a "religious" rampage) was published, something very strange happened. At first it seemed strange; while later on, it became almost predictable. Every time I spoke before an assembly of students, there would always be at least one boy who shyly requested permission to speak with me "in private." And what that boy and more than a half a hundred like him have now told me was so private that they dared not speak of it to their parents—no, not even to their closest friends.

From Berryville, Arkansas, to Manhasset, New York, the stories were all different, but yet they were all variations on the same disturbing theme: Our most creative young people are being tormented in every college, high school, junior high school, and, yes, grammar school in every state, city, and town in this nation. The reason for this always emotional and oftentimes physical oppression is that, try as they may, some boys simply cannot cram themselves into the mold befitting America's macho machine.

Although much of this force is generated by the fear of homosexuality, it isn't at all necessary to be homosexual to be persecuted as one of America's "designated victims." A designated victim is a boy, usually slender, usually thoughtful, who would prefer creating beauty to crushing bones. Because they might enjoy gymnastics, fencing, acting, writing, or band practice rather than football practice, these boys are called "faggots" and that's just for openers.

While it's true that the great majority of these young men, some sniffing back tears, who confided in me insisted that they weren't gay, yet each of them had had his manhood questioned. And they had it persistently and savagely questioned. Was it their fault, I wondered, that not one of these young victims had a face that one would expect to find amid the pages of *Sports Illustrated?* Is that

Reprinted from *The ALAN Review* 21.2, Winter 1994, pages 2–4, by permission of the author.

really what we as a great people on the cusp of the twenty-first century are needing? A nation of linebackers?

I would never have even guessed at the size and dimension of the "designated victim" problem if I had not written a book that opened a window onto the violence against homosexuals. But it has been people's extraordinary response to that book that has extended my window into an ever-widening vista.

In his introduction of me at the ALAN Workshop, Ted Fabiano, a young English teacher from Kansas City, flatly stated that homophobia affected everyone in his school. He broke it down: most obviously are those "designated victims," some gay, most not. Then there are those that verbally and physically oppress the victims, followed by those that egg on the oppressors of the "designated victims." And last there is the largest group of all: those silent observers who watch the people who egg on the people who brutalize the "designated victims." Forty years ago, a high school friend of mine with the improbable name of James Crowe committed suicide. What I did not—could not—understand then, I understand now. Jim Crowe was one of Central High School's "designated victims." In the best high school in Memphis, he was the best—the very best of the best! He had a fine baritone voice, was a gifted actor and a caring friend, and possessed a mind that reflected lights like crystal chandeliers at a royal wedding.

Oh, sure, I knew that he was "teased" because he had no interest whatsoever in sports, at least not in team sports. He much preferred his Saturday morning acting job on Memphis' premier station, WREC. That was his dream of one day acting, singing, and, perhaps, directing professionally. And any schoolboy anywhere can tell you that that's suspect. Very, very suspect! Some of the jocks, and would-be jocks, mocked Jim by nicknaming him "Sister Boy," which, incidentally, was the same name they hung on the suffering prep student in Robert Anderson's masterful play, *Tea and Sympathy.* In Anderson's play, however, the boy is "saved" by his physical union with Deborah Kerr, the headmaster's beautiful wife.

In "real life," I did not save Jim Crowe. Unlike Deborah Kerr, I lacked an understanding of the true depth and dimension of Jim's despair. In my eyes, he seemed to soar so far beyond his schoolmates that I chose to believe the pretty myth that a giant couldn't be brought down by a bunch of intellectual and moral pygmies.

If this society's constant preaching-railing-cruelty against homosexuality weren't bad enough (and, God knows, it is bad enough), it is hurting a great many more than the estimated 10 percent of the population that are gay and lesbian. It hurt Jim Crowe, and it's also hurting untold numbers of young males whose only crime is that they're suffering from what I've come to label the three

S's: Sensitive, Shy, and Slender. Jim Dodge, a New Hampshire police chief, suggested to me that there's a fourth S: Studious.

A psychiatrist who has achieved fame treating both sports heroes and literary lights once estimated that there were as many homosexuals in the American Football League as there are in the Authors League of America. But who would believe that? Myths die hard; and the prettier the myth, the harder it dies.

While researching *The Drowning of Stephan Jones,* I conducted over four hundred interviews during a twenty-month period in eight states, and I came to the sad conclusion that a lot of preachers, especially televangelists, are manufacturing hate from their pulpits. When, for example, I'd ask someone who had committed a crime against a gay why he did it, his answers were often shocking. Oftentimes the now-convicted felon would quote the Bible, his minister, and one or more of the nationally known televangelists to justify his violence. Reverend Jerry Falwell's words about homosexuality were, for example, once quoted to me in great detail by a teenager who had the week before opened up the skull of a man on his way to buy microwave popcorn at a convenience store.

When I'd follow a young criminal's thread back to his local pastor, the pastor, like all the clergymen I interviewed, would fervently proclaim, "Oh, no, I've never preached hatred. I only preach love. We hate the sin, but we love the sinner." For a long time, I thought about what so many ministers had told me about making that neat little dividing line between the sin and the sinner, and wondered if it really were possible.

To find out, I devised a psychodrama that I played with twenty-six people who had at least two advantages over the felons: They were at least fifteen years older, and they all had a reputation of being loving. With my Parker pen at the ready, I'd ask the participant to pretend that my favorite pen was a knife that I had just slid between his ribs. Then I'd ask my profusely bleeding victim if he hated me or the violence that I had done to him. It was no contest. Twenty-five had no trouble shouting out variations of, "No, I'd hate you, Bette."

A talk-show host on whose show I appeared labeled my book, "More than controversial, it's explosive!" While I may have been the first to write a popular novel about this shocking source of hate against gays and lesbians, I am most certainly not the first to be aware of it. Far from it: Practically every thoughtful person seems to be all too aware that this is happening—and it's happening now.

Of course, the clergy are far from alone in their hysterical homophobia with its broad-based consequences. But it is the voices of the clergy that resonate beyond the churchyard, past the villages, through the towns, and into all of our cities across this nation. If the "spiritual" voices are heard spewing hate and divisiveness, then where goeth our standards of decency?

In March of 1991, Boston was ready to explode over the issue of whether twenty-five gay and lesbian Irish Americans would be allowed to march in our city's Saint Patrick's Day Parade. Both *The Boston Herald* and *The Boston Globe* called to ask me what I think should be done.

Usually, I don't have answers, never mind instant answers, that I'm so certain of. But this time, I knew precisely what should be done: "Respectfully call upon the one person in all of New England who has the prestige, the power, and the authority to lead us Bostonians into a circle of brotherhood," I begged. "Bernard Cardinal Law could say 'no more violence' and make it stick." The Archdiocese of Boston came roaring back with five adjectives, all negative. They pointed out that *The Drowning of Stephan Jones* was "merely anecdotal and non-scientific" and that the author herself was "ludicrous, bizarre, and irresponsible."

To understand the oppression of the gays and lesbians by the religious community, I believe that it's instructive to look back on this 300th anniversary of the Salem Witch Trials. During that period, many people (including fifteen children) were put to death because they were, according to the parsons and priests, dancing with the devil.

The trials were stopped when the laity of the late sixteenth century rose up against the clergy chanting, "No more burnings!" Cotton Mather, the greatest preacher of the day, resisted, calling the laity "Devils or people who are talking with the devil." Ultimately, with the help of a Massachusetts governor, the clerics backed off, and, I'm pleased to announce, not once since, not in all these years, has another witch been found in the entire Commonwealth of Massachusetts!

I believe that it's way past time that we, the laity of the late twentieth century, should take our cues from the courageous laity of 1692. It took great courage, as well as great revulsion, for mere laymen to finally rise up against men who claimed to be God's earthly representatives. Well, we, the thinking laity of today, have already experienced the same revulsion experienced by our forefathers.

It is neither too early nor too late to do what they did: confront those un-lit minds, no matter how exalted be their station. Back in 1692, the people's questions to the parsons and the priests were, "Haven't we hung enough witches?" Today our updated question to these men of God is, "Haven't we brutalized and buried enough gays? Haven't we brutalized and buried enough of our creative young?"

Let us say "no" to oppression in the name of political expediency. Let us say "no" to oppression in the name of patriotism, and, for God's sake, let us say "no" to oppression in the name of religion.

Understanding Adolescent Homophobia: An Interview with Bette Greene

Lynne Alvine

I sat in the ALAN Workshop audience in the large hotel ballroom in Louisville, Kentucky. The speaker was describing "society's designated victim," a type of young boy who is sensitive, shy, slender and, often, studious.

I had not yet read her latest novel when I first heard Bette Greene speak about *The Drowning of Stephan Jones.* I picked it up one night a couple of weeks after returning from NCTE in Louisville. From the title, I knew Stephan Jones would die. I figured I'd just check out who drowned him, how they did it, and see if it was a book I wanted to include in the readings for my adolescent literature class at the university.

I should have known better than to begin one of Bette Greene's novels right before going to bed. I read into the night, knowing that Stephan Jones would die and knowing, too, that his brutalizers would not be punished, could not be punished, if the book were to have a credible ending.

I had heard the sensitivity and compassion in the author's voice as she talked about the young men for whom Stephan Jones was a prototype. I had heard the anger when she spoke of their brutalizers. I had not understood why she felt so strongly about such victimization. Why had she taken on such a potentially explosive topic?

A few months later, when I learned that Bette Greene was to be the keynote speaker at an English Festival for high school students

Reprinted from *The ALAN Review* 21.2, Winter 1994, pages 5–9, by permission of the author.

sponsored by the Western Pennsylvania Council of Teachers of English (WPCTE), I arranged for time to talk with her about her research for *The Drowning of Stephan Jones.*

We sat over room-service coffee at the Pittsburgh Ramada Inn. It had been several years since I had been first drawn into the story of Patty and Anton in *Summer of My German Soldier.* It had been twenty years since this woman across the table from me had first published that novel about intolerance and persecution in Arkansas during World War II.

I had enjoyed spending the afternoon with Bette Greene and those six hundred high school students at the English Festival. I was excited to have this opportunity to talk with her about her more recent work. She appeared to be tired, but I could tell she had been energized by the interaction with so many young people.

I asked Bette to talk about why she had written a novel about a gay couple and adolescent homophobia. I wanted to know something of her connection to this story. Her initial response sounded as though it might have been about *Summer of My German Soldier.* She spoke slowly, as if seeing her thoughts across the Pittsburgh skyline:

> I am bothered by injustice towards other people. The etiology of my hating hate probably has to do with two women whom I loved very much. One was our housekeeper Ruth, who was African American in a time and place where the Ku Klux Klan rode. In spite of this, Ruth was not a subservient person. For example, she would never have called you, "Miz Lynne." She would have called you "Miss Alvine." She protected her dignity at a time when it was neither popular or even safe to do so.
>
> The other woman was my grandmother, who also lived at that time in Wynne, Arkansas. She had emigrated from Lithuania where her brother was a superintendent of schools in a mid-sized city during WW II. Even though the Germans were murdering all intellectuals and Jews, my grandmother believed her brother, who was both a Jew and an intellectual, would be safe because he was so loved and respected in the community. I remember during the war my grandmother going every day to the Wynne Post Office waiting for a letter that would never come.

When I commented on the obvious influence of Ruth and her grandmother in *Summer of My German Soldier,* Bette explained:

> Oh, absolutely. . . . *German Soldier* was more of my own personal *violation. The Drowning of Stephan Jones* is personal in that I feel so personally violated by it, and yet it's not directly my story. I am straight and have been married to the same man for thirty-four years, but I don't understand brutalizing somebody because they are physically attracted to people in ways that I may not be. The first thing we do to destroy another human being is verbal. I destroy you

> by calling you things that take your personhood away from you. And then I may or may not do [physical] violence. I don't like verbal violence. I don't like things that people call people in this society: "Fat," "Skinny," "Four-eyes," whatever. I am offended by it. I'm deeply offended by injustice.

I turned our conversation toward her research for the book, asking about the interviews she had alluded to in the ALAN speech. Her subjects had been not only the victims and their victimizers. She had also talked with persons associated with the perpetrators of the crimes:

> I did about 485 interviews in eight states—California, Washington, Tennessee, Arkansas, New Hampshire, Massachusetts, Rhode Island, and Maine. I avoided anyone who stole from the victim because then you don't know if it's really a hate crime or a crime for gain. I talked to everybody who was available—their teachers, their Uncle Joe, their pastors, their coaches. Another criterion was that the brutalizers had to be generally considered "good boys," people who had never been in trouble before. I tried to isolate it as much as I could. I tried to find out where does the hate come from? Not all the boys were religious, but they all had been affected by religion. They knew it was OK to do violence to gay people because they thought it said so in the Bible.
>
> Once, just to get a reaction, I suggested that perhaps there was a better target. "Old people," I ventured, "they're much better targets than gay people. Even if they manage to strike you back, it's not all that hard. Chances are they can't run away. So go for the old people." The young men were horrified, insulted that I would suggest that they would do that. They said, "I'd never hurt an old person." So, somewhere out there through our religion and our culture they have learned that it is acceptable to hurt homosexuals, but it is not acceptable to hurt their elders.
>
> The trial lawyers help to make the situation worse. Invariably they don't have a real defense, so the attorney creates one: "The lone gay man 'came on' to this bunch of boys. The defendants were provoked in some way, sexually." I don't believe it! I've talked to a lot of people in the gay community, and they say to me, "Bette, we know what the world is out there. We don't come on to people unless there is first a subtle courtship back and forth. We don't come on to a football team, for God's sakes. We're interested in romance, not suicide."
>
> Had I done in every man who threw a pass at me when I was young, I'll tell you that there would have been any number of bodies floating down the Mississippi, the Seine, the East River, and later, the Charles.

Bette had implied that many of the abusers she had interviewed were quite young. I asked what rationale they had given for their actions against gays. Why did they believe that brutalizing gays was okay?

They quote the Bible. They quote their local ministers. I've talked with many of the ministers. They quote to me the Sodom and Gomorrah story. I may be the most expert person on Sodom and Gomorrah at this hotel, because I have studied it more than you want to know. It's not about homosexuality. It is about inhospitality. In the days before the Ramada Inn, when people were traveling, you had to take them in or they would be eaten by the wild animals or die of starvation. The man sent the daughter out instead of the guest. It has to do with gang rape. It has to do with inhospitality, but it has nothing to do with homosexuality. Jesus in all of his preaching never mentioned homosexuality—not once. The Ten Commandments are notably silent on it although they do talk about adultery. Preachers don't generally preach "We hate adulterers!" or half of the people in the congregation would walk out. If they're in a church, homosexuals are well closeted. So where is the issue? Who are they preaching to? Too many members of our clergy are preaching hatred. They send people out to kill the sin, but since folks don't know where the sin is, they kill the "sinner."

Earlier that day in her speech, Bette had held up a *USA Today* newspaper and had pointed to four front-page stories where religious fundamentalists were involved in killings. She referred to those examples as we talked:

Look at today's newspaper. A physician is gunned down. He's got three bullets in his back. The event in Waco, Texas, is another one. The [bombing of the] World Trade Center. All of this evil was done by religious fundamentalists. One was a Muslim fundamentalist. What does the Christian fundamentalist say? They say they're taking a collection up, not for Dr. Gunn, not for Dr. Gunn's two children who won't have a father, not for the grieving widow, but—you guessed it—for the murderer.

Any religious fundamental group (including Christian, Muslim, and Jewish) is a potential danger. The problem is that enlightened people are afraid to stand up and say that these people who spout pieties can also be terrorists and murderers. We're afraid to say it because they claim to be doing the work of God. None of us is so secure that we can speak against such a close buddy of God. There is no greater blasphemy in the world than these people who claim to be doing God's work.

I asked her to say more about her sense of how the world climate had informed her work on *The Drowning of Stephan Jones:*

Homophobia is endemic in America. The air we breathe is filled with homophobia. A great amount of it is coming from fundamental Christianity. I've gone to the churches of the young men who were the victimizers. On the tube I see the ever-grinning Pat Robertson. I watch the Trinity Network and the Eternal Word Network. What spews forth is a river of hate. Nobody can be more in error than when they insist that they, and they alone, speak for God.

Once again, our conversation turned toward those two men in the book who loved each other and who were brutalized for that love. I asked Bette to talk about Frank Montgomery and Stephan Jones and their attacker, Andy Harris.

> Stephan Jones was a composite character of many gay men, as was Frank Montgomery. I guess Frank Montgomery was, to me, a sort of Montgomery Clift character. They were both amalgamations of a number of people. [Andy Harris and his friends] picked on Stephan Jones because he was not a fighter. So who better to pick on? Andy Harris was just like so many of the young men, only a little bit more clean-cut. Andy was not a full person because he had picked up the stereotypes of his father, who used to batter him. The father would call him girl names and humiliate Andy. So, of course, Andy had a lot to prove. With the harassment of Stephan Jones, Andy could prove that he was really a man. That's what he wanted from Stephan. If he vanquished Stephan Jones, wouldn't that prove, once and for all, that he was a man?

It sounded as if she was suggesting that Andy Harris was confused about his own sexuality. I was curious as to whether she had found any evidence that the people who are the most active at the brutalizing are themselves troubled by their own unclear orientation. I asked her directly:

> No doubt. Here's one thing [the brutalizers] did, Lynne, which was fascinating. I am a grandmother. As I talked with them, they often tried to convince me how macho they are. Doesn't that grab you as being strange? Why would I be interested in how macho they are? I'm guessing that they're trying to prove something more to themselves than to me. In this society, violence is too often a shortcut to masculinity. Our coaches are involved. Our coaches brutalize the kids by yelling epithets at them when they fumble the ball, epithets that wound by telling these boys that they're not men, they're girls.

I asked about the characterizations of Carla Wayland and Carla's mother Judith, the librarian, who had stood up for intellectual freedom in the small Arkansas community where the novel is set:

> Carla was a lot like my daughter. I suppose there's something of me in Judith, and there is a lot of Judith in so many librarians that I have known. Librarians are a peculiar people. They don't make more money by getting you to take a book out and exercise your mind, yet they go through all of this trouble to get you to do so. Judith liked to feel useful and to provide an important service. Intellectual freedom was very important to her. This is one of the big issues in the book. Is it okay to have your intellectual freedom impinged upon if it's—say, for a good cause? For a religious cause? Judith didn't think so. Of course Carla was a high school student who wanted to be in the mainstream. She was proud of her mother, but she was also embarrassed by her mother. So Carla was torn by admiration, ambivalence, and love.

Clearly, Judith Wayland did not fit into the community where Bette Greene had set the novel. I asked her about her choices for that community.

> It's set near Fayetteville, Arkansas, in a mountain village that's noted for the diverse types of people who come there; it welcomes "nuts and berries." Parson Springs, Arkansas, proudly proclaims that this is a place where misfits fit. So, Frank and Stephan thought that they would fit in. And they did fit in. It was in the more typical neighboring town a few miles away that they ran into harassment. That community, like much of the rural South, too often snuffs out the intellectual curiosity because what they teach is that you're not supposed to think; you're supposed to believe, to go by faith. In growing up there, whatever I was told, I believed. Or, at least, I struggled hard trying to believe whatever it is that "nice" people are programmed to believe. The teaching was that you go by faith alone. And I really tried it. I mean literally. I never, for example, studied for anything. I spent my time praying that I would pass third-grade math. I prayed that I would just get a good grade. How do you deal with somebody like that?

The topics of gays in the military, homophobia, and gay and lesbian relationships had been everywhere in the press, on every talk show, in every sit com, on every news program. I asked Bette Greene about her sense of how the American public was responding to the gay rights in the military issue and/or this unprecedented focus on gay and lesbian lifestyles:

> I think the American people are going to get better about it. The polls are showing they're getting better. I would want to understand how it's going to work in the military. I'm sure there are going to be some difficult adjustments, but I would like to see it.

I suggested to her that Americans will get better on the issue only if the issue is talked about, only if the taboo is lifted. Many people who consider themselves to be very liberal, who would never make a racist remark, who would never make a sexist remark, will still tell a joke about a gay person. It seems gays and lesbians are the one group that it's still okay to pick on—sort of the last frontier of insensitivity and intolerance. Bette agreed:

> It is the last frontier. I think that it is a matter of being sensitized to it. If you tell a joke, it's to dehumanize. That's why I object to it. That's the first line in any battle. You dehumanize. I object to homosexual jokes. But it's not being gay that's the problem. The problem is being in the closet, because closets kill. Barney Frank and Gerry Studds in the Congress say, "I'm gay, and I'm okay." They do their job, and they still get reelected. But if Barney Frank or Gerry Studds were in the closet, then they could be blackmailed; they're half people. It's the J. Edgar Hoover syndrome. The former FBI head, according to a

> new book, was a man who was blackmailed by the Mafia because he was in the closet. I don't have objection to how people express their love if it doesn't hurt anybody else, but closets do hurt. I think being open takes a great deal of courage.

I believed *The Drowning of Stephan Jones* to be an important book. I knew the book had been received positively. When a high school girl came up to Bette earlier that day and said, "I loved your book," I asked her "What book?" I was not surprised that she said ". . . *Stephan Jones.*" I had seen students press forward to purchase copies of the book after her talk at the Festival. I wondered, however, what Bette Greene's perspective on the response was:

> Everyone who has come to me or who has written to me has been very positive. Everyone calls it a "powerful book," a book that is "memorable." Everyone I talk to who has read the book seems to have given it to somebody else to read. The only bad responses that I've received have been from people who have not read the book. When people read the book as opposed to hearing about it, [the response] is positive. I received one letter from a Methodist woman who said, "Your book gave me a whole new way of looking at gay people. Thank you for stretching the mind and the heart of a 64-year-old country woman."
>
> Last Christmas my husband brought home four books his secretary wanted signed. When she took *The Drowning of Stephan Jones* home, he thought she would be very upset. I sort of forgot all about it. I talked to her two weeks ago and she said, "Mrs. Greene, I want to tell you, [the book] changed my way of seeing things. Now I see homosexuals just like people a lot like you and me. I cried when Stephan Jones died."

As Bette shared her sense of the positive response from the readers of *The Drowning of Stephan Jones,* I began to be hopeful of its potential. I said to her, "If the sixty-four-year-olds can have that response, perhaps the young people can have a similar response. Perhaps it will help them ground themselves in a view that will stand up a little better against the barrage of hatred that is spewing from the religious groups":

> The designated victim is in every school in America. Ted Fabiano, who introduced me at NCTE, gave a very thoughtful presentation of why the book is important. He said that at his school in Kansas City, homophobia affects everyone. He pointed out that the core was the 10 to 20 percent of the kids who were thoughtful students, who would prefer to go to band practice than to football practice. They might very well be seen at academic competitions. They like to write or to act. They like things that are not considered "macho." This 10 to 20 percent of the students (some are gay, some are straight) are persecuted by an equal number who are the tormenters, a group of boys who want to show how virile they all are. The next group is the

> eggers-on. What they do is to act as cheerleaders to the tormentors. Then, there is the last group, the largest group of all: these are the onlookers who seek out a vantage point from which to stand and watch.

I thought again of *The Drowning of Stephan Jones.* "These are the 'Carla Waylands' of every school. After hearing your speech, perhaps the 'Carla Waylands' in the auditorium today will now have a different response when faced with situations where they must make a choice about how they will respond to the hatred":

> Again and again, I see a lot of physical courage, but so little moral courage. I see young people who will do all kinds of physical things to save people they don't know, but they will do little or nothing to save a friend if they have to stand up and say "Leave this person alone." We have to point out to them that real men are not the men who are doing violence. We can from a position of authority make statements about our personal beliefs. With our silence, we create a vacuum. What they need [for] us adults to say is, "It's wrong. It's wrong to bother people, to hurt people who are minding their own business." We need to have very understanding people who are going to be our leaders. I think it's important to talk about justice and injustice with them. There were 650 kids here today who listened as I spoke for justice, and there wasn't one snicker. No, not one.

My questions were answered. Bette Greene had written *The Drowning of Stephan Jones* because she believes that young people in every generation must confront the issues of intolerance and injustice toward others. She had come to Pittsburgh to raise those issues with high school students. Often, however, adults don't have an opportunity to take a stand when a young person is being victimized. A code of silence operates to protect the brutalizers in most schools. Those who would censor this book perpetuate that code of silence. *The Drowning of Stephan Jones* is an important book because it has the potential to develop sensitivity in young readers who might otherwise become one of the characters in the book, participating in such violence or standing by, watching it in silence. It also has the potential to reach out to society's "designated victims" who, in reading *The Drowning of Stephan Jones,* may come to understand that they are not alone.

Part I The Authors

Section 5
Richard Peck

Some Thoughts on Adolescent Literature

Richard Peck

Three and a half years ago I walked away from teaching in a school where curriculum had been effaced and literacy had become optional. I left a classroom completely in the control of nonreading talkers. And so I was attending NCTE meetings long before I ever knew I'd be writing novels for the young—before I felt the need to try communicating with them in any arena beyond the classroom.

But of course teaching English isn't really a job you can quit. I find myself walking up and down my silent study still giving fool-proof and brilliant lesson plans to non-existent students. And like any old teacher who ever was, I've prepared my lesson plan today and will give it though hell should bar the way.

Exchanging the hurly-burly of the classroom for the anxious tranquility of a writing desk was for me an overnight transition. I didn't at first know I'd find a publisher. But it seemed to me that teaching was drifting farther and farther into psychiatric social work—a field in which I wasn't trained—and a field which snubbed the most promising and receptive students. This was, of course, just after the tumultuous 1960s, when teachers were being told everywhere—including at NCTE Conventions—how to render themselves more expendable, how to water down an already minimal curriculum, and how to deal with attention spans that had no intention of stretching.

Because I didn't have your courage and constancy, I turned in my gradebook and said goodbye to the pension plan. But you never get far from your problems. Today I'm still trying to hold the attention of the young, to deal with a diminished attention span, to explore subject matter of immediate and manifest relevance, to vie with the distractions of television and peer-group pressure and the disarray of permissive home lives. I don't suggest that my novels are didactic—or dare to be. We live in an age and country in which we approach our young by indirection.

Reprinted from *The ALAN Review* 3.1, September/October 1975, pages 4–7, by permission of the author.

And so when I'm sitting alone at the typewriter, I sometimes lose heart. I've learned to combat this by getting out into other people's classrooms. Two weeks ago I was visiting school people in a California town with my publishers. We were discussing this new wave of novels directed mainly at a readership of younger adolescents. And one of the local librarians said, "What we need are books on the subjects we're getting now, but we need them rewritten for a third- or fourth-grade reading ability level." Not for third graders, of course, but for seventh or ninth graders with elementary school reading levels.

And evidently this problem of the lowering reading level isn't limited to us. I wrote a very light mystery novel that has been sold to a Copenhagen firm for Danish translation. The other day my publisher received a request to translate and abridge it for reluctant readers in a vastly simplified form. In my innocence I thought the novel was written in a highly accessible form.

And so the central educational problem of our time—the reading level—is a common cause for teachers and writers. We write novels for the young about their own concerns with characters drawn from their contemporaries. This has become a major publishing trend because so many of the young have not responded to adult reading—particularly the literature of the past. We have created a new form of reading, uncomfortably termed "Young Adult Fiction." And now we are being told that we must condense our narratives and simplify our vocabularies further. Surely, somewhere on the horizon ahead we will reach the vanishing point where writers along with teachers will be a terminally endangered species.

I think perhaps we have to think more about the needs of the young person who somehow has learned enough rudiments of reading to pursue books that will meet him halfway—the sort of student who can face a library that hasn't been renamed The Audiovisual Resource Center and is presided over by an illiterate technician who sees his future as the superintendent of schools.

We have already turned out a quantity of books directed to the nonreader. The late 1960s were full of them. Novels of special pleading—really very propagandistic tracts on the subjects of the drug culture, ethnic identity, embryonic political activism, and a number of other causes that made news. But I think we are learning that the aspect of the youth culture on which the TV news camera was fixated misfired in the hands of the young thoughtful enough to read by choice.

A book idea may sound very good to the self-consciously liberal editorial staff functioning in a New York City highrise, a staff who never go near a school. There is no such thing as a liberal teenager.

Adolescents are conservative out of psychological necessity, as you know. Though their rhetoric denies it, any school teacher knows that youngsters will say one thing and do the reverse. In my last teaching year, there was a seventh-grade girl in my class who assaulted the smallest student in the room and was excused the next day to attend a peace rally. It was also a school whose students demonstrated for integration and segregated themselves every time they sat down. Reports like these are sometimes written off by the publishing establishment as cynical.

The approach to a young black, Puerto Rican, Chicano, or Indian reader is usually patronizing. The emphasis is upon the wretched conditions or ghetto living and bigotry. This overlooks the fact that people of all backgrounds are continually rising in our upwardly mobile society. And it spurns the need for those who want out of present conditions and could use a hopeful story. In reading compositions by students of many ethnic backgrounds, I was never struck by their preoccupation with their group. They were ventilating personal and interpersonal concerns. They were more anxious to identify with the human race than with a particular segment of it. At the same time, there were student activists giving their all to racial or ethnic awareness. But again, they weren't readers.

It's no help to the youth novelist to be offended by the conservative, ego-involved inclinations of the young. He'd better spend his time trying to evaluate this conservatism because the young choose books as they choose their friends—more as mirrors than as windows.

While we writers are sometimes asked to water down our messages, a young adult novel is not a remedial-reading condensation of an adult book. In most attributes, it's a different genre. If I could only think of a perfect YA novel, I'd be home writing it at this moment. But there are some discernible traits.

First, a YA novel is unreality masked as realism. Setting, circumstances, and dialogue had better reflect a familiar world. But the protagonist generally must be able to do something that most of the readers cannot. He must rise up independently from his tribe and assert himself. Or he must work his influence on others. Most young people rightly enough feel trapped—by their institutions, by family structure, by a need for conformity.

They like to read about someone who's managed to work free. The first novel I ever wrote, *Don't Look and It Won't Hurt,* deals with a girl in highly unpromising circumstances—a broken home, poverty, anonymity. When her older sister goes to a home for unwed mothers, the slender webwork of family stability collapses. And so the protagonist must rise up and pull the family together again and find herself, not through conformist patterns, but by a kind of plucky individualism. In real life, the events are unlikely: in a story, they provide scope that a young reader may feel he doesn't have.

In any gathering of teenagers, the underdog or the offbeat youngster is an obvious outcast. But in a novel for the same readership, the underdog is slated for triumph. This serves both the reader who feels excluded by giving him some vicarious identity and the conformist reader who can experience tolerant impulses he wouldn't express in his own life. M. E. Kerr's *If I Love You Am I Trapped Forever?* is a clear example. A boy in it seems so eccentric to a provincial high school society that he's nicknamed "Doomed." Yet his extreme individualism transforms everyone's senior year in a variety of antic—and readable—ways.

Another distinguishing, feature of the YA novel is that it needs to end at a beginning. No author can in good conscience end his story with "and they lived happily ever after." For a fifteen-year-old, the best and worst of life still lie ahead. But the events of a YA novel must prepare both protagonist and reader for a lot of life yet to be lived. The events are a few experiences that nudge him or thrust him toward maturity. Here the author tries to walk the narrow way between fashionable ennui and pessimism and the parental urge to promise a pot of gold at the end of the rainbow of Right Living.

More than any other, I think, this present generation needs a sense that the future holds a great deal of promise for those who are free enough to face it. When you and I were adolescents we spent too much time wishing we were grown up. Too many of today's adolescents see no value in maturity. And in truth we live in a society in which maturity and responsibility appear to buy you very little.

A final attribute of the YA novel must be its emotional emphasis. While we novelists for the young lie awake nights trying to pull tight plots together and worry over the stylistic devices our editors and reviewers are conditioned to look for, our young readers seem far more interested in a book as an emotional outlet. To oversimplify, after a reassuring outcome in a story, I suspect they like best a good cry.

This doesn't mean that every story need be lugubrious, though many of them are. But the young feel very full of emotions they are hard put to express. The well-known sexual revolution hasn't seemed to liberate either the participants or the noncombatants.

Friendships are just as important. Many young friendships are painfully inarticulate, and yet those friendships are emotional to a degree rarely known in later life. In all their relationships—including family ties—most of the young are emotionally frozen. Novels in which characters actually express themselves by word and deed are very satisfying and necessary.

Another emotion is humor. And here we are on the shakiest ground of all because the young, like all people who laugh a lot, are essentially humorless. Analyze the laughter in a schoolroom, and you find it is motivated either by nervousness or derision. Writing humor for this readership is as perilous as it is needed. More truly, richly comic YA novels would be very welcome, though of course much harder to bring off than trendy relevance or grim situation.

We are well into a trend that is still finding its way. And it has emerged so suddenly from its ancient forebears, a Hardy boy and Nancy Drew, that examining where we are is difficult.

We're suddenly into a time in which college is losing its hold on the young, both as a place for academic excellence and as a promise for tangible future success. Another prop is being knocked out from under the young. Only a few years ago most of the young spent the end of their adolescence either in college or the army or in premature marriages. Today, masses of them will fall into none of these institutions when they leave high school. There are new options, new unknowns, new tensions.

What books about their bewildering world can do for young people I'm not sure, but it's very clear that the young are looking for something as palpable as a book in the hand.

Our goal as writers for the very young is of course to make them inveterate, chronic readers whose tastes will keep pace with their maturity. Right now our greatest problem is that we can only reach a small minority—those who read well enough to spend leisure time with a book. Television may be the obvious enemy, but the ultimate one is surely the early school reading program that is neither reading nor a program.

Probably it's not fair to deal television a glancing blow. After all, it's provided some useful hints to the YA novelist. Even young people who have arrived at the age of twelve without ever having to read a book through have a rudimentary sense of plot, characterization, and sometimes theme from TV. But its great contribution is pacing. The YA novel is informed by the thirty-, sixty-, and ninety-minute timing of TV programming, with time out, of course, for commercial breaks.

This briskness is evident in the shape of the novel's chapter lengths, reduced exposition, and the bracing need to characterize in a matter of sentences not pages. Is something lost in this acceleration? Unquestionably. But it makes good YA writing crisper and less self-indulgent than much current adult reading.

TV undoubtedly robs us of readers, but it has proved far less lethal than the school where reading limps along at the pace of the slowest student and the home where books—and ideas—are never mentioned.

Ten Questions to Ask about a Novel

Richard Peck

In a time when the written book report has gone the way of the diagrammed sentence, the class discussion of a book remains the usual way of eliciting reader response. Most discussion leaders could use some new questions, if only to discourage the "I liked it/didn't like it" reaction. Herewith, ten questions to ask about a piece of fiction. Herewith, too, the ulterior motive in asking each question:

1. What would this story be like if the main character were of the opposite sex?

(Ulterior Motive): to approach the thinking of the author, who must decide what kind of protagonist or narrator will best embody or express the viewpoint. Could the protagonist of *The Member of the Wedding* be a boy instead of a girl? Could Jerry Renault in *The Chocolate War* be a female victim of a female gang? Certainly, though each book would seem different in many superficial ways. Such a question might even temporarily defuse the sexual polarization rampant in junior high.

2. Why is this story set where it is (not what is the setting)?

(Ulterior Motive): to point out the setting as an author's device to draw the reader into the action by means of recognizable trappings. The isolated setting of *Lord of the Flies* is a clear, if negative, example. But why is a soap opera almost always placed in an upper-middle-class suburban setting? Why do so few YA novels occur in historic or exotic locales?

3. If you were to film this story, what characters would you eliminate if you couldn't use them all?

(Ulterior Motive): to contrast the human richness of a novel with the necessary simplification of a TV show. Confronted with the need to eliminate some of the characters who add texture, some readers may rise up in defense of their favorites.

4. Would you film this story in black and white or in color?

(Ulterior Motive): to consider tone. The initial reaction in this florid age is to opt for color in everything. But some young readers

Reprinted from *The ALAN Review* 5.3, Spring 1978, pages 1, 7, by permission of the author.

may remember the chilling Dracula films are in black and white, perhaps in part because dark shadows are always darkest and black blood is more menacing than red.

5. How is the main character different from you?

(Ulterior Motive): to relent for once in our attempts to get the young readers to identify on their own limited terms. Protagonists regularly embody traits for the reader to aspire to. In YA books, they typically have powers, insights, and surmountable drawbacks that readers will often respond to without possessing.

6. Why or why not would this story make a good TV series?

(Ulterior Motive): to contrast the shaping of a book's sequential chapters in the larger shape of the plot to the episodes of a TV series that repeat narrowly but don't rise from their formula to a central conclusion.

7. What's one thing in this story that's happened to you?

(Ulterior Motive): to elicit an anecdotal response that draws the reader into the book. YA novels typically deal in the shock of recognition in their depicting of highly realistic school, social, and personal situations. Science fiction and fantasy use very human situations to balance their more fabulous elements and to make room for the earthbound reader.

8. Reread the first paragraph of Chapter l. What's in it that makes you read on?

(Ulterior Motive): to begin a book where the author must, in assessing the need for immediate involvement in an age not known for its patient attention span. An even more wistful motive: to suggest that young people include in their own writing immediately attractive devices for gaining the attention of the reader, if only the poor teacher.

9. If you had to design a new cover for this book, what would it look like?

(Ulterior Motive): to consider the often-deceptive packaging of the book in this visual era, particularly the paperback cover, and to encourage a more skeptical eye among those who were being bombarded by packaging and commercial claims long before they could read.

10. What does the title tell you about the book? Does it tell the truth?

(Ulterior Motive): to remind the reader that the title may well be the most important words the author writes and to encourage their defenses against titles that titillate and oversell.

Social Protest in Young Adult Fiction

Hugh Agee

"Is this really literature?"

This is not an unfamiliar question for many young adult "problem" novels of recent years, and it is one some may ask of Richard Peck's *Are You in the House Alone?* In a sense, all YA novels are to some degree problem novels, for as Dwight L. Burton has noted in *Literature Study in the High Schools,* "Books for adolescents reflect various interests and concerns of young readers, but they have their greatest impact, probably, because of their connection with the personal problems of adolescents. . ." (244). Because it deals with the rape of its teenage protagonist, *Are You in the House Alone?* is a YA problem novel of special significance.

With the rise of the "new realism" in YA fiction, we have seen a wide-ranging treatment of sexuality. For example, we find the first awakenings of sexuality in the young teen in such books as Winifred Rosen's *Cruisin' for a Bruisin';* we find first love and first sex, often in explicit terms, in Judy Blume's *Forever;* we encounter the dilemmas of teenage pregnancy and abortion in such books as Paul Zindel's *My Darling, My Hamburger* and Winifred Madison's *Growing Up in a Hurry;* we find homosexuality treated in such books as Rosa Guy's *Ruby* and Isabelle Holland's *The Man Without a Face.* I daresay we could question the literary quality of most YA novels, and certainly none of the above novels are flawless, though some bear up better than others under close critical scrutiny. However, teenage readers with pressing personal concerns hardly make literary quality a major consideration when they pick up a YA novel.

What, then, of *Are You in the House Alone?* I have no sales figures to cite, so I can make no claims as to the novel's importance with its popularity. Yet *Are You in the House Alone?* is an important book.

Richard Peck's novel is the story of Gail Osborne, a sexually active high school junior who, after being subjected to obscene notes and phone calls, is raped and beaten by Phil Lawver, the son of the

Reprinted from *The ALAN Review* 6.2, Winter 1979, pages 4, 10, by permission of the author.

town's most prominent family. Peck dramatizes the notes and phone calls in a way that some readers may find a shade melodramatic, but young readers of mystery and suspense are familiar with these techniques and will not reject the story for them. Gail is able to identify her assailant, but she learns that nothing can be done because of the nature and the strong influence of the boy's family.

Peck's purpose of alerting young teens "to a serious sexual/legal/medical/social problem: the crime of rape, for which adolescents are the prime victims" puts the novel in the category of social protest ("Rape and the Teenage Victim," 173). Mainstream literature has long been a vehicle for social protest. Charles Dickens did a bit of crusading in the writing of *Hard Times,* and he took his lumps from the critics. Upton Sinclair was disappointed that *The Jungle* drew more attention to the handling of the meat supply than to the exploitation of workers, but we cannot disregard his novel for its literary shortcomings.

Peck acknowledges "writing a single-problem didactic novel, largely bereft of the techniques that had seen me through earlier novels" ("Rape and the Teenage Victim," 175). The challenge in writing such a novel is, of course, to keep it within the province of fiction, to avoid the tone and style of the documentary or the case study. We would agree that many teenage novels resemble case studies, but in a sense so do many outstanding adult novels. Flaubert's *Madame Bovary* is a masterful study of a woman bored with her marriage and her life in a small French village. Hawthorne's *The Scarlet Letter* is a powerful study of sin and guilt in a Puritan community.

I doubt Hawthorne researched the problems of adultery and its impact on the lives of a few people the way Richard Peck investigated the problems of teenage rape, but for Peck the research was significant. He writes:

> For me, writing about a rape victim was no exercise in self-expression, and I had to go beyond the books that had alerted me to the crime. I worked closely with Dr. Richard L. Hughes of the Northwestern University Medical Center. I did my best to follow the legalese of legislation, both current and proposed. I did time in a planned parenthood center serving teenagers.
>
> In each step toward the novel, I was more sickened by the crime and its disposition by law enforcement and the law; much more research and I would have been heading for yet another nonfiction book on the subject. I had to give my notes a final sorting and begin a novel, people with credible characters, not nameless statistics and faceless testimonials. ("Rape and the Teenage Victim" 175)

As narrator, Gail is a credible character. Her concerns are typical of many YA female protagonists. She has difficulties with her mother, who disapproves of Steve Pastorini, Gail's boyfriend and son of the local plumber. There is a communication gap between her and her parents that keeps her from telling them about the notes and phone calls. Moreover, Gail's father cannot tell her he has lost his job in the city; and even after Gail discovers the truth, her mother asks her not to let him know that she knows.

Gail is very conscious of the caste system that exists in her community: "There was something feudal about Oldfield Village and all its smug smugness" (Are You in the House Alone? 14). Thus Gail cannot forget that she is an outsider whose family has moved from the city. Gail is drawn in friendship to Allison Bremer because she, too, is an outsider. However, because Allison has been dating Phil Lawver and longs to become a part of the Establishment through her relationship with him, she rejects Gail when Gail identifies Phil as her attacker.

Gail's love affair with Steve is similar to those of other YA novels in that they assume "that making love was being in love" (9), but the permanence these young lovers presume is fleeting. In the hospital after she has been raped, Gail realizes that she and Steve "were really meant to be friends all along, not anything else. Maybe not even close friends. I'd admired him and liked him and we'd played at being lovers, and even that seemed an innocent experiment, and long ago" (120).

Gail's reevaluation of her friendship with Steve is minor compared with what she learns about the legal and social restrictions facing her. While she can identify Phil as her assailant, she has no witness to support her charge. Having been sexually involved with Steve also makes her even more vulnerable should she attempt to bring Phil into court. When questioned by the local police after she is raped, Gail is intimidated as the police chief attempts to imply that she has been tussling with her boyfriend. When she mentions Phil Lawver as her attacker, he tells her that she's asking for trouble.

When Gail later offers to resume sitting for Mrs. Montgomery, in whose house she was attacked, Mrs. Montgomery tells Gail she cannot use her any longer: "'Don't take it personally,' she said. '. . . I appreciate your help in the past, but things are different now'" (159). Then, too, Gail's mother wants to send her away to school, but Gail insists upon returning to her school: "'I'm going back because I have a right to go back'" (153). That Gail refuses to run from what has happened to her is a positive statement to young readers.

Given the nature of the book's audience and the ever-existing threat of censorship, Richard Peck has written his novel with appropriate restraint. The rape scene is left largely to the reader's imagination, but Peck does describe Gail's pelvic examination, of which he writes, "Research indicated that the typical rape victim never goes for medical treatment and attention. I wanted my readers to know what this treatment is and why it's vital." ("Rape and the Teenage Victim" 175).

That we do not see Gail's assailant brought to trial is but another reality of many rape cases. However, Phil attacks another high school student, the aftermath of which is a series of rumors of Phil's having a nervous breakdown and of his being "captain of the squash team in a boarding school in Vermont," the latter a rumor that Gail "could believe" (171).

The book ends on a less-than-hopeful note as Gail's mother observes that things have been worse, to which Gail responds:

> "It could have been worse, Mother, but not much. . . . We were all trying to protect ourselves as individuals and families instead of organizing to make everybody safe. There are more Phils out there, you know."
>
> "Don't talk that way," she said.
>
> "Well, there are. We should have done something else. We still should."
>
> *"But what?"* Mother said. "What could we do?" And then she turned her back to her work. (172)

But what? Peck does not provide answers, as is the case with many novels of social protest; but the issues he raises will echo in the minds of many young adults who read *Are You In the House Alone?*, for they are important in an ongoing struggle to uphold individual rights and human dignity.

References

Burton, Dwight. *Literature Study in the High School.* New York: Holt, 1970.

Peck, Richard. *Are You in the House Alone?* New York: Dell, 1977.

———. "Rape and the Teenage Victim." *Top of the News* (Winter 1978): 173–75.

Part I The Authors

Section 6
Hadley Irwin

18 Collaborative Writing for Young Adults

Hadley Irwin

Hadley Irwin (Lee Hadley, left, and Annabelle Irwin)

Photo by Shirley Walrod

Lee: I'm the Lee Hadley person; and, when I'm not standing here, I teach at Iowa State University. I'm associate professor of English there and that's the academic part of our program today. We're supposed to be talking about the joys and pains of collaborating. I am the joy, and there is the pain.

Ann: I'm Ann Irwin, and, as you can see, Lee will provide the topic sentences. I'll take care of the subheadings. I am a retired associate professor of English and now live with my husband on a lake in northwest Iowa.

Lee: We did bring Hadley Irwin with us. If you were children, if you were the people for whom we write and we were speaking to you as we have done so often, we would tell you that she is sitting right down there. And she is sitting down because she's well over a hundred and twenty-five years old.

Ann: And she has taught for seventy-five or eighty years, everything from kindergarten through graduate school.

Lee: She's a very tired lady. At one point, she decided she simply couldn't go on teaching. Why not do something simple? That is when she began to write. Or, if you don't like that story, there is another one. She was born . . . how long ago?

Ann: Eleven years ago. Her first book came out then, in 1979. However, we knew each other before Hadley Irwin was born. Now we'll tell you the truth. You know how it is when you're in academia—you're put on a committee. The head of our department said, "You're on a committee with Lee Hadley to arrange a summer workshop for a group of teachers." This was in April, and the workshop was to be in June.

Lee: A workshop for college credit.

Reprinted from *The ALAN Review* 20.1, Fall 1992, pages 2–7, by permission of the author.

Ann: It was a hopeless assignment. We did get together; I found out who Lee was and we met a couple of times and decided it was impossible. If you're in a department, you have to report on your committee's work, so we got together and wrote a beautiful report.

Lee: Twenty pages. Twenty pages on a committee of two people who tried but did absolutely nothing.

Ann: I was in English education, and I knew all the words to put in.

Lee: Do you remember behavioral objectives? Higher cognitive skills?

Ann: We used them all. And he didn't fire us. The head of our department.

Lee: Then we said, "Why don't we do this for money?" And that is how Hadley Irwin began.

Ann: Yes. It's sort of gross, though, to say we do it for money.

Lee: You didn't hear that. We do it for art. The first book we wrote was sheer sheer craziness. We lived, at that point, about a hundred miles apart and only met when we were teaching. So we didn't see each other often. You were gone that summer, and you saw the picture.

Ann: Yes. We have one newspaper in Iowa, the *Des Moines Register,* the newspaper Iowa depends upon. It happened to have a picture one Sunday of an older woman who'd been asked to leave her home because they were going to put a new highway through and they had to take down her house. She didn't want to leave her home, so a social welfare worker went to the D.O.T and asked if they couldn't make some arrangements to keep her in her home until she could no longer stay there.

Lee: There was a picture of this woman's face, an old woman's face, taken at the moment when the social worker told her she could stay in her own home. The two were embracing, and it was a beautiful picture of strength, beauty, triumph. Ann saw it, and I saw it. When we got back together, we thought: Isn't there something there that could be turned into a book? And then we started what turned into a collaboration, which is a word I hate. It sounds like World War II, doesn't it?

Ann: It's usually with the enemy.

Lee: What we did was to begin to learn how to write together. And it was a painful process in many ways.

Ann: When we get an idea or a germ of an idea, we put it in a sentence that will mean something in the book. It may never appear in the book, but it will certainly be implied in many ways.

Ann: So with this book, we thought, let's take an older woman who is no relation to the twelve-year-old girl who has spent the summer with her. The theme would be as the older woman says, "I'm going off stage. You're coming on stage. We ought to be able to see eye-to-eye." We tried to carry that theme throughout—that there isn't much difference between a twelve-year-old and a seventy-seven-year-old woman.

Lee: The idea was firmly in our brains of what we wanted to do. Now the question was, "How do we do this?" since we had never attempted to write a piece of fiction together. Annabelle would say, "I'd like to write a chapter about" whatever, and I'd say, "Gee, I'd like to write one about" something else. They weren't in any order, but we'd say, "Let's just go ahead and write it and see what happens."

Ann: I think we call it "episodic."

Lee: Very episodic.

Ann: She would give me what she had written over the weekend, and I would cut out her purple prose. Then I would give her what I had written.

Lee: Annabelle had taught too long at that point. So in her chapters she did what all of us do as teachers. She told us what she was going to tell us, then she told us, and then she told us what she had told us. All I had to do was go through and cut out the last paragraph of every chapter and she had a perfectly beautiful thing. We finally got something that kind of looked like a book, and *then* we discovered what we really needed to do in order to work together . . .

Ann: . . . was we had to sit down together and write—in the same room.

Lee: We said, "Okay we'll sit on this davenport with the manuscript in front of us and start from the beginning, and we'll write it together. And rewrite it together." How many times did we write the last chapter?

Ann: It's only about a page and a half. We couldn't figure out really the way we wanted it to end, and I think we revised it thirteen times. Finally our publisher at that time said, "Will you please send the last chapter?" We sent it, but forgot to keep a carbon copy.

Lee: Which is really stupid because we didn't know until we got the galley proof which one of the thirteen we had actually used. If that book hadn't worked, we would never, I think, have tried again.

Ann: I had an agent in New York, and I'd published one thing or a couple of things, I guess. So we sent this to her, and she said, "I just handle books for young adults. I think this is an adult book."

Lee: We got it back and thought, "Well, that's odd, since the protagonist is eleven or twelve years old." Somebody suggested to us that we try the Feminist Press, simply because the main characters are women in the book.

Ann: We thought, maybe we'd written for girls eight to eighty.

Lee: So we sent a letter and the first chapter to Feminist Press. They wrote back saying, "We don't take young adult books, and this is a young adult book, but we'll read it, if you'd like, and make comments." That was really very nice.

Ann: It usually costs to have a manuscript read.

Lee: After a while, we got a letter back saying, "We have just decided to start publishing young adult books." So they took it.

Ann: Two things saved the book. One was a review in the *New York Times Book Review* section.

Lee: And the Gray Panthers gave us one of the best reviews in the world. So I still don't know whether it's a young adult book, an adult book, or what it is.

Ann: Book-of-the-Month picked it up, too, that Christmas for selection.

Lee: Well, why not try writing another?

Ann: It's like when you were a child in school. You got one A, so maybe you could try to get another one. And of course, that was the challenge for us. We tried again.

Lee: Annabelle's a strange person. She's the kind of person who reads footnotes in history books.

Ann: And even bibliographies.

Lee: Why she happened to be reading about Native Americans I do not know. Do you?

Ann: I was reading an Iowa history book about the Mesquakies of Tama, Iowa. I got to thinking what it would have been like if you were an eight-year-old Mesquakie girl back in 1837 or so and the government sent in dragons and said, "Go on down to Kansas. We're taking over your land." What would it be like? Eventually the Mesquakies sold their ponies and all their belongings and walked back to Iowa and gave the governor of the Territory of Iowa enough money to buy eighty acres along the Iowa River for them. One thing about writing about historical events is that you have a plot outline—a framework.

Lee: Then you hang things on it and hope they match. It was a strange book, and, too, we changed our writing style. Annabelle and her husband live on this little lake. They have a house on one side of the lake where they live during the winter. They have a cottage on the other side of the lake where they go in the summer.

Ann: Now, there's a reason. All the summer people come back, you know, and you have to move out to see them.

Lee: So, that summer—why did I rent your house?

Ann: Maybe so you could take it off your income tax.

Lee: We sat down in the dining room with a typewriter and every history book or every reference we could find on Mesquakies. We read through them and ended up throwing them against the wall because most of them were written by either missionaries or military men who regarded the Mesquakies as something less than human. We couldn't use *them,* but we could reverse the facts and come out very nicely.

Ann: We did very well that summer: We got eighty pages.

Lee: We finished the book.

Ann: Yes.

Lee: We finished the book.

Ann: Eighty pages.

Lee: Eighty pages a book does not make. But, here's the joy. This is one thing I can count on Ann for. Given enough time, she can come up with that thing that the book needs, and she did in this case. She invented two new characters, and suddenly there was this marvelous subplot. Normally, what Annabelle does if the plot is in trouble is kill off one of the major characters. You could read through any of our books; and, if suddenly somebody drops dead, she did it.

Ann: When we are writing cross-culturally such as the book on the Mesquakies or the Japanese *Kim/Kimi* or *I Be Somebody,* we have to be very careful because we are not Black or Mesquakie or Japanese. We knew we would be criticized for attempting such books.

Lee: Even though you do your homework and do your research and have all these good feelings, it is so easy to make a mistake that you don't realize is a mistake. Certain colors, certain tribal names. When we finished the manuscript, we asked Alkaline Wanatee, a Mesquakie woman, if she would read the manuscript before we sent it off.

Ann: She agreed to come down to Iowa State. I think she was giving some demonstration on campus that weekend. We had sent her the manuscript, and we met her at the Union one afternoon.

Lee: This sounds stereotypic, I know, but it's the truth—looking absolutely impassive, just looking at us without a smile.

Ann: She said, "There's only one thing wrong." Of course, we thought, "Oh, we have to revise the whole thing." Then she said, "It didn't go on long enough."

Lee: She said, "We are still alive." We stopped the book in what was it?

Ann: 1846 or somewhere along there.

Lee: She said, "Why couldn't you just keep writing?" and we said, "Is that the only thing?" And she said, "Yes, everything else is totally authentic." Then, the book came out. I hate reviewers.

Ann: Unless the reviews are favorable.

Lee: Very favorable.

Ann: No doubt some of our bad reviews were good reviews, though.

Lee: I can't remember who did the review of the book, but they commented on the fact that the names of the characters were straight out of a Hollywood movie and not authentic. We had to laugh because they were so authentic that we had inadvertently chosen the name of a medicine man who was alive. And then the letter came.

Ann: Yes. Then we won a Jane Addams Prize.

Lee: Jane Addams Peace Prize International. They invited us to New York to the United Nations Plaza. They didn't send us any money so we couldn't get there, but it was nice.

Ann: But we got a plaque. Lee hangs all our plaques in her bathroom.

Lee: Where else could I be sure that everybody sees them? So we've done those two books, and we're still talking to each other and still enjoying each other, but we wanted to write something different. So, we wrote a book that dealt with divorce called *Bring to a Boil and Separate.*

Ann: We decided to go to a different publisher.

Lee: The strange part about this is, Annabelle and I created a class for the university called "Freelance Writing." One of the things we stress to our students is how much care you must take in choosing your market. You do research. You find out what kinds of things are asked for. When we got ready to look for a new market, I said, "Annabelle, you do it."

Ann: I took out the big *Writer's Market* for the year, and I opened it up to children's books, and I pointed.

Lee: With her eyes closed.

Ann: And I hit Atheneum Publishing Company. And Margaret McElderry.

Lee: And so we said, "Of course. We'll send it off and see what happens." That was very nice because . . .

Ann: I didn't have an agent any more.

Lee: No. Not since that first one. We got a letter back from Margaret saying, " I don't know if you're a man or a woman, but I think you're a woman. I really like this." And then the words that we will never forget: "I hope this is the beginning of a long relationship." And we said, "Oh, you have us for the rest of our lives. Take us, we're yours."

Ann: We're still with her. We got a good review on that book too. It said we wrote with "grace and wit." We liked that very much.

Lee: We took turns. She'd be Grace one week, and I'd be Wit the next, and then we'd turn it around. As a matter of fact, Annabelle refuses to look at any envelope that seems to contain reviews. She has me open them. If they're bad, I look at them and throw them away. If they're good, I read them out loud to her, and then later in the day she will read them out loud to me. Because I'll tell you, I don't know if other authors say this but we're always looking for reassurance.

Ann: The idea for our next book, *Moon and Me,* came from a junior high where we were speaking. For some reason—I'm not sure why—when a school asks us to speak they always put us the last period of the day.

Lee: Friday afternoon.

Ann: And they put us in a gymnasium.

Lee: It's spring outside, on the bleachers and on the floor—the kids that is, not us.

Ann: And no teachers around, only principals who stand around and say, "Sh! Sh!"

Lee: They really don't need to. There are always at least 500, 600 kids, and kids are inevitably just wonderful to talk with. There's never any problem, not if you're not their teacher. You see, when you come in, you're a break in the routine.

Ann: It helps if you have a good memory of when you were in seventh grade.

Lee: And have taught seventh graders.

Ann: We were awfully glad that hot day when the bell finally rang, and everybody ran.

Lee: And you know the locker sounds?

Ann: Bang, bang, bang. As we hurried by . . .

Lee: Dragging Hadley Irwin by one hand . . .

Ann: There were two little girls by their locker having an argument of some sort . . .

Lee: Disagreement, probably.

Ann: One had her hand on her hip.

Lee: She said, "He is *not* my boyfriend. He's just a friend who happens to be a boy." We looked at each other and said, "There's a book."

Ann: In fact that's the end of the book. The endings are often very hard to get, but this was our ending. All we had to do was write the book. Easy!

Lee: What happens normally is, after we get that notion, the idea, if we're lucky, we go up to the lake, and we sit out on the patio for a long time.

Ann: And the neighbors come by and say, "Why aren't you writing?"

Lee: We sit there and think of the characters. We don't plan what's going to happen in the book really. It's like your analogy. I've always liked the road map thing.

Ann: In planning a trip, you may know you are going to California. In this case, we knew where the book was going; but, like the trip to California, we didn't know whether we'd zigzag this way or that way or what route we might take before we reached the end.

Lee: And strangely enough in fiction—are you ready for this Annabelle?

Ann: No.

Lee: Strangely enough in fiction, a straight line isn't the best way to get there. It's the little side trips that you take—the things that occur to you that you didn't even know were going to happen—that make it work so much better.

Ann: We sit on the patio and play pretend games.

Lee: We said, "What's the most awkward age in the world for a girl to be?" And we decided probably a sophomore in high school.

Ann: Absolutely. I think they should eliminate the sophomore grade.

Lee: Just go freshmen, junior, senior, out.

Ann: Yes, it's a wretched time.

Lee: Girls at that point—this is a great generalization—have usually reached their height as far as growth is concerned. We thought, what if we've got this girl who's name is . . .

Ann: E.J.

Lee: And what if E.J. came from a family who was cosmopolitan, had traveled a great deal of Europe, and what if she got dumped with her grandparents in a little dinky Iowa town.

Ann: And where shall we put her in Iowa? Let's put her over on the Missouri among the loess hills.

Lee: Why don't we put her in this little tiny high school where—

Ann: Ninety in high school.

Lee: She's the tallest person in the whole school.

Ann: And she's the new girl.

Lee: And she has not yet had a date, a meaningful relationship. What if there's one person in the school . . .

Ann: Who's taller than she and is muscular. Then we had to think of a muscular name.

Lee: Right. Rich Adams is as muscular as we could come up with. He's, you know, he's . . .

Ann: Football . . .

Lee: A football hero. His saving grace is that, the thing he likes most in the world is hogs. He can tell you about pork bellies, and he's got a boar friend named Fred.

Ann: And he has a pickup truck.

Lee: Annabelle killed off Fred in the course of the book, by the way. Sad.

Ann: The pig had to die the night of the prom.

Lee: Yeah. A sad, sad, touching story. At any rate, he totally ignores E.J. She's only a sophomore after all.

Ann: But somebody is noticing her. He follows her around every place in school—

Lee: Down the halls . . .

Ann: Into the lunch room.

Lee: When she goes to the john, he stands outside and waits for her.

Ann: Yes.

Lee: He has the mind of a computer. He has the build of a professional football lineman. His name is Harmon Wells.

Ann: They call him "Moon" for short.

Lee: The only problem is, Moon comes exactly to her armpit because he's in the eighth grade. This is not the thing romances are made of.

Ann: No, but this is a friend who happens to be a boy . . .

Lee: By the end of the book.

Ann: And that's the way we write.

Lee: That's part of the way we write. Now comes the nasty part, you see, of sitting down and doing it. On paper. Annabelle goes to the typewriter while I find a comfortable chair—preferably with an Ottoman—in which I can lean back.

Ann: She doesn't spell very well.

Lee: And she types faster than the speed of light. We have changed our mode of writing again. We sit there like that, and Ann can inevitably come up with the first line of the first paragraph of the book, and she says it out loud. I hear that and say, "Oh, it's wonderful. That is so good." Meanwhile she's typing it, and I'm thinking, you could change a few words. Change from blue to green. Make that a weeping willow instead of a pine tree, which she may or may not do because she's at the typewriter. Then I try to add my little bit.

Ann: And you hope I type it the way you say it.

Lee: We go back and forth . . .

Ann: And, that works the best.

Lee: It really does. And if she gets tired of typing, I go over and sit down. We just take turns. Or sometimes, sometimes she will actually type a page or so without my hearing it, but I get to go over and read it right away.

Ann: I think what is happening is that we're both editors of whatever we write. I trust her and—and she trusts me sometimes.

Lee: Most of the time. We edit as we go along.

Ann: But that's just the rough draft.

Lee: Well, that's the ego thing too, though. Whenever I can say, "Oh, that's just terrific," you get an instant boost. If you can do a line and somebody laughs when they're writing it down, that makes you feel good. That's the process, and that's the first draft, which usually takes the summer.

Ann: Then, when we were teaching, we would spend the entire school year revising and changing. We are great revisers. I'll tell you how good revisers we are. We are now writing—what is this, the eleventh or twelfth book?

Lee: Twelve, I think.

Ann: We had a hundred and twenty-one pages done, and I dropped it off at Lee's to have her make some copies because, I don't have a copier handy. Before she got the pages copied, she threw away what she thought was a master thesis . . .

Lee: An old one.

Ann: When she got ready to read the 121 pages she was looking at a master thesis. She had thrown away the 121-page manuscript.

Lee: I cannot tell you how sick *I* felt.

Ann: I cannot tell you how sick *I* felt!

Lee: I called Ann—I put this off for a whole day; I couldn't believe I did it 'cause I'd just cleaned out—you know how student papers accumulate.

Ann: My husband and I were just packing to go to Florida for a month.

Lee: I called Annabelle finally and said, "Are you sitting down?" And she said,—my mother's 101 years old—so she said, "Is it your mother?" I said, "No, it's worse." And it was, it was.

Ann: We're up to 131 pages so we're moving on.

Lee: *Abby, My Love* is a book we didn't want to write. And we put it off, for how many years? Five?

Ann: At least five. We actually were thinking of writing about incest before you could say the word publicly.

Lee: One of the problems was the fact that we often write from our own experiences—if not experiences, at least feelings. Neither of us had had such an experience as incest.

Ann: The idea of the book originally came from a letter written by a teenage girl who was going through therapy for sexual abuse. It was probably as part of her therapy that she wrote the letter to Lee.

Lee: We dropped the idea of writing such a book for a year or two and even wrote another book instead, until one day an adult student of ours asked if she could meet us for lunch because she had a manuscript she wanted us to read.

Ann: While Lee was looking over the manuscript, the woman asked me, "What are you writing now?" I said, "We're trying to get started on a book about incest, but we aren't doing much with it." It was very quiet for a while and then she said, "What do you want to know about it? My father molested me from the time I was four." Lee looked up and said, "Do you want to talk about it?"

Lee: "Can you?" I asked. She looked at me and said, "If I went home now, it would start all over again." Then she said something that touched us both: "Did this ever happen to either one of you?" When we told her no, she said, "Why not?" I told her I couldn't answer that, but I said, "We were just lucky people, I guess." That question made us start the book.

Ann: Later that year we were speaking to the students in the Dubuque schools and were resting in the teacher's room. You know, to get that five-minute gasp of a breath between classes. The librarian came in and sat beside me and asked the same question, "What are you writing now?" I said we were trying to get started on a story about incest. "You know," she said, "it is a book that is certainly needed—not just for the victim but for the friend of the victim."

Lee: She went on to say, "There's always a best friend who has a sense that something is wrong but doesn't know what. And if the friend did know, would want to help but doesn't know how."

Ann: We like librarians!

Lee: We love librarians. The point of view in the book—the point of view is from the best friend. The reader and the best friend only know as much as the victim wishes to reveal. You have all the impact without being specific.

Ann: So we decided to make the best friend in the book a young man, and then we decided to start it as a friendship in seventh grade and allow a love relationship to grow between them that will counteract or counterbalance the terrible thing that she's going through. So, we finally wrote it.

Lee: I think the thing that pleases us most is an award that came from Spokane Public Libraries. It's one of the children's choice kind of things. The teenagers chose it as the best thing.

Ann: One librarian said that it is the book most stolen from her library.

Lee: Some of the things that happen in writing these books are really strange. Like, Abigail, the main character, I'd never use the name Abigail. I don't know anybody named Abigail. But we liked it. After we'd chosen it, Annabelle was poking around the back of the dictionary—you know, where it gives meanings for names.

Ann: In one place I found it means "joy of my father."

Lee: We look for omens. Any omen we can find. Abby and Chip, the young man, are playing a mind game. They want a vacation, but they don't want to call it anybody's birthday, so they decided to make up a day to celebrate—to do whatever they wanted to. A President—who is it?

Ann: Millard Filmore.

Lee: Millard Filmore's birthday. They are going to celebrate. Then they decide that is no good. Make it his wife's birthday. After we had written all this stuff, we decided we didn't know anything about Millard Filmore; so we called our local librarian and asked, "Was he ever married?"

Ann: After some searching she called back: "Yes. Twice. The first one's name was Abigail."

Lee: I don't know where you're from. But in Iowa so many high school kids are committing suicide. Just so many. After *Abby, My Love,* we decided, okay, why don't we try, a book about suicide.

Ann: We try to write a book that has some substance. We don't want a young adult to read it and end by saying, "So what?" We want them to think of what we were thinking of as a theme. It's what an eighth-grade girl said a theme of a book is: "It's what you remember about the book after you have forgotten who the characters were and what they did."

Lee: In this book we knew what we didn't want. We didn't want to explain how. We didn't want to write a how-to book—how to commit suicide. We didn't want to write a book that attempted in any way to explain the causes of suicide because we firmly believe it would be different for every single kid who ends up doing it. What we decided we really wanted to say was what happens to the friends, the other people who are left. The terrible impact.

Ann: So we copied the Greek dramatists, and we had the event take place—off stage.

Lee: Before the book begins. We meet the young man who was a very dear friend, and we see his escaping, trying to escape from the knowledge of what's happened, trying to understand what's happened.

Ann: We made the girl who did it brilliant.

Lee: Talented and gifted. These two kids have everything. They have money. They have a future that's incredible.

Ann: She wasn't pregnant. She wasn't on drugs.

Lee: Family doesn't beat her up. She's got everything in this world to live for.

Ann: The reason that we did this is that nobody knows the "why" of suicide. The only person who knows why is the person who did it, and they aren't here. We are not trying to explain why this suicide happened.

Lee: After the book concerning suicide, a strange thing happened and it does have to do with collaboration. We were talking about the thing that happens often in families between mothers and daughters, which is, well, you can say it better than I.

Ann: So often you get to the point that they can't stand each other. Suddenly along about fifteen or sixteen—I had three daughters—*you* change. *They* don't. *You* become naggy and nasty.

Lee: Stupid.

Ann: You don't know much. You just change. And then at about sixteen or seventeen you change.

Lee: You change back.

Ann: You change back into quite a nice person.

Lee: So we were talking about this kind of thing and wanting to write a book about it, and then we were speaking at a reading workshop. We had done a keynote speech in the morning talking about the books that we were doing. After we got through speaking, a man came up to us and said he'd liked our books and he thought kids responded to them. Then he said, "Have you ever written a book that deals with alcoholism or drug abuse?" And we said no.

Ann: His son, from the time he was fourteen, had gone from alcoholism to drugs.

Lee: He was an alcoholic at age fourteen or maybe earlier because they didn't discover it until he was fourteen.

Ann: He finally ended up when he was twenty-one burning himself to death in a van because he was . . .

Lee: His blood-alcohol level was so high it would have killed him. His father has been involved in drug education in the high schools. He said, "*If* you would like to come down someday for lunch, we'll sit and talk; and I'll tell you everything I can." So we did, and we used it in the book. We dedicated the book to his son. He said, "At least his life has done something. I can go to high schools and talk about drugs, alcohol. Kids won't listen to me, but, if they read something in a book of fiction, maybe they'll believe."

Ann: The hardest thing I think to do when we're writing on subjects that are deep and that sad and that awful is to keep a light touch.

Lee: Our notion is this. We know it, but I don't know if kids know it. No matter how awful it is for a moment or for a day or for a week or for a year, no matter if your world is crumbling underneath you, life is still going on around you. And there are still things to laugh at, to laugh about. I guess we believe in hope, and I think that's one of the things we try to show in the books.

Hadley Irwin: A White Writer of Colored Ethnic Fiction

Charles C. Irby

Hadley Irwin is more than a century old, and she is always present when Lee Hadley and Annabelle Irwin get together. Hadley Irwin was born when Annabelle asked Lee to look at a manuscript about a white woman attempting to write about the black experience in America. *Desk 15,* created by Annabelle, remains in manuscript form in a basement in Lakeview, Iowa. Since then, Hadley Irwin has published *The Lilith Summer; Bring to a Boil and Separate; We Are Mesquakie, We Are One; Moon and Me; What About Grandma?; I Be Somebody;* and *Abby, My Love.*

The following interview was designed to look into the minds of two people as one writer, to share their spirit and essence with an audience, and to demonstrate *how* they function as one. The interview was further designed to show what Hadley and Irwin learn from writing cross-culturally. The interview begins with their Iowa origins and concludes with the seeds of *Kim/Kimi,* a manuscript dealing with an aspect of Japanese American internment.

Lee Hadley: As a child I learned in a couple of ways. Mom took me to the library every Saturday, usually to two libraries, so I read a great deal. The other thing I did was listen to the radio, constantly. Mother was a dear person who didn't make me sit at the dinner table, who would let me take my plate and go in by the radio. The Lone Ranger was one of the heroes of my childhood. I can probably repeat whole scripts. So I grew up absolutely fascinated with the whole mystique or mistake of the West and, of course, with the Lone Ranger. With the Lone Ranger came Tonto. I was never around any Native Americans because there simply weren't any there, in the community, Bear Creek. My whole idea, aside from reading about

Reprinted from *The ALAN Review* 13.3, Spring 1986, pages 21–24, 50.

what an Indian was, was Tonto, who was limited to saying "Hiye Kemo Sabe," which I am not sure was any language at all, but it might be. So, it was a basic view of Native Americans and what they were like supposedly, and I never wanted to know that he was Jay Silverheels; that was not interesting at all; it was just Tonto. So that's where it all began.

Charles Irby: Tell me about "White Like Me."

Annabelle Irwin: I tried once on my own to write about black and white relationships in a book which was going to be called *Desk 15*. It was not very good and I think that is how Lee and I met. I brought *Desk 15* to her to see what we could do with such an idea. I suppose I was interested in writing about that because I was brought up in a little community in northwest Iowa called Peterson, and it was absolutely WASP. The interesting part was that after I had grown up and gone to college, I discovered that the man who ran our grocery store was Jewish, and I didn't even know what that meant. The other was that the sexton in our church, who rang the bell, was black and I didn't know it. He was Mr. Clark to me. So I was absolutely isolated as far as people being different. I thought that was the way the world was, the way it was in Peterson. I think that there are a lot of communities, particularly in the Middle West, where that is true.

CI: Let's integrate "White Like Me," and "Tonto Lied." (See Hadley and Irwin in *Explorations in Ethnic Studies* 7.2 (1984): 110.)

LH: Tonto didn't lie. The Lone Ranger lied.

CI: The Lone Ranger lied. Tonto lied too. Tonto carried out the stereotype. So let's move on to that in *We Are Mesquakie, We Are One*, because essentially what you are dealing with is the reality as opposed to the myth and stereotype.

LH: When talking about reality versus myth, I think it depends a great deal on the reader as much as the writer. We tried to be very careful with the book in a couple of ways. One was to be accurate and realistic without romanticizing Mesquakies, trying to be as clear and accurate as we could about elements of their culture which we do not, as white Quakers or white whatever, share. The research itself was terribly difficult because so little had been written that wasn't twisted in some sort of way. The twisting went on beyond that. The best source was "The Autobiography of a Fox Woman," which was an oral autobiography first recorded in Mesquakie and then translated into English. We tried to be accurate. We thought we had achieved that, but one particular reviewer was very annoyed with our choice of names, saying that they came straight out of Hollywood, which was not true because one of the first things we did was to understand how the clans worked and how the names would have to fit the clan structure.

AI: What we finally resorted to doing was getting a whole stack of history books that had anything to do with the Mesquakie and sitting down thinking just the opposite of what was said.

LH: We could almost turn it exactly around and come out with some approximation of the truth.

CI: So how did you feel once you had written the book?

AI: The book, honestly, almost wrote itself; it was probably the easiest book that we had written for some reason. We went to the annual powwow, and of course we talked to and had some Indian students in class.

LH: I think part of it was we became so fascinated with the history and with this whole world view that we had only seen very much from the outside. It assumed just absolutely fascinating dimensions. It made so much sense.

AI: And the whole settlement is something extremely unusual in Indian history in that the Mesquakie came back when Iowa was a territory and asked the governor to buy the land for them because they couldn't—they weren't citizens.

LH: I love the irony in that.

AI: They kept adding on and adding on and buying, and it was Quakers who helped them buy land. But the idea is that they bought their own land—the Mesquakie people don't live on a reservation.

LH: A favorite passage, and you probably have heard this before, is in a history book which is describing the lovely fertile fields of Iowa with green growing corn and suddenly you turn the corner and you find yourself in the "squalor and the filth of an Indian village, dogs and babies rolling in the dust on the street. A stew pot hangs over a fire. One wonders what is in the pot. Is it possibly a young dog?" This Iowa history book was read by thousands of school kids; those things are written down and some people, I suppose, still believe them, but to confront it in black and white on a page is just earth-shattering.

CI: Let me move into your class with the ideas that you have here. Do Iowa students, the students who come from rural areas in Iowa, really recognize that there are people other than white people, in spite of television?

LH: You mean inside, depth understanding. No, not now, even.

AI: Particularly when they come from smaller communities. I think that Ames and Iowa City are little cultural oases and what you see here is not what the rest of Iowa is like.

LH: And I am not sure that little cultural oases affect most of the students.

CI: How many black students do you have in class over a semester, one? How many Native Americans? How many Japanese Americans, Chinese?

AI: Very few.

LH: So, there is no interaction. Any reading we might give students in class: Maya Angelou, "never heard of her . . ."

AI: We took one of her essays and they were terribly affected, but they made absolutely no connections. Large gaps, fascinating! I taught Angelou in my adolescent literature class this year. Two of the young women in class—one white and one black—started talking to each other about being black in America. The young white woman said, "I didn't know that; I never thought that," as the other was telling what it was like.

CI: Now, I want you to discuss *I Be Somebody.*

AI: *I Be Somebody* was born from reading your manuscript on Amber Valley, Alberta. I had never heard of Athabasca or Amber Valley or Clearview. I wasn't aware that anything such as that happened. I was fascinated. So few people ever heard of it; it was like finding something that was hidden for a long time and I think that is what excited me about it. It is a historical fact, and, when you attempt to write historical fiction, it is sort of fun because you have the outline settled.

LH: Something else that we ought to toss in here that I think is important, not always important maybe to the reader of the book as much as the writers of the book, *is what happened to us as human beings.*

AI: Yes, I think if we got that across in the book it will be well worthwhile. We began to see beauty in black faces that we didn't know existed.

LH: Something even more than that though, and this is deadly, something from my good liberal background. I hate to admit I was literally seeing blacks for the first time.

AI: Yes, walking across campus.

LH: The awareness of a black girl, a black boy, where before I think I had said, which I thought was really liberal at the time, I don't know the difference; everybody is all the same. And they aren't. It was a real kind of epiphany.

CI: Tell me some more about *I Be Somebody,* as writers.

AI: Besides the manuscript, I think there were various little things that happened besides the fact that we tried to do something as we did in *We Are Mesquakie, We Are One.* I think we wrote the book not just for white students. It has a lesson for blacks and whites.

LH: Well, does it have a lesson? I'm not sure that it has a lesson.

AI: I don't want to make a division, but we didn't necessarily write *I Be Somebody* for white children.

LH: I never had a white reader in my head . . .

AI: I never did either.

LH: Obviously we want them to read the book, but no, I was thinking of a black reader rather than a white reader.

AI: I don't think I was thinking of either one.

LH: I think I was thinking black.

AI: Is that right?

LH: Well, we never talked about that, did we?

AI: No, that is fascinating because when you write you must be aware of your audience.

LH: Well, I know why I was thinking black because we were talking at your grandson's grade school. As a matter of fact, it was one of the first schools we had been in where there were both black and white kids, as well as several Asians. We had been going through all these books and the kids were interested, and then we mentioned the book we were writing.

AI: *I Be Somebody.* And you said it was about a boy and all the boys went yes, and then you said about a black boy.

LH: And the expressions on the white kids' faces were interesting too, but the expression on the black kids' faces was incredible.

AI: One little guy in the front puffed out his chest.

LH: And then we talked to them a little bit about the book and when we asked for questions, you know who asked the questions? The black kids. But the whole idea—hey, there is going to be a book about blacks—because I don't think there are that many. It was disillusioning to realize that. Oh, and the worries we had. Many of the same kind we had with Mesquakie, but primarily about language, our attitude. I think one of the things that we did in the first draft that we shouldn't have done was to be too kindly to whites.

AI: As we got through it, we discovered that most of the whites were good. We finally made revisions. All of us are part good and part bad, and we made it more realistic and added that episode in the woods with the "coon hunters."

LH: We asked three other people to read the book. We asked them because we felt they could have a better chance of being highly critical of the book.

AI: In fact somebody told us not to ask them to read it because they would be too hard on it.

LH: That's right. She said we would be crushed. Well, we weren't crushed. They did read it and took the time with it and thought with it and I talked with them and we spent about an hour together and they had a nice little list of things they felt didn't work.

AI: There were lynchings going on, they told us.

LH: Right, and of course in the idyllic confines of Clearview we didn't have anything with reference much to the outside world, and so I argued a bit with them. Well, I didn't argue, but I said, "Yes, I know you are right; I'm quite aware of that, but here in this particular place it wasn't that way"; and the more we thought about it afterwards the more convinced we became that there had to be some reference to what was going on outside. So, that added a reality.

AI: Back to stereotypes, we caught ourselves in a terrible stereotype.

LH: Which one?

AI: We had the white fellow driving his wagon selling things and we gave him a Jewish name.

LH: Yes, we had the Jewish trader, peddler. Which was accurate enough. Jona said just once couldn't he be something besides Jewish? Couldn't he be anything else?

AI: So we made him Irish.

LH: It is a lazy, lazy kind of thing to do. I was trying to think of other problems. I never felt that we approached stereotype with Rap or Spicey or with any of the black folks there. I don't think we did.

AI: No, I don't believe so. We tried very hard.

LH: It wasn't even so much of the case of trying hard, because when the people in the book became real to us, real human beings, then I don't think there was any danger of stereotype. It is the characters you are working with—I don't care if they are black, Jewish, or whatever, if they aren't real to you as human beings, that is when you lapse into the shorthand method of identifying things.

AI: Not that you don't have to once in a while with some minor characters.

LH: Oh, yes, that's fair game. But you also get caught up in that reverse thing which is just as bad in a way. I worried for a while about Nimrod Toles's gold tooth, glinting in the sun. And I said, "Oh my," is that a stereotype and I thought, "Hell, no": he has a gold tooth and he is smiling so naturally it is going to glint in the sun; so you work your way around those things.

AI: It is a book, though, that I am more afraid of what the reviews are going to be than any book that we have ever written. I think we are going to be in for a lot of criticism, both good and bad. I think it will be either very good or very bad. I don't think there will be any in between.

LH: I don't think there will be either. And yet, in a way, I want that book to go and I want it to do well and I want kids to read it and libraries to buy it, but in a way I don't really give a damn because I know it is a good book; I know it is an honest book; I know it isn't that book about going to heaven with the mule. Whatever that was. Honeybunch and somebody go to heaven [*Honeybunch and Jake*].

CI: Tell me about your next book concerned with ethnic folk other than white people.

LH: It is floating around in our heads. Japanese Americans and World War II.

AI: Of course the horrible thing about writing this next book for me is that I was living through it and knew what was happening.

LH: I didn't.

AI: Of course I was old enough and the hate that existed after Pearl Harbor was unbelievable.

LH: Now there is a reverse. We talk about Midwest and non-awareness of Blacks or Native Americans for that matter, but boy, awareness of Japanese Americans.

AI: Then you would suspect everyone you saw who might have a yellow-cast skin.

LH: The hate was there. How far removed from either coast?

AI: People didn't even know where Pearl Harbor was.

LH: And weren't too sure about Japan.

AI: That's right. How could I have lived through it and been so blasé about it? And I knew they were taking them to camps and I thought, "Good. Take them off that Western coast!"

LH: And well, what is different about that than sitting in the middle of Germany and saying, "Well I know over there, you got funny smoke coming up, but they deserve it." It is going to take work to write this book; it's going to be interesting.

AI: Isn't it funny, it never dawned on us that we were doing the same thing to the Japanese as the Germans were doing to the Jews. It never crossed our minds.

LH: Insofar as we know, we weren't burning anybody up in crematoriums. But who is to say? There is also spiritual death.

AI: But in the town where I was teaching when Pearl Harbor happened, there were seven boys who died on the Arizona.

LH: And the town was how big?

AI: The town was 2,500. Seven boys, dead.

LH: It would be bad enough to go from Seattle to someplace in Washington, but it seems to be a hell of a lot worse to go from California to Arkansas. And one of the things that I keep thinking that this book has to deal with is the disaffected quality of the Yonsei. They were robbed of a solid heritage that they might have received had things not disintegrated for them.

CI: In addition to that, there are a lot of third generation, Sansei, who seem to have significant mental health problems as a result of the camp experiences which their parents refuse to share with them.

LH: Which brings us right around the whole corner. We have to read a lot of Bettelheim, who worked with not only the Jewish survivors of the concentration camps but with their children and grandchildren. The same kind of thing. The parents wanted to shield them and in shielding them left them with nothing.

Part I The Authors

Section 7
Virginia Hamilton

20 Here's How It Goes: A Tale-Teller's Tale

Virginia Hamilton

Photo by Jimmy Byrge

I've said often enough that I write for youth because a part of me is perpetually twelve. I intend keeping forever certain marvelous memories from my childhood, including some having to do with my relatives outdoing one another by their wit with words. I was born in one of our bleaker states, the state of Ohio, and evolved into a scribbler, I suspect, out of a desperate need to create a less melancholy, dryer clime. My home state has some of the richest soil in the country, which is the reason a toilsome of laborers such as my relatives is beholden to it. I am descended from dirt farmers, eccentric individuals who never fail to see the humor in a monotonous Ohio landscape.

Here's how a bit of it goes.

Uncle L.E. saying that God, Himself, had seen Ohio but three times. The first time He saw it was when He created it, followed by the time He returned to apologize for what He'd done; and the last time (which was last week or last frost, depending on the whim of the uncle or aunt disguised as a farmer who is telling the tale) when God came to play the Ohio lottery and even lost His new bib overalls. Got them on sale at Sears, too.

Saying, if God would've won, he would've had the means and the leisure to move Lake Erie down from the upper tier so poor Cousin Lucrecia and Cousin Jason at Cleveland would get a rest from the confounded winds coming in off of that blasted Lake. . . .

The above is part of a rambling tall tale, known as a God Tale, and added onto over generations, like the ones I heard at age eleven or twelve from my uncles. Uncles did not talk to us children often, being so busy with farming, I suppose. At least, they did not talk in the manner of mothers and aunts.

"She's getting tall," aunts always did say. Or, "Sit up straight," said our mothers. "Take that rouge off your face. Acting just like Cousin Lolly Bell, and you know what happened to her."

Reprinted from *The ALAN Review* 6.3, Spring 1979, pages 1 and 8.

No, we did not know what had happened to Cousin Lolly Bell. But aunts and mothers know they had us close by them for the rest of the day, waiting eagerly to hear about what had befallen Cousin Lolly Bell. Any tale was a good tale when told by a relative.

I don't believe my childhood was ever as crystalline as I make it out to be. But it was awfully good in ways that remain important to me. Around it was abundant space and time. There was not the clutter of too much activity or activity for its own sake, and no hurry to be somewhere or to do some organized playing every single minute. There was time, and I remember it well, for my pals and me to be utterly bored. In fact, we grew so bored with fields, with dusty roads, clotheslines, feeding chickens, heat and flies, with all of the country sameness day upon day, that we would imagine anything, and make up whopping lies in order not to be bored. We spent endless hours at my cousin's house swinging on the porch swing, lazily thinking up things to do. An entire day might go by with us holed up in the shade, trying to imagine a special something that would be worth the supreme effort of getting up off our fannies. I do recall that one time, we did have quite a thought.

One of us got the bright idea to walk the oak crossbeam thirty feet up almost at the top of Uncle Willy's hay barn. I no longer recall which one of us had the thought, but I do know that my cousins and I had a serious discussion concerning the proper way to get across that beam, which was all of five or six inches wide. We decided, finally, that the best way to get across without falling was barefoot. The most exciting way would be going barefoot and running across. And, of course, the most daring, the scariest way had to be barefoot and blindfolded. We accomplished all three and in that order.

I recently related the experience to my daughter and received a withering look of disdain, followed by, "Dumb . . . dumb! Didn't you guys know you could've been killed?"

I don't think any of us even believed that we could have fallen. Not because we hadn't the sense to realize. But because we were by then terribly skilled at being kids. We didn't cross that high beam out of folly. I think we chose the beam because of the challenge it was to our abilities. In the same fashion, M.C. Higgins (from *M.C. Higgins the Great*) chose to swim the Ohio River; Buddy Clark (from *The Planet of Junior Brown*) chose to live on his own, overseeing his "planets" of homeless kids; and Arilla (from *Arilla Sun Down*) chose to sneak out at night to go roller skating. Much like characters from my novels, my cousins and I were as agile as cats, and in excellent physical condition at all times. We had to be. We traveled nowhere unless it was by our own locomotion. We were expert at fence walking, rope jumping, bike acrobatics (when we could locate decent bike chains and a pump to inflate our tires), and sleeping out at night on the slanted tin roof of the chicken coop without once sliding off or waking up from dreams. We stopped neighborhood tom-cat fights; we buried beloved pets struck by automobiles. We learned the piney woods, how to catch fly balls, how to turn back a pack of attacking dogs by the shrillness of our terrified yells and the accuracy of thrown stones. Rarely did we call our parents when we were in a bind; rather, we depended on the skill and courage of one another. My cousins and I were survivors. And the danger of the high beam in Uncle Willy's hay barn was for us considerably less.

Well, walking it was maybe a little dumb. But oh, how sweet the memory!

Without such memories as the high beam, several of my books would not have been written. A writer develops characters who reflect her own past experiences, while never needing to use the source of those experiences. For me, that source is inviolate. Never have I used the beam walk in a novel, for it would hardly be fair to put such a sweet truth into a fiction. However, there remains within me that twelve-year-old who gets loose, occasionally, long enough to influence characters I create with her daring.

She is coming along right now, with the scent of clover on warm breezes. With plenty of time and space to be herself. Remembering, nourishing the way it went.

Here's how it goes!

The Spirit Spins: A Writer's Resolution

Virginia Hamilton

A very good morning to everyone. It is a pleasure to be here. I want to begin this morning by having you listen to the voice in your head. Good advice, I think. Also, "Listen To The Voice In Your Head" is the title of a poem from a work in progress entitled *Teenage Heartbreak Blues,* by Arnold Adoff. I have been given special dispensation to dip into the *Heartbreak.* I'd like to read "Listen To The Voice In Your Head" to you now. It is dedicated to the adolescent within each of you and to young adults everywhere:

> You will never be tall
> You will never be slim
> You will never have a chest, male or female variety/
> That will cause excitement.
> You will break out with a huge
> pimple on your nose the afternoon
> of the Big Game
> The Evening of the Big Dance.
> You will break out/You will Break out
> No one will ever love you and the world will turn/
> Its great equatorial back on you and you/will live
> In a swamp of defeat and self pity and even your
> Mother
> will stop making sandwiches
> And
> You will never be tall/You will break out forever.
>
> (© Arnold Adoff, 1986)

That was my adolescence. Oh, how I cringe, remembering it even today. Oh, how I suffered through it and for it. Oh, how I cried over it and loved crying, looking at myself in the mirror at my pale, pinched face—I always found it lovely—and trembling lips, and loving the awful, delicious sadness of my dying for love, for wanting this *guy* I could never quite get who was on the varsity. Oh, my aching heart, my moans at being so skinny, flat-chested (believe it

Reprinted from *The ALAN Review* 15.1, Fall 1987, pages 1–4.

or not), too self-conscious to cross a room without tripping over my own bobbysox and falling on my face.

Who doesn't have vivid images of adolescence? It's amazing that any of us made it through. For then, we were earth's aliens. We, who mutated at puberty into these out-of-bounds, screeching/painfully shy, overbearing/underachieving, maniacal/angelic, poor, wretched teensters of the human condition.

To think it will and/or has happened to our own children is enough to cause an international ban on mother and fatherhood. Ban the bombs, I know what I was like. I could sleep sixteen hours at a stretch and be mystified why my mom refused to make me a grilled cheese sandwich. I could stare immobilized out of the window without blinking until my father came home and demanded that I do something, anything. I could eat two chocolate sundaes, drink a milkshake, eat a Mars bar before the movie, and two bags of popcorn inside during the movie and a large pizza with everything after the movie, and drink two Cokes along with it. "The waitress forgot our water, get some water." "Can I borrow your comb?" "Who's that with *her!*" And later laugh for days hysterically at the slumber party gossip over hotdogs and fries. Wake up at four a.m. on the floor and get sick in Agnes's bathroom. And be refreshed by one p.m. the next day in time to get home and have four hours to get ready for the big game that night.

My adolescence was far tamer than that of my kids. Theirs could be dangerous, and it was. Wild parties, car crashes that split the peace and tranquility of small-town Saturday night. Good friends died. Or big, dark cars *cruising* the neighborhood kid hangouts, selling nightmares, worse. My young adults grew up wary of strangers, knowing never to leave one house for another without calling home or telling a friend, and so on. They grew up, not quick to smile, almost angry that we had given them a world of danger, terrible weapons, little wars. They are slow to trust, but finally, are trusting and smiling. They are perceptive young people. They knew what they wanted to be at an early age, as I did and as their father did. That, our generations have in common. They grew up, avoiding the alienation from their parents that I and their father experienced with our own. I wonder why that is. What did their father and I do that was right, or did we have anything at all to do with it? Our young adults told us more than we sometimes wanted to hear. Perhaps they drew closer to us because their world was a tougher place; they needed to hold on longer to what they knew and whom they could trust. Yet, it's wonderful, those long conversations we had late at night, sometimes, that told us their fears and their dreams in their own words. What I have learned from my young people and, yes, from observing their friends has lifted my spirits up high and made my head spin, *changed* who I am and revolutionized the manner in which I live and think and work.

Long ago, I knew that when I had children they would be such and such a way. I would teach them this and that. They would of course want thus and so. Oh, they would want exactly what I had planned for them. I wouldn't make them do anything, but, knowing what was best for them, I would definitely lead them along the righteous way of their lives.

You know, all of us parents think like that, to some extent. We *do* believe we know what is best for our children.

We say, "Kid, I don't think those are the kind of young people you should be associating with."

Or, "Mary, why don't you try working on the school newspaper. You know, your writing is really wonderfully special, so like poetry, dear."

Or, "I think you should really consider becoming a lawyer. The papers you wrote on the American Revolution are like law briefs. Let me talk to Tim Donaldson, the lawyer, maybe a part-time job at his law office."

"Un, would you tell Michael not to call here after eleven o'clock, please Dear."

"And just suggest to Allan, please, not to go into my refrigerator like he owned it. Don't any of these kids ever eat at home? Why must I supply ten gallons of lemonade for the soccer team?"

"I have to drive how many to the state orchestra auditions? Where? But that's a 150 miles away. You have to be there at eight o'clock in the morning?"

Mine are two beautiful, headstrong, stubborn young people. They pay attention to everything I tell them and then turn right around and do precisely what they know is best for them. They have minds that they created, a condition, I think, that surely they inherited. Son Jaime is the youngest. Daughter Leigh is the oldest. Once, I thought to ask Jaime what he would be if he could be anything in the world. I expected him to say a seven-foot-tall basketball player or a millionaire or both. He said, "If I could be anything in the world, I would be born first before my sister."

Only in his later adolescence did Jaime resolve the conflicting emotions he had squaring his macho teen-boy image with the fact that his sister entered the world four years ahead of him. For him having Leigh for a sister was serious business. She was tall, willowy, talented, outgoing and manipulative, lettered in sports and sang like a bird. He was too short for his age, plump, nonverbal, never smiled willingly and was steadily argumentative.

It took them years to work it out, to become friends. The spirit spins, the revolution in mom and dad is the way they learn to let things be. They learn hands off, the philosophy of allowing the pain and holding back the comfort. Let the kids figure out how to comfort one another a bit, how to respect themselves.

In our family we believe in talking things out. And somewhere the muse, the art came to them. Somehow, they recognized talent for the wondrous possession that it is. They seized upon their artistry, recognizing it at an early age. And it became for them that bridge to knowledge and maturity. Not all young people are artistic, but most of them have sensitivity and are sensible, finally, concerning themselves.

I write for the adolescent and from adolescence and to it because I have seen its metamorphoses; I have witnessed this arch of destiny in countless young people carrying them from uncertainty to triumph as they learn to discover their selfhood.

It is a challenge for me as a writer to explore the often brave ways in which young people face themselves and one another and the adult world they must enter. Looking out from their junior and senior high school years, it must seem frightening, out here where we are. "If I can just be like you, mom," they might say, "If I can just be successful." "Oh," they say, "I'll never be anything—will I? Will I? I can't do anything. Where will I go? College is so big . . . too small. Too far away. Too close. I won't know anyone. No one will like me. Will I get in? Will I have friends? Who will I date? What will I wear? How much stuff do *I take with me?* I will never sleep in a noisy dorm with strangers. What will I do? Do *my own laundry?*" Now these are the kinds of fears that the successful, college-bound students invariably have. Imagine what sort of voiceless dramas go on within the students not so successful.

It is truly a long way for all of them from where they begin, on through their young adulthood.

It has been a long way, also, from where I started, perhaps farther than I would have dreamed, certainly farther than my own young people will have to go. I don't think I was designed to come this far. I am your garden-variety, farm-bred overachiever. Early on, I had a powerful sense that I wanted to write. And later, it was amusing to me that people were willing to pay me for what I had been doing for free.

Freedom is very important to me. What I remember most about growing up as an adolescent in Ohio was that I was free. Whether that is a true memory or a necessary fabrication is beyond my knowledge. But I took it upon myself to make regular visits, my cousin and I did, to my mother's friends and relatives who were old enough to be my mother's mother. These were missionary ladies of the church auxiliary, and I found them fascinating. They seemed to me to have lived in another time and were merely passing through my own. For me and my cousin, Marlene, it was a joy stepping into the half-light of silent, perfectly neat front parlors with blinds drawn against the heat in the late afternoon. The back of the sofa and the arms of easy chairs were protected by lace antimacassars they'd crocheted themselves. Polish gleamed on the oak floors and the dining table. I remember the slow, somnific ticking of the grandfather's clock. "Why were there no grandmother's clocks?" I wondered as I watched the stooped-back Miss Wing, an elderly missionary lady, rummage through her ancient calfskin purse, over there at the breakfront hunting up the right amount of change. And finding it, holding it between delicate thumb and finger out to me, she would speak, "Dear, take this to your mother, if you will. Etta put in for me last Sunday when the plate came around, as I'd forgotten my money."

"Yes, ma'am, Miss Wing," I would answer and gingerly take the change, blackened by time. I remember Miss Wing in her formal gray, silken dresses down to her ankles. And it is fitting, I think, that the essential family in a book of mine, *Willie Bea and the Time the Martians Landed* should be named Wings, too, in order to keep the memory of Miss Wing final and safe.

It is my habit to crystallize memories important to me within a fiction. The real Miss Wing was a tiny, bird-like woman, softly wrinkled and yellow in skin coloring. I adored her. The fictional Wing family have the same coloring, but their service to the fiction is much harsher in tone, in character and content, than the real Miss Wing would have been. What remains constant, I think, is the point of view from the real experience into the fictional portrayal. I saw the real Miss Wing through steady, vibrant, adolescent eyes. One views the fictional condition through the same eyes. If the portrayals seem at all vivid, it is because the extreme clarity and vitality of youth, that extraordinary young energy, *is* the seeing eye.

If I may return to freedom for a moment, I think what my parents did for me without my realizing it was to give me the sense that I was free to *create my own mind.* It is a belief that I cherish, that allowed me to bring to my own young people that same belief for them. And it further allowed me to find my own way in the literature I create. What rules I go by have come from my lack of concern for rules or proper ways of doing things. I feel free enough to deal in fantasy, for example, while not writing fantasy in particular. In this way, I am able to go beyond realism to aim a fictional world beyond itself.

I am most successful at this in books that are classified as adolescent, young adult literature. *Junius Over Far* and *A Little Love* fall into this category. *Sweet Whispers, Brother Rush* does not quite; and yet, I see it as sort of a pretrial for *A Little Love,* and I will have something to say about it a little later. *Junius Over Far* is an adventure romance; *A Little Love* is a "love" romance. *Junius* adheres closely to the formula, "Boy meets girl, boy loses girl, boy wins girl." But the love angle is hardly central to this story. The adventure plot is more significant. But more important than either is the marvelous journey that the character Junius must take and which is essential to any traditional romance. In the novel, Junius and his father, Damius, begin a journey to find out about the trouble Grandfather Jackabo is having. There is a generational test, or struggle, and all three male members of the Damius Rawlings family, the son, Junius, the father, Damius, and Grandfather Jackabo, seem to be warring with some inner turmoil. In the end, they will return to the point at which the journey or inner struggle began. The traditional reality romance is aimed somewhat beyond in the sense that the book's main characters are black and the predominant speech is West Indian, and the traditional locus or setting is the black milieu of a Caribbean island.

The romance of the novel *A Little Love* is traditional in the "love" romance sense. The love is symbolically related to spring and spring green, new growth and beginnings. Sheema Hadley's ordeal will be overcome by a happy ending. But not before she embarks on a journey in search of her missing father, which symbolizes her search for selfhood, definition, and maturity. In this book, the boy meets girl formula is altered in that from the very beginning, Sheema has someone who loves her. The young man, Forrest, never falters in his love for her. By the end of the book he loves her more, enough to ask her to marry him. And, by the end, our heroine will be victorious in her awareness of her own value and acquiring the tools she needs for a better life.

Sheema Hadley from *A Little Love* is not a traditional romantic heroine. She is overweight; she is not particularly pretty. She is black. She is poor and speaks a street language that adults would find offensive. But Forrest Jones loves her. Her Grandmom and Grandpop love her without qualification. She doesn't know why anyone would love her, since she sees herself as totally unlovable.

I love Sheema, too. I created her and it's my fault that the world seems stacked against her. But my own quest was to make the reader love her without qualification, as well.

The Sheema Hadleys of our society are not often subjects for serious young adult fiction. They do not fall into Western acceptable norms for romantic matter. That is why I choose them as my subjects. They are the forgotten whom I will not forget, and I hope you will not forget.

Now, I would like to substitute the novel, *Sweet Whispers, Brother Rush,* for *Junius Over Far* in forming with *A Little Love* a kind of literature triptych with a third romantic novel. First, *Sweet Whispers, Brother Rush* is not exactly a young adult novel; its subject matter is at times difficult and complex. There is a young man who, let us say, is love literate. There are two young people who are largely on their own. Teresa Pratt takes care of her older brother Dabney who is retarded and physically ill. But the romantic formula boy meets girl is altered here to the strong affection between a loving brother and sister. Boy loves girl because sister loses brother when Dabney dies suddenly and tragically. Teresa is so upset by his death that she plans to run away, perhaps to find her father, whom she remembers only vaguely. But she does not run away, yet thinks that maybe someday she will go off on her own. We know that in the middle book of the tryptych, *A Little Love,* Sheema Hadley does take the romantic journey in search of her father. *A Little Love* was meant to be a sequel to *Sweet Whispers,* but then I realized that Sheema was older, different, and both she and Teresa were really individuals in my scheme of teen romances.

The third book is entitled *A White Romance.* It is a traditional love romance, but again with large exceptions to the romance formula. Here there is a dual love angle. The central characters are black and some are white. Here we have genuine friendships. And the traditional, romantic love, usually only suggested in the romantic novel is quite clearly consummated in *A White Romance* as it is in *A Little Love.* The formulaic boy meets girl, boy loves girl, boy wins girl is again altered to girl meets boy, girl loses boy, but finds a different, perhaps better boy. The quest or adventure is present, but here it is rough and dangerous and takes place at a heavy metal rock concert in a huge arena in the Midwest.

The traditional narrator is almost non-existent in this novel. And there are few orthodox transitions. Except for the beginning, the book is almost totally dialogue. We are plunged into the world of a magnet school seen through the eyes of one main character, Talley Barbour, and we are gripped by her vibrant and vivid young adult psyche.

Again, my aim is to have the reader pay attention to and have sympathy for nontraditional characters and lifestyles through patterns of the traditional romance. These characters and their lifestyles are a metaphor for the real world. We Americans need to consider all of us essential to the total fabric of our society. This concept of humanism, the belief in the welfare of us all as one world, is central to my writing.

Our young adult literature tends to remove from the young adults, themselves. The slim presence of parallel culture literature would give the impression that such large parallel cultures have no presence and do not exist in America. I wrote *A Little Love, Sweet Whispers* and *A White Romance* with the concept of voiceless, somewhat hopeless young adults, who never have enough words, money, love. Before they are out of their teens they seem beaten, dispirited, characterized by unease.

Will the young people about whom my triptych books are written ever read them? Are these young adults capable of reading books; do they have the mental ease to concentrate long enough; do they care to read?

Most of the time, I avoid such questions. What I must remember is that if there is a young adult somewhere who wishes to extend his or her comprehension of life and lifestyles, who wants to find something between the covers of a book that reflects his or her personal struggles, dreams, or even to find a new sort of entertainment, then these three books will be there for the reading. They are also there for me. Because somewhere deep within, the Sheemas, the Teresas, the Talleys have long since touched me with their special magic.

My son's generation of young adults grew up knowing that books were more important than the flickering images on television. He may love MTV, but he and his friends know that knowledge still comes from the printed word. This may not be true for the next few generations, who may have more difficulty with reading as the glut of videos, computers, and cassette tapes finds more room in their consciousness. It is hard for me to conceive of a world without writing and reading at its center. I hold to the Jonathan Kozol ideal that literacy represents "some sort of answer to a universal need for vindication and for self-perpetuation." And, yet, three-fourths of the world does not have food to eat, and in terms of that deprivation, reading does seem elitist, if not meaningless, and self-perpetuation seems doomed to failure.

American young adults bear the burden of relative ease in their lives. They have endless choices beyond to read or not to read. Moreover, the writer must contend with the large problem of national illiteracy, and black illiteracy in particular. Illiteracy hurts the writer of the parallel cultures most directly. But quite often, nice things do occur cross-culturally and racially. A woman who is white related to me this story of her experience in reading *A Little Love* before giving it to her teenage daughter with the single comment, "I think you will find this book interesting." The daughter read *A Little Love*, enjoyed it.

"But didn't you find the Black English difficult?" asked the mother.

"What Black English?" said the kid, "Mom, that's the way kids talk."

Well, we know that all kids don't sound like Sheema Hadley. But there is a kind of American hipness among our young adults which comes from following trends on television, in magazines, music and concerts, favorite young stars from a variety of culture stations. All teenagers speak the same language to a great extent, more so than do we adults speak one another's language. Go into a city school, a midwestern vocational school, any American high school, really, and you will discover that young adults use the same symbol words and sign words no matter what class they come from or what their color. They will inflect key words in the same manner. Young adults all over the country speak of "dweebs" and "wusses" and "nerds." "Chill out" is a watch phrase. One will say, "Jerry is taking Terry out and she's not even pretty" with the emphasis on *even*. As teachers of English, you might find my acceptance of colloquial speech simplistic. But young adults use a rich, expressive language. The hope is that they will know standard English and its value, but continue to create their own minds, so to speak, which is expressed through creative English. It was from listening to my son and his friends that I first got the idea for *A White Romance*. They are keen observers of the young adult society and eager participants. They touch me with their honesty and integrity. Jaime has a friend, Chris, who is a wonderful guitarist, who loves most heavy metal music, his choice for himself. He attends, as does my son, any heavy metal concert within a hundred miles of home. I wanted Chris to hear the new cassette by one of my favorite pop singers. He listened to a cut, respectfully, and then struggled with himself as I asked him, "Well, what do you think of it?" Poor young man. Here was Jaime's mother, this writer, asking him something about pop music. He struggled; I could see it on his face. But finally, his sense of himself shone in his eyes. He would tell me the truth and he said, looking me dead in the eye, "I'd rather listen to nothing, *loud*.

He just gave me one of the best lines I'd heard in a long time. My mind couldn't have created that sentence. His did.

We come now to the part of the breakfast talk set aside for the writer's announcements. I have written a sequel to a book entitled *The House of Dies Drear*, which I mention because it is a two part "Wonderworks" (PBS) telecast. The sequel is entitled *The Mystery of Drear House*, Book II of the Dies Drear Chronicle.

Also I'd like to announce a work-in-progress, rather like a tragic romance, part fiction and part fact, that takes place in 1854. I believe it is pertinent to the present. It is a slave-rescue case taking place in Boston; it became a famous national cause at the time. I mention it because the past for me is always present. I write largely from the black experience, for an audience as large and varied as I can find. I am not only a black writer for black people, rather I am a writer for people. I believe in the decency of us all. I write from a love of life and fabricating, in search of truth. Sounds silly to say it, but there it is. And to say one thing about the folktale book, *The People Could Fly*. Young adults often enjoy having the tales read out loud to them. I had good results reading to kids at a local college not too long ago. These folktales I developed as a metaphor for present-day struggles and accomplishments of parallel culture. These folktales from the plantation era demonstrate that tale-telling is not merely a thing of the past, but a continuing cultural imperative.

People of the parallel culture are an oppressed people. There is little American black writing that is not socially conscious or race-conscious writing. In it is thesis and antithesis in search of synthesis. My young adult characters live within a fictional social order characterized by tension and struggle. The final resolve is for awareness, growing consciousness. History teaches us that the progress of civilization is for the growth and refinement of human consciousness, or so we hope.

Imaginative use of language and ideas illuminates for us a human condition which we all share, which reminds us to care who we Americans are. Who are these black people? Who are these white people? Who are all these people; where do they come from; how do they dream; how do they hunger? We are then reminded to value the young, young adults, and to understand what they desire and dream.

Those are my pronouncements. I am awfully pleased to have this opportunity to share some of my reasons for being with you.

Gothic and Grotesque Effects in Virginia Hamilton's Fiction

Anita Moss

At the 1983 Conference of the Children's Literature Association at the University of Alberta, Virginia Hamilton participated in a discussion of her novels and acknowledged that William Faulkner's fiction had been a major influence upon her own. One of the important ways that Faulkner has had an impact on many twentieth-century American writers has been through his masterful and complex use of Gothic conventions. In this essay I intend to explore Hamilton's uses of Gothic and Grotesque conventions and effects, especially as these traditions have come to her through American Gothic, a line which leads back to such eighteenth-century British writers as Horace Walpole, Ann Radcliffe, Matthew Gregory Lewis, and others, and later perpetuated and refined by such nineteenth-century British writers as the Brontës and Charles Dickens and in America by George Branch Cabell and Edgar Allan Poe.

In his classic work, *Love and Death in the American Novel,* Leslie Fiedler describes the "naturalization" of Gothicism in American fiction, of which Faulkner's novels have been the most distinguished examples. Flannery O'Connor and Eudora Welty have followed Faulkner's example by using the Gothic mode to explore psychological and moral horror. Ralph Ellison's *Invisible Man* uses surrealistic effects and Gothic images—dream, nightmare, etc.—to depict the complexities of minority experience. Most recently, the African American writer, Toni Morrison, has made brilliant use of Gothic and Grotesque effects as she attempts to express the virtually unspeakable stories of black women in her novel *Beloved* (1987). In Virginia Hamilton's novels, too, the Gothic mode has been an abiding feature whose conventions have enabled her to tell stories of intense psychological power and moral complexity.

Reprinted from *The ALAN Review* 19.2, Winter 1992, pages 16–20, by permission of the author.

Gothicism and the Drear Books

Hamilton's most explicit venture into Gothicism occurs in *The House of Dies Drear* (1970) and its sequel written almost twenty years later, *The Mystery of Drear House* (1987). The earlier novel is gloriously imbued with specific Gothic effects. As the action in early Gothic romances occurred in deserted castles filled with ghosts and tortured spirits from dungeon to attic, so the central image in both of the Dies Drear novels is the house of a famous abolitionist, an important station in the Underground Railroad, and hence inhabited by its own anguished ghosts. Spaces within and without Drear House resonate with supernatural possibilities. Dreams, surrealistic qualities, and fantastic images abound in both novels. Drear House is likewise a maze of mysterious spaces, tunnels, hidden passages, recesses, and surprising connections.

The opening paragraph of *The House of Dies Drear* describes a strange dream of Thomas Small, the central character of both novels. Though Thomas walks a familiar path in the dream, he experiences a dreadful sense of claustrophobia as evergreen trees appear to become gigantic and threaten to engulf him. In this frightening dream Thomas encounters a white-haired, satanic old man, whose "eyes glowed red and then spewed fire" (2). The reader knows, however, that such a dream may represent some sinister foreboding that the move from North Carolina to Drear House in Ohio may not be fortuitous.

As Thomas's father, Mr. Small, begins to describe the house, both Thomas and the reader feel more and more uneasy about this remote, big, pre–Civil War house, with its hidden rooms and lost plans. Hamilton repeatedly stresses the secrecy, strangeness, remoteness, and potentially supernatural qualities of Drear House. It is an absolutely central metaphor in both novels, and it is for Thomas a way to make connections with his cultural past. His experience in Drear House helps Thomas to imagine what it really meant that "between 1810 and 1850, forty thousand of them [fleeing slaves] had passed through Ohio" (10).

Weather usually plays a prominent role in establishing an atmosphere of dread in Gothic novels. Likewise, the Small family arrives at their new home amid "a gloom of mist and heavy rain" (25). The house itself seems to share these atmospheric conditions:

> The House of Dies Drear loomed out of mist and murky sky, not only gray and formless, but huge and unnatural. It seemed to crouch on the side of a hill high above the highway. And it had a dark, isolated look about it that set it at odds with all that was living. (26)

No wonder Thomas realizes at once that his new home is haunted. The house of Dies Drear sits broodingly within a heavily Gothic landscape: a muddy stream gushing near the house looks to Thomas as if it is bleeding; trees near the house are "bare and twisted by wind" (27). Also Thomas immediately associates the house with a castle, drawbridge, moat, war, and a king. All of this strikes him as sinister and alienating: "the hill and house were bitten and frozen. They were separated from the rest of the land by something unkind" (29). Thomas also realizes that, like all Gothic houses, this one harbors secrets.

Thomas's fearful musings focus finally upon the eccentric Mr. Pluto, the same old man who had figured prominently in his initial dream. Called "Mr. Pluto" because he lives underground, this character remains terrifying both to Thomas and to the reader for more than half the novel. Thomas is certain that Mr. Pluto is giving the Small family warnings to flee. His suspicions about Mr. Pluto's nature are strengthened by local superstitions; many families in the community not only believe that Drear House is haunted; they also think that Mr. Pluto is a cohort of the devil. Ultimately, Thomas's intuitions about Mr. Pluto are wrong. The boy's reading of Gothic romances has caused him to misread both Mr. Pluto and Drear House.

The house does indeed possess a hidden underground chamber, a natural cave made eerie with fabulous stalactites and stalagmites, and Mr. Pluto is the keeper of Dies Drear's secrets. But the secret revealed finally is not a Gothic horror—but a treasure. Before the Small family shares Mr. Pluto's secret, however, Thomas must endure an initiation into the house. When he accidently falls into a secret tunnel under the front steps, Thomas begins to feel the heaviness of the house: "The idea of the whole three story house of Dies Drear pressing down on him caused him to stop a moment on the path" (47). Yet these lost, dark, cramped, and bewildered moments in the tunnel in which he believes he hears cries of despair enable him to imagine the true condition of the many slaves who had hidden there before him.

In experiencing the isolation and alienation from community, the secret signs, nightmares, and darkness of Drear House, Thomas begins to understand at the deepest human level the abstract facts he had read in the historical account of the House of Drear. While the power of the past is often expressed through the Gothic ghosts as a destructive force impelling characters in Gothic romance toward irrevocable disaster, Hamilton uses these conventions for very different purposes in *The House of Dies Drear.* Her Gothic narrative suggests that, for African Americans, the confrontation with their collective cultural past is almost intolerably painful but also essential in order to face the future and grow. To be sure, Mr. Small and Thomas discover terrible secrets—murder, revenge, greed, obsession—but they also discover the treasures of their own cultural past which help to heal the pain and reconcile breaches between neighbors and within families. Like so many of Hamilton's fine novels, this one powerfully affirms the values of the African American family and community symbolized in the church, which, as Thomas discovers, has played such a profound role in the road to freedom for his people.

Many scholars have noted that Gothic novels in America have often shown the disintegration and decay of cultural identity (Faulkner's *Sanctuary, Absalom, Absalom,* and *The Sound and the Fury* are notable examples); Hamilton, however, uses similar narrative strategies for very different purposes. Her novel does not end with a burning house or a howling idiot but with her young protagonist's father happily recording treasure upon treasure. Thomas' father is not a mad Gothic villain, greedy for treasure, power, and forbidden pleasures of the flesh, but a humane scholar who teaches his son and other members of his community that cultural treasures are to be shared, not hoarded. Nor is Mr. Pluto a Gothic villain but a keeper of stories, secrets, and treasures. In 1970 when this novel was published, Hamilton held up a luminous and hopeful vision for young readers who must have wondered if they could survive the present at all, much less explore the painful secrets of the past and brave the uncertainties of the future.

Gothicism in *Junior Brown* and *Sweet Whispers*

While Hamilton employs Gothic conventions in her two novels about Drear House essentially to explore and reveal cultural identity, she also uses them to express intense tensions within families and painful psychological realities in *The Planet of Junior Brown* (1971) and *Sweet Whispers, Brother Rush* (1982). Neither of these novels contains such explicit features of Gothicism as the Drear House books; rather the Gothic conventions in these novels are what literary historians have sometimes called the "Grotesque." Alfred Appel writes in *A Season of Dreams:*

> The Grotesque is characterized by a distortion of the external world, by the description of human beings in nonhuman terms, and by the displacement we associate with dreams. . . . The Grotesque is heightened realism, reminiscent of caricature, but going beyond it to create a fantastic realism or a realistic fantasy that evokes pathos and terror. (74)

Another distinguishing characteristic of this kind of "New American Gothic" is its use of enclosures and a claustrophobic sense of space. Irving Malin writes in *New American Gothic* that this kind of fiction often features an "other room" or a "final door through which ghost-like forces march." This final room, according to Malin, is the coffin, or analogous thereof—tightly constrained spaces where growth, freedom, and identity are impossible to achieve. One of Hamilton's most potent uses of Gothic technique is in her treatment of space as a metaphor for oppression and imprisonment as well as a possible source of creative inspiration—secret, hidden, sheltered places where characters may somehow grow despite the constraints.

In both *The Planet of Junior Brown* and *Sweet Whispers, Brother Rush* Hamilton uses images of confinement and enclosure, as well as images of creative, sheltered space (see Gilbert and Gubar). Tomblike spatial metaphors in these two novels are also closely associated with illness, madness, and creative art. The spatial metaphors function symbolically within the novels themselves and also offer some provocative insights into the writer's sense of identity.

In *The Planet of Junior Brown* Mr. Pool's hidden basement room is the location not only where creation takes place but also where Mr. Pool and Buddy imagine whole new spheres of being and knowing. Mr. Pool senses in Buddy Clark "a whole new being lying in wait" (20). Homeless, Buddy Clark has learned to take care not only of himself but of others as well. He escapes his homelessness and sense of isolation by caring for younger boys in the dilapidated basements of abandoned buildings. Buddy calls this network of shelters his "planets," and he teaches the boys to take care of themselves, to survive in a hostile world. These underground homes provide food, shelter, companionship, and even new names for the boys. In his homeless condition, Buddy Clark has evaded the institutions of an oppressive culture. He and the boys whom he shelters have chosen to live underground in both a literal and metaphorical sense. Like the characters of Dostoyevsky and Richard Wright who choose to live underground, Hamilton's Buddy and his "planets" have chosen to live outside society and in a sense beyond it. Though Hamilton does not idealize this existence, she suggests that it is preferable to the mad or diseased spaces in which Junior Brown is imprisoned.

Junior Brown lives with his asthmatic mother in a comfortable and beautifully kept apartment. Junior's father, the reader is told, lives in Jersey. Junior hopes his father will visit, a wish that never comes true. Clearly Junella Brown has imprisoned her son and herself in their nice home. Though she professes to be proud of Junior's musical talent, she nevertheless deprives the boy of his art. Junior must practice on a piano whose wires have been detached. Junior is a prisoner in a house where his desire to create is repressed and killed. The hammers silently strike the air. Junior is silenced in a tightly constrained space.

When Junella suffers an asthma attack, Junior must care for her. Afterward as his mother sleeps in exhaustion, Junior paints. His rage finds expression on the canvas. Before he paints, Junior feels "red" under his skin. He dances exuberantly. He contemplates Buddy Clark's freedom and resents it. Noise and redness burst within him. Both external and internal spaces for Junior are intolerable.

To relieve his inner struggles, Junior fills the empty spaces on his canvas to create "The Red Man." "The Red Man" contains other people; and Junior enacts on the canvas his fervent fantasies of freedom and escape: "He had everyone flowing free—Mr. Pool and his daddy and Buddy's daddy and games and busses and old people and trees" (138). Like Charlotte Gilman's female character of *The Yellow Wall Paper* who imagines that she sees a despairing woman trapped and creeping within the paper's pattern, Junior imagines his own mad double in "The Red Man," with his dark red pulsing brain and his barely contained energies. Hamilton makes it clear that this alter ego is essential to Junior Brown, the fat boy who imagines his own monstrosity and succeeds in making himself monstrous by devouring all the food in the house, as if to occupy all of the space in that tightly constrained and repressed home of illness and despair.

Junella herself both seeks confinement with her own illness and self-pity while trying to escape it. She admires Miss Peebs, Junior's music teacher, not only because she has been a famous concert pianist but because Miss Peebs's ancestors had never been slaves. She tells Junior that they should go downtown more often and not confine themselves so closely to the black community. They should not be such hermits, she says. Nevertheless, Junella continues not only to confine her son but to invade his inner space as well. As he walks with Buddy Clark, Junior can hear his mother's voice: "Junior's mother reached into Junior's mind and tried to take it over . . . 'Mama, why you always have to bust in on me?'" (35–36). Junior at least finds some respite on the bus, a neutral space where he can hide: "He could sit down. Hiding himself there in the rear of the bus, he could look like anybody else of ordinary size" (41).

The other adult who profoundly affects Junior Brown is his piano teacher, Miss Peebs. Trapped in her parents' home, this gifted pianist has rejected her art. She has locked herself away with decaying books, dust, and piles of furniture. Like Junior, Miss Peebs also perceives a mad double, a filthy relative who has infected her claustrophobic home. Though Junior longs for the freedom of the ebony and ivory spaces of the piano, Miss Peebs has violently attacked the piano, a pathetic emblem of her self-hatred and rejection of her own art. Miss Peebs thus forces Junior to enact a pitiful caricature of his art by beating out his lesson on a chair. Saddest of all, she imprisons herself.

Readers can only speculate as to why these two women have confined themselves with their illnesses and madness. One can only guess that both characters are reacting to oppressive forces in their culture as well as in their own families. Mrs. Brown reacts to the apparent abandonment by her husband and to the cultural forces making such a situation necessary by enslaving and confining her son. Junior's vital creative self thus struggles for freedom, but Hamilton dramatizes how this vital self is encased in layers of fat and trapped by centuries of oppression. Miss Peebs has allowed her parents to determine her identity. Her apartment, with its crumbling books and crowded paraphernalia from the past, strongly resembles a tomb rather than a home. Junior, Miss Peebs, and Junella Brown each seem to be locked into dreadful isolation. Junior expresses his feeling of alienation poignantly, as he feels curiously shut out even as he is shut into the basement room with Buddy Clark and Mr. Pool: "Across the span of planets, Junior Brown thought, 'Who am I? What can I know? It's Friday. Outside me, it might be Monday. Or nothing. Or something terrible'" (23).

Neither Miss Peebs nor Junior and his mother appear in any way connected to a community. Buddy Clark, on the other hand, has learned to reach out to others and so free his creative self. Though he has no father or mother, he finds a parent substitute in his mentor, Mr. Pool. Buddy moreover has many "brothers"; yet he longs for one special brother—hence his attachment to Junior Brown. He is equally at home in the dark streets, running free and easy, or inhabiting his underground enclosures. His existence has given him inner strength and inner vision: "In the dark he had taught himself to see with his mind" (73).

Buddy is "Tomorrow Billy" to his "planets," and, as Mr. Pool has hinted and the name suggests, he may indeed be a new being who has learned that the old law of living only for oneself will no longer suffice. Lacking a family, the homeless boys must create their own families. As Buddy explains, "We are all together because we have to learn to live for each other" (206).

When Junella Brown destroys Junior's "The Red Man," which she considers obscene, she has removed all of the space Junior had left. He must find a new space or explode from the inside with all the violence he had expressed on his canvas. Likewise Mr. Pool and the boys come close to losing their secret basement room and decide that their marvelous solar system must be dismantled. Junior's enormous bulk, the reader notes incredulously, is lowered into the basement with a pulley, a grotesque scene reminiscent of a similar scene in Faulkner's *As I Lay Dying.* Junior takes his filthy mad double with him into the basement; he has relieved Miss Peebs of her diseased and horrible relative at last. In his new home, however, Junior finds that he no longer needs the filthy alter ego. As he rests in the closeness of his new family, comforted by the music of Buddy's resonant voice, he can no longer see the diseased relative.

Hamilton's ending in *The Planet of Junior Brown* is tough-minded to say the least. But she strongly suggests that being shut out by a society is to be shut into ourselves, our illness, and our madness. Only a true liberation can free us to discover ourselves, our independent spirits, and our creativity. Only recognizing that the mad double is an evil thing we create out of our own rage and despair will enable us to dispel it.

In *Sweet Whispers, Brother Rush* Hamilton also gives her readers an intense apprehension of the central character's claustrophobic existence. In this powerful novel about child abuse and child abandonment, the central character Teresa, or "Tree," has been left by her mother, Vy, to care for her brother. Vy cannot tolerate her son's illness and mental retardation and leaves her two children quite literally imprisoned in an apartment. They share their aloneness and survive without their mother's presence. Tree must cook, clean, plan, and care for her childlike brother, Dabney. The reader meets Tree as she is beginning to mature. She hides her budding breasts as boys tease her. Meanwhile she has seen a "gorgeous dude" on the street and has fallen in love with him. It is important to the novel's structure that Tree is poised on the brink of womanhood. Before she can grow into maturity, she must retreat, even regress, to rediscover the sunny spaces of her own childhood, the house of her parents which contains its own terrifying secret in an attic room.

Teresa and Dabney have lived without parents and without any knowledge of their past. Their intensely enclosed apartment seems to be the beginning and end of their existences. Indeed Hamilton's novel may remind readers of Edgar Allan Poe's famous Gothic tale, "The Fall of the House of Usher." Madeline and Roderick Usher are closed within a Gothic house, doomed by a mysterious inherited disease just as Dab is doomed by porphyria, the strange disease afflicting the male members of Vy's family. Like Roderick Usher, Dab is the last surviving male member of his family. Vy and Brother Rush had been unusually close and enclosed with illness, just as Tree and Dab are. We also learn that Brother Rush died in an accident on the day that all the ivy fell from the house, as if to symbolize that the best hope of the Rush family and the house itself had fallen, a detail strongly reminiscent of the eerily floating vines which cover the Usher house before it falls and disintegrates. Finally, the name "Rush" seems to be inspired by Poe's doomed Usher family. Tree, then, must retreat to a terrifying Gothic domain to learn how to live while her brother must also return to the past to learn how to die.

In her study *Archetypal Patterns of Women's Fiction,* Annis Pratt has stressed the frequency with which female heroes in women's fiction are accompanied in their voyages of self-discovery by an ideal male guide, whom Pratt calls the "Green World lover." Brother Rush seems to serve this role in Tree's quest for knowledge of her past. She clears her own sheltered space in the apartment—a tiny alcove with a table where she draws pictures of trees, open spaces, families—all of the things missing in her own life. As Junior Brown expresses his mad desires and exuberant vitality by painting, so Tree expresses her own deep needs and wishes in her drawings. Brother Rush, Tree's "Green World" guide, takes her back to childhood and allows her to complete the tragic story of her own past, a necessary if painful knowledge she must have in order to understand her brother and her mother.

Holding a gleaming sphere—a window to Tree's past—the ghost of Brother Rush appears at just the point when the household becomes more than Tree can handle. Traveling into the open spaces of her past, Tree discovers disturbing secrets: her father's abandonment of his family, inherited illness, and most terrifying of all, Vy's physical and mental abuse of her son. To her horror, Tree learns that Vy has often confined Dab, tied him up, and beaten him. Gradually Tree realizes she is trapped with a Dab who is becoming more and more seriously ill. Inner and outer space become increasingly intolerable for Tree, a conflict which climaxes in the scene where she runs around the apartment in grief and madness after Dab's death. Tree receives one final glimpse of Brother Rush—as a decaying corpse riding away in his car with Dab, Hamilton's graphic way of assuring both Tree and the reader that both Dab and Brother Rush are dead, that Tree's place is yet among the living. Only twice does Tree feel a reassuring sense of community to alleviate her terrible sense of loss and alienation. As she rides in the sheltered space of Vy's car, she feels protected and cared for as the car moves through the dark streets, just as she had felt as a baby girl riding securely behind Brother Rush's protective shoulder. In the final scene of the novel, Tree dines with Vy, her boyfriend Silversmith, and Silversmith's son Don, after Dabney's funeral. Though the ending seems a bit too happy and contrived, it represents the hope that both Vy and Tree may yet come to terms with their losses in the future.

In *The Planet of Junior Brown* and *Sweet Whispers, Brother Rush,* Hamilton's Gothic and Grotesque uses of space suggest that the characters' experiences in actual space are emblems of drama enacted within psychic spaces. She also reveals that our most precious spaces—our homes and our very selves—may be invaded by destructive forces beyond our control. Whereas the Small family attempts to restore cultural treasures in *The House of Dies Drear,* the protagonist in *M.C. Higgins the Great* experiences a terrifying claustrophobia as his Appalachian home is threatened by the destruction and pollution of strip mining. As in other American Gothic novels, *M.C. Higgins the Great* depicts the disintegration of a cultural order in which people seem literally to be haunted by ghosts from the past, paralyzed by present conditions, and powerless to confront the future. Such a situation results in grotesque behavior: Mr. Killburn tries to heal the wounded mountain by laying his witchy hands upon the damaged earth; M.C. swings high on his forty-foot pole waving a burning mop as he fantasizes about his mother's future as a singer and plots to hunt the girl he has seen on the mountain; finally M.C., his father, and his friend use the tombstones of dead ancestors as a possible stay against the dangerous spoil heap which threatens to slide down the mountain.

But Hamilton's uses of confined spaces do not always suggest psychological or cultural disorder and disintegration. As we have seen, Buddy Clark in *The Planet of Junior Brown* and Tree in *Sweet Whispers, Brother Rush* use enclosures as havens for creative activity. According to Gaston Bachelard, such enclosures may not only serve as regressive retreats; they may also shelter dreams, imaginings, and the most significant creative work. Hamilton expresses this kind of "felicitous space" (Bachelard, 3031) in *The Time Ago Tales of Jahdu* (1969):

> Mama Luka liked to sit in her tight little room in a fine good place called Harlem. She liked to sit with the window blinds drawn against the sunlight. And Mama Luka did this every day. (4)

Mama Luka's tight little room is not the "final room" of Gothic fiction. In this magical half-light she imagines the exuberant Jahdu—how he found his power, how he took care of trouble, how he finally became himself. In this good place Lee Edward listens as the stories shape themselves in the imaginations of both teller and listener. In darker expressions of the Gothic, the enclosed room is the place of nightmare and horror, such as the terrible room in which Vy beats and confines her small son, but such places may also shelter hopes in the direst circumstances. Survival for African Americans has often required silence, secrecy, and concealment—going underground spiritually, emotionally, and even literally. In *The Magical Adventures of Pretty Pearl* (1983), Pearl, the god child, experiences the horrors of the worst possible nightmare space—the hold of a slave ship containing captured Africans. Later she finds shelter in the forest: "'Oh, that is a hiding place,' she told herself, 'better than a rock or a cave. Who gone wander around in there? Robbers on the edge of it, I bet. But deep inside, I'll find me a find'" (43).

Indeed the forest serves as a symbol of home and self in *The Magical Adventures of Pretty Pearl.* Like the forests in Gothic fiction, it is mysterious and terrifying, yet for African Americans the forest yields good things—treasures in fact—and it was the hiding place for countless escaped slaves making their way north to freedom.

As we have seen, Hamilton has made imaginative use of explicit features of the Gothic and Grotesque tradition in her rich and varied body of young adult fiction. These techniques have allowed her to explore psychological and cultural dimensions of character which social realism does not usually allow for. While the characters examined in this discussion vividly inhabit Gothic spaces haunted by ghosts of the past, demons of the present, and imagined spectres of the future, characters in Hamilton's more recently published books have taken to the open road. Hence, the journey rather than the house serves as the central metaphor in *A Little Love* (1984) and *Junius Over Far* (1985). Hamilton's work in any event reflects a remarkable blending of well-established traditions in American literature with African-American folklore and myth, just one of the reasons why she has created some of our most distinguished works of young adult literature.

References

Appel, Alfred. *A Season of Dreams.* Baton Rouge: Louisiana State UP, 1965.

Bachelard, Gaston. *The Poetics of Space.* Trans. Maria Jolas. Boston: Beacon, 1969.

Fiedler, Leslie A. *Love and Death in the American Novel.* New York: Stein and Day, 1966.

Gilbert, Sandra, and Susan Gubar. *The Mad Woman in the Attic.* New Haven: Yale UP, 1979.

Hamilton, Virginia. *The House of Dies Drear.* New York: Macmillan, 1970.

———. *Junius Over Far.* New York: Harper, 1985.

———. *A Little Love.* New York: Philomel, 1984.

———. *The Magical Adventures of Pretty Pearl.* New York: Harper, 1983.

———. *M.C. Higgins the Great.* New York: Macmillan, 1974.

———. *The Mystery of Drear House.* New York: Macmillan, 1987.

———. *The Planet of Junior Brown.* New York: Macmillan, 1971.

———. *Sweet Whispers, Brother Rush.* New York: Philomel, 1982.

———. *The Time Ago Tales of Jahdu.* New York: Macmillan, 1969.

Malin, Irving. *New American Gothic.* Carbondale: Southern Illinois UP, 1962.

Pratt, Annis. *Archetypal Patterns of Women's Fiction.* Bloomington: Indiana UP, 1982.

Part I The Authors

Section 8
Sandy Asher

23 Best Friends: Talking with Young Readers through My Books

Sandy Asher

Courtesy of Drury College

An important difference between writing for adults and writing for adolescents is that when you write for adolescents, there's a very good chance some of your readers will take you seriously.

It's a rare day when a book changes the perceptions or value system of an adult. Generally adults choose books that reflect and reinforce attitudes they already hold. Very young children enjoy books the way they enjoy cookies: while a story's going on, it's a physical delight—the sounds of the words, the colors of the pictures, the closeness of the adult sharing it with them—but, like a cookie, when it's gone, it's gone. They're either full for the moment, or they want another one. They don't reflect on the themes and values imparted by the story and the relevance of all that to their immediate and future lives.

Young adult readers, on the other hand, are very definitely in search of ideas, information, and values to incorporate into their personalities and into their lives. The books they read become a very real part of them.

I know for a fact that my value system was heavily influenced by the books I read as a child. My attitudes toward many things, religion, politics, life expectations, are appreciably different from my parents'—and were already changing way back in elementary school, when I first read Louisa May Alcott's *Little Women.*

Through feisty Jo March, Alcott made writers out of many young dreamers, and I am among them. Jo wanted to be special—and so did I. She actually said those words, "I want to be special," and for the first time on this earth, I heard my secret thought, my private, rebellious little dream, put into words. Even better, Jo had a plan: She would be a writer. Well, I already loved to write. But I didn't know that had a name, I didn't know you could do that, be a

Reprinted from *The ALAN Review* 17.1, Fall 1989, pages 1–4, by permission of the author.

writer, until Jo gave me those words, too. Best of all, Jo succeeded, and that gave me courage and hope.

Not many of us can hope to write books that affect readers for over a century, but knowing how vital a part I may play in even one young person's life, I feel a heavy responsibility to be careful about what I say and how I say it. I'm not talking about censorship of my words or ideas, but about thoughtfulness: What do I really think about things, and what do I want to say to the next generation?

This becomes an even greater challenge when I consider that the majority of readers of young adult fiction are girls. What can I possibly do for them that would even approach what Louisa May Alcott did for me, especially in the face of the mixed messages they receive daily from society? As we set women free from stereotypes, young girls need more guidance than ever through what must seem an overwhelming array of choices.

The majority of readers of fiction are girls, but that doesn't mean they all are. And the boys reading serious fiction along with them are bound to be those sensitive enough to realize they, too, are caught up in an exciting and terrifying time. They, too, are searching, but not for easy, pat answers.

Let me define what I mean by serious fiction. I don't mean humorless fiction. By serious fiction, I'm talking about stories that examine the human condition in a thoughtful way. Please note two important words here: "human condition." Not male condition, not female condition. In serious fiction, there is no such thing as a boy's book or a girl's book, and I think I speak for all serious writers when I plead with librarians, teachers, and parents to stop labeling books that way. First of all, writers have to choose one gender or the other for their main characters. We do not choose one with the intention of turning our backs on the other half of the human race. Second, how are the two halves ever to understand each other if they are encouraged to see the world only from the same-sex point of view? And finally, male and female, they are searching for answers to important questions about life—about love and death and joy and grief and all the rest of it. There really aren't and shouldn't be two mutually exclusive sets of answers. More than one successful male writer has said, "It all began with Jo March."

I don't claim to have all the answers, but the questions young people must ask of themselves and the world as they grow up provide me with fascinating themes to explore. The questions that most interest me fall into two categories: how to separate from other people and how to connect with them.

Much attention has been paid, in my own books and others, to the first and often most dramatic work of growing up: separation from parents. I'm especially intrigued by the problem of girls separating from their mothers and boys from their fathers. To grow up, you have to become more like that same-sex parent. To become an individual, you have to become less like that parent. It's a tricky situation, and often an explosive one. How do you break free without destroying the relationship entirely?

This dilemma forms the basis for a variety of conflicts in my novels. In *Summer Smith Begins,* Summer attempts to separate herself from a highly competitive mother. Stephanie, the narrator of *Just Like Jenny,* struggles against her mother's perfectionism. Three teenagers in *Missing Pieces* search for themselves in the rubble left behind by parents who are gone either through death or divorce. In *Daughters of the Law* and *Everything Is Not Enough,* youngsters are unfairly asked to make up for their parents' suffering and to live out their unfinished dreams.

"I'd like to say we lived happily ever after," Summer muses, when she and her mother have finally confronted their differences. "But we didn't. Not exactly. We fought and made up and fought and made up again and again. But it was okay. It didn't kill us." What she means is, it didn't destroy the bond between them, and it didn't crush her own, fledgling sense of self.

There is a second, related, challenge young adults must face: As they separate from and reorganize their relationship to the family, they must connect to the greater world. As they discover who they are, they must find out where they fit in. The media—movies, television, magazines—suggest only limited ways of connecting outside the family: romance and sex, not necessarily in that order. The YA shelves of bookstores are increasingly stocked with fiction proclaiming and extolling the same limited choices.

This is particularly true of material aimed at young women. There is a nod toward meaningful work as a way of connecting—a briefcase here, an American Express card there—but young women are still shown in an endless hunt for romance—for men who alone can complete and define them.

It is no accident that the much-touted movie *Working Girl* has been dubbed "a modern Cinderella story." Prince Charming no longer gallops in on horseback. He hails a taxi. He no longer whisks Cinderella off to his castle, where all problems will be solved by the perfect marriage. Today, when we know marriages fail, they ride off together toward a perfect career. But our heroine still has to win her prince. Before, she did it with her beauty, innocence, kindness, and honesty. Now, she does it with "a head for business and a body for sin." But she does it. The modern wicked stepmother/witch is a female executive with a "bony ass"—who loses, not her life, not her career, but her man, the real measure of her success as a woman.

Certainly, romance and sex are important ways of connecting; the survival of our species depends on them. (And meaningful employment may be way out ahead of young readers; they first have to get through the here and now.) But there is another way of connecting: friendship—supportive, nurturing relationships that have to do with human kindness and caring, but not necessarily with romance or sex. ". . . I thought it over," Murray Gordon tells Debbie Palermo in *Things Are Seldom As They Seem,* as they discuss moving their friendship into romantic territory, "and I told myself, 'Mur, if there's anything in the world you do not need right now, it's an ex-girlfriend. What you do need is a friend. And you have one, the best in the world. Don't mess with a good thing.'"

It's assumed that children know all about making and keeping friends, that they're born knowing how. But something strange and puzzling interferes with the process; children are often very cruel to one another. It begins with fourth-grade cattiness and goes on straight through fraternity hazing. Why? I didn't understand it at those ages and I still don't, so friendship has become an important theme in my books.

Part of the reason for the cruelty may be rooted in powerlessness. Feeling powerless in the adult world, some children exercise what little power they do have over each other. The enclosed world of the school building reenforces this tendency. Bullies prosper where their victims can't simply walk away and stay away. Schools don't mean to have anything in common with prisons, but both give rise to the same struggle for pecking order.

Some of the cruelty among children is probably due to the natural testing of limits—how far can you push before somebody pushes back?

And some of it is due to the fact that genuine friendship doesn't get a lot of publicity in our society. In spite of the traditional, rose-colored image of childhood pals, I'm not sure children know all that much about it.

Adults know how much they depend on—or long for—trusted friends, but that's not a sentiment we often communicate to children. We talk about family a lot. Blood is thicker than water, we say. But families aren't what they used to be. More than ever, we need friends.

Most adult friendships are carried on at work, or after the children are asleep, or when they've been left at home with the babysitter. What we talk about with dear friends is often exactly what we can't talk about with our families, especially the children. (Sometimes it is our families, especially the children.) We know there are times we just couldn't make it without our friends, but how much of that do our children actually witness? They're in school or asleep.

Friendship as it appears in the media is often superficial—friends are the other people in the party scene or at the game, faces in a crowd. And it's temporary—friendship is something to do until romance comes along.

In the world of movies, TV, magazines, comic books, and certain kinds of genre fiction, crime and war have a curiously heartwarming aspect to them: Soldiers and crime fighters are allowed to have buddies, people whom they can trust with their lives and most intimate thoughts and feelings. Even criminals (Butch Cassidy and the Sundance Kid, for instance) have buddies to rely on.

"Buddy movies," by definition, are about male bonding. Whole wars seem to be fought, on screen at least, so that men can discover each other as friends. An ironic example of this is feminist Alan Alda's classic TV series, *M*A*S*H.* From episode one, Alda's character, Hawkeye Pierce, has a best friend, Trapper John. The very day Trapper John leaves Korea, B.J. Honeycutt shows up to be Hawkeye's even better best friend. But nurse Margaret Houlihan goes through eleven years of war without once getting close to another woman!

"Female buddy movies"—and TV shows—are increasing as more women take on producing, directing, and writing roles, but they're still the exception that proves the rule. Friendship, if it shows up in the media at all, is a male prerogative and, even then, permissible only under extreme "macho" conditions. Bullets *must* be whizzing overhead. Under ordinary circumstances, girls compete with each other for guys, guys compete with each other for the fun of it, and romantic love is offered as the only alternative to loneliness.

But a real life without friends, male and female, is emotional poverty indeed. Friendship doesn't come cheap; it doesn't come easy. It takes practice, and maybe that's a final explanation for the cruelty among children. They're beginners. Rank amateurs. They need more practice.

They also need role models to know what their practicing is supposed to lead to. Friendship is often confused with being liked or being popular. Being liked may be a result of conformity, of simply not being offensive; popularity has everything to do with quantity, but not necessarily anything to do with quality. The difference is critical. People compete for popularity. There is only one Homecoming Queen. They work together on friendship. (And yet there's no crown for it, no flowers, no applause.)

The friendships between Murray and Debbie and between a variety of characters in all of my books endure enormous hardships, undergo great testing strains, but they hold, and they grow. They're important, central to the characters' daily lives. As Jenny says the first time Stephie fails her, "It was awful without you, Stephie. Even with other people there, I kept coming around to the edge of this big hole where you should have been." That's my way of letting young people in on the big secret, that friendship is vital, to both sexes, even in peace time, and that it takes considerable effort. In making that effort, we grow—and we grow up.

Adolescence is particularly hard on friendship. Wanting to appear grown up, young people go to extraordinary lengths to mask their vulnerability. That doesn't make for the kind of open communication friendship requires. A letter I received from a British teenager begins, "I hope you don't mind me writing to you, but I have read your book, *Just Like Jenny,* and in some ways have problems like Stephanie, and I feel I can't talk to anyone about them."

As a way of talking, she writes:

> . . . Gradually my friends' attitudes changed, and a barrier was put up between us, especially between one who was once my best friend. She is still my best friend, but I don't know about her. . . . I don't want to force myself on her, if she doesn't like me, but it's so hard to tell . . . even after weeks of trying to be just as good as she is, so she actually recognizes me, and trying to hide when I feel upset. I hate to feel jealous, but whenever I see her she's always surrounded by a crowd. At the show near home this summer, I ran when I saw her, I felt so ashamed.
>
> This term, she was separated from me in speech, and when I was asked if I minded, because my teacher had spent so long working out a complicated timetable, and because I didn't want to seem childish, I said I didn't mind, but really I could scream. I wish they . . . could see how they hurt me. I just smile—it's all I can do, but I really want to cry. Oh, please, please help me.

Well, I sent as supportive a letter as I could and months later got back a short note, saying in part, "I'm better friends now with them than ever before. It's not always perfect but I feel a lot better now. Thanks so much for all your help and advice. It was much easier when I felt someone was 'backing me.'"

Imagine being so insecure that you have to reach out to a total stranger, clear across an ocean, to ask for help. If I'd shown up on her doorstep the next morning instead of answering in a letter, she'd have been mortified. But I don't think that possibility ever occurred to her, because I don't think she was writing to me at all. She was writing to Stephanie Nordland, a character in a book. (Did I know or care about Louisa May Alcott years ago? Not a bit. Jo March was far more real.)

Books, novels, stories, are one way we can reach out to one another without losing face, one way of saying, "We are not alone, not in our fears, not in our hopes, not in our nightmares and not in our dreams."

A story that says that can be the best friend a young reader has. In a turbulent time of changes and choices, the characters in that story understand—and they never let you down. They're there whenever you need them; they don't smother you with attention when you don't need them. They never tell a living soul which parts of their story made you cry and which parts helped you laugh. And they give you the words to explain yourself to yourself, words such as those Jo March gave me, "I want to be special. I am going to be a writer." Words you can use to create your own life, to separate as an individual and to reconnect as a member of the human race.

No wonder young readers are the most loyal audience any writer could ever hope to have. As writer and reader, we act separately, but through the books, we connect. We become best friends.

Works Cited

Alcott, Louisa May. *Little Women.* New York: Knopf, 1968.

Asher, Sandy. *Daughters of the Law.* New York: Beaufort, 1980.

———. *Everything Is Not Enough.* New York: Delacorte, 1987.

———. *Just Like Jenny.* New York: Delacorte, 1982.

———. *Missing Pieces.* New York: Delacorte, 1984.

———. *Summer Smith Begins.* New York: Bantam, 1986.

———. *Things Are Seldom What They Seem.* New York: Delacorte, 1983.

The Problem with Realism

Sandy Asher

I was assigned a topic for today, "The Problem with Realism." It's been a long time since I was the assignee. As a teacher, I've grown accustomed to doing the assigning. Everything that follows, therefore, is Mike Angelotti's fault.

Well, I thought, what is the problem with realism? Simple! Every time you try to take a nap, the phone rings.

No, I reminded myself, that's the problem with reality. Realism is an entirely different thing. As we all know, bad things travel in threes, so before long, three problems with realism had cropped up: one for the writer, one for the reader, and one for the go-betweens who bring young people and literature together.

The Writer's Problem, or Truth Is Stranger Than Fiction

Incredible things happen in real life every day. Right here in Detroit, for instance, over 300 fires were set throughout the city the night before Halloween. And yet, no one wrote a review stating that October 30, unlike many of God's better days, was poorly constructed and unconvincing. The fires burned, we were convinced. Drop 300 unexplained fires into the middle of a novel, however, and see where that gets you. Even your own mother is likely to express doubt.

In real life, the more inexplicable the occurrence, the harder we work to compensate, to impose logic, to find meaning. This is, in fact, why we invented stories. Life, in case you haven't noticed yet, is generally chaotic. People in three-piece suits carry briefcases and dash around the world telling every one they're in charge, but they're not. Just when they think they've got it all together, someone shoots Mrs. Gandhi, or a child disappears without a trace, Mount Saint Helens blows its top, or we discover the last three things we ate, drank, and breathed cause cancer. We would go stark, raving mad, I think, if we had to deal with reality exactly as it comes. It's too hard, too fast, too overwhelming, and far too complex. Since the days of the cave dwellers, we have told and listened to stories as a

Reprinted from *The ALAN Review* 12.3, Spring 1985, pages 1–3, by permission of the author.

way of making life hold still long enough for us to make some sense of it. Myths, legends, folk tales, Bible stories and novels are all our way of biting off only as much as we can chew, and then chewing it over and over again in the hope of digesting it, coming to some conclusions about it and deciding where we fit in.

Stories impose order on the otherwise unbearable chaos of our lives. Fiction is not a luxury. It's an absolute, rock-bottom, sanity-preserving necessity.

And because it is, we demand of our writers that realism be more than a reflection of reality. Realism is an entirely different thing. It's an arrangement of the components of reality—people, places, events, ideas, and emotions—into patterns that facilitate analysis and understanding. Realism is an enriched reality that in turn enriches our lives. At least it should be. When it is not, writers face reviews. The Creator of reality does not.

The Reader's Problem, or "Whose Life Is This, Anyway?"

I read realistic fiction as a teenager, wanting to be entertained, of course, but also searching for answers to my questions about real life and for role models to pattern myself after. But the best a girl in those stories could hope for was to get a boyfriend and grow up to become a nurse. That was the best—more often than not, it was just get the boyfriend, with the clear implication that that was really all the growing up she'd ever need to do.

Those stories are back in fashion, I'm sorry to say, but fashions change, so I remain hopeful. Still, a thoughtful young reader today, one who has noticed, for instance, that a woman was recently nominated for vice president of the United States, could only look at these formula books and wonder, "Whose life is this, anyway?"

In the 1960s, writers of realism for young adults started dealing with other, perhaps more serious, issues facing teenagers: death, divorce, alcoholism, child abuse and so on. YA novels, like everything else at the time, became relevant. And then they became, perhaps, too relevant. If you were a voracious reader—and many are at that age—you got the distinct impression that if there were no dead, divorced, drunk child abusers in your family, you weren't normal somehow. Many, perhaps even most, of the young people reading out there were being left out of the picture. Readers, more often than not, are nice kids. They are the other statistic, the ones who are not doing whatever happens to be making the news. (For one thing, they're too busy reading!) And these very readers were being told they were too boring to write about. Hoping for books to cheer them on in their search for ways to lead decent, useful, and meaningful lives, for books that encouraged them to go with their own best instincts, they could only look around at many of the deadly serious novels available to them and wonder, "Whose life is this, anyway?"

It was in response to this need that I found my own place in young adult literature. I wanted to center my work on nice kids, not reverting to the simplistic stories of the past, but involving them, as characters and as readers, in complex, sometimes humorous, sometimes unpleasant examinations of reality. I wanted to draw them in, working from the familiar to the unfamiliar, and help them to understand that this life, strange though it may be at times, is truly their own. Not only is there a place for them in it, but much joy to be had, and work to be done.

This is not to suggest that all novels should be like mine. I've come up with one solution to what I perceived as a problem. For some, there is no problem; for others, there are different solutions. That's fine. I would ask only that realism be presented as a search for truth, rather than as an escape from it.

The Problem for Adults Who Lead Young People to Books, or "Read Two Books and Call Me in the Morning"

The problem with realism here is often the problem itself. Human beings were born to categorize: animal, vegetable, mineral, vertebrate, invertebrate, all of the above, none of the above, eenie, meenie, minee, and/or moe. And I grant it's a necessary tool for organizing the vast amount of material we must process in the course of a lifetime.

But can one honestly say of a novel, "this book is about death"; "this book is about learning disabilities"; "this book is about child abuse?" When teaching a unit on spiders, we might well read *Charlotte's Web* during story hour, but when teaching *Charlotte's Web* as literature, can we say, "It's a book about spiders?"

Would we suggest, as adult to adult, that Tolstoi's *War and Peace* is a book about war? Or a book about peace? Or even a book about war and peace? I think not. What good adult literature is about is its unforgettable characters, Natasha and Pierre, among others, the richness of their lives, the value and meaning of their existence.

Unfortunately, children's realistic novels are not only classified by problem, they are often also limited to problem. The "problem book" approach encourages some publishers and writers to produce quasi-novels in which stick figures act out an example of this year's sensational topic. It serves neither literature nor children well to have character development secondary to the life of the problem. Children do not want, need, or deserve watered-down literature any more than they want, need, or deserve watered-down life. Realism is an enriched reality; the problem book approach is reality—and realism—diminished.

Categorizing novels according to problems can also diminish the reader. Parent, teacher, and librarian, willing or not, are cast as bibliotherapists and encouraged to match subject matter to child: divorce to divorce, abuse to abuse, handicap to handicap. It is a well-intentioned effort to help children in trouble, but I fear it's misguided. Sometimes it helps. True. But sometimes anything helps, including chicken soup. Often as not, nobody really knows why.

Was it the book itself that helped; or was it the attention? It's powerful medicine to have an important adult care enough to say, "Here, I'd like to share this with you. It matters to me that you're unhappy." "It" could be a book or a Hershey bar. A little stroking does go a long way. I don't know about you, but when I'm depressed, a depressing book is about the last thing I want to read. Coming from the bedside of a dying friend or relative, for instance, I do not want to curl up with a book about a dying friend or relative. And, if by some chance, I do find myself in the company of such a book, I'm as likely to be offended by it as comforted. It may miss the mark and fail to do justice to my pain, or it may come too close to bear.

In the throes of making a disastrously poor decision about some aspect of my life, I am rarely open to learning about decision making. Afterward, maybe. Before might have been preferable. During the catastrophic maneuver, I am usually far too busy setting a career record for closed-mindedness, and no book is going to tell me what to do.

Maybe I'm unusual in this. Maybe children are more open to facing hard facts at difficult moments. I suspect not. One's timing, therefore, would have to be exquisite to match book, reader, and optimum moment for effectiveness.

More important, though, a child should not be categorized by problem any more than a novel should. There is far more to each, nuances of feeling and myriad reactions and interpretations, and that diversity must be respected. It is unfair to both child and book to reduce them to a formula: "Got a problem? Read two books and call me in the morning."

A lifetime reading habit, on the other hand, can build up a healthy resistance. Bruno Bettelheim, in his *Uses of Enchantment,* points out that fairy tales, through countless repetitions, stamp a pattern of success into our youthful minds. Characters with whom we can identify struggle and strive and try, try again until they succeed. And we learn, from glass mountains scaled and witches and ogres defeated, that whatever life demands of us, we can do.

No one expects fantasy to match reality, glass mountain to physical handicap, ogre to abusive parent. Fantasy doesn't lend itself to that as easily as realism. But, it still does important work. We learn, in a general way, the value of hope, determination, and effort toward a goal, and this becomes the foundation upon which we build our lives.

Bettleheim limits his theory to fantasy for the very young, but I believe realism for older readers has the same health-promoting properties. Bettelheim warns us that children should not be made aware of the effect this or that aspect of a story may be having on their psyches: "You think your mother's an old witch. That's why you enjoy 'Hansel and Gretel' so much!" The work must proceed subconsciously and at a steady, individual pace. The same could be said for realism. It can help, it can affect lives, but it works best when taken internally as a steady diet, and only rarely when applied externally as first aid.

"The Problem with Realism"—a negative topic by definition. Not being a negative person by nature, I prefer to turn it around and see all three problems as challenges: to the writer, a commandment to honor the best traditions of our craft; to the reader, an invitation to venture outside the familiar, the safe, and the all-too-often trite; and to the go-betweens, a call to a renewed commitment beyond expediency to the slow, careful, loving enrichment of entire lives through literature.

Hard work for all, but essential. Perhaps it's a good thing, after all, that in reality—and in realism, as well—every time we try to take a nap, the phone rings.

Sandy Asher Discusses Writing, Reading, and Teaching

Genny Cramer

Q: I'd like to begin with some questions for those of us in the classroom who are interested in promoting writing for our students. If you were to advise teachers about encouraging and developing children's writing, what would you suggest?

A: I would emphasize attitude. A positive attitude, an open, accepting, enthusiastic attitude is probably the most important thing. Many students I see at the college level have completely lost confidence in their ability to write creatively. What they're worrying about, of course, is getting the answer right. When there isn't any one right answer, they're at a loss for what to do. They respond very well to an atmosphere of acceptance: Whatever is inside of them to write about is valued because it's important to them; and, if it's important to them, it's important to me. I think that attitude is vital to encouraging children to write creatively.

Q: How do you suggest teachers provide mechanical corrections without intruding on students' creativity?

A: I try to have a separate time for my students to write for the sheer joy of it: to listen to what's going on in their own head, to watch it pour out onto a piece of paper and to have someone read it who's not going to criticize. There's plenty of time later for rewriting and proofing, and even then, only certain projects, chosen by the writers themselves. I firmly believe there's no interest in learning to do something better that's no fun to do in the first place. So I very much want to get students excited about their own writing. Then I think it follows naturally that they want to make it as good as it can be.

When I work with young children and we put out a journal, and I only have a short time with them, I do all the mechanical

Reprinted from *The ALAN Review* 15.1, Fall 1987, pages 44–46, 54, by permission of the author.

corrections when I type it up so they do not read back their own mistakes. I explain to them that when we share writing with other people we want it perfect, so I've had to make little changes here and there. If I had more time with those kids, after they'd decided what to share, I'd help them work on mechanics. But not every time they set pen to paper. It becomes an agony when they begin to see only spelling words and commas instead of their own thoughts.

Q: Are there some particular activities, procedures, or assignments you recommend elementary teachers use to help foster that joy of writing?

A: Oh, I think there are plenty of available idea starters and any that the teacher can honestly get excited about would be useful. Kids can tell when you're doing an activity by rote and when you're doing it with some enthusiasm yourself. Anything you find truly appealing can be used. One that I use frequently begins: "You're on a bus and you overhear only one line of a conversation between two people: 'I'll never forgive you as long as I live.' Who are these people? What has led up to this point? What is going to happen next?" I've had good luck with that with a lot of different age groups, so I love doing it, seeing what new responses turn up.

Q: Could you estimate how much class time is needed by a teacher who wants to provide time when children are writing for the joy of writing?

A: It depends on the age group and on the kids themselves. When I was working with gifted children in Summerscape (a summer program in Springfield, Missouri), they could easily write for an hour at a time. With other children, twenty minutes is about all they can handle. I think it's probably just as well to stop a little too soon than to have it drag on too long. If you get them started and interested, they'll go back to it. Many times, I've seen notebooks and pencils carted to the lunchroom or out to recess.

Q: Should this kind of writing be a daily activity?

A: Again, it would depend on the kids. You don't want to turn it into a chore. It might be something you do two or three times a week so that it stays special, or once or twice a semester for extended blocks of time.

Q: Is there anything else along the line of journals or books that teachers might take advantage of to promote writing?

A: Kids love to read what they've written and what their classmates have written, so I've always tried to finish up with something in print that they could keep and refer back to. I've seen lovely poems and short prose pieces done on poster board with illustrations. When

I was in school I made up plays and my teachers let me rehearse them with my friends and perform for the class. Any chance to show off is great. It feels good, knowing that someone cares enough about what you've written to shine a spotlight on it.

Q: How did your teachers influence you in your early writing?

A: To this day, I still see them standing over my desk smiling down at me, at what I'm doing. They were very approving and very caring. They knew that I liked to write, and they'd find ways all day long for me to do it. I'm sure I was one of those kids who finished the regular work earlier than anyone else. I can remember one teacher handing me an African folk tale and saying, "Could you make this into a play for the class?" So, I did. The day of the play, my friends and I were all decked out in costumes, ready to go, and I made this huge relief map of Africa. The principal walked into the room, looked at the map, and said, "You misspelled Tanganyika." I was devastated! That's all I remember about the entire day. I had left the "y" out of Tanganyika. With any creative act, your heart is right on the line. You've created this thing, you're all excited about it, and you're vulnerable. And he just came out with this sledgehammer! Most of my teachers, however, saw what was important to me and made sure I knew it was important to them, too; they drew it out.

Q: When did you realize that you wanted to be a writer?

A: At birth! I was always writing. I think I must've actually realized I was "a writer" when I read *Little Women.* When Jo said she wanted to be something special, I knew I wanted to be something special, too. She chose to write; I was already writing; our fates were sealed. Later, I married a professor, just as she did!

Q: Were there other writers or books that you can recall as having important shaping influences for you?

A: Peter and Wendy. All Louisa May Alcott's books. Any fairy tale by anybody, any time, and all the Oz books. Later, Salinger's *Catcher in the Rye* and Blume's *Are You There, God? It's Me, Margaret,* because of the honesty—and humor!—they brought to the concerns of young people.

Q: Why have you chosen young adults and children as your audience?

A: I didn't start out thinking I was writing for adults. A friend read several of my poems and said, "Do you realize there's a child or a reference to childhood in every poem you've written?" I was totally unconscious of it. But at that point I began to realize—well, maybe I have a special affinity for childhood. I was writing plays for adults until I saw another friend performing in a children's play. I had never seen live theater for children, and these kids in the audience were jumping out of their seats, screaming and laughing, booing and cheering. I thought, "this has got to be the most wonderful fun in the world." And that's how I started writing children's plays.

Every time I think of a story, the child's viewpoint of whatever's happening interests me much more than any of the adult viewpoints. When I first tried writing a novel, the voice that came out was the voice of a teenage girl. So it chose me.

Q: How do you begin a new book?

A: First, I eat everything I can get my hands on. And when I can't find anything left to eat, I clean the whole house. What haunts me, though, even as I avoid the issue in every way I possibly can, is a very clear feeling about a conflict and how I want to resolve it, so I have the beginning and the end. I spend a lot of time thinking about who this is going to happen to, who the characters are, and that often changes the plot, the conflict, and the ending.

Q: Do you complete an outline before you begin writing?

A: Yes. I let the idea simmer for a long time, partly because that's a good thing to do and partly because I'm too lazy to start. It eventually reaches the point where I really cannot hold it back anymore. "I've got to do something with this or it's gonna drive me crazy." That's when I sit down, write the outline and begin my five pages a day.

Q: At the height of the writing you're doing, when you're past the simmering point and you're into a schedule, about how many hours a day are you writing?

A: Usually, I do about three hours of actual typing each morning in my office, then I'm stiff and sore and tired of staring at the print. There's no way of knowing how much time I spend writing in my head, though, while I'm washing dishes and driving the car and so on. I do an awful lot of mental juggling of what I've written or what I want to do the next day.

Q: How many drafts do you generally write?

A: I do a lot of rewriting, a lot. I rewrite each day's work the next day before doing the next five pages. The I'll go through the whole thing at least half a dozen times. When it gets to the point where I've lost all objectivity, I type a clean copy and give it to my husband, Harvey. Then he makes suggestions, and I rewrite it all again. If it gets past him, it goes to New York. Then, of course, my editors have suggestions and I may rewrite another two or three times between the contract and the time the book goes into production. Fortunately, the rewriting is the part I like best. First drafts are the killers.

Q: What advice would you have for aspiring writers?

A: Read. And write. A lot. Someone said you have to write a million rotten words before you can write any good ones, so you have to get your million rotten words out of the way. Write the kinds of things you enjoy reading. If you like mysteries, try mysteries. If you like realistic fiction with humor—that's what I do—that's probably what you ought to be writing. And don't give up. But I don't think I need to mention that. The ones who are really interested won't. The rest probably should!

Q: Why?

A: There's a good chance your work will never be published. Much of what is published is quickly forgotten.

Q: How do you deal with the frustration?

A: A friend who writes once said that if he ever finally got a book published, he'd want to win an award; and then when he'd won an award, he'd want the Pulitzer, and if he got the Pulitzer, he'd want the Nobel Peace Prize, and if he got that, he still wouldn't be happy. That was really kind of frightening, to think you could work hard all your life, get to your deathbed, and still feel you'd never "made it." The truth is, you're not likely to become rich and famous. But there is one guarantee: You can spend every day of your life doing something you love doing. Interesting enough, about the time I reached that understanding, I sold my first book. It must've been a point where I matured both as a person and a writer.

Q: Do you want to say anything about censorship?

A: Yes. I'd like to have my work on any list of censored books available, because it's a sure way of getting them read. It's wonderful publicity.

Seriously, for the first time ever, with my latest book, my publisher asked me to soften the language. It really upset me because when other writers have complained about that sort of pressure, I've always been able to say, "My publisher has never asked me to do that." It's dangerous to let a very small minority of people who are agitating have such a big influence. Now, I'm all for them agitating. They can carry on all they want, and I will defend to the death their right to do so. I do think they keep the pendulum from swinging too far toward easy vulgarity, which just weakens our vocabularies. Being aware of opposition doesn't hurt. It keeps us honest. But bending to it out of fear alarms me. Are there teaching activities teachers should avoid? I recently heard that in one high school students were assigned to read the first and last chapters of *The Scarlet Letter* and were then shown the movie. I was horrified. Seeing a movie has nothing to do with reading a book. I would rather have those kids read just about any book in the world even if it's not a classic, for the experience of reading a book, that very special pleasure.

Reading requires you to do at least 50 percent of the work. You have to imagine the story; you have to bring yourself to it and participate. You "do" a book; a movie or TV show is "done unto you." The experience of reading a book should be kept whole and treasured for the unique thing that is.

That applies also to censorship, to the idea of putting warnings on books to rate them like movies. When a kid watches a movie, she or he sees, in vivid color and with stereophonic sound, an adult representation of sex or violence or whatever. There is nothing in a book but words. A child can only interpret those words according to previous knowledge and experience. Where an adult reader forms an adult's mental representation, a child is likely to form a simplified image, or to dismiss whole passages as meaningless.

A child can also close a book and put it away if she or he feels threatened by or not ready to deal with what's in it. She or he can reread or stop and ask questions. The child is in control. Children are bigger than books. A movie screen's a lot bigger than a child, and the action keeps coming, ready or not.

Q: Is there anything else you would like to say to teachers?

A: Keep reading to kids. It may well be that nobody else is. Stay aware of what they're being exposed to in the media, and provide them with alternatives. If they're overdosing on *Rambo,* read them books with antiwar themes, so that they have a balance. Give them other viewpoints, new ways of looking at things; choose nonstereotypical material.

My biggest disappointment with children's book clubs is that they've gone so much toward movie and TV spinoffs. And posters—kittens and puppies and ducks. As my kids grew older, it seemed there were fewer and fewer "real" books being offered, serious books. The rationale is, "This is what the kids want; this is what they'll buy." I think a teacher might use reading aloud time best to give them what they don't yet know they want. That's what teaching is all about, isn't it?

Part II About Young Adult Literature

26 Twenty Years of YA Books: The Publisher's View

Laurel Barnard
Jean Feiwel
Marilyn Kriney

Laurel Barnard of Bantam Books

When I received the word that one of the topics of the ALAN Workshop at the 1987 Annual Convention of the National Council of Teachers of English in Los Angeles was to address the best, the worst, the past, the present, and the future in the field of young adult books during the past twenty years, it seemed particularly propitious. The media had been full of coverage of events celebrating the 1960s. At Bantam, we too were focusing on those volatile times as the result of two events. The first was the fall 1987 publication of Todd Gitlin's Bantam book, *The Sixties, Years of Hope, Days of Rage.* Coincidentally, we were reminded of the decade and its uniqueness in a way that was very special for us in the departments that deal with YA books. For March 1988 marks the twentieth anniversary of the publication in hardcover of Paul Zindel's *The Pigman*—a true milestone.

I began to think about the longevity of the great YA novels, the true classics of the genre and how they have endured. *The Pigman,* for example, was published originally an age away from today, light years ago, it seems. In April 1968 up to a million college and high school students took part in a national student strike in an antiwar gesture, Todd Gitlin reminds us in *The Sixties.* Martin Luther King, Jr. and Robert Kennedy were assassinated that year. The accepted dress of the day was miniskirts, bell-bottoms, love beads and head bands. *The Pigman* was published before Kent State, before Woodstock, before man made history on the moon. It was well before MTV, Sting, and AIDS. And, *The Pigman* helped to alter the complexion of

Reprinted from *The ALAN Review* 15.3, Spring 1988, pages 48–51, by permission of the author.

what young adults would read indefinitely. Now, twenty years and lots of history, trends, milestones, and school graduating classes later, it is still being read, taught, felt, and enjoyed by so many.

Besides providing the backlist mainstay of a publishing company's YA list and hopefully finding a niche in the classroom, these true classics are also part of the foundation on which what is new has been built. A *Horn Book* editor, librarian, educator, luminary, Ethel Heins has written, "One of the striking aspects of the books published for children and young adults during the past ten years is that so many of the observable trends were logical and emphatic continuations of what had begun in the mid-1960s." She goes on to say that although in the 1950s the unpleasantries of life were not ignored, the stress was most certainly on "traditional good taste." A real revolution came with the onset of the '60s. In a sentence that may seem to capture the essence of '60s YA literature for some, Heins names the all too familiar and almost laughable litany of problems that the YA novels of the era tackled and that faced those woeful characters:

> What with the social upheaval and the preoccupation with popular psychology, the writers' eager acceptance of liberated subject matter and emancipated vocabulary generated an explosion of fiction dealing with alcoholism, child abuse, death, divorce, drugs, murder, psychotic patients, suicide, teenage pregnancy—with or without abortion—and various diseases, from anorexia nervosa to cancer, until it appeared that adolescents were indeed suffering all "the heartaches and the thousand natural shocks that flesh is heir to."

Then came the 1970s. In an *English Journal* article, Stephen Tchudi talked about his tenure as *English Journal* editor and wrote, "There was steady interest in literature during the '70s too, particularly in student-centered and individualized reading programs. These developments were perhaps best represented by the cover of the February 1974 *English Journal* showing a kid in sneakers and bell-bottom jeans engrossed in a paperback book."

Now it is the 1980s with a new decade ahead. Has the tide turned away from the trends of the '60s? Has enough grief been heaped upon those hapless, catastrophe-prone characters? Some think so. According to *The Writer Magazine,* at a meeting of the Children's Book Committee of the Authors Guild in 1987, "children's librarians and booksellers revealed that problem novels dealing with divorce, drugs, disease, and other weighty social issues are declining in popularity."

This past September marked the launch at Bantam of a new hardcover imprint called "Starfire Hardcover Books." Perhaps this list helps to represent, in part, the face of young adult literature today. It is an eclectic and diverse list. It is not a list of "fluff," nor is it one of "problem" novels. Rather it is what we like to call "intelligent entertainment." Humor and fact-based historical novels. Books about teens facing peer pressure dealing with adults, making decisions. The drama of the family of a teenager who leaves home one afternoon and never returns. The humor of a group of boys who belong to a nonclub of self-proclaimed "obnoxious jerks."

Since young adult literature is an indicator and reflector of the times, it is interesting to speculate about what factors will impact the future of the genre. A recent article in *NEA Today,* written by Jane Power and called, "The Generation Zap," focuses on the "baby boom" generation who are now ages 24 to 42 and number 70 million. The article notes that the baby boomers' values are influencing the shape of the public schools as their children fill the nation's classrooms. Power goes on to say that the boomers as parents are older than the generation that came before, they're twice as likely to have gone to college, they make high demands for their children's education and although they want to help their children do well, they have little time to devote to that cause. "In 1986, more than 60 percent of youngsters aged six to 17 had mothers in the job market." Last year more than a fourth of U.S. families and more than a third of U.S. children—that's 8.8 million families with 23 million children, cites the article—were headed by a single person, usually a woman. The article concludes by stating,

> Just as American childhood still bears the changes stamped on it by the millions of boomers in their passage, so American parenthood will likely never be quite the same as before the baby boom generation changed the country, and families along with it. Fewer children, new family structures, high expectations, tight schedules—they may not all be permanent, but today they're the forces shaping the parents of tomorrow.

It will be fascinating to see what the children and teenagers of baby-boom parents who are being taught by baby-boom educators—who read *The Pigman* as teenagers themselves—will be reading in the future and what other myriad societal influences will impact young adult literature and become a topic for discussion at ALAN 2007.

Jean Feiwel of Scholastic, Inc.

Twenty years ago I was fourteen years old. At that time I was more interested in getting my hair stick straight with an iron than in spending time in bookstores or libraries. So I can't tell you about the history of YA publishing with the wisdom of two decades. I can speak confidently, but mostly personally about the last ten, and what I don't know, as my little brother used to say, I can make up.

As I was mulling over the highs and lows of what I've seen over the years, I found it could best be summed up by Charles Dickens when he wrote, "It was the best of times. It was the worst of times." Isn't it fitting that any discussion of YA books has an ambivalence about it? Or at least any overview that I'm going to give you. Because rather than be historical or academic, I've chosen to highlight some of my own highs and lows in publishing as a way, of course, of giving you a picture of YA books then and now.

To start, let me give you a thumbnail evolution of young adult books, beginning when I had graduated from the sophistication of straightening my hair by using gunk that smelled like rotten eggs to blissfully (and finally) cutting it short. The year was 1972. It was the time of the teenage problem novel. A time of a candor about the difficulties adolescents had growing up. Books could be about divorce, sex, pregnancy, drinking, or drugs. Interestingly, for all their honesty about addressing the realities of teenage life, the books were thinly disguised morality tales. The genre was best exemplified by the grandmommy of them all—*Go Ask Alice.* Alice, who started out as a well-meaning teenager, took a wrong turn somewhere and spiraled down into a loose life of drug abuse. She had the good sense to die at the end of this "true"story, and as the back of the book cover said, "You can't ask Alice anything, anymore." Now I'm not sure if this is the high point (you'll excuse the expression) or a low point. Let's say it was a turning point because the material uncovered by this genre of bookmaking would lead better writers to the same ground. But when authors like Norma Klein or Judy Blume or S. E. Hinton are writing about the problems of teenage life the focus is not so much on the issue as on the characters. The turmoil of the sixties led to the honesty and realism of the seventies which led to a surprising (and yet not new) genre of teenage novel. Some critics speculate that the origination of the teen romance was simply an outgrowth of what publishers had been doing so successfully in their adult books. Others say it was a backlash to the realistic fiction that was painting too grim a picture for readers to enjoy. I think it was simply a recognition that books for young adults couldn't be limited to one kind of fiction. While teens recognized and responded to themselves as depicted in the work of Mazer, Cormier, Peck, and Zindel, there was also within those readers and in another segment of the population teens who didn't spend a lot of time in libraries or bookstores but would read something if it seemed to speak to them.

There is one very significant factor that galvanized the sales of the teen romance and YA books in general. It was the decision of the B. Dalton Bookseller chain, at that time some three hundred stores strong, to separate YA books out from the children's book section in their outlets. This meant that YA books would have their own section of the store, their own merchandising campaigns, special promotions built around books and/or authors, and for the first time a bestseller list to track sales in this marketplace. This was a revolutionary concept, and the sales soared. What was gratifying at that time, which began in 1979 or so, was that individual titles by individual authors—a book by Harry Mazer or Julian Thompson—could sell as strongly as a teen romance. Young adults who never spent time in bookstores took to hanging around their sections in the B. Dalton stores. Of course many of the stores were situated in the local malls so it was a perfect location to attract the YA audience. And attract them they did. There is research to support that the teenage population in the early eighties was at a swell, but even so, no one said that they had to be in bookstores.

Waldenbooks followed the lead of Dalton's identification of the YA market, but their merchandising strategy always favored the romance over the individual title. They felt it was more cost effective to promote many books in a series rather than a single title. And when you're dealing with low price tags like $1.95, you can see (but maybe not agree with) their approach.

This move by B. Dalton I consider the most important high in YA books. At that time I was the editorial director at Avon Books. And there I had created a YA imprint called Flare. It was not only a heady time in terms of the sales of books, but it was an exciting time in terms of publishing. At Avon I began publishing original paperbacks by authors who were well known and unknown, and the results were probably the most satisfying in my career. A highlight of the list was Norma Fox Mazer's *Taking Terri Mueller.* It was the first and I believe only time Norma would be published first in paperback. She took a leap of faith when she signed with me. The book sold very well, and it went on to win the California Young Readers Medal and the Edgar Mystery Award.

Julian Thompson's *The Grounding of Group 6* was my personal best. I will never forget the editorial meeting where I presented that title to our esteemed board. I explained that the book was just about these parents who wanted to kill their teenage kids, and so they sent them to this boarding school to be exterminated. And I said the book was sort of funny, too. I'll give them all a lot of credit. They let me buy that book and publish it. And Avon's first printing was 105,000 copies. The book went on to establish Julian as the brilliant and unconventional writer he is.

Last, on my own list, and noteworthy not for its sales but for other things that happened to it was a manuscript that came to me under the title "Black Girl in a Manger." I thought, this book is going nowhere with this title; but you know what, that book was so good that maybe even if we hadn't changed the title to *Marked By Fire,*

Joyce Carol Thomas would have won the American Book Award for Children's fiction. The book was also named an Outstanding Book of the Year by *The New York Times*—a first for a YA paperback original.

My point is that sales weren't the only part of the burgeoning of YA fiction. There *was* an American Book Award for children's fiction. It doesn't exist today. *The New York Times* did single out a paperback original to review and highlight. Authors could be published effectively in a paperback original format. I don't think that's true today.

What happened? Well, it's like I said at the opening of these notes, the best of times led to the worst of times. Maybe not at the same time, but one can lead to the other.

While Avon was developing Flare, Scholastic created Wildfire, Bantam Sweet Dreams, Silhouette First Love and the teen romance industry was born. Then every publisher in creation decided to get into the YA book business, and that's when trouble started. The book chains had made their YA sections very profitable, but they began to be wary of the multitude of series starting every hour. They also began to intrude their opinions in the creation of the covers of the books—and some went so far as to suggest book and series ideas. If a chain skipped one of your titles because they didn't like the cover, you could lose so much business that you were inclined to change the cover. This is a period I call the tail wagging the dog, and it's very much in operation today. But I can't blame B. Dalton and Walden for becoming somewhat tyrannical in their buying practices. I blame us, the publishers. I think we started looking at books from the outside in. It was not only the covers, but the "series" idea which the chains had always found easier to merchandise that took hold with a vengeance in 1984. Sweet Valley High has got to be one of the smartest concepts to come down the pike, but it spawned such a glut of low-level imitations, and involved a whole lot of publishers who were only in it for a fast buck, that the face of publishing seems forever changed.

Many books seem little more than covers wrapped around ideas that aren't very well written. I think there are better series and worse series. I wish people could tell the difference. What the proliferation of the series has done is to really fill the bookstores with category books, and leave not as much room any more for those single titles by people like Klein, Brancato, Bridgers, Ellen White—or whomever. This is a low point for the paperback.

When I went to Scholastic in 1983, I knew the days of publishing paperback originals as a means of getting the attention for the writers that they deserved were over. And as I'm learning the ropes of hardcover publishing, I'm hoping that by the time the books get out in the world in paperback, they'll be armed with the review attention and the word of mouth that will help them on their way in the fiercely competitive paperback market.

When Scholastic published Julian Thompson's *A Band of Angels* in hardcover in 1966, it met the same kind of controversial reviews his previous books had endured. So it was especially gratifying when the novel was named an ALA Best Book for Young Adults. Somehow the teenage readers had gotten their message through. Because it was not the librarians who wanted that book on the list, it was the young adult readers. And in the same way it's not the buyers at B. Dalton or Walden whom we should be appealing to; again it's the teenage readers. Whether we reach them through teachers or librarians, I know they're out there. I just hope we can hear them. And I hope we as publishers listen to what they have to tell us.

Marilyn Kriney of HarperCollins Junior Books

I'm going to start off by making two points about low points. The first is a personal low point: the day I ran out of books to read in the children's room. How did I know? I walked the fiction shelves from A to Z and couldn't find a single book I wanted to read that I hadn't already read. I was graduated to the adult room, where I found books like *Gone with the Wind, Pride and Prejudice,* and *The Good Earth.* But I was eleven years old, and I also wanted more of Mary Stolz and Maureen Daly and Jean Webster and—I admit it—Cherry Ames, student nurse. There simply weren't any more books like that. So you won't catch me dwelling much on the low points in young adult literature over the past twenty years or so. I think the true low point came earlier, in the years before there were books for teenagers.

For some years, and even now, I think, a favorite low point has been the problem novel. Conventional wisdom tells us it is dead. But what are we saying? What is a book without a problem? It's the Sears catalog and the telephone book. We're really saying a particular form of the young adult novel is looking shopworn. I happen to think this is true. There have been too many books on divorce, suicide, hopelessly insensitive step-parents, and so on, written with what appears to be very little in the way of spirit or commitment.

There was a program recently on public television about the evolution of rock and roll. Pat Boone said he didn't really want to record a song whose lyrics made no sense. But his manager talked him into it and naturally they both made a lot of money. There he was on the screen singing "Tutti Frutti" with the joy and the conviction of a rag doll. And there was Little Richard, the song's creator, not being overly serious about it, but singing the same nonsense lyrics with all his heart and soul. And the song made perfect sense.

Perhaps the half-hearted air of some problem novels comes from their being written to fill a perceived demand in the marketplace, not out of conviction or passion or playfulness. I don't know.

Still, we should be careful not to throw out the baby with the bathwater. Mediocrity isn't unique to the "problem novel." It can infect books of all sorts. So when I think about low points, I'm more comfortable doing so on a book-by-book basis. As an editor, I worry that if I become categorical about what I'm dismissing—oh, no, not another book on that subject—I'm probably just about to overlook the most authentic, most endearing, most illuminating book on teenage pregnancy ever written.

The high points? Well, I'm going to be sweeping about this. By my lights, it's the very existence of the splendid body of young adult literature that has grown up over the past twenty years. People sometimes say young adult literature isn't a legitimate form. That by the time a child is twelve or thirteen he or she should be reading adult books. I suspect their adolescence was different from mine. Being a teenager is not at all like being a child, and I am very grateful adolescence is not a model for adulthood. It's a unique and tumultuous time. It's a period of doubts and fears, of joy, of a fierce and sometimes overwhelming need to sort out where one stands, as an individual, in relation to one's peers, to the larger world, ethically, emotionally.

It is, of course, true that many books published for adults find a large audience among teenagers. But that hardly diminishes the importance of writers like Robert Cormier, S. E. Hinton, M. E. Kerr, Robert Lipsyte, Norma Fox Mazer, Harry Mazer, Katherine Paterson, Richard Peck, Laurence Yep, and Paul Zindel. The explosive popularity of their books is the best evidence of the needs they fill in the lives of adolescents. I have always wished as publishers we could find a way to market these books to adults. Simply because the best books are books for all ages, and to pigeonhole them is to deny what makes them excellent—their universality.

Where are we headed? I'm going to address the question by singling out several books. Each of them a high point in the recent literature. The writers are all exciting new voices published for the first time within the past three years. I admit to a bias: three of the four are Harper authors. Their work, I think, represents very well the great vitality and originality of young adult fiction today.

Bruce Brooks. His first novel, *The Moves Make the Man,* was a 1985 Newbery Honor Book. His second novel, *Midnight Hour Encores,* is about a journey, literally and figuratively, as Sibilance T. Spooner, a prodigiously talented cellist, and the father who has raised her travel cross-country to meet the mother who, in the throes of the sixties, gave her up at birth. It's not possible to encompass the richness of this or any of the books I'll be mentioning, so I've chosen to focus briefly on one or two of the qualities that give each book its distinction.

Two things about *Midnight Hour Encores:* First, the characterization of Sib is breathtakingly articulate, full of energy and daring and conviction, cunning, indecently self-assured, arrogant, impatient of the flaws of others. There is something extraordinarily liberating in this portrait of a young woman who is not altogether likeable, but who is so fully and unabashedly herself. Second, the relationship between Sib and her father is as one reviewer stated, "one of the finest father/daughter portraits in all of young adult literature." At first Taxi seems to be a bit of a whimp—overindulgent and dominated by his daughter. But gradually the truth emerges. Unconventional, generous, and selflessly loving, in a sense the embodiment of all that is fine about the sixties, Taxi has given Sib the freedom to be. He has a kind of strength we don't value nearly enough in this world and which this book compels us to consider. In the end, Sib takes a decisive step into adulthood, shedding that quintessentially adolescent conviction that she has raised herself and recognizing how deeply responsible her father is for who she is. A greatly rewarding book.

Brock Cole, whose novel *The Goats* describes the developing relationship of two outcasts, teenagers, a boy and a girl, who are left naked and without food on an island. Their fellow campers have decided they are oddball enough to be the victims of the annual practical joke. At first the two of them are paralyzed with embarrassment and rejecting of each other. Nonetheless, they decide to make a risky escape and run away from camp, and soon they start to rely on each other. The relationship that emerges is based on nothing less than profound kindness, respect, playfulness, love, a mutual concern for the well-being of people outside the relationship. Cole portrays it with such simple truth and "raging tenderness" (to use his own phrase) that one wants to cheer for the insight and example it offers to teenagers.

Pam Conrad. Her award-winning first novel, *Prairie Songs,* was a 1985 Best Book for Young Adults. A stunning book, it is set in Nebraska near the turn of the century. The story is about Louisa, a young girl, who comes to see her life in a new light when a fragile young woman from the East comes to town. Louisa is enchanted by Emmeline, who treasures books and poetry and beautiful things. But in the end the rigors of prairie life are too much for her. Emmeline loses her grip on reality and finally dies. She leaves behind for Louisa not only a love of books, but an even deeper appreciation for Louisa's own sturdy family—her hardworking, homely, nurturing family—and for the harshness of the land she's always loved.

The book is a kind of unsparing love song to life on the Nebraska prairie, and in a way, it asks us as readers to look with a fresh eye at our frontier past. It is an extraordinary evocation of the demands the life made on people and the physical and emotional ruggedness of those who survived it.

Bruce Stone. His first novel, *Half Nelson, Full Nelson,* published in 1985, was also an ALA Best Book. On the surface it's a fast-paced and zany entertainment about a boy who kidnaps his bratty younger sister and has a run-in with the FBI. But there's an important subtext here. Yes, the hero's father is a clown. He wears a leopard-spotted strongman's suit and wrestles alligators for a living—Gator Man, he's called.

So significant is he in the social order, the family lives in a rundown trailer camp in the tackiest part of the state. But Nelson loves his father dearly, and he'll do anything—go to jail if he must—to get him back together with Nelson's mom. Adolescents can be terribly embarrassed by their parents. I think it's part of their biological program. One of the things this book reminds us of is that what's valuable in a relationship has very little to do with surface appearances.

Other new voices to look out for in the future. *Elizabeth Frank,* whose first novel *Cooder Cutlass,* Harper published last year. She's all of twenty-four-years-old and a very promising writer.

Julie Reece Deaver, whose graceful and moving first novel, *Say Goodnight, Gracie,* will come out this spring under the Charlotte Zolotow imprint. And *Thelma Hatch Wyss,* whose young adult novel *Here at the Scenic-Vu Motel,* manages to be funny and substantive and clean and wholesome. No one swears, for goodness sake. And I swear it's not dull!

Works Cited

Gitlin, Todd. *The Sixties, Years of Hope, Days of Rage.* New York: Bantam, 1987.

Heins, Ethel. "A Decade of Children's Books: A Reviewer's Response." *Newbery and Caldecott Medal Books 1976–1985, The Horn Book* 1987. Rpt. *Trends in Children's Book Publishing: Editors' Views.* Ed. Linda Fein Abby. *Catholic Library World* (September/October 1987).

Power, Jane. "The Generation Zap." *NEA Today* (November 1987).

Tchudi, Stephen. "Lessons from the Decades: Former *EJ* Editor Speaks." *English Journal* (September 1987).

The Writer Magazine. (December 1987).

Rural Youth: The Forgotten Minority

Lin Buswell

Throughout much of the history of the United States, this nation has had a predominantly rural population consisting of farmers, hunters, trappers, and small-town business people. When the country was young, many went west to reap the abundant harvest of furs. Later the Homestead Acts lured many families west in search of better land at cheap prices and the chance for a brighter future for their children. For that early rural population, life meant uncertainty and constant struggle. Those who survived long winters, plagues of grasshoppers, violent spring and summer storms that destroyed months of work in minutes, and the loneliness became as tough and resilient as the land on which they lived. That independent breed who worked the land and loved its changeability learned to respect and adapt to the fickleness of nature, to make an ally of the potentially hostile force.

Although only a small percentage of our population still lives and works in the country, rural culture is stubbornly alive in the United States. Ignorance about this culture was revealed by an item in the *Cedar Rapids Gazette* (March 18, 1982):

> **POLICE LEARN RURAL TERMS**
>
> PLAINFIELD, Ind. (AP)—Police could have trouble tracking down a dozen missing barrows if they don't know they're looking for a neutered male hog and not a wheelbarrow.
>
> So David Wantz is developing a course on rural crime for the police.

The article went on to give examples and explain how police could be more effective in combatting rural crime by being more knowledgeable about rural life.

This blindness to our rural heritage is not restricted, of course, to police matters. It can be found in most aspects of our modern existence, English classrooms included. It is small wonder that one of my

Reprinted from *The ALAN Review* 11.2, Winter 1984, pages 12–14, by permission of the author.

students commented that "nobody writes books about people like me." To this student the world of subways, elevated trains, taxis, highrises, and multicultural populations is as strange as the world of feedlots and confinement sheds is to city youth.

In response to students' requests for books with a rural setting, I began to search. Robert Newton Peck's *A Day No Pigs Would Die* was the only piece of quality writing, with which I was familiar, that had a rural setting. Knowing there must be more out there somewhere, I looked through card catalogues and such reference books as *The Junior High School Library Catalogue* (4th ed. H. W. Wilson, 1980) and *The High School Library Catalogue* (11th ed. H. W. Wilson, 1977). What I found was both enlightening and disheartening. It appears that this is one minority group that has not claimed a great deal of attention lately. The findings are as follows:

1. Over 50% of the books with a rural setting take place before 1900. (This is not surprising since the big drop in rural population occurred after 1900.)
2. Most books that have a rural setting have an animal as a focal point. (Students often tend to lose interest in animal stories after age twelve.)
3. Of those books taking place after 1900, most take place during the Depression and during the 1940s. (The present generation of authors were growing up during this period.)
4. Most books with a rural setting for the older adolescent have a female protagonist.
5. The Ozark Mountains area appears to be fertile ground for novels about rural life.
6. None of the books with a rural setting describes farming as it is in the Plains states today. (None mention such equipment as tractors whose dual wheels dwarf a large man and are equipped with stereo cassette players, air-conditioning, and power steering; equipment that can plant, cultivate, or harvest sixteen rows of crops in a single pass; modern scientific farming methods such as minimum tillage or contour plowing.)

The bibliography at the end of this article concentrates on books set after 1900 without an animal as the main focal point. The novels listed were chosen for their probable appeal to adolescents. For the most part, they tend to deal with an adolescent who is moving into adulthood and trying to establish a personal value system.

Three of the novels offer sensitive portrayals of rural adolescents struggling to find their places in a changing and predominantly urban society. Although Mildred Walker's *Winter Wheat*, Lynn Hall's *The Leaving*, and Luke Wallin's *The Redneck Poacher's Son* take place in markedly different contexts, each realistically recreates the tie to the land experienced by rural youth and the pull exerted on them to leave the rural areas for a "better life." Despite the fact that these novels are set in rural America, the themes of search for self-identity, self-worth, and values have universal appeal.

Winter Wheat is the lyrical story of Ellen Webb, who had grown up on a Montana dry-land wheat ranch. In 1940 Ellen graduated from high school. Because the year's crop had been good, her parents, Anna, a Russian war bride, and Ben, an educated Easterner, decided to send her to Minneapolis for a year of college. Until Ellen met Gil, a senior from Minneapolis, she was homesick. Although life in the city frightened Ellen, she felt that she could be happy there with Gil. Only after Gil's visit to her home in Montana, did she know that their backgrounds were too different. Gil could not see the stark beauty and the goodness of life in Montana. Ellen allowed him to leave without a word, knowing that he would never return:

> The kernels shelled out of the sheaf when you rubbed them. They tasted sweet and hard between your teeth, the way life should taste to you in the morning when you wake up and at noon when you're hungry and again at night when you're through for the day—only mine didn't, I thought, and spit the grain out of my mouth.

For Ellen life revolved around the ranch and the life cycle of the tough winter wheat.

Once Gil left, Ellen began to look at her parents and her home through Gil's eyes. She saw the barren loneliness of the land, the impoverished existence. Her parents appeared to her as two bitter people who had learned to tolerate each other from a sense of duty. Only after she began teaching at an isolated school near Prairie Butte, did she start to see the nature and depth of her parents' relationship. It was a relationship that needed few words and little demonstration of affection, but one that was strong and durable from hardship.

After coming to terms with her loss of Gil and her negligence in the death of one of her students during a blizzard, Ellen was able to think of going on with her life. Because of what the school board thought was an illicit affair between Ellen and Warren Harper, the father of one of her students, the board dismissed her. Since Ellen had been close to the motherless Harper boy and his father had enlisted, she returned home with the boy and, for the first time, she saw the strength and love of her parents. Her mother explained: "We get mad, sure! Like ice an' snow an' thunder an' lightning storm, but they don't hurt the wheat in the ground." The conflict that Ellen felt between choosing a life on a ranch and a life in the city allowed her to change and to grow into a woman who understood that "it takes cold and snow and dryness to make the best wheat" or people or relationships.

Like *Winter Wheat,* Lynn Hall's short but powerful book *The Leaving* offers strong characterizations of the people in a small rural Iowa family and the relationship between Thora and Cletus Armstrong and their daughter Roxanne. Thora married Cletus Armstrong during World War II when she was running the farm alone for her aging parents. Because the farm needed a man, big-boned Thora married the first man who drifted through and offered her marriage. Cletus wanted to be his own boss on a place of his own. Unfortunately, Cletus knew little about good farm operation.

After several years Cletus forced Thora to move to Waterloo, a larger town, where he took a factory job. Because of Roxanne, Thora stayed with Cletus in the city even though she was unhappy. When they eventually moved back to the farm that Thora inherited, Cletus returned to the farm for the same reason Thora had remained in the city—Roxanne.

Roxanne loved the land and the lifestyle as much as Thora, but she did not want to stay on the farm because that was the only option open to her: "She felt suddenly as though she were a repeat of her mother, starting over again with a new life, and it was crucial that she know what mistakes to avoid."

To prove to herself that she could survive in an environment other than that of the farm, Roxanne moved to Des Moines. She successfully found a job, established a relationship with a young man, and managed her own money.

Cletus, his reason for staying no longer present, departed shortly after Roxanne had moved to Des Moines. Because Thora knew the importance of what Roxanne was doing, she did not ask her to return to help with the farm. Once Roxanne satisfied herself that she would not be settling for less, she returned to the farm, no longer afraid that she was a "repeat" of her mother. She knew now who Roxanne was and what was best for herself.

Luke Wallin's *The Redneck Poacher's Son* is the fast-paced story of sixteen-year-old Jesse Watersmith. All his life Jesse had been waiting for an escape from the Alabama swamp where he lived on the wrong side of the law with Paw and his two brothers. Although Jesse loved the outdoors and the way of life in the swamp, he hated what Paw and his brothers did to make money—things like selling moonshine flavored with shaving lotion and selling poisonous, rotting fish to cheap restaurants.

In the spring of his sixteenth year, Jesse and his family were offered jobs in the sawmill. Jesse went to live with a friend of his aunt's and, for the first time in his life, is free of his crafty, villainous father, who Jesse believed had murdered his mother. Through his friendship with Ren, the mill owner's daughter, and through the education he received from Miss Elmilly, Jesse began developing a set of values contrary to those of his father and brothers.

When his older brother was killed in a bar by a jealous husband and Paw vandalized the mill with a chain saw, Jesse realized he had to choose between his values and his family. He told the state police about the poison fish, but the police doublecrossed Jesse by telling the sheriff, who wanted Paw dead. As he held a gun on Paw and his brother, the posse closed in. Realizing that he had nothing to fear from Paw anymore because he had stood up to Paw, Jesse let Paw and his brothers escape.

Winter Wheat, The Leaving, and *The Redneck Poacher's Son* offer the adolescent reader a realistic portrayal of rural life. The search by Ellen, Roxanne, and Jesse for an integrated system of values is sensitively and artistically presented in these three works. In addition, the reader vicariously experiences life in rural America and the pressures faced by individuals who are moving from adolescence to adulthood from dependence to independence. These books represent quality fiction for the adolescent reader.

Bibliography

The South

Branscum, Robbie. *Johnny May.* New York: Harper, 1984.

———. *Toby Alone.* Garden City: Doubleday, 1979.

———. *Toby, Granny, and George.* Garden City: Doubleday, 1976.

———. *Toby and Johnny Joe.* Garden City: Doubleday, 1979.

Bridgers, Sue Ellen. *Home Before Dark.* New York: Knopf, 1976.

Burch, Robert. **D.J.'s Worst Enemy.* New York: Viking, 1965.

Glasgow, Ellen. *Barren Ground.* New York: Modern Library, 1933.

Heck, Bessie Holland. **Golden Arrow.* New York: Macmillan, 1981.

Hinton, S.E. **Tex.* New York: Delacorte, 1979.

Lee, Mildred. *The Rock and the Willow.* New York: Lothrop, Lee, & Shepard, 1963.

Paterson, Katherine. *Bridge to Terabithia.* New York: Crowell, 1977.

Rabe, Berniece. *Naomi.* Nashville: T. Nelson, 1975.

———. *Rass.* Nashville: T. Nelson, 1973.

Rawls, Wilson. *Where the Red Fern Grows.* Garden City: Doubleday, 1961.

Swarthout, Glendon, and Kathryn. **Whichaway.* New York: Random, 1966.

Wallin, Luke. **The Redneck Poacher's Son.* Scarsdale: Bradbury, 1981.

The East

Farrow, Rachi. **Charlie's Dream.* New York: Pantheon, 1978.

Meader, Stephen W. **Blueberry Mountain.* New York: Harcourt, 1941.

Peck, Robert Newton. **A Day No Pigs Would Die.* New York: Knopf, 1972.

Rich, Louise, D. **Summer at High Kingdom.* New York: F. Watts, 1975.

The Plains

Brown, Irene Bennett. *The Willow Whip.* New York: Atheneum, 1979.

Cleaver, Vera and Bill. *Dust of the Earth.* Philadelphia: Lippincott, 1975.

Engebrecht, P. A. *Under the Haystack.* New York: Dell, 1975.

Graber, Richard. **Black Cow Summer.* New York: Harper, 1980.

Hall, Lynn. *The Leaving.* New York: Scribner, 1980.

———. *Too Near the Sun.* Chicago: Follett, 1970.

Lenski, Lois. **Corn-farm Boy.* Philadelphia: Lippincott, 1954.

Pellowski, Anne. *Willow Wind Farm.* New York: Putnam, 1981.

The West

Corcoran, Barbara. *This Is a Recording.* New York: Atheneum, 1971.

O'Hara, Mary. **Green Grass of Wyoming.* Philadelphia: Lippincott, 1946.

———. **My Friend Flicka.* Philadelphia: Lippincott, 1941.

———. **Thunderhead.* New York: Lippincott, 1943.

Steinbeck, John. **The Red Pony. The Short Novels of John Steinbeck.* New York: Viking, 1953.

Walker, Mildred. *Winter Wheat.* New York: Harcourt, 1944.

*Male figure as a major character.

28 The Hispanic in Young Adult Literature

Patricia Tarry-Stevens

In young adult literature, Hispanic characters take on usually one of three roles: indigenous American, newly arrived immigrant, or historical participant. A smaller number of books now available from American publishers show us life in other Spanish-speaking countries.

Unfortunately, an abundance of examples from any one of these categories does not exist. However, novels about adolescent Hispanics represent a variety of writing styles and reading interests.

Novels that show the Hispanic as an integral part of the American experience are somewhat more common than the other roles Hispanic protagonists play in young adult literature. The experience of growing up Hispanic in rural New Mexico is told in two novels: *. . . And Now Miguel* by Joseph Krumgold and *Bless Me, Ultima* by Rudolfo Anaya. Newbery Award-winner *. . . And Now Miguel* tells the simple story of Miguel, who wishes more than anything else to journey into the mountains with his father and brothers on their annual sheep migration to higher ground. As he is finally taken into the camaraderie of the older sheepherders, Miguel makes the longer journey within himself, from boyhood to manhood. Although not predominately written for the young adult market, *Bless Me, Ultima* revolves around seven-year-old Antonio and his relationship with his grandmother, Ultima. Ultima is a *curadera*—a healer. Antonio and his grandmother grow to have a rare and special relationship, one that transcends time and even death. It is a novel for mature teenagers, but one that realistically shows the coming of age of a rural-born and raised New Mexican.

Red Sky at Morning by Richard Bradford, also set in New Mexico during World War II, gives us such memorable characters as Chango Lopez, Chamaco (the sheriff), Tarzan Velarde (the town *pachuco*), and Victoria Montoya, the beautiful and intellectual daughter of the main character's housekeeper. When Josh Arnold is sent

Reprinted from *The ALAN Review* 17.2, Winter 1990, pages 31–32, 3, by permission of the author.

from Mobile, Alabama, to northern New Mexico to live for the duration of World War II, he cannot foresee all the cultures and beliefs which will soon intertwine with his life. On his first day of school in this new environment, a fellow classmate tells Josh,

> "We only recognize three kinds of people in Sagrado: Anglos, Indians, and Natives." What about the Negro? "I already explained that to you. He's an Anglo. That is, he's an Anglo unless you're differentiating between him and an Indian. Then he's white. I admit he's awfully dark to be white but that's the way it goes around here . . . If there's a minority group at all around here, it's the Anglos."

Setting his novels in modern times, P. J. Petersen uses many Hispanic characters to round out his scenarios. In *Corky and the Brothers Cool*, it is Alfredo who shows Tim, the main character, the truth about his new friend, Corky. At the beginning of the book, Alfredo asks Tim, "You think he likes Mexicans?" Tim seals their friendship answering, "He'd better." Corky's attitude toward Mexicans, however, is less than admirable. To an illegal alien who understands little English, he yells, "You ignorant greaser. You're a real pain in the butt, you know that?" Corky then smiles politely as the man smiles back at him, not comprehending the words. In the end, although Corky provides an excitement unequaled in the dull little northern California town, Tim recognizes there are more important values than excitement. Bigotry and "getting back at people" are very cruel jokes, no matter who is involved.

In *Would You Settle for Improbable?* also by Petersen, the main character, Michael Parker, writes in his journal that he really admires Salvadore Sanchez: "He's the oldest of eight children, and he can speak both Spanish and English. But me? I am typical, average, normal and blah." In the same book, there is a teacher named Mr. Hernandez, one of the few teachers respected by teachers and students alike.

In *The Spanish Smile* by Scott O'Dell, we follow the life of Lucinda de Cabrillo y Benivides as her father tries to hide her from twentieth-century life on their island off the coast of California. Her father has contempt for Anglos and vehemently tells her: "Five million Hispanics know little of their heritage. But they grow angry at being people of the second class—*de clase sequnda*—looked down upon by the Anglos, underpaid, preyed upon by the unscrupulous, galled that their children attend schools where they are taught in gringo words the children do not understand." Lucinda must disentangle the truths and mysteries in her father's plans for her life. Lucinda's life as an heiress and ruler of the island is continued in *The Castle in the Sea* by O'Dell.

The character of the poor, newly arrived immigrant is one that can be dramatic and very memorable. More than twenty-five years ago, the play *West Side Story* gave viewers and readers alike a vivid picture of the conflict of young Puerto Ricans trying to find a niche in American society. Readers not only could see the conflict of dreams and reality in this and other stories, but they also could see the ramifications that accompany those unrealistic dreams—poverty, gangs, poor education, crime. Gary Paulsen in *The Crossing* writes of Manny Bustos, a poor youngster of the streets of Juarez, Mexico, whose dream is to cross the border into the United States. As he meets Sergeant Robert S. Locke, Manny states: "I cannot live in the streets much longer. I am too small. . . . Would you help me?" Manny dreams of crossing into the United States, and Sergeant Locke seems to be his only hope. In the last chapter, small Manny Bustos is seen fleeing north, leaving death and despair behind.

This character's hopes and dreams are continued in the character of David Garcia found in Paulsen's *Sentries.* David has crossed the border and looks with hope toward work in the beet fields of Nebraska. Quite simplistically, he states, "I am fourteen and I am in the United States and things will become right now. I will find work and there will be money to send home and there will be food for them." As David hitchhikes through New Mexico and Colorado, he is surprised at the immensity of land. In Mexico, the men had never talked of the land one must cross to get to the work fields. Finally after reaching Nebraska, David is excited as he finds work almost immediately on a beet farm. Puffed up with pride, he considers himself very lucky indeed to have a job. A pregnant woman also working the fields tells him, "Lucky people do not hoe beets. Lucky people own the farms that hire us to hoe the beets." Later she explains the unfairness of working the fields but also sadly acknowledges that it is work, and in Mexico they cannot even do that. As this modern-day Madonna gives birth to her child in the fields, David starts to see his great dream diminish and feel anger at the unfairness of life.

Viva, Chicano by Frank Bonham realistically tells of life in the Los Angeles barrio. Joaquin (Keeny) Duran wants to continue the pride in *la raza* that his father gave him as a child. In the midst of a chaotic home life, the pressures of gang membership, and the unfairness of juvenile authorities, Keeny searches for a better life and a better way to find that life. Led by the wisdom of Emiliano Zapata, the great revolutionary figure of Mexico, Keeny learns to face his problems and start anew.

Writer Scott O'Dell has become known as a master storyteller and many of the novels that show the Hispanic in history are his novels, such as *The Captive, The Feathered Serpent,* and *The Amethyst Ring,* describing the Mayan civilization. In *The Captive* we follow Julian Escobar, a young, idealistic Jesuit seminarian as his life becomes entwined in the Mayan culture of sixteenth-century Mexico. In *The Feathered Serpent,* his life continues within the intrigues and mysteries of first the Mayan culture, then the Aztec culture. The final book in the series, *The Amethyst Ring,* follows Escobar as he leaves the Mayan culture and travels further south into the land of the Inca, joining the exploits of the explorer Pizarro.

In *The King's Fifth* by O'Dell, the reader journeys with Coronado and a Captain Mendoza through the unknown territory of Cibola in New Spain. Told through the eyes of Esteban de Sandoval, a fifteen-year-old mapmaker, we see the greed that men have for gold treasure and conquest, both of land and human souls. Because Esteban has not paid the required "king's fifth" of the treasure he has helped locate, he is imprisoned and awaits the trial as he writes his story.

The young heroine in *Carlota* by O'Dell finds herself caught in the middle of the Mexican-American War in California in 1846. Carlota and her father want nothing from Spain nor the United States. They want their own land, left undisturbed. For this, Carlota goes to battle with her father, only to realize she is not necessarily just an extension of her father or a copy of his beliefs.

Young adults can experience life in other Spanish-speaking countries in two books: *The Honorable Prison* by Lyll Becerra de Jenkins and Scott O'Dell's *The Black Pearl.* In *The Honorable Prison,* readers live through a violent revolution in a South American country in the 1950s. The adolescent heroine, Marta Maldonada, becomes a prisoner, along with her entire family, because of her father's outspoken journalistic writings. They are given a crude house on an army base, their "honorable prison." Marta and her brother must find diversions from the tedium of living under constant guard. They have their family together but that is about all they have. Because of a lack of medicine, Marta's father becomes dangerously ill as the rest of the family suffers from near-starvation. At the end, the civil war is over, Marta's father is in a coma, and Marta looks to an unsteady but more favorable future.

In *The Black Pearl,* Ramon Salazar grows to manhood in a small Mexican village in Baja, California, as he finds the Pearl of Heaven—a black pearl. His overnight fame and respect are soon tainted by ruin and revenge.

In conclusion, there are many excellent examples of young adult literature with Hispanic protagonists. The problem lies not in quality, but in quantity. For the student who wishes to read about Hispanics in gang warfare, there are only a few books. For young females who wish to identify with a female protagonist, there is nineteenth-century Carlota, the heiress Lucinda, and minor characters found in other books. For a minority group that is one of the largest in the United States, it seems neglectful that so little is written about Hispanic lifestyles. Unfortunately, young adult literature is not keeping pace with the views, feelings, and frustrations of Hispanic Americans.

Books Cited

Anaya, Rudolfo. *Bless Me, Ultima.* Berkeley: Tonatiuh, 1972.

Becerra de Jenkins, Lyle. *The Honorable Prison.* New York: Dutton, 1988.

Bonham, Frank. *Viva, Chicano.* New York: Dell, 1970.

Bradford, Richard. *Red Sky at Morning.* Philadelphia: Lippincott, 1968.

Krumgold, Joseph. *. . . And Now Miguel.* New York: Thomas Y. Crowell, 1953.

O'Dell, Scott. *The Amethyst Ring.* Boston: Houghton, 1983.

———. *The Black Pearl.* Boston: Houghton, 1967.

———. *The Captive.* Boston: Houghton, 1979.

———. *Carlota.* Boston: Houghton, 1977.

———. *The Castle in the Sea.* Boston: Houghton, 1983.

———. *The Feathered Serpent.* Boston: Houghton, 1981

———. *The King's Fifth.* Boston: Houghton, 1966.

———. *The Spanish Smile.* Boston: Houghton, 1966.

Paulsen, Gary. *The Crossing.* New York: Orchard, 1987.

———. *Sentries.* Scarsdale: Bradbury, 1986.

Petersen, P. J. *Corky and the Brothers Cool.* New York: Delacorte, 1985.

———. *Would You Settle for Improbable?* New York: Delacorte, 1981.

Schulman, Irving. *West Side Story.* New York: Pocket Books, 1961.

29 Why the Success of the Teen Romance Depresses Me

Alleen Pace Nilsen

In the 1970s, many of us thought that adolescent literature was finally coming of age. Paul Zindel had won a Pulitzer Prize and still seemed pleased to write for teenagers. Vera and Bill Cleaver wrote consistently good books, and so did Robert Lipsyte, M. E. Kerr, Norma and Harry Mazer, Robert Newton Peck, and Barbara Wersba. The power of the new realism was shown in such books as Glendon Swarthout's *Bless the Beasts and Children,* John Donovan's *Wild in the World,* Isabelle Holland's *Man Without a Face,* and Alice Childress' *A Hero Ain't Nothin' But a Sandwich.* Robert Cormier's *The Chocolate War, I Am the Cheese,* and *After the First Death* were read and reviewed as serious literature for both teenagers and adults.

Now at the beginning of the '80s, it's depressing to come off this high and find that the attention getters are series of softcover love stories—what our library science students have dubbed "training bras for Harlequin romances": *The Wildfire* and *Wishing Star* books from Scholastic, *Sweet Dreams* introduced by Bantam in September, and the *First Love* books introduced by Simon and Schuster in October. Aimed at readers of age eleven or twelve and up, the series appear to be on their way to the same kind of financial success as their adult counterparts, which now account for 30 percent of mass market paperback sales.

Scholastic was first to discover the market, which last year brought them 1.8 million dollars through school and bookstore sales. According to editor Ann Reit, the thirty *Wildfire* books have been consistently at the top of Scholastic sales lists, except when occasionally displaced by a media tie-in or a cartoon book. *Christy, Superflirt,* and *Beautiful Girl* are among the favorites. *The Wishing Star* line is being added this year for slightly older girls.

Reprinted from *The ALAN Review* 9.2, Winter 1982, pages 12–14, 39, by permission of the author.

Nancy Pines at Bantam admitted that their *Sweet Dreams* line was "inspired" by Scholastic's having "uncovered a market that is seemingly endless." Bantam hopes to compete by having their stories more tightly written and by having "brighter, punchier, and more sporty" covers. Their first six titles are *Laurie's Song, Little Sister, California Girl, The Popularity Plan, Princess Amy,* and *P.S. I Love You.* Two more books will be released each month.

Simon and Schuster has the advantage of being able to make a tie-in between their new *First Love* series and their already well-known *Silhouette* line for adults. Over the summer, ads appeared in trade journals and tags were appended to *Silhouette* television commercials so orders were already in from schools and libraries before the first six titles were printed. All carry the identifier "First Love from Silhouette," and include *Serenade, New Boy in Town, Kate Herself, Please Let Me In, Flowers for Lisa,* and *Girl in the Rough.*

The books are a pendulum swing away from the realism of the last decade. They feature beautiful high school girls, usually only-children from white, upper-middle-class homes. The audience is strictly girls (Bantam has received 2,000 letters, not one from a boy) attracted to the easy reading, the beautiful-people covers, and the wish-fulfilling plots.

A Simon and Schuster representative explained, "If there are problems, they have to be normal ones—no drugs, no sex, no alcohol, no bad parents, etc." The problems don't seem so normal to me, but at least they are ones that most girls could dream of coping with. In *Beautiful Girl* by Elisabeth Ogilvie (Scholastic) the problem is that April is so exquisitely beautiful that people are either jealous or afraid of her, but she finally learns that being beautiful is simply a part of her life she will have to cope with, and "If boys flocked—or didn't flock—what difference? Besides, there was Matt. More and more I looked forward to being with him."

The problem in *The Popularity Plan* by Rosemary Vernon (Bantam) is that Frannie is too shy to talk to boys, but her friends draw up a plan in which she is assigned certain ways to relate to a boy each day. Sure enough, she is asked for so many dates she has to get a wall calendar to keep from getting mixed up. But by the end of the story she is happy to "give it all up" and settle for Ronnie, the boy she really liked all along.

In *That's My Girl* by Jill Ross Klevin (Scholastic), Becky is an ice skater who has to fight off getting ulcers while worrying about the upcoming Nationals, her chance at the Olympics, and whether she will lose her boyfriend who feels ignored. Bantam's *California Girl* by Janet Quin-Harkin has an almost identical plot except that Jennie is competing for the Olympics as a swimmer.

A key difference between teenage and adult reading has been that books for young people are mainly purchased by or through schools and libraries for some educational value. Taxpayers feel a right to say where their dollars are being spent. So publishers must first please librarians and teachers who act as agents for the taxpayers, and *then* please a young audience who has the final say by simply refusing to read.

But creators of romances bypass traditional adult critics and reviewers by coming out in paperback editions only, which never receive as much critical attention as hardbacks, then marketing books directly to young readers through newsstands and chain bookstores. Even Scholastic, which courted teachers for decades and sold through school book clubs, made half of last year's sales through commercial channels.

Direct marketing is crucial to the success of romances because they will not get the approval of many adults. Those who do approve will most likely follow the reasoning of Vermont Royster in the *Wall Street Journal* (June 24, 1981) when he compared romances with his reading of books his mother considered trash—*Tom Swift, The Rover Boys, Detective Nick Carter,* and *Wild Bill Hickock.* He admits the plotting of the romances is banal and monotonous and the writers can probably turn them out wholesale, but at least, "The spelling is correct and they do manage mostly to abide by the rules of English grammar." He recommends the books as an aid in helping a generation of television-oriented kids acquire the habit of reading. Once they are hooked, "call it an addiction if you will . . . young people can be led by good teachers to enlarge their reach."

I'm sympathetic to Royster's point, but I'm also depressed by the success of the romances. Part of it is purely personal. As someone devoting my professional life to literature for young readers, I'm embarrassed. I feel like a betrayed wife with an *I gave you the best years of my life, and this is what it comes to* reaction.

A second reason has to do with my sons and my daughter and what such books do to their expectations about boy/girl relationships. My boys would never read such books, but if the girls they want to date have read them, their lives may be affected. In young romances, boys are models of psychological perfection much as pinup girls in men's magazines are models of physical perfection. I suspect boys can't stand to read romances because the books force them to compare themselves with the idealized boys in the stories and they end up feeling awkward—and inferior.

When I called one of the editors and told her I was thinking of writing an article entitled, "The Jocks in Girls' Fiction—Characters without Support," she said, "Oh, these aren't jocks. They're very nice boys." Yes, they are very nice boys, far too good to be true. They have more wisdom than the girls' parents, more patience than all the adults as well as the girls' friends, and are so in love that even when rebuffed they wait on the sidelines until their true worth is recognized. Examples from the books illustrate some of the other characteristics of the dream boy.

He is mature and unselfish: At the end of *That's My Girl* after the celebration party, Jed is grateful for a few minutes of Becky's undivided attention:

> "It's good to have you all to myself for a change. From here on that won't happen too often. I'll have to get used to sharing you with the whole Olympic figure skating team, the reporters, the photographers, Vera, your hairdresser, your dressmaker, your business manager, your . . ."
>
> "Hey, I'm skating in the Olympics, not going to Hollywood!" Becky interrupts.

He is there when he's needed: In *Beautiful Girl,* Brendan, who throughout the story plays big brother, protector, and consultant to his beautiful cousin, shows up on a deserted country road just in time to rescue her from being harassed by three teenage hoods. His explanation of knowing that he was needed is simply, "I had funny feelings all day. I didn't know whether it was the flu coming on or if I've got psychic powers from my Irish great-granny who could read tea leaves."

Just by being, he solves problems: Also in *Beautiful Girl,* April says, "I went back to bed wishing I could call Brendan. Once I heard his voice I would feel like *me* again, not someone cut off forever from all dear, safe, daylight things."

He has inner qualities: In *The Popularity Plan,* after the girl has decided to give up trying to go with all the boys and to settle for the quiet, shy boy in her art class, the two spend a day on the beach and, "That enigmatic boldness that Frannie had glimpsed only in Ronnie's vibrant painting was now very evident in his personality. What she had thought was contradictory and puzzling was simply another dimension of the same, fascinating Ronnie."

He is competent: When two acquaintances are hurt in a motorcycle accident in *Beautiful Girl,* April's mind is chaos, but Matt runs and shuts off the motorcycle and then puts his head down to Bobby's chest and announces that he isn't dead:

> "I'll get an ambulance," Matt said. "I may be a little while getting to a telephone if I can't flag down a car. So don't panic." He was talking to me. "And don't move or touch him. Oh, here." He unzipped his jacket and put it over Bobby's chest and shoulders. "It's not much, but it'll help." He looked intently into my face. "Will you be all right?"
>
> "Yes," I said, knowing it had to be so.

Just as my boys are unable to compete with these dream boys, my daughter is unable to find a boyfriend who has all of these qualities. It's small wonder that boys retreat to fantasizing through the false bravado of locker-room talk while girls daydream with the romances and hope to get a boyfriend who is two or three years older than they are. The age difference gives the boy some chance of having had time to develop at least a few of the expected qualities.

The view of life portrayed in the romances puts just as much pressure on my daughter, but in a different way. This is best illustrated through a quiz, "Does He Like Me?" which was written by the Scholastic *Wildfire* editor and printed in a promotional magazine distributed last spring. The quiz tells the reader that if a boy likes her, he will:

1. comment on her appearance,
2. remember what interests her,
3. ask her what she would like to do,
4. call her sometimes just to say "Hello,"
5. really listen to her,
6. confide in her about something that worries, scares, or pleases him,
7. never put her down, especially in front of other people,
8. keep talking to her even when one of his friends comes along,
9. notice when she is upset or sad or depressed, and
10. ask her for a date.

This sounds wonderful. The only problem is that not a single boy that my daughter meets will have read this quiz. So even if she follows the exact outline given in *The Popularity Plan,* it's highly unlikely that she will find a desirable boy who behaves as the quiz says he will. In reality such behavior is a matter of training and experience in social situations rather than emotional attachment.

The quiz is a distillation of the attitudes expressed throughout the romances. If my daughter takes it seriously, she is likely to conclude that there's something wrong with her. She can come to this conclusion via two routes: (1) No boys like me because no boys act as the quiz says they should, or (2) The only boys who like me are clods because they don't act as the quiz says they should.

Another aspect of the romances that damages the self-image of readers is their false portrayal of dating. High school is made to appear a continual round of parties and dates, when in reality 10 percent of the kids do 90 percent of the dating. Unless teenagers are going steady (and this may be why so many kids go steady), their social life is mostly made up of group activities rather than of arranged dates. And when a couple breaks up, seldom is another boy waiting to ask the girl out.

That the retreat from realism and the embracing of the romances should come after a decade of feminist consciousness-raising also depresses me. Apparently many girls are simply rejecting as too difficult the demands that were placed on them. I tried to raise my daughter to feel responsible for her own happiness, but she might justifiably question why I expect more from her than the world expects from the idealized girls in the romances. If even they—with their brains, good looks, and perfect parents and homes—must wait for boys to bring them happiness, then why does she have to find it for herself?

It's interesting that even though the very existence of the books and their stress on boys convey the idea that nothing could be more important in a girl's life than popularity, the romances give a passing nod to feminism in that the girls have career ambitions. For example, in *P. S. I Love You,* Mariah is a writer. In *Beautiful Girl,* April says she's going to be a lawyer instead of a model, and then of course there are the Olympic stars in *California Girl* and *That's My Girl.*

What depresses me the most about the romances is their treatment of sex. Each company's representative used the term "squeaky clean" to imply there is no sex. But sex is their *raison d'etre,* and their creators use hidden persuaders to appear "squeaky clean" *and* at the same time sexy. Individual book titles and trademarks are full of sexual connotations. Each beautiful young model on the poster-like covers has her own come-hither look. The cover of Scholastic's *That's My Girl* features a braless skater in a white dress carefully posed so that the shapes of three nipples—two on her and one in her mirrored reflection—are clearly visible.

The books are teases. Authors set up sexy situations and then skip to the next chapter. It's easy to titillate but difficult to write about sexual feelings honestly to help girls know what it's like to have a real boyfriend. I'm not bothered that romances make young women think about sex. That's natural. What I don't like is their incompleteness, their hypocrisy, and their one-sidedness.

A basic difference between these books and the "innocent" teen novels of the 1950s is that today's readers do not belong to an innocent generation. They have real-life heroes such as movie stars Kristy McNichol, Tatum O'Neal, and Brooke Shields. Shields has no image other than sexuality, but even the relatively "wholesome" McNichol and O'Neal co-starred in *Little Darlings* as two girls at summer camp bent on "freeing themselves" from the burden of virginity. And walking by a magazine stand, anyone can spot headlines about live-in boyfriends and Marie Osmond "wanting a baby."

In the midst of such media acceptance and—promotion—of youthful sexuality, what today's teenagers need from adults is not more commercial exploitation of their good looks and their awakening feelings. What they need is help in understanding themselves and their relationships. The success of the soft-cover romances will be noticed by authors, editors, and publishers of other young adult books. Imitation is inevitable, but I hope that it will be done selectively. Young readers appear to be tired of depressing, problem novels. They want some happy stories. Let's hope that better writers can provide these without the falseness, the setting up of impossible expectations, and the sexual titillation that fill the romances. Is it too much to hope that someone might even write a happy love story so honest that boys as well as girls will read it?

Adult Midlife Crisis in Adolescent Novels

Richard F. Abrahamson

Young adult literature and teenage developmental tasks have been linked for years. Teenagers seem to enjoy reading books in which the main character surmounts developmental tasks that the reader is attempting. In G. Robert Carlsen's new edition of *Books and the Teenage Reader* (1980), he writes:

> In the search for identity the young use books, particularly fiction and biography, as a main source of information. Through them they try on different roles, and sometimes they discover people like themselves whom they can observe handling their lives. . . . Unless the books they read offer them experiential encounters, most will be turned off by reading. (13)

When we focus exclusively on teenagers and developmental tasks, we neglect other characters in YA books who are also trying to surmount developmental tasks of a sort. Parents in YA books are usually in their late thirties and forties and are struggling through a time psychologist Daniel Levinson calls the "Midlife Transition" and Gail Sheehy calls the "Midlife Crisis." It is the time when many adults reevaluate their lives and struggle for an identity in a parallel way to the struggles of their teenage children.

It seems there are three questions that surface here. First, do the authors of current YA books depict parents in midlife crisis? Second, what effect do parents going through midlife crisis have on their teenage offspring? Third, is the parallel parent struggle worth pointing out to teenagers?

Let's take the last question first. In *Teaching Adolescent Literature: A Humanistic Approach* (1979), Sheila Schwartz writes, ". . . secondary school literature can help students develop sociological and psychological consciousness" (7). Discussing the adult task of midlife transition will aid students in developing this psychological consciousness. Certainly one goal of education is to help move youngsters from a totally ego-centered world. By looking at the

Reprinted from *The ALAN Review* 8.2, Winter 1981, pages 29–30, 38, by permission of the author.

adults as well as the teens in YA fiction, adolescent readers get to walk vicariously in someone else's shoes—in this case someone older but with many of the same concerns. Far too often parents are not looked upon by teenagers as real people. To consider the adult midlife tasks is to shed some fresh light on parents. To get adolescents to view parents as vulnerable human beings just like themselves, capable of being disillusioned and still searching for an identity, is to present parents in an often-neglected way.

Do YA authors depict parents in midlife crisis? The answer is yes. Alice Bach, Paula Danziger, M. E. Kerr, Norma Klein, and Sandra Scoppettone write about a teenager's struggle for identity and growth that is paralleled by a parent in midlife. The parent's struggle through this crisis very often affects the teenager in the family. Before we get to the books, however, a short discussion of midlife transition seems necessary.

Daniel Levinson's *The Seasons of Man's Life* (1978) grew from his study of a group of men in the middle of their lives. He maintains that men's lives are made up of eras lasting approximately twenty-five years with five-year overlapping transitions between eras. During these transitions, men come to terms with the past and prepare themselves for the future. What Levinson calls the midlife transition extends from roughly forty to fifty years of age and serves to terminate the period he calls early adulthood and to initiate middle adulthood. It is the period in the middle of their lives when adults realize their mortality and reappraise the past in order to plan better use of their remaining time.

In *Passages* (1976) Gail Sheehy claims that women enter what she calls "the Deadline Decade" between thirty-five and forty-five years of age. They become cognizant of physical deterioration and search for authenticity in their lives. Women often see a whole new realm of opportunities open up to them at this time:

> Up from the years of having small stumblers affixed to their hand, able now to walk at an adult pace, better at organizing her time and integrating her priorities, she is released to soar into realms undared on wings untested, and while seeking her originality, to sing with unaccustomedness of all that she attempts. (418)

Both men and women make significant changes in their lives as a result of the process of midlife. These may involve divorce, remarriage, occupational shifts, lifestyle changes, progress in creativity or social position. Sheehy says, "The consensus of current research is that the transition into middle life is as critical as adolescence and in some ways more harrowing" (360). Like their parents, adolescents are experiencing great changes. Physically, mentally, and emotionally, the teenage years are times of growth and development. Adolescence is the period of transition from childhood to adulthood, when young people face tasks similar in some ways to those of their parents. It is interesting to look at the ways novelists for young adults have looked at this confluence of adolescence and midlife.

In Alice Bach's book *The Meat in the Sandwich* (1977), Mike's mother reappraises her life and considers how different it has been from her expectations. Like the men in Levinson's study, she seeks "to modify the life structure of the thirties and to create the basis for a new structure appropriate to middle adulthood" (194). She says,

> I don't know why life is so different from what I had imagined fifteen years ago. . . . Your father planned to be an engineer and he is an engineer. I don't know exactly what I thought I'd be, but now I picture myself as the central switchboard lady of the house—every day answering the same questions: "Where did I put my keys?" she said in Daddy's deep voice. "Where are my magic markers?" . . . I didn't realize that every day would be the same, three meals to fix, vacuum extra-hard near the front door, scour the bathroom sink. . . . Most of what I do all day is boring. (26)

Mike's mother is at a crossroad. She sees herself at a point in her life where she needs to make a decision about how she will spend the next half of her life. She wants to make changes:

> I want to live with all of you—but I want to live differently in the same house with the same people. I want to have my private projects to work on, to look forward to, like you all do. (27)

This midlife crisis of Mike's mother has a definite effect on his life. In an effort to help Mom, the family decides to share the household duties so that she might have time to develop her painting skills. This is fine until Kip Slater moves in next door. Kip feels laundry, vacuuming, and dishes are "woman's work." Kip wants to excel in sports and to that end his entire family supports him. They buy him expensive athletic equipment. Mike wants to compete with Kip in sports, and he wants Kip's approval and friendship. Mike's need for Kip's approval is in direct conflict with his mother's needs. In comparing both families, Mike feels his family is being unfair to him. Bach does a good job of paralleling Mike's need to prove his masculinity and win Kip's approval with his mother's midlife search for individuality. It can certainly be seen here that the parent's midlife transition has a direct effect on the central teenage character. In fact it is the head on collision of parent developmental tasks and teenager developmental tasks that causes a central conflict in the book.

Much of M. E. Kerr's work involves the parent and teenager in transitional tasks. In *Is That You, Miss Blue?* (1975), fifteen-year-old Flanders Brown is sent to boarding school because her mother has run off with a young research assistant. Gail Sheehy says that thirty-five is the most common age for runaway wives. Women who have devoted their lives up to this point to their husbands, childbearing, and housekeeping, suddenly realize that their children need them less and less; and, like Mike's mother in *Meat in the Sandwich,* they feel a need to be individuals. Flanders' mother says, "I left your father because I want to be someone in my own right. . . . I didn't give up my right to individuality once I had you" (158). The young research assistant Mrs. Brown ran away with served only as a catalyst for her breaking away from her family. Mrs. Brown's real need was to stop being simply a support for her husband and daughter and to start a career and life of her own.

Flanders's own developmental crises are speeded up as a result of her mother's search for individuality. Being forced into boarding school made it not only possible, but necessary, for Flanders to stand on her own, to sort things out, and to start making her own decisions. As a result of Mrs. Brown's midlife crisis, Flanders is forced into discovering her own individuality. By the end of the book, Flanders goes to visit her mother after a year of boarding school. Flanders says, "I couldn't believe all that I had to tell, all that I'd seen and heard and been a part of, and for the first time in my life, I'd been seen and heard on my own" (159). Again, we see a situation in which the adult transition was the catalyst for the teenager surmounting developmental tasks.

Dinky Hocker Shoots Smack (1972) is filled with parents in midlife transitions. What is most interesting here is that Kerr portrays two sets of parents handling midlife adjustments in very different ways. On the positive side are Tucker Woolf's parents. Tucker's father, fired from his job as a professional fund-raiser, tries to start a new health food business and his Ph.D. mother, dissatisfied with her job of grinding out true love romances, starts law school. It is typical of both men and women in midlife to rethink their life goals and begin a new career or business. During the process of career change, Tucker's parents work at keeping communication open with him. His mother says, "I want you to understand why your father and I haven't been paying much attention to you lately" (91). She apologizes for teasing him and tries to help him through his emotional tangles with Mrs. Hocker and Natalia. His father tells him, "From now on, I want you to feel like an equal around here" (135). A full family effort is necessary for Mrs. Woolf to go to law school. The family discusses problems and includes Tucker in its decision-making process. Although Tucker's parents are clearly in a period of stress and change, they still manage to maintain a close relationship with their son.

In the same book, Mrs. Hocker exemplifies the parent who is so engrossed in her own quest for fulfillment that she ignores the cries from her teenage daughter Dinky. Mrs. Hocker is portrayed as a community do-gooder who makes her own life meaningful by doing volunteer work with drug addicts. She is so involved with helping the addicts that she does not hear her own daughter's plea for help that takes the form of overeating. Marcus, a reformed drug addict, gets more of Dinky's mother's attention than Dinky: "The best way to get Mrs. Hocker's attention was get into some kind of trouble" (169). Dinky's trouble is not drugs, but food, and a need for her parent's love and support. In a desperate last attempt to get her mother's attention, Dinky paints the words "Dinky Hocker Shoots Smack!" on the walls, sidewalks, and doors of automobiles in her neighborhood while her mother is at a banquet receiving a Good Samaritan's award.

In *Dinky Hocker Shoots Smack,* a mother's search for meaningful identity keeps her too busy to give adequate time to her own daughter. This parent quest also provides the basic conflict in the story. The contrast between the Hockers and the Woolfs in their reaction to their children during midlife strains seems obvious. The Woolfs face their own problem of identity and career and still maintain a positive family relationship. The Hockers are so involved in their own individuation processes that their own daughter's needs are ignored.

The midlife task of reappraising the first half of one's life is a prelude of mental illness for Geri Peters's mother in Sandra Scoppettone's *The Late Great Me* (1977). Unable to admit to her husband and then to her children that she had been an unpopular outcast in high school, Mrs. Peters invents a successful and popular high school career complete with a yearbook signed by many close and adoring friends. She constantly pushes Geri to follow in her footsteps. She pressures her to make new friends, smile, be more popular with the "in-crowd" instead of the freaks. Geri's own insecurity and her need to please her mother by being popular leads her to good-looking Dave Townsend, a boy who escapes his own sordid home life with liquor. Geri begins drinking heavily and lying to her parents to protect her drinking. Geri's lying precipitates her mother's illness. Mrs. Peters says,

> When I saw that you were lying and drinking I started to get disoriented. I didn't know what the truth was. I didn't know what was real and what wasn't. I stopped talking because I didn't want to lie any more and I couldn't face telling the truth. (246)

In *Passages* Sheehy says, "Letting the dark side open up will release a cast of demons. Every loose end not resolved in previous passages will resurface to haunt us" (358). Her own unresolved problems as an adolescent haunt Geri's mother during Geri's adolescence. Geri's mother's life was so limited to illusions about her past that when her own children reach high school, she is no longer able to handle the realities of life. As she realizes the distortions she has created in her own life, she cannot cope with the lies, drunkenness, and alienation in her daughter's. Mother and daughter reinforce each other's sickness and only professional institutional care can help Mrs. Peters while Geri is finally saved by an understanding former alcoholic teacher. *The Late Great Me* provides the classic example of just how much a parent's midlife crisis can affect the life of the teenage offspring.

In all the novels discussed so far, it has been the parent's midlife problems that have served as a catalyst for change and conflict in the life of the adolescent. Paula Danziger, however, provides a different picture. In *The Cat Ate My Gymsuit* (1974), Marcy Lewis causes her mother to begin to reevaluate her position as a woman and as a wife. Thirteen-year-old Marcy has a poor self-image brought about by her size and her father's constant criticism. Marcy says, "All my life I've thought that I've looked like a baby blimp with wire-frame glasses and mousy brown hair" (1). When the principal fires Ms. Finney, Marcy's favorite English teacher, Marcy gets involved in a student campaign to reinstate her. Ms. Finney had started to undo some of the thirteen years of intimidation Marcy had experienced under her authoritarian father. She was gaining self-confidence. When she disobeys her father and joins the student group, she has made a positive move toward self-esteem, individuality, and control of her life.

Marcy's dramatic decision to join the student group serves as an inspiration to her mother. Her mother wants to get involved but faces her own self-doubts and the authoritarian spouse. Nevertheless, following her teenager's example Mrs. Lewis gets involved. Mother and daughter go to the school board meeting defying Mr. Lewis. As a result of this positive action, both mother and daughter learn to value themselves and Marcy learns to handle her father's criticism.

In conclusion, it can be said that authors of current YA fiction do portray parents in midlife crisis or transition. As Sheehy's and Levinson's works show, these parents in their late thirties and forties are involved in their own set of developmental tasks that include a search for identity and a reevaluation of their lives. In a parallel manner, the teenage main characters in these books are striving to surmount their own developmental tasks that are often quite similar to their parents' problems. In most cases it is the parents' transitional struggle that causes some type of conflict for the adolescent in the family. The majority of YA books focus on the midlife transition of the mother in the family. Adult males are not overlooked, but their search for identity is not portrayed as dramatically in YA fiction as is that of adult females. In books like Norma Klein's *It's Not What You*

Expect (1973), we find a father who leaves home, grows a beard, and spends his summer in a bachelor pad in Greenwich Village where he works on a novel. In M. E. Kerr's *Love Is a Missing Person* (1975), we find a father in midlife crisis who gets divorced and marries a young woman only two years older then his own teenage daughter. So adult males are depicted reappraising their lives but not as often or as dramatically as are women.

Finally, we go back to the last of our initial questions: Is the parallel parent struggle worth pointing out to teenagers? To ignore the parents in YA books is to ignore an important group of characters. The parent midlife struggles in the books and in real life do affect the teenager's life. If a look at midlife transition only gets adolescents to view parents as human beings who have problems, dreams, and uncertainties just like they do, then the look will have been beneficial for both parties involved in parallel struggles.

References

Bach, Alice. *The Meat in the Sandwich.* New York: Dell, 1977.

Carlsen, G. Robert. *Books and the Teenage Reader.* Rev. ed. New York: Bantam, 1980.

Danziger, Paula. *The Cat Ate My Gymsuit.* New York: Dell, 1974.

Kerr, M. E. *Dinky Hocker Shoots Smack.* New York: Dell, 1972.

———. *Is that You, Miss Blue?* New York: Dell, 1975.

———. *Love Is a Missing Person.* New York: Harper, 1975.

Klein, Norma. *It's Not What You Expect.* New York: Avon, 1973.

Levinson, Daniel H. *The Seasons of a Man's Life.* New York: Knopf, 1978.

Scoppettone, Sandra. *The Late Great Me.* New York: Bantam, 1977.

Schwartz, Sheila. *Teaching Adolescent Literature: A Humanistic Approach.* Portsmouth, NH: Boyton-Cook, 1979.

Sheehy, Gail. *Passages.* New York: Bantam, 1976.

31 The Image of Working Blacks in YA Novels

Margaret Bristow

In *Shadow and Substance: Afro-American Experience in Contemporary Children's Fiction* Rudine Sims devotes her last chapter to important black writers she calls imagemakers. She mentions Lucille Clifton, Eloise Greenfield, Virginia Hamilton, Sharon Bell Mathis, Walter Dean Myers, Lorenz Graham, Mildred Taylor, Rosa Guy, Julius Lester, and Brenda Wilkinson, among others. She says, and I agree, that black writers find it necessary to be witness to the African-American experience so that African-American children can find themselves and their experiences mirrored in the fiction. She also indicates that this witnessing is necessary so that African-American children can understand "how we got over" in the past and recognize and develop the inner strength that will enable them "to get over" in their own time. Hence, she calls these black writers for young people—the image makers.

In our society the black unemployment rate is more than double the national average; one out of every three blacks lives below the poverty level; fifty-two percent of black teenagers are unemployed. Economists warn of occupational obsolescence in a society in which the young unemployed black male represents the fastest growing population. The questions arise: What is the image of the black world of work as seen in novels written for adolescents? Does it create a positive image for young black readers?

To ascertain the image of the working black in adolescent fiction, I examined forty books with teenage black protagonists written by black authors between 1964 and 1982. The year 1964 marks the passing of the Civil Rights Acts and the creation of the Equal Opportunity Commission and, thus, represents the start of the modern era of work for black Americans.

Robert Havighurst in *Human Development and Education* lists ten developmental tasks imposed by society upon the adolescent. Two of these tasks require the teenager to prepare for the world

Reprinted from *The ALAN Review* 13.1, Fall 1985, pages 38–40, 55, by permission of the author.

of work: (1) achieving assurance of economic independence and (2) selecting and preparing for an occupation.

As a teacher who uses adolescent literature as bibliotherapy, directly or indirectly, I cannot overlook the portrayal of work in novels with black protagonists. Hence, I examined the black working world as portrayed in young adult literature in five ways: (1) preparation of male black teenage protagonists for a career, (2) preparation of female black teenage protagonists for a career, (3) occupations of black teenage protagonists, (4) occupation of female parent, and (5) occupation of the male parent.

Preparation of the Teenager for the Job World

Some emphasis is given to preparing the male protagonist for the job world. Recall the incident from Mildred Taylor's novel *Let the Circle Be Unbroken* when Cassie Logan says:

> The next morning Mr. Morrison hitched up both Lady and Jack. Then he and Mama climbed into the wagon seat and Stacey {her brother} climbed on top of the cotton bin. Frankly I was surprised that I was going. I had pointed out to Mama several times that Stacey had been allowed not only to observe business since he had been ten, but to take care of some of it as well. I supposed I had finally convinced her that my education in practical matters was just as important as his. After all, she had had to run the farm and sell the crops; perhaps I would too some day. (81)

Taylor's novel has a 1935 setting; therefore, the lack of job training for the female is understandable. We would not expect this same viewpoint to continue in the novels of the 1970s and 1980s. In the forty novels I surveyed, however, little attention is given to preparing the female protagonist for work, in spite of statistics which avow that black women are the primary bread winners in 41 percent of black families. David in *Return to South Town* by Lorenz Graham explains what it is like to be a doctor to sixteen-year-old Junior while nothing is said to his fourteen-year-old sister Angie. Calvin in *Ruby* by Rosa Guy owns a restaurant, but never gives second thought to preparing his daughters to work in it or to own it. Peter Aimsley invites sixteen-year-old Imanu, whom he has known only a week, to come to his shop and learn the trade, but nothing about the shop is ever said to Gail, his oldest daughter, who is going to college to be a fashion designer.

Job talk between the black male young adult protagonist and an adult is limited. However, there is even less between the black female protagonist and an adult in the forty books surveyed. The longest piece of advice about a job is given by Steeple to Stone wall in Jesse Jackson's *The Fourteenth Cadillac.* The job discussed involves keeping horses in shape for horse shows. This is the only novel of those surveyed in which the plot centers around a black teenager's search for a place in the world of work. Only Joyce Carol Thomas and Brenda Wilkinson devote more than a page to dialogue in which a black female protagonist is given advice for success in the job world. In *Marked by Fire* (Thomas) Mother Barker gives Abbysinia Jackson, who wants to be a medical doctor, advice: "You stay with me two months and when I get through you'll be a special doctor" (80). Ironically, she is talking about preparing her to be a root doctor. In *Ludell and Willie* (Wilkinson) Ludell is given advice by her grandmother:

> She told Ludell that when she started working for Miss Henley, Miss Henley had tested her honesty by placing a dollar bill on the kitchen floor for an entire week. In spite of the fact that mama would pick it up and lay it on the cabinet, it would be back there the following. So on the fifth day, she took the dollar to Miss Henley and said, "Miss Henley I done been down five times to pick up this dollar. Now next time it's mine!" And mama said after that the two of them got along just fine. True to mama's warning Ludell was tested by the woman she went to on Saturdays however more cheaply with fifty cents. (55)

Types of Jobs Held by Black Teenage Protagonists

Of the forty adolescent novels surveyed, only two have protagonists whose summer work helps them in their later careers. David in *North Town* by Lorenz Graham works summers in a hardware store, learning to put on aluminum siding and evaluate the quality of roofing and flooring. Later, as a medical doctor, he builds his own office and is able to do some of the carpentry he learned working in the hardware store. Juannetta Mackklin in *Lessons in Love* by Tracy West is able to get a summer job as a teacher's aide at Simmons School for the handicapped. At first, she is uncertain of her career goal, but after working successfully with handicapped children, she decides to become a teacher.

Robert B. Hill, research director for the National Urban League, in *The Strengths of Black Families* documents the high goals exhibited by black parents toward their offspring by encouraging them to seek a better job through a college education. This is true in all forty novels except one. Mama in Kristin Hunter's 1968 novel *Soul Brothers and Sister Lou* says to Louretta, "I never went beyond the eighth grade but I'm smart enough to raise all of you" (10).

Of the forty novels surveyed, only ten have working teenagers. This is not surprising in view of the high level of black teenage unemployment. Perhaps, the most atypical jobs are held by five black teenagers, Gloria, Dean, Bubba, Omar, and Jeanne, in *The Young Landlords* by Walter Dean Myers. These teenagers, through a twist of fate, become landlords of an apartment complex and are able to hire an accountant and do extensive repairs.

A question arises: How many teenage protagonists in the forty novels had parents who were landlords? None. However, one minor teenage character, Buck Taylor in the novels *North Town* and *Whose Town?* (Graham), had a father who sold houses. Dora Belle, an adult character in Rosa Guy's *The Disappearance*, had acquired several houses by somewhat shady means, such as from her boy friends. Other more traditional jobs were held by nine teenage protagonists. In *Hoops* (Myers) Lonnie works in a run-down hotel. Mary Ann, his girl friend, has a job keeping track of the liquor and other goods used in a bar. In *The Planet of Junior Brown* by Virginia Hamilton, Buddy works for the owner of a newspaper stand. In Sharon Bell Mathis's *Listen for the Fig Tree*, Muffin's boyfriend Ernie works as a clerk in the grocery store. Francis, the protagonist in *Fast Sam, Cool Clyde and Stuff* (Myers), works in the A&P after school. Ludell in Brenda Wilkinson's books works as a cleaning woman and babysitter. In *Arilla Sun Down* (Hamilton) Arilla's brother waits on tables in a dining area where his father works as a supervisor. Edith, the main character in *Edith Jackson* (Guy), works as a maid and factory worker. However, there is very little space in the forty novels devoted to the search for summer employment, although that is a question which surely confronts most teenagers.

Occupations of Parents of Teenage Protagonists

The increase in middle-class black families, which is largely due to the increase of black professional working women, has been largely overlooked in adolescent fiction. Very few black novelists give attention to the black female professional despite the fact that almost 41 percent of black households are headed by females. Only one novel of those examined, *Arilla Sun Down* by Virginia Hamilton, devotes two paragraphs to a favorable description of the mother's job by the teenage protagonist. What is the lack of positive comment on the work of black women saying to the adolescent who reads these books?

Likewise, only six teenagers in the forty surveyed books have parents who are self-employed. Arilla Adams's mother owns a dance studio. Mother Peters, Edith's foster mother, owns a beauty shop. Mrs. Josephine, Rainbow Jordanis's foster mother, is a seamstress. Ruby and Phyllistia Cathy's father in Rosa Guy's books owns a restaurant, which he relinquishes. Frank, Fonzie's father in James Baldwin's *If Beal Street Could Talk*, owns a tailor shop, which he later loses. Gil in *The Disappearance* has a father who owns a car-repair shop. Since the numbers are few, what subtle message is being delivered to the black teenagers? It is that blacks are basically consumers, not owners. In fact, this message is true, but there is a need for more positive, nontraditional occupational role models for black youth.

Of the books surveyed, most teenage protagonists' parents are in service jobs as laborers; but I did find one protagonist in *Arilla Sun Down* whose father is a supervisor. He is, however, a supervisor of cooks at a technical college. In *Hoops,* the protagonist's father is a social worker, one of the few male professionals observed in the surveyed books. With the rising black middle class, there seems to be a greater need for more black novels which depict middle-class professional parents, such as the medical doctor father and social worker mother in *Because We Are* by Mildred Walter.

Only one black teenage protagonist's father has a nontraditional job. Justice's father in *Justice and Her Brothers* (Hamilton) is a stonecutter. Only one black teenager, through her talents, makes considerable money. Louretta Hawkins in *Soul Brothers and Sister Lou* is a vocalist. Only one black teenager in the forty novels successfully fulfills his ambition to be a medical doctor, David Williams in *Return to South Town* (Graham).

In conclusion, the literary merit of the junior novel with major black characters, attested to by Robert Small in his dissertation, is still seen in most of the forty novels. The black cultural heritage is also evident in most of the novels, indicating that these black writers have lived the black experience and add positively to its dimension. However, as an imagemaker for adolescents, the black writer must not forget the message he or she may subtly deliver to the teenager concerning the world of work.

References and Titles Mentioned

Baldwin, James. *If Beal Street Could Talk.* New York: Signet, 1974.

Graham, Lorenz. *North Town.* New York: Crowell, 1965.

———. *Return to South Town.* New York: Crowell, 1976.

———. *Whose Town?* New York: Crowell, 1969.

Guy, Rosa. *The Disappearance.* New York: Delacorte, 1979.

———. *Edith Jackson.* New York: Viking, 1978.

———. *Ruby.* New York: Viking, 1976.

Hamilton, Virginia. *Arilla Sun Down.* New York: Greenwillow, 1976.

———. *Justice and Her Brothers.* New York: Greenwillow, 1978.

———. *The Planet of Junior Brown.* New York: Macmillan, 1971.

———. *Sweet Whispers, Brother Rush.* New York: Philomel, 1982.

Havighurst, Robert. *Human Development and Education.* Longman, Green, 1953.

Hill, Robert. *The Strengths of Black Families.* New York: Emerson Hall, 1972.

Hunter, Kristin. *Soul Brothers and Sister Lou.* New York: Scribners, 1968.

Jackson, Jesse. *The Fourteenth Cadillac.* New York: Doubleday, 1971.

Mathis, Sharon Bell. *Listen for the Fig Tree.* New York: Viking, 1974.

Myers, Walter Dean. *Fast Sam, Cool Clyde and Stuff.* New York: Viking, 1975.

———. *Hoops.* New York: Delacorte, 1981.

———. *The Young Landlords.* New York: Viking, 1979.

Sims, Rudine. *Shadow and Substance: Afro-American Experience in Contemporary Children's Fiction.* Urbana: NCTE, 1982.

Taylor, Mildred. *Let the Circle Be Unbroken.* New York: Dial, 1981.

Thomas, Joyce Carol. *Marked by Fire.* New York: Avon, 1982.

Walter, Mildred. *Because We Are.* New York: Lothrop, Lee and Shepard, 1983.

West, Tracy. *Lesson in Love.* Boston: Silhouette, 1982.

Wilkinson, Brenda. *Ludell and Willie.* New York: Harper, 1977.

32 Christianity in American Adolescent Realistic Fiction from 1945 to 1981

Julia H. Nixon
Robert C. Small Jr.

Adolescents are in a transitional period affecting all aspects of their lives. Based on the background of all the teachings they have received, they must begin to make decisions on their own, to question what adults have taught them, and to form their own beliefs in relation to other teenagers, their own particular personalities, and the world in which they live. The value systems that they develop will influence their decisions for the rest of their lives. Many adolescents have received extensive instruction in religion throughout their childhoods. As adolescents begin to struggle against adult control of their lives in other areas, they also begin to question, lay aside, or doubt their religious heritage. In *The Search for America's Faith,* for example, Gallup and Poling (1980) indicate that adolescents show an interest in spiritual questions and a high level of personal involvement in religion.

It seems logical to assume that young adult literature would attempt to meet the needs and address the interests of adolescents in general, as well as the individual needs and interests of different young people. However, in spite of the traditional influence of the Christianity in America, very little has been written in the literature available to adolescents that reflects this influence. It is, in fact, difficult to think of more than a handful of young adult novels that treat religion with any depth. To test this impression, we decided

Reprinted from *The ALAN Review* 12.3, Spring 1985, pages 9–12, 53, by permission of the author.

to examine a large selection of young adult novels for their religious content.

To find the novels that included religious content, we looked at all available editions of the following widely used selection sources:

Basic Book Collection for Elementary Grades, American Library Association

Basic Book Collection for High Schools, American Library Association

Basic Book Collection for Junior High Schools, American Library Association

Best Books of the Year, Selected by the editors of School Library Journal

Books reviewed by the *School Library Journal*

Books for the Teen Age Reader, G. Robert Carlsen

Books for You, National Council of Teachers of English

Books for Young Adults, An annual book poll compiled by G. Robert Carlsen and others

Children and Books, Zena Sutherland

Children's Books Too Good To Miss, May Hill Arbuthnot

Children's Catalog, The H. W. Wilson Company

Children's Literature in the Elementary School, Charlotte Huck

Junior High School Catalog, The H. W. Wilson Company

Literature for Today's Young Adults, Kenneth Donelson and Alleen Pace Nilsen

Literature Study in the High Schools, Dwight Burton

Newbery Medal Winners and Honor Books, 1945–81

Senior High School Catalog, The H. W. Wilson Company

Your Reading, National Council of Teachers of English

We considered realistic adolescent novels published between 1945 and 1981 that contain serious concerns of adolescents, according to the annotations in the selection sources. We then developed a sixteen-item checklist with 142 subtopics which reflect various aspects of Christianity in the culture. The checklist included such topics as church attendance, sacraments, prayer, death, Christian holidays, the Bible, clergy, hymns, and denominations. This checklist was used to analyze each of the 201 most frequently recommended novels.

Findings

Adolescents are quite concerned about their religion and have many questions about it. They want to know how the religious teachings they have received at home and at church affect their lives. However, if the books in this study are indicative of all realistic adolescent fiction, readers will not find the answers here. Instead, they will find superficial discussions of Christianity and references to the same traditional practices that they question. Although middle adolescence is the most common time for a religious experience to occur, only two characters in the books in the study have such an experience: Mr. Slater in *Strawberry Girl* (Lenski 1945) and Jiro Ito in *The Moved Outers* (Means 1945). Both are minor characters; however, some protagonists such as Louretta in *The Soul Brothers and Sister Lou* (Hunter 1968), Louise in *Jacob Have I Loved* (Paterson 1980), and the title character in *Santiago* (Clark 1955) become more positive in their attitude toward Christianity or toward Christian practices. However, none of them is shown as having an intense religious experience.

Although all but eight of the 201 books in the study refer to Christianity, most of the books do not actually treat the subject of Christianity in depth, nor do they address the religious issues of concern to adolescents. Most of the references to Christianity in the books relate to cultural issues and traditional ritual, rather than to theological issues such as the nature of God, God's role in the history of mankind, or how Christianity has or should affect moral decisions.

For example, when contemporary issues such as abortion or sexual relationships outside of marriage are portrayed in books such as *Mr. and Mrs. Bo Jo Jones* (Head 1967), *My Darling, My Hamburger* (Zindel 1969), *Morning Is a Long Time Coming* (Greene 1978), *The Girls of Huntington House* (Elfman 1972), and *Father Figure* (Peck 1978), Christianity's role in moral decision making is not discussed.

The portrayal of death is discussed in relationship to Christianity in such books as *The Ceremony of Innocence* (Forman 1970), *Stub, a College Romance* (Bro 1952), *The Soul Brothers and Sister Lou* (Hunter 1968), *Home Before Dark* (Bridgers 1976), and *May I Cross Your Golden River?* (Dixon 1975). In most instances, however, such as those in *Father Figure* (Peck 1978), *The Friends* (Guy 1973), *Where the Lilies Bloom* (Cleaver 1969), and *A Day No Pigs Would Die* (Peck 1972), the conversation centers on the religious funeral service or the necessity of praying at the time of a death. Ministers are called, scripture is quoted and hymns are sung. Life after death, however, is most often portrayed as a concrete, literal interpretation by an individual who seems to be characterized as immature in his/her concept of Christianity. Rarely is life after death treated in depth, except in *Stub, a College Romance* (Bro 1952), in which Stub and his college friends discuss their differing concepts of an afterlife.

Pierre Babin in *Faith and the Adolescent* indicates that many adolescents are hostile toward organized religion, while at the same time feeling an intense interest and need for religion. This hostility toward organized religion is shown in some books as boredom with church services or resentment in being required to attend. Kit in *The Witch of*

Blackbird Pond (Speare 1958) and Ludell in *Ludell and Willie* (Wilkinson 1977) resent being required to attend what they consider to be boring worship services. Their objections are portrayed as superficial—the church service could be any dull adult gathering—and there seems to be no deeper dimension to their drift away from religion. In addition, adolescents' intense interest and need for religion is not, for the most part, dealt with in the books that we reviewed.

Many Christian symbols are visible in American churches, homes, and literature. Mary Wilcox in *Developmental Journey* states that her studies indicate that adolescents are concerned with, but confused by, these symbols. However, adolescent realistic fiction virtually ignores the symbols. A few crosses, church bells, and church steeples are mentioned, as are the ordinances of baptism, confirmation, and the eucharist. However, the references are almost always unimportant and a part of the setting. Of the twenty-six novels that mention baptism, most refer to the christening or baptism of infants. In *The Witch of Blackbird Pond* (Speare 1958) and *Wilderness Bride* (Johnson 1962), baptism in icy water is indicated as the source of serious illness. In *A Spy in Williamsburg* (Lawrence 1955) the christening of an infant is used as a social event as elaborate as the one the English Governor had for his child. Most of the eight novels that mention the eucharist simply refer to someone taking communion. An exception to this is *The Moved Outers* (Means 1945), which mentions the "lifted up peaceful feeling" communion always gives the protagonist although she is being forced to live in a Japanese internment camp during World War II. *The Rock and the Willow* (Lee 1963) mentions that Enie cannot take communion because she does not belong to the church. However, there is practically no discussion of the abstract meaning of these symbols in the lives of adolescents, nor of the referent of the various symbols.

Adolescents are also concerned with the Bible and its teachings. The Bible is quoted many times in the young adult novels that we studied. Books like *The House of Fifers* (Caudill 1954), *Orphans of the Wind* (Haugaard 1966), *Fogarty* (Neville 1969), and *Jacob Have I Loved* (Paterson 1980) contain numerous quotations throughout. Several books contain rather long quotations from the Bible: *Moccasin Trail* (McGray 1952) quotes Psalm 91:4,7; *The House of Fifers* quotes Isaiah 58:9,12; and *South Town* (Graham 1958) quotes Psalm 27:1,14. *Tree of Freedom* (Caudill 1949) quotes numerous passages in French from the Huguenot Bible. One hundred eleven of the novels contain references to a total of sixty-four biblical characters. The Bible is also used to decorate a bedside table or a church pulpit in many of the books we studied. However, the importance of the teachings of the Bible, the arguments concerning the symbolic nature of the stories or the infallibility of the Bible, and diversity in interpretation of the Bible are largely ignored.

Some historical novels for young adults contain references to the conflict between various denominations and to the conflict between government and/or society and the religious practices and beliefs of the characters. When the Amish young people in *Plain Girl* (Sorenson 1955) are required to attend a public school, they are faced with conflicts between their religious customs and the customs of the school. Conflicts between customs in the Indian culture and Christianity are shown in *Maggie* (Breck 1954), *Santiago* (Clark 1955), and *River of the Wolves* (Meader 1948). Differences between Christianity and Chinese customs are discussed in *Su-Mei's Golden Year* (Bro 1950), and differences between Japanese customs and Christianity are discussed briefly in *The Moved Outers* (Means 1945). However, books with contemporary settings rarely treat this problem. In the books studied we found no contemporary protagonists or minor characters who struggle with a conflict between milieu and religious beliefs. None are taunted by peers for wearing or not wearing certain clothing, for saying a blessing before a meal, for attending church or for refusing to participate in some social event or school activity because of religious beliefs.

Although many theological issues and Christian traditions were debated, discussed, and questioned during the late sixties, the only issue within the church to be reflected in books for adolescents of that period is the racial issue. In *Classmates by Request* (Colman 1964), *North Town* (Graham 1965), and *Tolliver* (Means 1963), churches were used for civil rights meetings. The minister in *South Town* (Graham 1958) tried to serve as spokesman for the Williams family when vigilantes were about to attack them. The ministers in *Anchor Man* (Jackson 1947) and *Willow Hill* (Whitney 1947) spoke at public meetings on behalf of having blacks attend white schools. In *Edgar Allan* (Neufeld 1968) the minister attempted to adopt a black child but changed his mind when social pressure became too great for him. However, the relationship between civil rights and Christian teaching about love or concern for the welfare of others is not discussed. The books tend to address only outward practices such as integration. Other issues of the sixties such as the "God Is Dead" movement, situation ethics, separation of church and state, and controversies concerning church hierarchy and the role of the lay people in the governance of denominations are not mentioned in the books.

Jesus is the foundation of Christianity, but He is usually mentioned in the books as a historical character. His relationship to His teachings and their relationship to the ethical or moral decisions of the protagonists in the books are not discussed. Only Mark Brian in *I Heard the Owl Call My Name* (Craven 1973) expresses a personal relationship with Jesus. The failure of adolescent fiction to show a relationship between the protagonists and Jesus's teachings indicates a need that should be met realistically in books for adolescents, since so many adolescents believe that they have such a relationship or are struggling to deal with their loss of a childhood sense of closeness to Jesus.

Some Possible Causes of the Problem

It is clear, therefore, that the Christian religion appears only infrequently in novels for young adults and then generally in a superficial fashion. Religion is a part of the setting but rarely a part of the theme. Although many controversial subjects that relate to adolescents have been dealt with in recent young adult fiction, religion rarely has. There are several possible reasons for the failure of adolescent books to address Christianity. In the period from 1945 to 1959, although Christianity was very important in the United States' culture, many people tended to treat it superficially. They focused on traditional practices, church attendance, and stewardship, rather than theological issues, how Christian beliefs affect the moral issues of society or how literal and symbolic interpretations of the Bible might conflict. This, in addition to the tendency of writers and publishers of books for adolescents to avoid controversial issues, caused the books to include frequent passing references to religious practices but not exploration of theological issues.

In the '70s there was a trend toward the production of books for adolescents dealing with many controversial issues, but Christianity was still not treated with depth in adolescent realistic fiction. Possibly this lack of depth was related to some people's interpretation of the Supreme Court decisions concerning religion in the schools. Publishers may have believed that, in their zeal to avoid purchasing books about religion for schools, librarians and teachers would refuse to purchase books that emphasized religious issues for fear of not complying with the law.

Another reason for the tendency of adolescent realistic books to avoid the concerns of adolescents relating to Christianity may be the discomfort that the authors feel in writing about religion. Many authors may find the subject embarrassing. It would be necessary for an author to have an interest in Christianity and to be fairly knowledgeable of its theology, though not necessarily be a believer, in order to write effectively about Christianity and to raise the issues of concern to adolescents. On the other hand, authors who are themselves believers in Christianity may find that they have difficulty avoiding didacticism in the presentation of the subject. There may also be a tendency on the part of the authors and publishers to underestimate the interest of adolescents in religious beliefs and practices. Without knowledge of studies of adolescents' opinions and concerns about religious matters, authors might get the impression, from casual conversations with adolescents, that they are not interested in reading about Christianity.

Children's literal Biblical interpretations and concrete concepts of religious phenomena often conflict with scientific information learned in adolescence. Adolescents need and seem to want exposure to realistic characters who face the transition from concrete to abstract or spiritual interpretations of Christian teachings.

There is an unmet need for well-written adolescent fiction which deals realistically and reasonably with Christianity since many adolescents want to see how other adolescents adjust to the conflicts of thought within the Christian community, as well as the conflicts between Christian beliefs and practices and society in general. What is being proposed here is not the writing of religious tracts, nor the converting of teenagers to a particular religion, nor, for that matter, the writing of books that carry a message opposed to Christianity. Rather, what is being suggested is the writing of sensitive, thought-provoking young adult novels that deal with the theme of religion in the lives of teenagers. Therefore, the difficulties involved in writing and publishing such books should not be allowed to keep them from becoming available.

References

Babin, Pierre. *Faith and the Adolescent.* New York: Herder and Herder, 1965.

Gallup, George, Jr., and David Poling. *The Search for America's Faith.* Nashville: Abingdon, 1980.

Wilcox, Mary M. *Developmental Journey.* Nashville: Abingdon, 1979.

Titles Mentioned

Breck, Vivian. *Maggie.* Garden City: Doubleday, 1954.

Bridgers, Sue Ellen. *Home Before Dark.* New York: Knopf, 1976.

Bro, Margueritte Harmon. *Stub, a College Romance.* Garden City: Doubleday, 1952.

———. *Su Mei's Golden Year.* Garden City: Doubleday, 1950.

Caudill, Rebecca. *The House of the Fifers.* New York: Longman, Green, 1954.

———. *Tree of Freedom.* New York: Viking, 1949.

Clark, Ann Nolan. *Santiago.* New York: Viking, 1955.

Cleaver, Vera and Bill Cleaver. *Where the Lilies Bloom.* Philadelphia Lippincott, 1969.

Colman, Hila. *Classmates by Request.* New York: Morrow, 1964.

Craven, Margaret. *I Heard the Owl Call My Name.* Garden City: Doubleday, 1973.

Dixon, Paige. *May I Cross Your Golden River?* New York: Atheneum, 1975.

Elfman, Blossom. *The Girls of Huntington House.* Boston: Houghton, 1972.

Forman, James. *Ceremony of Innocence.* New York: Hawthorn, 1970.
Graham, Lorenz. *South Town.* New York: Follett, 1958.
Greene, Bette. *Morning Is a Long Time Coming.* New York: Dial, 1978.
Guy, Rosa. *The Friends.* New York: Holt, 1973.
Haugaard, Erik Christian. *Orphans of the Wind.* Boston: Houghton, 1966.
Head, Ann. *Mr. and Mrs. Bo Jo Jones.* New York: Putman, 1967.
Hunter, Kristin. *The Soul Brothers and Sister Lou.* New York: Scribner, 1968.
Jackson, Jesse. *Anchor Man.* New York: Harper, 1947.
Johnson, Annabel, and Edgar Johnson. *Wilderness Bride.* New York: Harper, 1962.
Lawrence, Isabelle. *A Spy in Williamsburg.* Chicago: Rand McNally, 1955.
Lee, Mildred. *The Rock and the Willow.* New York: Lothrop, Lee and Shepard, 1963.
Lenski, Lois. *Strawberry Girl.* Philadelphia: Lippincott, 1945.
McGraw, Eloise Jarvis. *Moccasin Trail.* New York: Coward-McCann, 1952.
Meader, Stephen W. *River of the Wolves.* New York: Harcourt, 1948.
Means, Florence Crannell. *The Moved Outers.* Boston: Houghton, 1945.
———. *Tolliver.* Boston: Houghton, 1963.
Neufeld, John. *Edgar Allan.* New York: Phillips, 1968.
Paterson, Katherine. *Jacob Have I Loved.* New York: Crowell, 1980.
Peck, Richard. *Father Figure.* New York: Viking, 1978.
Peck, Robert Newton. *A Day No Pigs Would Die.* New York: Knopf, 1972.
Sorenson, Virginia. *Plain Girl.* New York: Harcourt, 1955.
Speare, Elizabeth George. *The Witch of Blackbird Pond.* Boston: Houghton, 1958.
Whitney, Phyllis A. *Willow Hill.* New York: David McKay, 1947.
Wilkinson, Brenda. *Ludell and Willie.* New York: Harper, 1977.
Zindel, Paul. *My Darling, My Hamburger.* New York: Harper, 1969.

33 Touchstones in Nigerian Youth Literature

Osayimwense Osa

Matthew Arnold used the term "touchstone" in *The Study of Poetry* (1880) to denote short passages of literary excellence which can be used to test the true strength and worth of other literary works; a procedure he considered more objective than merely valuing a work on personal or historical grounds. Today "touchstone" is used to mean a test or criterion for quality. To assert that some literary works are "touchstones" is a big claim. Likewise, considering a work a "touchstone" is an opinion. Frank Kermode (1985) asserts that "opinion is the great canon maker" (74). Inherent in that statement is "works of art come to be considered important not because of some shared inherent quality in them, but because they happen to seem valuable in terms of current taste and opinion" (Nodelman 1985, 3).

Today's youth (adolescent/young adult) literature is contributing immensely to the richness of all Nigerian literature, which hitherto has been a preserve of the adult world. Likewise, it is revolutionizing the reading habits of Nigerians. Young adult novels that are popular among Nigerian youths are steadily increasing in number. Some are mediocre, some are poor, and others are not really young adult literature. However, a few stand high above the rest in texture, style, thematic thrust, and presentation.

Three "touchstone" young adult books are Jide Oguntoye's *Too Cold for Comfort*, Agbo Areo's *Director!* and Buchi Emecheta's *The Bride Price.* They manifest a refreshing effortlessness, clarity, sureness of characterization, mastery of dialogue, and readability. In this article reference will be made to other young adult novels such as Buchi Emecheta's *Naira Power,* Chukwuemeka Ike's *Toads for Supper,* and Agbo Areo's *The Hopeful Lovers* to highlight and illustrate the strength of the three "touchstone" books.

Reprinted from *The ALAN Review* 15.3, Spring 1988, pages 56–58, by permission of the author.

Too Cold for Comfort, Director! and *The Bride Price* are not structurally complicated. The artistic temperament of the authors is not geared toward obscurity. The relatively simple structure of the works represents a deliberate decision to recreate their fictional world pictorially and chronologically. The novels maintain a consistently controlled style. It is only in the bid to capture various levels of language use in Nigeria that some form of pidgin English is used. However, the use of pidgin English does not obstruct the reader's understanding. In spite of the didactic stance of quite a number of young adult novels, these authors maintain an objective presentation of material. The young adult characters convey a sense of "felt life," rather than becoming instruments to illustrate a particular position or theory. The novels' themes are rooted in the Nigerian youth world as well as in the general world of young adulthood.

Unlike many young adult novels which tend to depict action mainly on a physical plane, *Too Cold for Comfort, The Bride Price,* and *Director!* attempt to delve into the psychological state of the young adult protagonists, and the result is a full roundedness of characters. According to Rebecca J. Lukens (1986), "we may know a person's height, weight, hair, color, ethnic background, and occupation. This is information. But until we are aware of the temperament, joys, and ambitions we do not know that person" (4). The protagonists in these novels are lifelike, and we are aware of their temperament, joys, and ambitions; we "know" them.

The narrative methods employed in these novels help ensure some ready sympathy for the protagonists. The heroes and heroines are the central consciousness of the novels, through whose eyes and with whose point of view readers look at events of the story. This is very true of *Too Cold for Comfort* where the reader is kept so close to the hero's consciousness that it seems as if the narrative emanates from the reader's mind.

We travel with Kolade Omola from the eve of his marriage through the time of his matrimonial problems. Like most youths, Kolade is quite excited about his coming wedding. Like most, he regards sex as an "instinctive thing, despite the lessons of the story of Adam and Eve, too natural for a timetable." His wife Hannah regularly denies him this sexual gratification, to which he believes he has a right, due to her warped conception and understanding of Christianity. Even on the night of their wedding day, when newly married couples typically consummate their marriage, Hannah's misunderstanding of Christian morality comes to the fore and ruins the night:

> Kolade had kissed her passionately and dragged her down to bed. She noticed her iro falling off and . . . "That is temptation," her voice rang out. She had some inner caution, a sort of voice akin to the

> "voice of God" which had cautioned her against falling for the lustful advances of Dr. Kole Tokulo over the years. As she had then reached obediently to this voice, so she would now.
>
> "Stop that, Kolade," she said in a high, hard and resolute tone, pulling him off and gasping, her eyes flashing in bewilderment.
>
> "What? Why?" perplexed, Kolade asked.
>
> "Don't you know what you are doing?"
>
> "What if I know? Is it anything wrong?"
>
> "Wrong. Yes. Don't you know right things should be done at the right time? That otherwise they become wrong?"
>
> "Wonderful. What time is better than now?"
>
> "You don't know. Man of small faith."
>
> "Hannah . . . Hannah . . . you . . . you are beating me hollow," Kolade stammered and trembled, full of sudden doubt.
>
> This was not the Hannah he had dreamt of a few days before his wedding but a fanatic of the sort he would least like to encounter.
>
> "Are you loose sexually?" Hannah rebuked him. "I arrived only few minutes ago; now you come to pounce on me. You didn't even mind leaving the door unfastened. This is unlike the follower of Jesus Christ you claim to be. No true Christian rushes into things. We should pray, consult God, seek His approval and blessings."
>
> "Good sermon," Kolade snapped back, shaking his head pitifully. He could see Hannah's mind was enslaved to dogma. He kept his distance on the bed and gazed at her, "Have you forgotten that our marriage was blessed by God and man in a memorable wedding ceremony only today?" (25–26).

This passage shows the atmosphere of Kolade's and Hannah's relationship, even on the night of their wedding—an atmosphere which henceforth pervades their love making, or lack thereof. Regular denial of Kolade's sexual gratification frustrates him. Consequently, he begins to regard his matrimonial home in terms of an enclosed state (marital bondage). His purchase of a "Liberate Yourself" T-shirt indicates his desire to get out of the claws of his marriage with Hannah, whom he soon regards as "an incorrigible bigot" (57). The theme of love and marriage among youths gives *Too Cold for Comfort* its strength. The novel can be acclaimed for the tremendous vitality exuded by the character of Kolade Omola through whose consciousness the reader feels his plight. Oguntoye paints a picture of an irrepressible, ebullient youth.

According to Eustace Palmer (1981), Emecheta adopts in *The Bride Price* "the technique which E. M. Forster referred to as 'bouncing'—demonstrating remarkable dexterity in shifting the focus, with the result that a good many of the characters, and not just the heroines, are powerfully presented" (21–23). Akunna, the female protagonist, is developed in considerable depth, and, unlike a welter of paper thin adolescent characters featured in many young adult novels, she emerges as a rounded character (Osa 1983).

The Hopeful Lovers, Toads for Supper, and *Naira Power* provide a good counterpoint for the three "touchstone" novels. They are like sermons on the mount, reflecting the shortcoming of philandering by giving a subtle warning to youths to shun such lifestyle. In spite of the fact that Tade Eji in *The Hopeful Lovers* and Amadi in *Toads for Supper* are living characters, true reflections of Nigerian playboys who recall for the reader Thomas Hardy's Sergeant Troy in *Far From the Madding Crowd,* these novels are didactic. Emecheta's *Naira Power* indicates to youths what will happen to them if they attach unnecessary importance to money. Putting such value on the naira, Young Ramonu steadily goes into stealing and graduates into an armed robber, only to be burnt alive when finally caught. *Naira Power*'s importance lies mainly in its topical nature. The naira was very strong in the 1970s—the oil boom era in Nigeria. Unfortunately through mismanagement and stealing, even in high quarters, the naira collapsed, and Nigeria now experiences the pang of economic squeeze. If money was not stolen, Nigeria still would be very viable. Emecheta shows that naira power is not permanent, especially when thieves are present in society.

Unlike such simplistic moralizing pieces, Agbo Areo's *Director!* is complex and dense; the author wants the reader to be attentive and put two and two together to get to the core of the novel's theme. Superficially, *Director!* seems to explore the theme that stealing results in retribution. But Areo's presentation is complex and lifelike. Akinduro Falana, the protagonist, is not a complete devil. The novel shows how his values are misguided. The novel's moral value lies in its ability to help the reader understand a moral predicament such as the condemnation of materialism. This kind of moral value lies in literature cast in the mold of realistic fiction.

Unlike the didactic pieces mentioned earlier, Buchi Emecheta's *The Bride Price* is a good example of a nondidactic Nigerian youth novel. The relationship between content and form appears simple, but is quite dense. A superficial reading of the novel may lead one to conclude that it is didactic, stressing the need for conformity to traditional cultural ways of life. Actually, to reach such a conclusion is a misjudgment of the importance of the plot and the role of the narrator.

The narrator says nothing positive about traditional ways of life. The novel considers the traditions of "osus" (outcast) and "bride price," showing the destructive side of such customs. In spite of the fact that Chike's father is one of the wealthiest and best-educated men in Ibusa community, he and his family are regarded as slaves (osus) because one of his ancestors had been sold into slavery. Because of tradition and custom, Chike, an osu, cannot marry the freeborn Akunna. Despite this social taboo, Chike and Akunna elope. Their rebellion brings about the death of their baby in childbirth and later the death of Akunna. Akunna, even on her deathbed, however, insists that her marriage was happy, and the choice of the child's name "Joy" should reflect the happiness of the union. Certainly, in this case, one may say that Akunna's short-lived happiness brought more joy than a marriage arranged by tradition. Such a marriage would have been determined by material (the bride price), not human, gain. Not only does tradition in this novel never take a step in the right direction, but those who rebel against tradition—the girl, the young man and his father—are always seen in the best light. They are the ones who make the human moves, even at the cost of material sacrifice. And, their shortcomings, if they can be viewed as such, are forgivable. In other words, the plot seems to say—a short and sweet marriage is better than a drawn-out life of misery with the wrong partner. Even this, however, is not the point of the novel.

The narrator's role in the novel is significant. Her comment at the end, "If a girl wished to live long and see her children's children, she must accept the husband chosen for her by her people, and the bride price must be paid," does not mean that people ought to conform to tradition, as a superficial reading of the novel may lead one to conclude. Rather, given the plot, it means—and this is the point of the book—nonconformity to inhuman customs seems to lead to disaster. However, this is something we should protest and fight against, perhaps unto death. Akunna plays the classic role of omniscient narrator and leads us into the thoughts of those with whom we should sympathize. However, it seems the author does not want her work to be obviously didactic. Therefore she makes the narrator hold back when it comes to direct criticism. Emecheta, in other words, wants readers to be active, wants them to put two and two together—for then their sense of revulsion will be realized. In short, the book, for all its protest, seems a beautiful example of nondidactic art.

Emecheta is a serious and committed writer, committed to exposing the plight, trials and tribulations, predicaments and predilections of the unfortunate and cheated: "For Emecheta, women constitute the most oppressed, the most underprivileged and the most unfortunate of all the underprivileged groups, and she has made the championing of the cause of womanhood her own peculiar territory" (Palmer 1981).

There can be no mistaking the tremendous wave of sympathy Emecheta arouses in the reader towards Akunna in *The Bride Price.* This note of responsive sympathy between heroine and creator leads, at times, to an overidealization of female protagonists, a certain blindness towards or refusal to contemplate their faults (Palmer 1981). This blunt portrayal of a young adult female is also apparent in the portrayal of sexual promiscuities in both traditional and modern Nigeria. *Too Cold for Comfort, The Hopeful Lovers,* and *Toads for Supper* deal with love affairs and philandering in urban areas, whereas *The Bride Price* deals with the topic in a traditional African society. The point is, whether in an urban or a rural society, widespread promiscuity is present. In spite of the fact that Chike, the local casanova in *The Bride Price,* is an osu (an outcast), he glories in his amorous relationships with local girls; some of his sex partners are married. In this way, Chike is like Akinduro Falana in *Director!* who sneaks out of school to have fun in brothels with free women; he is also like the female students who become harlots in order to make money in the city. Likewise, Chike's philandering is similar to that of Tade Eji in *The Hopeful Lovers* and Kolade Omola in *Too Cold for Comfort.* While Tade Eji is a playboy, Kolade Omola is compelled into sexual promiscuity because of the uncooperative nature of his wife, Hannah. Contrary to the impression conveyed by Chínua Achébe and some other African novelists, some of these young adult novels, like *The Bride Price,* indicate that there is widespread promiscuity in traditional society.

Some Nigerian adults condemn these books for using foul blunt language. But, the novels seek reality; and, of course, good literature should reflect life.

Too Cold for Comfort, Director! and *The Bride Price* are successful works of literature. Because of the depth of their characters and non-didactic nature of plot and theme, one can safely say that these three books merit serving as critical standards, "touchstones," and as frequent examples of good Nigerian young adult novels.

Works Cited

Areo, Agbo. *Director!* London: Macmillan, 1977.

———. *The Hopeful Lovers.* London: Macmillan, 1979.

Emecheta, Buchi. *The Bride Price.* London: Fontant Collins, 1965.

———. *Naira Power.* London: Macmillan, 1982.

Forster, E. M. *Aspects of the Novel.* London: Edward Arnold, 1927.

Ike, Chukwuemeka. *Toads for Supper.* London: Fontant Collins, 1965.

Kermode, Frank. *Forms of Attention.* Chicago: University of Chicago Press, 1985.

Lukens, Rebecca J. *A Critical Handbook of Children's Literature.* Glenview: Scott, 1986.

Nodelman, Perry. "The Art of the Children's Novel." *ChLA Quarterly* 11.1 (1986): 2–4.

Oguntoye, Jide. *Too Cold for Comfort.* London: Macmillan, 1980.

Osa Osayimwense. "Adolescent Girls Need for Love in Two Cultures." *English Journal* 72.8 (1983): 35–37.

Palmer, Eustace. "A Powerful Female Voice in the African Novel." *New Literature Review* 11 (1981): 21–33.

34 The Image of the Teacher in Adolescent Fiction

Mary Ann Rygiel

As a teacher, I am interested in the image of teachers. As an English teacher, I share the English teacher's faith that the written word is powerful, remaining after the chimera of television and film have faded. One of the most prolific, widely read—and hence, potentially influential—groups of commentators on teachers in the past decade has been the writers of adolescent fiction. Because the novels in this genre focus on the lives and problems of teenagers, they are frequently set in schools for at least some of the events of the story, and they depict teachers as constituents of the literal and psychological landscape of their teenaged protagonists. Through this fiction, these writers have articulated their views on the qualities of the good teacher and the bad teacher.

I have chosen fifteen adolescent novels for an examination of the characteristics of the teachers portrayed in them. In some novels, teachers are a relatively minor element of the adolescent's landscape. In others, teachers are far more prominent in the terrain of the teenager's world. Despite this difference in degree of importance of the teacher to the novel, the writers, though working independently, have reached an artistically expressed consensus on the traits of teachers who are portrayed positively and teachers who are portrayed negatively. The characteristics of each group are instructive.

Imagination

The first characteristic of teachers who receive favorable treatment is that they are imaginative and innovative. Imagination finds its uses in all subject matters. Ms. Barbara Finney, English teacher in Paula Danziger's *The Cat Ate My Gymsuit,* has a light show in class, Friday Finney flicks with snacks, and a bearded guitar-playing visitor who shares his poetry with the class. Miss Blue, a science teacher

Reprinted from *The ALAN Review* 8.2, Fall 1981, pages 12–15, by permission of the author.

(M. E. Kerr, *Is That You, Miss Blue?*), makes science more intelligible to her students by her idiosyncratic approach. One instance is her characterization of inert gases as "snob gases," for their property of not combining with other elements. Ms. Larson, art teacher in Paula Danziger's *The Pistachio Prescription*, makes the subject of American art history come alive for her class through the assignment of such projects as the making of a class quilt.

Insight and Involvement

A second characteristic of the good teacher is insight into the behavior and feelings of young people. Through her characterization of gases, Miss Blue has also managed to make an oblique comment on the social life of the girls at Charles Boarding School. Yet Miss Blue's religious zeal makes her remote from the student body and the other faculty, so her perceptive view of the girls is undetected by all but the sensitive narrator. For other teachers portrayed in other novels, insight is coupled with involvement. For example, Miss Peabody, English teacher in Isabelle Holland's *Heads You Win, Tails I Lose*, does not simply recognize overweight Melissa Hammond's misery at the sight of her handsome, insensitive neighbor and his giggling girlfriend at the town library. Miss Peabody tells Melissa with studied casualness that Ted MacDonald will be all right in about ten years.

A corollary to involvement with students is that the teacher is energetic. An apt image of this energy occurs in Frank Bonham's *The Nitty Gritty*, in the person of Mr. Toia, who drops by on his motorcycle to visit truant Charlie Matthews at his home. In this story, the boundaries of Mr. Toia's teaching domain are not the four walls of the classroom; he is capable of reaching out to "street people," in the "street" if necessary, in order to convey his message about the power of education to lift people out of the trap of poverty.

Degree and kind of teacher involvement varies with the kind of world the novelist has created and those who inhabit it. Mr. Toia is not a significant part of most of the events of *The Nitty Gritty* because this novel is really a story about how wise "street wise" is. Therefore, most of the episodes in the novel show people hustling. Yet, Toia's visit to the Matthews family in the beginning of the story and his discussion with Charlie of his "story" at the end of the novel provide a structural frame and perspective on all that happens.

By contrast, in both *Winning*, by Robin Brancato, and *The Man Without a Face*, by Isabelle Holland, the focus is on the critically important relationship of an adolescent with a teacher. In each case, the teacher does not put a limit on the relationship either in terms of time spent or emotion invested. In *Winning*, the teacher, young Ann Treer, recently widowed, reluctantly agrees to tutor Gary Madden, a star football player who has been hospitalized after a paralyzing injury in a game. Treer's relationship with Gary keeps him mentally alive during his months in the hospital, by her faithful visits, by her awareness of his need for independence, and not least by her assignment of a psychological novel (*Crime and Punishment*) and probing written work. She also saves Gary quite literally in his moment of depression during a lonely New Year's Eve, when she persuades Gary not to take his own life.

Interestingly, Justin McLeod (*The Man Without a Face*) also consents quite reluctantly to tutor fourteen-year-old Chuck Norstadt, a boy who needs to escape his female household but cannot pass the entrance exam at St. Matthew's boarding school. McLeod has a past which has left him emotionally bankrupt and self-punishing. But unlike Treer's widowhood, which provides a respectable curtain of detachment, McLeod's past would not meet conventional tests of social probity. His reclusive life protects a past of secrets and a present emotionally barren by choice. Chuck's life, too, has been emotionally incomplete, spent with a mother whose hobby is husbands. Charles learns enough during his summer of studies to be admitted to the boarding school. But more important, through the developing relationship between Chuck and McLeod, both man and boy turn toward personal commitment and away from a life stance of ironic detachment.

Talent

McLeod also exhibits the third major characteristic of the good teacher: the possession of talent, or in some instances, scholarly ability. Although his mysterious life gives rise to the whispered absurdity that he writes pornography, he is in fact a writer. He reveals to Chuck that he has published under the pseudonym Terrence Blake, a writer of highly regarded fantasy and science fiction.

In *Heads You Win, Tails I Lose,* also by Isabelle Holland, the drama teacher and coach, Miss Ainslie, has been in English repertory, appeared on Broadway, and directed a high school play favorably reviewed by a New York newspaper. Brian Griffin, in Lois Duncan's *Killing Mr. Griffin,* has sacrificed his status as tenured faculty member in a university English department to teach where he sees greater need, in high school. Barbara Finney (*The Cat Ate My Gymsuit*) leaves Dwight D. Eisenhower Junior High School to pursue a doctoral degree in bibliotherapy.

Adherence to Standards

Writers of adolescent fiction delineate a fourth major characteristic of good teachers—adherence to standards. They distinguish between fair standards and gratuitous cruelty, and expect mature readers to do the same. The penultimate example occurs in *Killing Mr. Griffin,* in which a group of adolescents present a distorted view of their English teacher. Yet author Lois Duncan makes clear the altruistic nature of Griffin's career choice and his personal code: The basis for his strict standards in class is his consuming desire to see students become independent thinkers and writers. He does not tolerate late papers, plagiarized work, or vacuity of thought in student writing. Nor does he like the latter any better in colleagues.

Justin McLeod is also faithful to high standards. He announces to Chuck Norstadt his uncompromising terms for the summer tutoring: three hours of tutoring a day, followed by Chuck's three hours of independent study. Any violation, and the arrangement is finished. In Mildred Taylor's *Roll of Thunder, Hear My Cry,* Mrs. Logan, a black teacher in a segregated school in the Mississippi Delta of the 1930s, maintains standards in a difficult setting. In fact, her failing the unscholarly T.J. for cheating leads to the loss of her job and financial crisis for her family.

Because individuals vary in what they see as having importance, two teachers may both have high standards even if their specific values clash. This is made clear in Alice Childress's *A Hero Ain't Nothin' But a Sandwich.* Bernard Cohen, a seventh-grade teacher in a Harlem school, emphasizes traditional academic learning. Nigeria Greene, also a seventh-grade teacher at the same school, teaches civics and social studies with a social message. He wants to imbue his students with a sense of personal pride and brotherhood.

Bad Teachers

Bad teachers can be defined by the contrapositive to assertions made about good teachers. Teachers who are not imaginative are not good teachers. Similarly, teachers who are not involved with students, not intelligent, not faithful to high standards, are not good teachers.

Miss Appel, in Robert McKay's *The Troublemaker,* provides a simultaneously comical and rather pathetic example of a teacher lacking in imagination. Her first writing assignment to a class of high school seniors is on the topic, "The Most Delicious Meal I Ever Ate." When rebel Jesse Wade responds with his enigmatic poem on boiled beans, Miss Appel runs scandalized to the principal.

As indicated earlier, degree of teacher involvement with students varies a great deal. Brian Griffin, a good teacher, feels a strong commitment to his students. But expressions of commitment which come easily to a character such as Barbara Finney, who even plays volleyball with the girls in P.E. in order to reach a girl, are incompatible with Griffin's reserved nature. However, Griffin cares sufficiently about his students to risk his career for them; he cares enough about them to discuss them so frequently at home with his wife that she feels she knows them; he cares enough to be exacting.

In Barbara Wersba's *Tunes for a Small Harmonica,* Harold Murth offers an appropriate instance of a teacher who can be condemned for his lack of insight and involvement. Wrapped in a cocoon of his own feelings, Murth is unaware throughout the entire novel of the adolescent passion J. F. McAllister bears toward him. He seems oblivious to the significance of her nursing him through an illness and showering him with gifts, and takes astonishingly little notice of her presenting him with one thousand hard-earned dollars for a trip to England to complete his dissertation on Christopher Smart.

One fictional teacher has the unhappy distinction of combining lack of intelligence with a lack of high performance standards for herself or her class. Dolly Luna, in *Killing Mr. Griffin,* lets herself be "kidnapped" in her pajamas by her students, who then take her to breakfast. This makes her popular. To Brian Griffin, Dolly Luna is just that, a "dolly" with a head full of sawdust. The author later makes it clear that she concurs with Griffin's assessment of Dolly's intelligence. On the day Dolly substitutes for Griffin in class, she shows herself blithely unaware of what the students are studying, of where they are in their text, or of any need to present a coherent lesson.

Rosa Guy offers one of the most searing portraits of any teacher, in her Miss Lass in *The Friends.* Miss Lass not only remains aloof from her ghetto class, she actually fears and despises them, using her well-practiced technique of deflecting student hostility from herself by selecting a victim from the class as the focus of everyone's dislike or ridicule. The other portrait of a teacher without redeeming virtues occurs in the figure of Brother Leon, in Robert Cormier's *The Chocolate War.* For Brother Leon, the accomplishment of his own sales goal for a school fund drive is far more important than the resistance offered by any lone student to the sale. In fact, such resistance must be crushed. His brutal efforts to break Jerry Renault are unethical and terrifying.

Some teachers who are reading this and measuring themselves against the yardstick offered by writers of adolescent fiction may feel that what is upheld is an impossible ideal. But this is not so. Good teachers in these novels recognize their own flawed natures and do not parade before unsuspecting adolescents as paragons. Miss Ainslie tells Melissa, who views her as a substitute for her own alcoholic mother, that she was not successful with her own daughter. Admissions of weakness or of need are made by McLeod, by Treer. Like real, complex people in other professions, the good teacher is someone who can admit a mistake and who is capable of growth.

It was noted earlier that some teachers are relatively minor elements of some of these novels. The more the teacher is shown as a functionary who takes roll, makes and collects assignments, and gives punishments for misbehavior, the more likely it is that the portrait is negative or at best neutral. Such teachers are not central as individuals to the thoughts, feelings, and development of the adolescents in the novel.

Often, such a teacher is shown as part of a group. In *The Troublemaker,* Mrs. Parsons is shown in charge of a large study hall with several other teachers present. Mrs. Parsons would like to play the role of "loving tolerant mother person sitting down for a guidance session with wayward children" (115). Yet, when an opportunity for honest discussion occurs, Mrs. Parsons shows that her real aim in any "dialogue" is to bring students around to an unquestioning acceptance of school policies. She tries to enlist the help of other study hall teachers in a suppression of dialogue. In Nat Hentoff's *This School Is Driving Me Crazy,* Mr. Kozodoy, who is seen as substantially concerned with his own career advancement, has class control but pinched sympathies for his students. Mr. Kozodoy is shown in several lengthy scenes drinking coffee in the faculty lounge and complaining about student Sam Davidson. In speaking directly to Sam, Mr. Kozodoy stands behind an unvarying shower of dictums: "He who is a slob in his personal habits is also a slob in his thinking habits. And he who is a slob in his thinking habits is a slob in his moral habits. It is all tied together. A clean boy is an honest boy. And vice versa" (37).

By contrast, in novels presenting good teachers, the teachers are distinguished from their colleagues not only in their character traits but in the actual structure of the novel. They are shown talking individually with adolescents, they are shown working at their desks, they are shown looking at books, and they are shown teaching with zest. It was said of Mrs. Logan that she was a "disrupting maverick" and that "more traditional thinkers like Miss Crocker were wary of her" (22). This does not mean, however, that these teachers undermine the nature and purposes of education in their classrooms. In fact, they reinforce the true goals. While their colleagues cooperate blindly with an unwritten law that says it is all right to bore children in the classroom day after day, these teachers make efforts to present stimulating, intelligent classes, to understand the problems of their students, and to uphold standards.

In making this composite portrait of the good teacher, I have drawn on the traits of many individual fictional characters. If we view literature not only as a reflection of reality but as an ideal toward which we should tend, this composite is obviously not a rigid mold. For each characteristic of good teachers, there is wonderful variation—"pied beauty"—in the way it is individually expressed. Good teachers are male and female, black and white, young and not-so-young. They are found in public schools and boarding schools, in junior high schools and high schools. They do not quit when the closing bell rings, but teach at home and in a hospital setting and in a school auditorium and on the street, if necessary. Good teachers make English class and art class exciting; they can make geometry and science and classics exciting, too. They may differ with each other as to what they see as important. But what can be said of all good teachers was said of Cohen and Greene by their principal (*A Hero Ain't Nothin' But a Sandwich*): ". . . the kids fare a bit better because they're both here" (55).

References

Bonham, Frank. *The Nitty Gritty.* New York: Dell, 1971.

Brancato, Robin. *Winning.* New York: Bantam, 1978.

Childress, Alice. *A Hero Ain't Nothin' But a Sandwich.* New York: Coward, 1973.

Cormier, Robert. *The Chocolate War.* New York: Dell, 1975.

Danziger, Paula. *The Cat Ate My Gymsuit.* New York: Dell, 1975.

———. *The Pistachio Prescription.* New York: Dell, 1978.

Duncan, Lois. *Killing Mr. Griffin.* New York: Dell, 1979.

Guy Rosa. *The Friends.* New York: Bantam, 1974.

Hentoff, Nat. *This School Is Driving Me Crazy.* New York: Dell, 1978.

Holland, Isabelle. *Heads You Win, Tails I Lose.* New York: Dell, 1973.

———. *The Man Without a Face.* New York: Bantam, 1973.

Kerr, M. E. *Is That You, Miss Blue?* New York: Dell, 1976.

McKay, Robert. *The Troublemaker.* New York: Dell, 1972.

Taylor, Mildred D. *Roll of Thunder, Hear My Cry.* New York: Bantam, 1978.

Wersba, Barbara. *Tunes for a Small Harmonica.* New York: Dell, 1977.

The South in Recent Young Adult Novels

Robert C. Small Jr.

For generations, Americans from the North, Midwest, and West have had an ambivalent attitude toward the South, its culture and its people. They have sometimes seen the South as populated by fair maidens and chivalric gentlemen, sometimes as a peaceful rural paradise, sometimes as a dark world of poverty and violence. Over the years, literature for teenagers often has reflected this ambivalence.

Romantic South

On the one hand, readers and authors have idealized a region that they believe is filled with lovely ladies and handsome gentlemen surrounded by the scent of magnolias and living in gleaming plantation houses with columned porticos. Fantasizing about and reading about a graceful and dramatic world of beauty, gaiety, heroism, and grandeur, those Americans who do not live in the South—and, indeed, quite a few who do—have thus accepted the Romantic South as a real rather than a fictional place. They have remembered the first chapters of *Gone with the Wind*, but not the last ones.

Poverty South

At the same time, many who are not Southerners have viewed the South as an area of ignorance and bigotry. Caricature sheriffs with big bellies, lynchings, hillbillies, and sloppy speech have been the bases of that other view of the South. Seen from this perspective, all black Southerners and most poor white Southerners live in terror of the Ku Klux Klan, the Boss, the Sheriff, the Mine Owner, the Mill Owner, and the Banker. Most Southerners live in rural poverty in dirt-floored cabins on worked-out farms or in isolated mountain valleys called "hollows" by the rest of the world and "hollars" by the natives. In this view, mostly stupid, mostly illiterate, mostly hopeless, these Southerners speak, not the sweet accents of Scarlet O'Hara, but a mumbled mush that is impossible to understand and regularly interlaced with odd expressions.

Reprinted from *The ALAN Review* 13.2, Winter 1986, pages 62–66, by permission of the author.

While the Romantic view of the South is largely a single view and a positive one, this one, which might be called the Backward South, actually consists of two quite different responses. First, there are those who react by emphasizing the grimness of Southern life and do so with moral outrage. Like the abolitionists before them, they are determined to bring about change. They, the books they write and the parts of books they remember, give as one dimensional a view of the South as the novels of the Romantic School. They tend to see 99 percent of Southerners as good-hearted but oppressed poor, and the other one percent as evil, powerful Bosses. They stress the wickedness of the Feudal South as the Romantics stress the virtues of feudal relationships.

Another set of believers in the Backward South see the ignorance, poverty, and strange speech habits of the region as funny rather than tragic. In this view, when Southerners remain in the South, they spend most of their time running moonshine or wrecking cars. *Smokey and the Bandit* and *The Dukes of Hazzard* depict this version of the South. On the other hand, if Southerners leave the South, their encounters with the sophistication of the world is seen as hilarious. Reruns of the *Beverly Hillbillies* show naive emigre Southerners befuddled by the modern world.

Literary South

There is a third stereotyped view of the South. Although not nearly as widespread as the other two, it is, nevertheless, a very powerful one. It is also one in which many Southerners are closet believers, as many are also closet Romantics. In this view, the South is filled with fine poetry and great novels. The literate write those novels; the less literate compose folk songs and enrich the English language with their colorful speech. No less a stereotype than the Romantic South and the Backward South, this view, held mostly by the literate, the educated, and the cultured, sees the Southerners who can read and write as consisting largely of people like William Faulkner, Carson McCullers, Thomas Wolfe, and Jesse Stuart.

Each of those stereotypes has a touch of the real and as much of the unreal as any unified view of a diverse people. The South is no one place or people. Geographically it slips over into West Virginia, western Virginia, parts of Kentucky and Tennessee; that is, it includes Appalachia. This region from which Granny and the other Beverly Hillbillies are supposed to have come is a different world from that of Plains, Charleston, Richmond, and Savannah. The mountainous South that spreads over beautiful, rugged, coal-rich but isolated and poverty-burdened Appalachia is viewed, even by other Southerners, with a mixture of romance and scorn similar to the attitudes of the rest of the country toward the entire South. Eastern North Carolina looks north and south to other states that make claims to aristocracy and west to its mountainous other half, whose people are incomparably different from the fishermen of the coast and the tobacco farmers of the Piedmont.

The Young Adult Novel and the South

These stereotypes marred the treatment of the rural South in most young adult novels until the last few years. Early in the development of the young adult novel, many authors used settings in rural areas and small towns, particularly in the South. These young adult novels, usually dealing with horses and dogs, hunting and teenage love, had little to do with Southern people and their culture. They rarely made contact with the social and economic problems of the South; they were merely set in the South. The problems of the South were part of the taboos that Dwight Burton identified in *Literature Study in the High School* (1970). There were few exceptions. In *Shuttered Windows,* Florence Crannell Means rose above the sentimentality of the young adult novel of her time to picture the strength of Southern black culture, as well as the invidious effects of racial prejudice and the resulting suppression of black people. However, few teenagers were given the chance to read her books.

In most cases, however, the young adult novels of the 1940s and 1950s set in the South reflected either the Romantic or the Funny Backward stereotypes. They bore little relation to the stark reality of the region during these years. Authors of these novels seemed to use the South to create a nostalgic world of country living, hunting, farming, riding a dearly loved horse, and living with treasured dogs. It was the teenage version of the Romantic South, but with even less that was truly Southern than adult novels that were formed from the stereotype. Or, the books were about a funny world of hicks, hillbillies, and rednecks. Certainly, they showed no influence from the splendid Southern writers of those decades such as Flannery O'Connor, Faulkner, and McCullers.

In the 1960s, attention in the young adult novel to an idealized rural South was largely replaced by a concern with such topics as drug addiction, illegitimacy, divorce, and homosexuality. Although it is likely that such problems existed in the rural South as much as anywhere else, the settings of the young adult novels written in the '60s and especially the early '70s shifted from the small towns and farms of the earlier novels to large cities and their suburbs. Indeed, most of the settings were outside the South. A few young adult novels did deal with the problems of racial prejudice in Southern towns. *South Town* by Lorenz Graham and the other novels in his series looked at black life in the South and at the black expatriate in the North. Bella Rodman's *Lions in the Way* also tried to explore the problem of school integration. A few authors like Vera and Bill Cleaver (*Where the Lilies Bloom*) specialized in Southern and Appalachian regional stories, and in *Where the Red Ferns Grow* Wilson Rawls depicted an essentially Southern mountain story set in the Ozarks. The fare was pretty thin, however. The typical young adult novel of this time seemed to deal with either a black drug addict or a gang leader living in the ghetto of a major city or with a middle-class white teenager whose parents were contemplating divorce. More recently, however, a number of young adult novels have been set in the South and in Southern Appalachia. In fact, there seems to be a renewed interest by young adult authors in the people and customs of the American South. Unlike the superficial, sentimental novels of the '40s and '50s, many recent young adult novels set in the South deal in profound ways with the Southern people, their culture and problems. Some treat the modern South; some look to the recent past; some, to the distant past. Authors like Sue Ellen Bridgers, Katie Letcher Lyle, Mildred Taylor, and Katherine Paterson write in the tradition of Southern literature—in the tradition, that is, of Eudora Welty and McCullers. They write from the South; they do not merely place their stories there.

The tragedy of black Americans was largely ignored in the literature of the South until recently, and authors of young adult literature were also guilty of that omission, Means's *Shuttered Windows* being a notable exception. Mildred Taylor in *Roll of Thunder, Hear My Cry* filled that gap with a novel so beautifully written that it won the Newbery Award in 1977 and, more important, gave readers a young adult novel that genuinely appealed to adults. Earlier, Paula Fox produced the agonizing *Slave Dancer,* also a Newbery Award winner; and Virginia Hamilton captured a Newbery Award for *M. C. Higgins, the Great,* set on the edge of strip-mined Appalachia. In two novels about Ludell Wilson, *Ludell* and *Ludell and Willie,* Brenda Wilkinson presented the Southern black world, on the verge of drastic change, but, despite its hardships, possessing its own integrity and power.

Characters

Southern literature has always been famous for its treatment of characters, especially bizarre characters and those driven by dark forces within their world and themselves. Faulkner, O'Connor, and Harper Lee show us those people and the forces that drive them. So do Bridgers, Lyle, and the Cleavers. Think of Mary Call of *Where the Lilies Bloom* and *Trial Valley* with her proud determination—or Stella, of Bridgers's *Home Before Dark,* also proud, also determined. Both are characters of the South, like the women, old and young, of Welty's stories. Bizarre characters abound. There is the wild boy in *Trial Valley;* the long-courting, briefly married, almost-never-married old couple in *All Together Now;* the father and the wild Indian in *A Ballad for Hogskin Hill* (James Forman). They are as true to the South and to themselves as the dwarf and giantess in McCuller's *Ballad of the Sad Cafe,* the characters that form the family in *The Heart Is a Lonely Hunter,* and those in O'Connor's stories.

Language

The speech of the South has been looked at with the same ambivalence as its culture and people. Badly reproduced in movies and television programs, it is often found charming. Actually spoken by real-life people, it produces scorn, laughter, or pity. Yet it represents a wide scope of linguistic varieties: the African-influenced speech of coastal South Carolina and Georgia, the French-influenced speech of parts of Louisiana, and the early modern English still appearing in the mountains of the Appalachia. There are the forward or broad sounds of rural Georgia and Mississippi, the many varieties of black speech found throughout the region, and the old, nearly lost, pockets of antique upper-class accents found in Virginia and South Carolina.

More important, the literature of the South is as much a literature of language as it is one of character of setting. The Elizabethan richness of Faulkner, the wild variations of O'Connor, the deceptively naive prose of McCullers, the pure Southern rhythms of Welty are matters of conscious style, of careful attention to language. Dialect operates not only in the speech of their characters but also in the magic of their narrative. Their stories are one fabric from the language of their South. Lyle has captured that Southern richness in some of her narratives. Mildred Lee subtly contrasts the Southern mountain speech of Lanthy Farr to the Boston accents of Drew Thorndike in *The People Therein.* Bridgers is a master. Taylor in *Roll of Thunder* depicts dialect magnificently. Style and language from and of their region mark these new Southern novelists as they enrich the young adult genre.

Setting

Southern literature has also been the epitome of literature of setting. The small towns of McCullers, the rural environs of O'Connor and Faulkner, the towns and country of Welty, and the cities, towns, and country of Robert Penn Warren dominate and control the characters, lives, and plots of their novels. The literature of the South is as much a literature of setting as it is a literature of language, people, and events.

Hogskin Hill is as much a character as any of the humans in Forman's novel, as, in its way, is the giant steam shovel that drives like a relentless force across the land and people. The farm and tenant house of *Home Before Dark,* the rural Virginia landscape of William Armstrong's *Sounder,* the slave ship as an extension of the South in *The Slave Dancer,* and the Great Smoky Mountains of *The People Therein* are all actors in their stories, not merely backdrops. The power of the land is, in many ways, a living force for such authors. Faulkner's Yawknapatopha County invades and dominates the lives of those who live there; and, in many recent young adult novels, place is an equally powerful force.

Plot

Finally, the Southern novel of the twentieth century has been marked by a belief in uncontrolled and uncontrollable fate. Even in the midst of laughter, Faulkner and O'Connor see Southerners driven to their actions by fate. In their darker moments, they and McCullers, Warren, Harper Lee, Katherine Ann Porter, and Wolfe seem to believe that the tragedies of the South—slavery, war, repression, poverty—have created a fated people. Although individual and frequently bizarre, these Southern people are, nonetheless, trapped by the power that moves their world, like characters in a Greek tragedy. The modern young adult novelists of the South seem to recognize the power of fate, although they are usually willing to let their characters master that fate, a mastery more exciting and moving than any mere conquest of simple events. Perhaps the most impressive example of the power of fate among these novels is the force that moves the black family of *Roll of Thunder, Hear My Cry* toward crisis and confrontation. They are successful, even prosperous. They cope with the prejudice of their white neighbors. They are protected by reasonably decent, influential white people. Yet one knows that, ultimately, the power of fate operating in their time is driving them toward disaster. It seems that they cannot survive, that the social forces of the time will not let them survive. One might guess that they are not in control of their own lives. Fate seems to move them toward ruin as the people in *Absalom, Absalom!* cannot change the fate that rolls them forward, like a wave, on the wave of Faulkner's prose.

But these new Southern writers rarely reject the power of the human spirit to survive and control fate. Thus Stella in *Home Before Dark* will not let fate dominate her, although her mother is a slave to it. In *All Together Now,* Casey and Dwayne, despite their mostly joyful summer, are ultimately overcome by the fate that moves to put Dwayne in a home for the retarded. At the same time, however, Hazzard and Pansy struggle against their fate to love, but never to be together—he, in his tent, she, in her soul. Bridgers once said that Hazzard and Pansy nearly took the novel away from her, and in the end they forced her to bring them back together. Perhaps, then, they were so determined to control their fate that they took charge of the writing of their novel, to be sure that fate was not in charge of them.

Conclusion

Southern literature has a magnificent tradition. In the twentieth century authors like Wolfe and Faulkner, Warren and McCullers looked at their region and produced works of greatness. They used the language, the fears, the world, the culture of their people as the clay to shape an image of men and women, the blacks and whites, the rich and poor, the mountain folk and the tobacco farmers of the rural South. In that great tradition write Mildred Taylor, Sue Ellen Bridgers, Katherine Paterson, and the other authors of this new young adult literature of the South. They meet the challenge well.

Suggested Readings

Armstrong, William. *Sounder.* New York: Harper, 1972.

Branscum, Robbie. *Johnny May.* Garden City: Doubleday, 1975; New York: Avon, 1976.

Bridgers, Sue Ellen. *All Together Now.* New York: Knopf, 1979; New York: Bantam, 1980.

———. *Home Before Dark.* New York: Knopf, 1976; New York: Bantam, 1977.

Cleaver, Bill and Vera Cleaver. *Trial Valley.* Philadelphia: Lippincott, 1977; New York: Bantam, 1978.

———. *Where the Lilies Bloom.* Philadelphia: Lippincott, 1969; New American Library, 1974.

Crook, Beverly Courtney. *Fair Annie of Old Mule Hollow.* New York: McGraw, 1978; Avon, 1980.

Forman, James. *A Ballad for Hogskin Hill.* New York: Farrar, 1979.

Fox, Paula. *The Slave Dancer.* Scarsdale: Bradbury, 1973; Dell, 1975

Lee, Mildred. *The People Therein.* Boston: Houghton, 1980.

Lyle, Katie Letcher. *Finders Weepers.* New York: Coward, 1982.

———. *The Golden Shores of Heaven.* Philadelphia: Lippincott, 1976.

Paterson, Katherine. *Bridge to Terabithia.* New York: Crowell, 1977; Avon, 1979.

———. *Jacob Have I Loved.* New York: Crowell, 1980; Avon, 1981.

Rawls, Wilson. *Where the Red Ferns Grow.* Garden City: Doubleday, 1961; New York: Bantam, 1974.

Rockwood, Joyce. *Enoch's Place.* New York: Holt, 1980.

Taylor, Mildred. *Roll of Thunder, Hear My Cry.* New York: Dial, 1976; New York: Bantam, 1978.

Wilkinson, Brenda. *Ludell.* New York: Harper, 1975; New York: Bantam, 1980.

———. *Ludell and Willie.* New York: Harper, 1977; New York: Bantam, 1981.

Wallin, Luke. *The Redneck Poacher's Son.* New York: Bradbury, 1981.

Appalachian Literature and the Adolescent Reader

Carolyn L. Mathews

The book had sat on my desk since first period, forgotten momentarily by its reader, who had hurried off without bothering to pick up either it or the frayed orange notebook from a desk by the window. Just before lunch an exiting student stopped and picked it up, saying, "Oh, are you reading *Queenie Peavy?* It's the best book I ever read. I read it once in the sixth grade and four times since then." No, I wasn't reading *Queenie Peavy,* but I wondered what it was that would make an eighth-grade student read a book five times. "It's so good," Lisa informed me. "It's about this girl named Queenie Peavy who lives way out in the country—kinda like around here—and her father's in jail. And she's real mean, but really all she wants is for her father to come home. But when he does, he doesn't pay attention to her, and he's real mean an' all, and she realizes she's got to be somebody all on her own. It's a real good book." So I read *Queenie Peavy.*

Part of the appeal of *Queenie Peavy,* an adolescent novel by Robert Burch, can be attributed to its theme, a theme referred to by G. Robert Carlsen as "The Search." In his article, "For Everything There Is a Season," Carlsen says that adolescents choose books about individuals who are looking for a direction in life.[1] Thus, Queenie is appealing in that she is a character who is caught in a values conflict and who struggles to overcome that mean and defensive streak in her nature that keeps her in constant trouble at school and in the community. Her struggle is one in which she, in Carlsen's words, must "come to terms" with herself and her life.[2] But this pursuit of values is not the only reason that teenagers in my school would find Queenie appealing.

When I rethink what Lisa told me about *Queenie Peavy,* I remember that the first thing she mentioned was not Queenie and

Reprinted from *The ALAN Review* 11.1, Fall 1983, pages 11–12, 47–48, by permission of the author.

her meanness and her change, but rather that "Queenie Peavy lives way out in the country, kinda like around here." Thus for Lisa, and for many teenagers, I think, there is a need to read novels whose settings and characters are regional. Teenage readers want to see themselves in the novels they choose to read, and a very important, but often overlooked, part of this sense of self is the self that we are because of where we're from.

Queenie Peavy is from rural Georgia, a place likely to be familiar, if not known, to anyone who lives in the rural South and knows that "sorry" doesn't have to do with apologies and that being "smart around the house" has nothing to do with IQ. Something in the dialogue and in the descriptions of biscuits and fatback makes the reader say, "Yes, that's how it is here." Yet, readers in Southwest Virginia, in western Kentucky, in that whole mountain region from West Virginia to Georgia—to these readers Queenie Peavy lives in a place just "kind of like it is here." The element of setting absent from this book, but so important to the people of these areas, is the mountains. That Appalachia is a distinguishable region within the body of literature set in the South is a premise set forth by many scholars of the Appalachian region. Among these is Wilma Dykeman Stokely, who refers to this as "subregionalism" and notes that there have been differences between the "reality of the mountain experience and that of the rest of the South."[3] Jim Wayne Miller makes this distinction between Southern literature and Appalachian literature by pointing out a "cultural separateness" of the Appalachia.[4] Jack Welch takes this notion further by stating that "the test of whether or not there is such a thing as Appalachian literature will lie in whether or not we can find examples of the sociologically defined characteristics of the region in the literature . . . about the region." He concludes that "fortunately for the sake of the future of Appalachian literature, it is possible to find abundant examples of these sociological characteristics in the literature."[5]

Appalachian literature, then, is literature set in Appalachia, the southern highland region of the United States that extends from West Virginia, follows east of the Blue Ridge in a southwesterly direction into Georgia, and turns to include northeastern Alabama, Tennessee, and Kentucky. Welch refines this definition by qualifying that Appalachian literature is literature which "reflects certain qualities of Appalachian culture and which concerns itself with the land as it impinges on human life."[6]

Using Welch's definition, which takes into account cultural qualities reflected in the literature, the reader of adolescent novels can find examples of Appalachian literature within the body of young people's literature. This culture is reflected within a limited number of adolescent novels, five of which will be discussed here as a representative sample. Four of these, published within the past five years, are *Trial Valley,* by Vera and Bill Cleaver; *Fair Annie of Old Mule Hollow,* by Beverly Courtney Crook; *A Ballad for Hogskin Hill,* by James Forman; and *The People Therein,* by Mildred Lee. *Trial Valley* is the sequel to *Where the Lilies Bloom,* by Vera and Bill Cleaver, published in 1967. If the reader were to apply some sort of sociological measuring stick to these novels, he or she would likely determine that all reflect to some degree a true picture of the Appalachian experience.

Consideration from a Sociological Perspective

One of the traits which sets Appalachian attitudes and culture apart from that of mainstream American is a fierce individualism.[7] With this in mind, the reader is not surprised when Roy Luther in *Where the Lilies Bloom* gives his daughter strict instructions to provide for him a "simple homemade burial when the time comes" in a hole he dug himself. Mary Call is directed not to send for the undertaker who "can be ill-humored . . . when the times comes to divvy up" or for the preacher who "has a mighty voice in these mountains but expects to be paid."[8] Individualism can mean a refusal to accept charity. In *Trial Valley,* the sequel to *Where the Lilies Bloom,* Mary Call continues to carry out her father's wish that the family never accepts charity. Kiser, her brother-in-law, "does not give us money support," she says. "I will not let him. We earn our living from the gathering of salable medicine plants and their parts."[9] This same attitude is expressed by Fair Annie's Pa in *Fair Annie of Old Mule Hollow.* Pa, opposed to government handouts, says, "A man shouldn't ast the govermint to take care of him when he can take care of hisself."[10] The disdain of charity is in part a need to be self-reliant and in no way beholden to others. Thus, when Fair Annie's Pa is released from jail, a visit due to an explosion aimed at driving out strip mining, Fair Annie sees "no reason to spoil his homecoming by telling him that his daughter had asked an outsider for help."[11] Similarly, Drew, a visitor and naturalist in the Smoky Mountains, writes to his sister that he periodically provides first-aid for mountain families who always offer him a meal or a present in return for his treatments, for they have "a horror of being beholden."[12] In *Ballad for Hogskin Hill,* individualism takes a strange turn, one described by Weller in *Yesterday's People* when he says that public welfare serves individualism by allowing a man to accept a check, but go on living as he has always done. The government is "serving individualism's need," and for some getting a check becomes a challenge, and "ingenious ways of qualifying" are devised. This, Weller calls "self-reliance gone to extremes."[13] Thus, it is not surprising that in *Ballad for Hogskin Hill,* David's grandfather, Jason, asks seventeen-year-old David to accompany him for his performance at the county health clinic. The old man pretends to be blind in order to qualify for more government relief; and, when he succeeds he laughs, ". . . We did it. You and me," then continues, "Seriously, Davy, I had it comin'. I'm not restin' here just for show. That was a day's work an' more."[14]

A second characteristic of Appalachia is a strong sense of family. Wilma Dykeman Stokely sees this as an important quality which distinguishes much Southern Appalachian literature.[15] Thus, the number one rule set down for Mary Call by her father is "always to take pride in having the name Luther." Her number two rule is to strive with everything in her "to keep the family together."[16] In *Ballad for Hogskin Hill,* the importance of family is shown when the grandmother, Zorah, tells David, "There's Stuart blood in your veins,"[17] thus beginning an account of the family's history. She makes David promise to keep track of it once she's gone. Strong family ties and clannishness take the form of a feud in *Fair Annie of Mule Hollow.* Here values are in conflict for a teenage girl, Fair Annie, who has been taught to hate and fear the "wild McFarrs," but who has come to love one of them.

Other traits related to family feelings and family structure are also demonstrated. Weller notes that families in Appalachia exhibit an emotional dependence on each other and that the death of a family member brings great and often exaggerated grief.[18] Thus, when the grandmother dies in *The People Therein,* her daughter Ora takes to her bed, "from mourning her ma."[19] Another characteristic noted by Weller is the unique place of babies in the mountain family. Always, he said, they are welcome. Thus, the reader sees Sharon, the sister in *Ballad of Hogskin Hill,* happily supported by her family when she births an illegitimate baby. Illegitimacy is also addressed in *The People Therein.* Laban, the very religious father of pregnant Lanthy, says she is blaspheming when she says her love had been something "holy." He holds a grudge against the unknown father but accepts the child, saying "what's done's done."

A third trait related to families is the distinct separation of the male and female roles. These roles prescribe daily tasks, the separation of the sexes, and certain social behaviors.[20] Thus, in *Fair Annie of Mule Hollow,* the men and boys hang around the grocery store while the women and children go to church. The existence of distinct roles is also shown when "for the first time that they could remember, Ma offered the blessing." Within Fair Annie's family, offering the blessing is "Pa's prerogative as head of the table and of the family."[21]

A final characteristic to be discussed here is the Appalachian person's sense of fatalism, the belief that the events of a person's life are determined by powers beyond his or her control.[22] Coal mining is an occupation that is fatalistic in nature, and such fatalism is demonstrated in *Ballad for Hogskin Hill* when David dreams of the ghosts in the mines. Forman writes,

> All coal mines had ghosts, malevolent phantoms ready to push the unwary into near-bottomless shafts. Most miners were religious, but when the earth gave a tremor it was not God at work, but Big John or Sad Sam rumbling down there, for a soul lost in a mine remained there forever, cursing its ill fortune and seeking disaster for others.[23]

Weller notes that fatalism allowed the mountaineer to live without feeling guilty that he was to blame for his lot in life, and indeed it was often the harshness of the land that overcame the man.[24] Thus Mary Call says in *Where the Lilies Bloom* that Roy Luther has "let things beat him . . . the land, Kiser Pease, the poverty." She goes on, "Now he's old and sick and ready to die and when he does, this is what we'll inherit—his defeat and all that goes with it."[25]

Considerations from a Literary Perspective

Thus, all five of the adolescent novels mentioned above reflect the qualities that sociologists have determined as characterizing the Appalachian region. Does sociological mirroring mean, then, that all five in this representative sample are books which teachers of Appalachian young people should recommend to their students? The answer is no, and the reason for this answer has to do with the purposes of sociology as opposed to the purposes of literature. When we use only a sociological measuring stick to determine the effectiveness of the literature, there comes a point where a good piece of literature becomes immeasurable, too big in a sense, to be scientifically matched with a list of social traits. Jim Wayne Miller is writing of this distinction between sociology and literature when he says that the nature of sociology is to form generalizations and its concern is with group rather than individual behavior. Literature, on the other hand, is concerned with individuals and with the "unique knowledge to be derived from this emphasis."[26]

A test for determining *good* Appalachian literature for young people, then, should be not that different from tests for any sort of literature. To be considered "good," the novel should first be free of stereotyping. Second, it should deal in depth with individuals, and it should show those individuals involved in universal conflicts or learning some universal truth. Wilma Dykeman Stokely emphasizes a third criterion reminiscent of Welch's definition of Appalachian literature as literature dealing with the land as it "impinges on man." This criterion, one which applies specifically to Appalachian literature, is what Stokely calls "a heightened sense of place."[27]

In determining the literary effectiveness of the five aforementioned novels, the reader recognizes early in the reading of *Fair Annie of Old Mule Hollow* that this story is made ineffectual by stereotyping of characters and situations. Beverly Courtney Crook treats a contemporary subject, strip mining, against a backdrop of mountain feuds and antiquated social customs. That Crook tries to make characters who stand for "typical" mountaineers is obvious; in fact, she tells us several times over that her characters behave as they do simply because they're mountaineers. "In true mountain tradition," she writes, "he [Pa] never revealed his feelings in words or expression."[28] Likewise, Crook uses the generalization of "patriarchal family structure"[29] to create a picture of mountain women and girls that is far from believable. She writes,

> Ma and the girls got dressed and heated coffee to keep warm. The men were gone and they were suddenly faced with a void of leadership. No one knew what to do. Although they sometimes resented being bossed by the men, they still depended on them for decisions.[30]

Only in the end when Fair Annie resolves to finish school and then study to become a lawyer are the stereotypes broken, but these events happen too late to salvage the story. Even though teenage girls would likely become involved with Fair Annie and her love for the hated McFarr, girls in Appalachia would not recognize, as similar to their own, the place where Fair Annie lives or the family that surrounds her. Few families, if any, still have "play parties," and the reader would be hard pressed to find any modern mountain girl who, like Fair Annie, has never been out of her cove or who has never ridden in a car.

The stereotyping in *Fair Annie of Old Mule Hollow* leads to a very romanticized picture of mountain life, for Fair Annie's life has an archaic quality in which nights are spent singing the old ballads in the family's cabin, and the days are spent lost in the mountain thickets. The strip mining seems terrible in that it threatens this quaint scene.

Such is not the case in James Forman's *A Ballad for Hogskin Hill.* Forman is aiming for a more realistic picture of mountain life, but the novel fails on several counts. Forman wants to show the reader the devastation of strip mining and the exploitation of the Appalachian land and people by large coal companies, but this admirable cause is overshadowed by some obvious flaws in the book. Just as in *Fair Annie of Old Mule Hollow,* the author has been satisfied to let generalizations dictate the characters and their actions, and the reader is left wondering what these people are *really* like. Anyone who has read Weller's *Yesterday's People* can easily imagine Forman rereading particular sections from this sociological representation of Appalachia before sitting down at his typewriter to clack out the next chapter. When one reads Forman's account of Paradise on "welfare-check-cashing day," he or she is struck by the similarity to Weller's description. Forman writes,

> David has seen nothing to beat the jam-up of vehicles . . . International Harvester pickups, mud-caked Fords and Chevy's clogged what was normally a deserted street.[31]

This is very like Weller's statement that "it is . . . common . . . to see the streets filled but once a month, and then with slow moving, mud-spattered old cars, pickup trucks, and jeeps. . . ."[32] Similarly, when Sharon, the teenage sister, unmarried and pregnant for the second time, says,"Reckon I can't get on without another life kickin' away inside. I feel so no-account, otherwise,"[33] the reader remembers Weller's statement, "I am confident that one reason for the high rate of illegitimate births in the mountains is that the arrival of a child gives a young girl a new sense of her own purpose and worth. . . ."[34] Obviously, there is some truth in the picture that Forman gives us, but the characters are flat, one-dimensional depictions of what he imagines mountaineers to be like. The reader knows nothing about Sharon other than the information provided, and I, for one, wondered why Forman bothered to depict any situation in such a superficial way.

Because of the stereotyping, the overall image of Appalachian people in this novel is a very negative image. We see the characters through the eyes of seventeen-year-old David, who refers to his family as the "Kincaid Carnival," a carnival complete with his mother, the fat lady who never steps away from the TV except for a Moon Pie; Joseph, his dim-witted brother; his grandfather who runs a still and cheats the government; and his father who roams at night with an outcast who speaks broken English. Young people in Appalachia *might* identify with David, but in any such identifying they would feel, I'm afraid, shame, and they would understand all too well David's leaving the mountains at the end of the novel. Although David must leave to escape possible imprisonment and even though Forman says that David and his girlfriend, Verna, went "as people who do not flee but seek,"[35] the reader feels that Forman gives no one a reason for staying in this depressed and depressing region. Forman writes, "The forest and the mountains might one day exist no more, but what then would remain to nourish the souls of men?"[36] His *sentiments* tell the reader that a sense of place is important, but unfortunately the reader sees nothing in his characters to suggest that they have been so nourished by the mountains.

A third novel, *The People Therein,* succeeds where the above two novels failed. Mildred Lee, in this book, presents characters who display mountain qualities but whose actions and speech are a part of the author's use of characterization rather than of setting. We see Lanthy's father, Leban, embarrassed, then enraged, and finally accepting of her pregnancy, and these reactions are a part of his character rather than being simply an announcement that he acts "in the mountain tradition." Set at the turn of the century, the book does not dwell on the quaint and picturesque, but shows the sweat and sting of hours in the sun, day after day in the cornfield or the quiet loneliness of winter's early bedtime when Lanthy lies listening for her dead Granny's night sounds. Isolation, that main fact of mountain life in the past, is revealed throughout by strong images, and the reader feels it as he or she reads of the wind "sad in the cedar boughs." This story, basically a love-romance, follows the usual plot line in that Drew and Lanthy meet, are separated, and finally reunite. Teenage girls, particularly, would become involved with Lanthy's feelings and with her long wait for Drew's return. It is the fine characterization and careful attention to setting that make this Appalachian novel one to be recommended to teenagers.

The novels by Bill and Vera Cleaver, *Where the Lilies Bloom* and its sequel *Trial Valley,* depict a life "which means good despite all its sorrow and mistakes and confusions."[37] The Cleavers successfully demonstrate the two qualities identified by Stokely as qualities which distinguish the best of Appalachian literature. These two, the "heightened sense of place" and "an awareness of the continuity of life," are central to both of these adolescent novels.[38]

Forces of nature have always played an important part in mountain life, and Mary Call speaks of this when she speaks of those "who lived and hoped, hungered, froze, endured isolation, monotony, who hated, fought, despaired and died."[39] She experiences these forces during the harsh winter after her father's death when piled snow caves in the roof of one part of their house and Romey insists that the long winter will never end, that "The Lord has forgotten us. This land is forgotten."[40] But finally the winter ends with spring, a "rebirth . . . turned tender green"[41] and the Cleavers show that, while mountain life is hard, there is a promise of some sort that keeps life from being the totally depressing occupation that Forman sees.

Trial Valley deals thematically with life's promise as it is revealed through the coming-of-age of Mary Call. At the beginning of this book, Mary Call poses a question about the purpose of life. "We are here for a reason," she says. "We are not here just to watch ourselves and each other rattle around like stones in a bottle."[42] Through the course of the story she finds Jack Parsons, a child abandoned near her home; and, though she works to establish the child with her sister and brother-in-law, this child's trust and love of her make him cling to her. Mary Call moves from viewing Jack Parsons as just another invasion on her freedom to seeing the raising of Jack as part of her purpose. Her change is revealed in this conversation in which Mary Call tells of her friend Gaither's feelings for the child and then for her own:

> "Sure. He thinks you're what it's all about."
> The child frowns, uncomprehending. "Do you?"
> "Do I think you're what it's all about? Well, yes, I guess I have come around to that nutty way of thinking. But don't let it go to your head."[43]

Mary Call's purpose, then, is tied closely to the Appalachian sense of family, an awareness that has to do with the family's rootedness in the region, rootedness based on a concept of the "continuity of life."[44]

Mary Call's ties to her purpose and family are shown in her rejection of a young social worker who has come to love her:

> He asked me to marry him.
> I said, "I can't."
> "Is that your full answer?"
> "We don't believe in the same things. I have my kids and I believe in them. You don't."
> "I see," said the Virginian. . . . And then he became angry. He told me my views were "elemental." That my opinions were base and out-of-style. . . .
> Well, the Virginian knew about the stars. He was educated and polished but what was missing in him was too much for me. And now I dream no more dreams of him.[45]

The Cleavers give no romanticized view of mountain life, but that this life is good is reflected when Mary Call says, "So this, then, is the promise, clean and simple. It is a strange one, this compensation that speaks of life ongoing. There is no confusion in its consolation. It is positive."[46]

Each of the five adolescent novels discussed above reflect Appalachian life, but simple reflection of mountain life is not the only quality to be considered when helping Appalachian students choose literature. The recommended books, free of stereotyping and overgeneralization, should show the characters influenced by their surroundings and by their sense of family roots and ties. Readers should discover in their reading of these books the part of themselves that is there because of their mountain roots.

References

1. G. Robert Carlsen, "For Everything There Is a Season," *Literature for Adolescents,* ed. Richard A. Meade and Robert C. Small, Jr. (Columbus: Charles E. Merrill, 1973), 118.

2. Carlsen 118.

3. Wilma Dykeman Stokely, "The Literature of the Southern Appalachian Mountains," *Mountain Work and Life* 40 (Winter 1964), 12.

4. Jim Wayne Miller, "Appalachian Literature," *Appalachian Journal* 5(Autumn 1977), 82.

5. Jack Welch, "A Sociological Rationale for the Existence of Appalachian Literature," *Appalachian Journal* 3 (Winter 1976),169.

6. Welch 168.

7. Jack Weller, *Yesterday's People: Life in Contemporary Appalachia* (Whitesburg: UP of Kentucky, 1965), 29.

8. Vera and Bill Cleaver, *Where the Lilies Bloom* (Philadelphia: Lippincott, 1969), 13. Hereafter referred to by book title.

9. Vera and Bill Cleaver, *Trial Valley* (New York: Bantam, 1977), 4. Hereafter referred to by book title.

10. Beverly Courtney Crook, *Fair Annie of Old Mule Hollow* (New York: Avon), 13.

11. Crook 113.

12. Mildred Lee, *The People Therein* (Boston: Houghton, 1980), 47.

13. Weller, 31–32.

14. James Forman, *A Ballad for Hogskin Hill* (New York: Farrar, 1979), 65.

15. Stokely 13.

16. *Where the Lilies Bloom* 14.

17. Forman 36–37.

18. Weller 59–60.

19. Lee 132.

20. Weller 75.

21. Crook 112.

22. Weller 37.

23. Forman 25.

24. Weller 37.

25. *Where the Lilies Bloom* 15.

26. Miller 88.

27. Stokely 12.

28. Crook 11.

29. Cratis Williams, "Who Are Southern Mountaineers?" *Appalachian Journal* 3 (Autumn 1975), 34.

30. Crook 87.

31. Forman 60.

32. Weller 91.

33. Forman 226.

34. Weller 62.

35. Forman 228.

36. Forman 226.
37. *Trial Valley* 1.
38. Stokely 13.
39. *Trial Valley* 2.
40. *Where the Lilies Bloom* 143.
41. *Where the Lilies Bloom* 172.
42. *Trial Valley* 2.
43. *Trial Valley* 116–117.
44. Stokely 13.
45. *Trial Valley* 114.
46. *Trial Valley* 117.

Bibliography

Carlsen, G. Robert. "For Everything There Is a Season." In *Literature for Adolescents.* Ed Richard A. Meade and Robert C. Small, Jr. Columbus: Merrill, 1973. 113–22.

Cleaver, Vera and Bill. *Trial Valley.* New York: Bantam, 1977.

———. *Where the Lilies Bloom.* Philadelphia: Lippincott, 1969.

Crook, Beverly Courtney. *Fair Annie of Old Mule Hollow.* New York: Avon, 1978.

Forman, James. *A Ballad for Hogskin Hill.* New York: Farrar, 1979.

Lee, Mildred. *The People Therein.* Boston: Houghton, 1980.

Miller, Jim Wayne. "Appalachian Literature." Appalachian Journal, 5 (Autumn 1977): 82–91.

Stokely, Wilma Dykeman. "The Literature of the Southern Appalachian Mountains." *Mountain Work and Life* 40 (Winter 1964): 7–18.

Welch, Jack. "A Sociological Rationale for the Existence of Appalachian Literature." *Appalachian Journal* 3 (Winter 1976): 168–179.

Weller, Jack E. *Yesterday's People: Life in Contemporary Appalachia.* Whitesburg: UP of Kentucky, 1965.

37

The Search for Identity: A Theme Common to Adolescent and Native American Literature

Raymond D. Kemp Jr.

The need to find oneself—to be one's own person—is perhaps the strongest and most traumatic drive of adolescence. The adolescent faces a transition from the dependence of childhood to the independence of adulthood. The teenage years are an extremely turbulent time, where the values of one's parents, peers, and society often conflict. Adolescence forces an identity crisis, where each individual must come to terms with the questions: "Who am I?" "Where did I come from?" and "Where am I going?"

The search for identity amid conflicting cultural values is a common theme in literature written by and about Native Americans. Their identity crisis is brought on when the cultural values of the Native American and those of the white world conflict. This theme offers adolescents many parallels to their own identity crisis and is illustrated by five novels: *A Girl Named Wendy* by Beverly Butler, *A Country of Strangers* by Conrad Richter, *Arilla Sun Down* by Virginia Hamilton, *When the Legends Die* by Hal Borland, and *House Made of Dawn* by N. Scott Momaday.

The protagonists in each of these novels are strongly influenced by the values and culture of the Native American. All spent at least part of their childhood living on the reservation. When forced

Reprinted from *The ALAN Review* 16.2, Winter 1989, pages 10, 13, by permission of the author.

to "keep their real self half-smothered between the layers of conformity that didn't wholly fit" (Butler 208), all face an identity crisis. The protagonists all find that they do not fit wholly in the Native American culture or in the white man's culture. In these novels, there is a depth of character that draws the reader into the protagonist's world.

Fifteen-year-old Wendy in *A Girl Named Wendy* faces her identity crisis when her parents are divorced. She is taken from the reservation to Milwaukee to live with her aunt and uncle. Here she is caught between her relatives, who attempt to reject her aunt's Native American heritage, and Russell, an openly militant Native American who lives with them. Wendy also faces additional pressures to conform when her aunt and uncle attempt to mold her into their deceased daughter's image. When she runs away and returns to the reservation to live with her mother and medicine-woman grandmother, she feels torn between two worlds. Wendy faces this crisis and discovers who she is and what she is in this fast-moving, perceptive novel.

Twelve-year-old Arilla in *Arilla Sun Down* perceives her self as a "throwback." She doesn't look like her black mother or her part-black/part-Native-American father. She feels intimidated by her fifteen-year-old brother, Jack Sun Run, who calls himself an "Amerind" and acts out a stereotyped Indian role. By outward appearance, her father rejects his Native American heritage, but its influence is apparent. Arilla's life changes when she saves her brother's life. She develops confidence in herself. When she must go to the reservation to get her father, she learns just how much her father's Native American heritage influences him and how he has attempted to withhold this influence from his family. She discovers that her brother acts the way he does to hide the hurt and insecurity caused by the conflict of the two cultures. She realizes that she, too, must someday come to terms with her Native American background. Arilla's fascinating story is interspersed with dream-like free association of her earlier childhood.

Mary Stanton is kidnapped as a very young child and raised as Stone Girl in *A Country of Strangers*. She is young enough so that she forgets her white heritage and becomes in her mind a Native American. She marries and bears a son. Her life is happy until she is forcibly returned to her natural parents and the white world. She resists this return until she learns of her husband's death. Her natural parents reject her and her son, and she works for them as a servant. Her son is killed when she saves her younger white sister from a fate similar to hers. Stone Girl recognizes a bond with her white parents, especially her dead mother, but remains a Native American in her heart. She is caught between the two worlds, not totally fitting in either. With her husband dead and parents' rejection, she has lost all sense of roots. She sets out for the wilderness with True Son, who faces a similar dilemma, to live in a country of strangers. Richter is sensitive in his characterization of Stone Girl in this intriguing, fast-moving companion novel to *A Light in the Forest.* In *A Light in the Forest,* the similar story of True Son is chronicled.

Thomas Black Bull sets out to eradicate his past in *When the Legends Die.* Betrayed by his own people and the whites, he succeeds in killing all of his past (the legends) except his childhood on the reservation (the bear). After a successful career in the rodeo, he returns to the reservation to recuperate from an injury. He relentlessly hunts the bear, which symbolizes his childhood, but cannot bring himself to kill it. He realizes that he cannot kill the bear, because in doing so he is symbolically killing himself. He begins to accept his past and remember feelings that he has long suppressed. He realizes that he will never be the same "clout Indian" that he was in the past, and for the first time since his childhood begins to make peace with himself and who he is. We share Thomas Black Bull's childhood, his rodeo life, and his return to the reservation in this powerful and vivid novel. The Native American life of his childhood is exceptionally portrayed.

In *House Made of Dawn,* Abel returns to the reservation after World War II to find that he doesn't fit in anymore. He kills a white man in a drunken brawl and is sentenced to prison by the white man's court. He is relocated to Los Angeles after his release. Here his mental state deteriorates. Two friends attempt to help him adjust to urban life, but they realize they are powerless. After he is almost killed in a fight, he returns to the reservation for a "second homecoming." When his grandfather, who raised him, dies, he finds solace in his heritage and the land itself—the "house made of dawn." Momaday, a Kiowa Indian, vividly and realistically portrays Abel's struggle. His wide use of Native American legends adds to the rich imagery and detail.

A turbulent search for identity caused by cultural conflict is the common denominator for these novels. The Native American culture, view of life, and respect for the spirituality of nature are also addressed to varying degrees.

The five protagonists ultimately triumph when they face their identity crises and come to terms with themselves. They all emerge with a stronger resolve of who they are, where they came from, and where they are going.

Introduction of these and similar novels into the classroom will greatly enrich any adolescent literature program. In addition to expanding the adolescent's world by presenting another culture and dispelling many stereotypes, the students will be drawn into the characters and identify with them. It may be possible for the adolescent to address affective feelings, not openly addressed otherwise, through these Native American characters.

Bibliography

Borland, Hal. *When the Legends Die.* Philadelphia: Lippincott, 1963. (Senior High.)

Butler, Beverly. *A Girl Named Wendy.* New York: Dodd, 1976. (Middle School/Junior High.)

Hamilton, Virginia. *Arilla Sun Down.* New York: Dell, 1976. (Middle School/Junior High.)

Momaday, N. Scott. *House Made of Dawn.* New York: Harper, 1968. (Senior High.)

Richter, Conrad. *A Country of Strangers.* New York: Knopf, 1972. (Middle School/Junior up.)

38 Before "Teaching" a Novel: Some Considerations

Patricia P. Kelly

Literary critics and our own reading experiences tell us that the novel provides a closer representation of real life than any other literary group. Through novels students can explore other cultures and other times; can broaden their views beyond the boundaries of their own communities; and can see how characters handle problems or fail. The vicarious nature of literature, best provided by novels, is an important reason for having students read these longer works. Although we should encourage extensive reading based on students' own choices and have students with common reading interests share their reading in small groups, teaching longer works, specifically novels, as a whole-class endeavor can serve several purposes. But before I describe what I think are the values of having some works read in common, let me explain what I believe are not appropriate reasons for "teaching" a novel.

Novels should not be assigned in order to prepare students for college or "the future." Such goals are shortsighted, leading both teachers and students to viewing literature as something to be administered in doses—it's good for you, it will socialize you, or it will make you successful. With this approach, we expose our students to the great writers so that it's much like getting the measles; once you have them, you don't have to worry about it anymore. The point is that, although many students gain what I call a "cocktail" knowledge of literature, they by and large remain untouched by the *experience;* others just tune out, and in all probability do not become lifelong readers, which is perhaps the overriding goal for teaching literature. It is critical that the novels selected for study focus on what students can learn *now;* the novels should say something important to them in this stage of their lives. This assumption, of course, may justify some classics as well as make us rethink using

Reprinted from *The ALAN Review* 11.2, Winter 1984, pages 36–37, 48, by permission of the author.

others, but it certainly means that good young adult novels belong in the curriculum.

We want to challenge students, but at the same time we don't want to make them struggle to the point that it is, as one teacher put it, like "pulling teeth" to get them to respond or worse yet tell them what it all means. There must be something in the novel that touches their own lives, something to which they can relate. Students can handle what might indeed be a more difficult novel if they have the context, a store of understanding, to bring to the work. That is one reason why I think a novel such as *The Old Man and the Sea* probably should not be taught at the high school level. Although the words are easily decoded, the situation is one in which most students cannot immerse themselves. An old man's agony, his sense of being past his prime and useless but trying one last time to triumph, is not a character with whom they can identify. Also, the plot moves slowly and much of the conflict is subtle, whereas Cormier's *The Chocolate War* reveals a similar existential view of man but in a different context that students find appealing.

Neither is teaching a novel to an entire class an opportunity to use a text-analysis approach, more appropriate for English majors and others committed to the study of literature. Teacher-directed novel study, however, should provide critical and evaluative thinking experiences which extend students' understandings beyond those normally gained through independent reading.

Having in-common class novels is not returning to the basics in its often-misapplied approach of just pushing difficult literary works down into the lower grades, which results in students' attempting to deal with ideas and worlds unconnected with their own experiences. We cannot ignore readiness, a complex set of variables involving more than reading levels, as we select novels for study.

Why then do we want students to read some of the same novels?

Whole-class reading experiences help students develop a more critical eye, help them gain the skills that will, in fact, make reading a pleasure. I avoid theme finding, however, because students somehow have come to believe that is the ultimate question that must be answered from literature and that teachers actually have these gems written down somewhere to mete out at appropriate times. I focus, instead, on character and the complexity of motivations and decisions that characters make. I want students to understand the characters in relation to the time and the situation. For example, *Home Before Dark* by Sue Ellen Bridgers, although essentially Stella's story, goes beyond the coming-of-age theme. Toby's love, conflicts, hurts, and inner feelings are so poignantly told that boys as well as girls enjoy the novel. The complexity of the adult characters also makes the novel more than a teenage story—Stella's mother, not her father, has kept them on the road in poverty; Stella's father wrestles with his feelings of inferiority as he lives in the tenant house and his brother lives in the homeplace; Anne fears that she will have to assume responsibility for the children; and Maggie realizes that loving and giving are more important than owning things. These and other well-developed minor characters make this novel rich for classroom discussion.

The characters in fiction then become part of the student's storehouse of experiences—not themes in the abstract. Whole-class discussions of the same novel can help students become independent critical readers, making them realize that a literary work cannot be boiled down to a single satisfying sentence or phrase, a nutshell to be stored away for some future use, and developing their skills for evaluating a writer's craft. Many students are indiscriminate independent readers, putting one book aside and picking up another without much purpose except the experience of a new story. But class activities, in which students share views, hear a variety of perceptions, and explore possibilities, deepen the understandings that they in turn can take back to their independent reading.

Another reason for a class to study some novels is to provide some common reading experiences that can serve as "touchstones" for discussions. Students can compare and contrast the ideas in other literary genres to those in the novels, thus connecting their study of literature rather than viewing it as discrete experiences.

A final purpose lies in the value of engaging in a sustained reading experience. It is valuable for students to develop the capacity to deal with longer works, not only because it is an important reading skill but because those same sustained efforts carry over into lifelong learning. All entertainment cannot and should not be half-hour television shows, broken by commercials, or short stories, designed to be read in one sitting; neither do headlines and capsulized reports reveal the details and implications of important issues. We cannot let students become satisfied with snippets if we can make them thirst for more by teaching the process of dealing with longer works.

In selecting books for whole-class reading then, I look for good-quality novels that appeal to adolescent interests. At the same time that I value the importance of adolescent interests, I attempt to choose books that most students probably would not select to read independently; or if they might, I believe that the students will emerge from the class reading experience with considerably broader dimensions. Because the characters in Katherine Paterson's *A Bridge to Terabithia* are elementary school age, the novel is appropriate for independent reading at that age but also as an in-common reading experience for older students, who will not be put off by the ages but instead see the universality of experiences—rejection, fear, envy, death. Jess's initial reaction to Leslie's death is complex, involving a sense of his own importance because his best friend has died, liking the attention he is receiving, experiencing the inability to express his grief partly because death is an abstraction, the finality of which he cannot understand, and partly because grieving means accepting death. The quality of writing and the breadth of characterization make the book an excellent choice for older students' whole-class reading.

The books selected should represent a balanced connection between where students are and where we want to take them. If a literary work doesn't bridge that gap, if there is too much or too little distance between the two, then the study will be mostly unproductive—either because the novel is too easy to use for teacher-directed class reading or because it requires understandings beyond the students' personal and academic experiential levels. There also should be some consideration of providing a balance between the light and dark sides of life. Of course, many good choices tip more one way than the other; but if literature is something to which teenagers can personally relate and through which they broaden their experiences, then the total year's study of literature should present a fairly balanced view of life.

Some consideration might be given to the differences in reading preferences between girls and boys although adapting to these differences is more important in earlier reading stages. However, both late adolescent girls and boys like novels with sociological and psychological overtones.

Whether certain works are acceptable for whole-class reading within the context of community standards is an issue that teachers must decide for themselves. I do believe, however, that in selecting novels for in-common reading we need to consider this factor but always in relation to our educational purposes. For example, *The Chocolate War* contains the language and behaviors of teenage boys, causing some adults to view the book as inappropriate for classroom use, particularly with junior high students. Perhaps a more compelling reason for using the book in senior high classes, however, is the level of conceptual thinking necessary to comprehend the novel beyond the facts of the plot. The novel can provide for some students an excellent introduction to other existential works or for other students, the major study of existentialism.

When we assess the purposes for using novels as a teacher-led activity and the criteria for selecting such novels, many young adult books clearly meet those purposes and criteria. Why then do many of us continue to view them as pap rather than substantial sustenance or as the second-rate substitutes for students who cannot handle the first-rate classics?

Derek's Story: The Complex History of One Adolescent Reader

Margaret Mackey

I met Derek when he volunteered to participate in a study of teenaged readers. He was four months short of his seventeenth birthday and a very affable, easygoing young man. One reason he had offered to assist me, he said, was that it was "better than sitting in English class." He laughed often and appeared to be very relaxed about the reading I asked him to do.

The purpose of my study was to investigate the association between a teenager's current reading strategies and that same person's reading history. I tried to keep an open mind about any such linkage, though it was tempting to assume that a good reader would more likely be an enthusiastic reader with a long history of reading for pleasure. At the beginning of the study, I was convinced that my own views of how reading works were open-ended and plural, and that they made due allowance for the idiosyncrasies of individual readers. My experience with Derek challenged these assumptions and showed me that the varieties of individual learning are far more complex than I had thought.

Derek's Reading

As I had with other readers, I asked Derek to read two short stories. One was a science fiction story, "Impostor," by Philip K. Dick, and the other was "The Doll's House" by Katherine Mansfield. The stories were chosen to contrast with each other. One was a genre story, set in the future, with many turns and twists of plot; the second placed less emphasis on plot and concentrated on presenting a vignette of social life in the early part of this century.

Reprinted from *The ALAN Review* 20.3, Spring 1993, pages 39–42, by permission of the author.

Derek read these stories in sections, silently; and, at the end of each segment, I asked him to comment on what was happening, to predict what might happen next, and to reflect on what he had earlier thought.

Derek read well. He made thoughtful and subtle comments on the characters. For example, he noticed in "Impostor" that the people who arrested the hero "actually weren't sort of the enemy; they were on Olham's side." In "The Doll's House," he observed of the heroine's bossy sister, "Isabel is more of a leader but a follower at the same time. She does what people think is right." He made comments that indicated he was thinking of the stories as constructs; his predictions included phrases like, "They'll describe," and, "They'll develop," and he made more than one explicit remark about "the way this story was written." He made easy use of such terms as "setting the scene," "description," "symbolism." At one point, he retrieved a detail he had passed over, or forgotten, earlier in the story: "Sutton Woods seemed to say something to him, and I didn't pick up earlier in the story, but it's obviously got some significance to him." It seemed to me that ability to read as if he had noticed the initial mention was a kind of reading sophistication that gets little credit in reading manuals but that is nevertheless significant in the real world.

Derek was flexible about tactics. In the first story, he made a decision early on about the likeliest way the plot would develop and stuck to his prediction even when the author twisted the plot in very intricate directions. He was right about the ending, and he was not to be decoyed. After reading the first section of "The Doll's House," however, he made an erroneous decision that the story was set during the 1930s or 1940s. This time he was very ready to change when further evidence presented itself. He said, "I think my first prediction of the time was a little too late; I think it was probably earlier, in the early 1900s or the late 1800s." Asked why, he produced evidence from the text: "The town house, the town school type of thing, and the way they were dressed, and the social structure of the time."

By the end of our first meeting, I had gained a very positive view of Derek as a reader. He was astute and observant for the most part; he made adjustments where they were clearly called for; but he registered very early on that, in "Impostor," Philip K. Dick was playing a game with the readers and engaged his wits accordingly. He was flexible, intelligent, subtle. I looked forward to a follow-up interview.

Derek's History

The second time we met, I asked Derek to describe his own history as a reader. Again, he was very pleasant and articulate. It was what he said that was surprising.

Derek learned to read without any trouble and said, "It seems like I've always sort of known how to read." As a child, he was read to occasionally and liked Dr. Seuss. There were always books in his home and from time to time he was taken to the library. He is one of four children, and they all owned books. Derek's friends liked to read and encouraged him to join in with them, recommending titles and inviting him to readathons.

Yet from the outset Derek resisted reading. His brother owned *The Hardy Boys* series, but Derek didn't bother with them. His cousin, who loves to read, made serious efforts to engage him with books, but Derek just fell asleep. He didn't get many books for presents because everybody knew he couldn't be bothered to read.

Derek's present reading involves the occasional flick through the *National Geographic* on the way to bed, reading captions rather than full articles, and an annual reading of a single title chosen from a set of *Reader's Digest Condensed Books,* which he reads in the car while traveling on his summer vacation.

In spite of this severely limited engagement with reading for pleasure, Derek was able to make quite sophisticated comments on how reading works. Asked what makes a good reader, he said:

> Trying to understand every aspect. A lot of people I know read through things but they don't really bother to sit there and figure things out if it doesn't come to them immediately. . . . And I think picturing what you're reading in your mind is really helpful. Sort of watching the play go by as you read.

Furthermore, his level of low-grade acquaintance with a number of book titles was higher than such a reading background might suggest. As part of my project, he looked at a number of first pages of a wide range of novels written for children, adolescents and adults; and as these pages were identified, he was able to comment on many of them, although his comments were social rather than literary. For example, in a conversation about the *Sweet Dreams* romances, he said, laughing, "I remember the girls reading a lot of that. I used to try and find them dirty scenes." Of *Pride and Prejudice,* he remarked, "I saw part of the movie and . . . my sister read it in university so I had to type up her essay." He observed that he had always meant to read something by Stephen King but never quite got around to it. Similarly, he had actually read *The Lion, the Witch and the Wardrobe* as a child, and enjoyed it so much he contemplated reading more, but somehow he had never managed it.

The contradictions of Derek's reading story do not end here. Since he was about eleven or twelve, he has spasmodically felt an urge to improve himself and made a stab at reading a very challenging book. He tried *Huckleberry Finn* at the end of Grade 6 and made little sense of it. A year or two later he had a go at *Moby Dick* but failed to finish. When asked what book he had read most recently, he was stymied: "Hmmm. What was it?" Looking at the first pages reminded him that he had borrowed a copy of *Great Expectations* from his future brother-in-law and read some of it but again had not finished.

Derek seemed to have few illusions about himself. Asked if he would describe himself as a good or a poor reader, he replied, "I think I'm a good reader but not really a reader. . . . I don't do much of it, but, what I do, I enjoy and I like to think I do well."

Some Contradictions

If I had met Derek in my classroom, I would have been very impressed with his reading abilities. Certainly, of the group I saw for his little project, he was one of the strongest readers.

If I had met Derek socially, in a framework that allowed me to be aware of his daily habits and preferences, I would have registered him as a nonreader. As he said himself, he has many activities which he prefers to reading; and he was very hard pressed to imagine a situation in which he would actually voluntarily read, although he doesn't dislike it. Knowing Derek thus, I would have supposed that his reading talents were as limited as his interest.

Yet in the artificial situation where I did encounter Derek, he revealed that either of these analyses would have been inadequate. Derek is a much more complex reader than most standard paradigms allow for. He seldom reads, but he doesn't actually dislike it. He prefers to do almost anything else; but when he chooses to concentrate, he can produce subtle, flexible readings.

Robert Protherough has described five modes of reading: "These five can be arranged on such a scale of 'increasing distance,' without suggesting that the fifth mode is necessarily 'better' than the first" (21). These five modes are as follows: projection into a character, projection into the situation, associating between book and reader, the distanced viewer, detached evaluation. Derek certainly described himself as a distanced viewer, almost in so many words, and provided examples of detached evaluation when asked. What seems to be missing in his reading history is much evidence of engagement. Apparently as a consequence of this affective vacuum, he has very little enthusiasm for an activity he can actually do quite well.

Jack Thomson, in a major study of Australian adolescent readers, also attempted to outline a developmental model of response to literature. He worked out a six-point scale of stages through which readers develop, though no level is exclusive. These levels are described thus: unreflective interest in action; empathising; analogising, reflecting on the significance of events (theme) and behaviour (distanced evaluation of characters); reviewing the whole work as the author's creation; consciously considered relationship with the author, recognition of textual ideology, and understanding of self (identity theme) and of one's own reading processes.

On this scale, Derek would most easily fit at level 5, "reviewing the whole work as the author's creation." According to Thomson's analysis, this level involves such strategies as "drawing on literary and cultural repertoires, interrogating the text to match the author's representations with one's own, recognition of implied author" (360–361).

The value of such developmental models may be arguable, but they serve as some guide to the observation that Derek was a relatively sophisticated reader, able to make detached observations about the workings of the text and at the same time drawing support for his reactions from his own experiences. If we subscribe to the idea of readers developing as they pass through school, then, on these scales, Derek would seem to be making good progress. Yet he achieved this despite a substantial indifference to the whole idea of reading.

Some Questions

The first question that must be asked of Derek's approach to reading is, does it matter? Derek's reading life now comprises compulsory reading for school, the occasional encounter with a condensed book, and a few very spasmodic attempts, usually incomplete, to read something more challenging. From this approach to reading, he has developed a reading style that enables him to pick up cues in the text, make successful extrapolations to the implications for the text as a whole, and bring his own life experience as well as his literary experience to bear on the project of making sense of a story. What more could be asked of him? If he prefers to spend all his free time on sports and hobbies and social life, why should anyone worry or object?

Aside from that question, there are some more pragmatic issues. Derek's story of his reading past was utterly consistent. Even when his friends and relations were reading all around him, he could always find some better way to spend his time. Was there an optimum point when a more active attempt to engage him with stories would have paid off? No answer to this question is possible in Derek's own specific case, but the implications of any answer are obviously important for other children.

In Grade 9, Derek's English teacher expected him to produce regular book reviews. Once more, the *Reader's Digest* came to his aid, and he wrote many of his reviews on condensed books. In his eyes, obviously, the product was more important than the process. Yet if the Grade 9 teacher had insisted that, instead of producing artifacts to attest to assignments completed, the students must truly and sincerely *enjoy* their reading, what kind of tyrannical atmosphere would that have engendered? Enjoyment, amusement, entertainment, or engagement must be volunteered; no amount of conscription will create them. It is a classic example of leading a horse to water. Even if your classroom offers the best environment possible for the creation of reading pleasure, there is no way of decreeing or guaranteeing that it will occur.

Some Attempts at Answers

Paradoxically, it seems to me that one way of improving our chances of getting students who like to read is to increase our respect for their right not to enjoy it. This is more likely to be achieved if we are clear what kind of readers we have in our classroom. If I try to imagine myself as Derek's teacher, I can all too readily picture a situation where I assumed, on the basis of his reading performance in class, that he was a cheerful and enthusiastic reader. Our inability to find titles that interested and involved him, which would have been almost inevitable, would have puzzled and frustrated me.

Most of the ways we have evolved of monitoring somebody else's reading occur during or after the reading itself. It is difficult to think of ways to investigate a reading of a text before that reading actually takes place. Yet what the reader contributes to the reading of a text is of prime importance—and already in place before the reading begins. If we base our assessment of a reader solely on what happens while the reading is going on, or after it is finished, we are in danger of ignoring a large ingredient in the whole exchange.

Thus with Derek, by the end of our first meeting, I had asked him to read stories in sections, commenting on the development of the story as he finished each section. This technique was one way of assessing how he read as it actually occurred. At the end of each story, I asked him to comment on the story as a whole, engaging him in retrospective summary and comment. I could at this point have asked him lots of other school-exercise kinds of questions, such as giving him a comprehension quiz, or asking him to write an alternative ending, or asking him to write the diary of one of the characters, and so forth. All of these exercises have in common the fact that they occur after the event.

Yet the most interesting fact about Derek as a reader was not what kind of post-reading conclusions he could reach: it was the contradiction between his poised and relaxed reading and his history of almost complete indifference to the charm of printed fiction. Working on the basis of class activities, I might never have picked up this contradiction, and my reactions to Derek's reading activities would have inevitably been inadequate.

Dealing with him as a librarian, I might have taken in only his indifference, and assumed that his reading abilities were as vestigial as his interest. I would still have been seeing only a partial picture. Yet it is a librarian who has put his finger on at least part of the problem in the classroom. Frank Hatt has argued that we should expand our idea of the reading act to include the finding of the book:

> It might be useful to locate the beginning of a reading act at the point when the reader *decides to read,* and starts attending to messages about a text, or clues for relevance putting aside other claims on his attention. At this point in time he chooses to prefer certain of his needs over others, and sets about asking the store [of available books] which texts will match those needs. . . .
>
> One effect of extending the reading act to include the "finding" of the text is to draw attention to the shortcomings of much of the reading done in educational situations, where students are obliged to read prescribed texts. "The finding" in these cases is highly artificial. The students [*sic*] does not go through the process of selecting a preferred need, nor of matching a text to it on the basis of descriptions or clues. Having had the first part of the reading act done for him, he has to behave as if it were his own work and assume the right set for the rest of the reading act, and so reading becomes a kind of simulation game. (65–67)

Derek's Grade 9 teacher made an effort to get students to include the finding of the book as part of the project of producing book reviews. However, once again, the mental "set" could not be induced from the outside. Derek's attitude in his Grade 9 reading was quite clear: His sole purpose was to produce a book report at the end. "A kind of simulation game" is a good description of the activity he described.

There are no easy answers to the questions raised by students like Derek. A lack of engagement was the dominating feature of Derek's reading history, but engagement is the most personal reaction of all. Understanding can be intellectual alone, enjoyment can be superficial; engagement requires some surrender and involvement on the part of the reader and cannot be decreed by an outsider.

Being aware of this limitation and respecting another reader's right to withhold a final commitment to a text is probably a step forward for teachers and librarians both. In dealing with young readers there is an argument in favour of having a more complete picture of their reading histories than has sometimes seemed necessary, provided it is coupled with respect for those readers' rights to be as enthusiastic, hostile, or apathetic as they choose. Remembering that the reading which begins now is only a fragment of the reader's whole experience is vital.

Long before I met Derek, I thought I had concluded to my own satisfaction that reading is a complicated, messy, unpredictable and fascinating activity. Talking to him made me realize how much I had oversimplified.

References

Dick, Philip K. "Impostor." *Spectrum Two: Modern Short Stories.* Ed. Bruce Bennett, Peter Cowan and John Hay. New York: Longman, 1970. 128–40.

Hatt, Frank. *The Reading Process: A Framework for Analysis and Description.* London: Clive Bingley, 1976.

Mansfield, Katherine. "The Doll's House." *The Doves' Nest and Other Stories.* Toronto: Macmillan, 1923. 1–13.

Protherough, Robert. *Developing Response to Fiction.* Milton Keynes, England: Open University Press, 1983.

Thomson, Jack. *Understanding Teenagers' Reading: Reading Processes and the Teaching of Literature.* New York: Nichols, 1987.

Familiarity with Reference

Donald J. Kenney

Familiarity with reference and bibliographical sources in the field of children's and young adult literature can provide a gateway for enhancing a teacher's and librarian's ability to provide better guidance in selecting books for students to read and study. Knowledge of the review and biographical sources related to the field of young adult literature can also help teachers create meaningful assignments and projects for their students.

This issue's column is devoted to selected reference sources and tools in the field of children's and young adult literature that classroom teachers should find helpful in selecting and teaching young adult literature in their classes. While many of these sources may suggest by their title and use "children's literature," they are, however, broader in scope and include young adult literature. Within the past few years many reference tools have begun to appear devoted exclusively to "young adult literature." This apparent divergence of "children's literature" and "young adult literature" is an important landmark. An essential ingredient for the development of a discipline is the codification of its literature. The emergence of reference sources devoted to young adult literature is a signal that young adult literature has come of age.

Many of the sources listed should be available either in the school or public library and certainly at an academic library if one is nearby. While some of the sources listed will be of interest only to a teacher or librarian, others may be helpful to students preparing assignments or projects related to the study of a literature unit or individual young adult novels.

Reprinted from *The ALAN Review* 19.1, Fall 1991, pages 48–54, by permission of the author.

Professional Reading and General Sources

The sources listed in this section will probably be of interest to teachers and librarians as professional reading in advancing their knowledge of the field of young adult literature. Two notable books listed are *Literature for Today's Young Adults* and *Nonfiction for Young Adults. The Literature for Today's Young Adults* by two well-known scholars in the field of young adult literature, Kenneth L. Donelson and Alleen Pace Nilsen, has gone through three editions and has become a standard textbook for many courses in the field. Betty Carter's and Richard Abrahamson's *Nonfiction for Young Adults* is the first major work dealing with how to evaluate and select high quality nonfiction for young adults.

Beyond Fact: Nonfiction for Children and Young People, compiled by Jo Carr. Chicago: American Library Association, 1982.

This collection of essays, by noted authors and critics of informational books, points out the need for greater awareness of the "literature of fact."

Beyond the Happy Ending: The Pedagogy and Promise of African American Literature for Youth by Dianne Johnson. Westport, CT: Greenwood Press, 1990.

Examines the development of African American literature for young people, looking specifically at current themes and underlying philosophies from 1920 to the present.

Celebrating Children's Books: Essays on Children's Literature in Honor of Zena Sutherland, edited by Betsy Hearne and Marilyn Kaye. New York: R. R. Bowker, 1988.

Essays on children's literature by some of the major writers of children's and young adult literature, including Lloyd Alexander, Paula Fox, and E. L. Konigsburg on such topics as imagination, women, and reality in children's literature.

Children's Literature in the Classroom: Weaving Charlotte's Web, edited by Janet Hickman and Bernice E. Cullinam. New York: Lothrop, Lee & Shepard, 1981.

Divided into three sections: understanding the use of literature in the classroom; celebrating books and authors in the picture book, fantasy, historical fiction, poetry genres; and developing literature-based programs.

Choosing Books for Children: A Commonsense Guide by Betsy Hearne. New York: Delacorte Press, 1990.

The author offers commonsense guides to selecting books for children at different developmental stages. Includes an excellent chapter on censorship.

For Reading Out Loud! A Guide to Sharing Books with Children by Margaret Mary Kimmel and Elizabeth Segel. New York: Delacorte Press, 2nd ed., 1988.

The authors make the case for reading out loud to children and offer tips on how to do it effectively. Included is an excellent annotated bibliography with some 300 titles of books to read aloud to both children and young adults.

Literature for Today's Young Adults by Kenneth L. Donelson and Alleen Pace Nilsen. Glenview, IL: Scott, Foresman and Company, 1989.

One of the few scholarly, readable books on the emerging field of young adult literature. Especially thorough on historical and critical aspects of the field.

Nonfiction for Young Adults: From Delight to Wisdom by Betty Carter and Richard Abrahamson. Phoenix: Oryx Press, 1990.

The authors analyze nonfiction for the young adult audience in terms of interest, accuracy, content, style, organization, format, and uses. Valuable guidance for teachers and librarians on how to appreciate, evaluate, and select high-quality nonfiction for young adults. Also includes seven interviews with such nonfiction authors as Lee J. Ames and Milton Meltzer.

The Voice of the Narrator in Children's Literature: Insights from Writers and Critics, edited by Charlotte F. Otten and Gart D. Schmidt. Westport, CT: Greenwood Press, 1989.

Professional authors and illustrators of books for children discuss writing, specifically the narrative line and how they created it. Professional academics examine theory and technique in books for children and young adults.

What Do Draculas Do? Essays on Contemporary Writers of Fiction for Children and Young Adults by David Rees. Lanham, MD: Scarecrow Press, 1990.

The author examines the work of fourteen contemporary authors and their relationship to other fiction. Among the authors included are Mary Norton, Joan Aiken, Madeline L'Engle, Maurice Sendak, and Roald Dahl. A concluding essay looks at why authors choose to write for young people.

Writers on Writing for Young Adults: Exploring the Authors, the Genre, the Readers, the Issues, and the Critics of Young-Adult Literature, edited by Patricia E. Feehan and Pamela Petrick Barron. New York: Omnigraphs, 1991.

Essays that discuss the content, writers, and nature of young adult literature. Along with librarians and critics, such notable YA authors as Engdahl, Klein, Guy, and Paterson are among the distinguished contributors to this work.

Worlds Within: Children's Fantasy from the Middle Ages to Today by Shelia A. Egoff. Chicago: American Library Association, 1988.

This work traces the development and history in children's literature from the Middle Ages to the 1980's. Has an excellent bibliography of children's and young adult works dealing with fantasy in children's literature on pages 311–327.

Critical Sources

A recent article in *The Chronicle of Higher Education* points out the transformation in the way scholars look at children's and young adult literature. As pointed out in the article the amount and variety of scholarly work in the field has increased dramatically. Each year the *Children's Literature Association Quarterly* publishes an annual bibliography of research done in the field of children's literature, and it has doubled in size every year since the bibliography was first published in 1987.

The best sources for the documentation of children's/young adult literature can most easily be found in sources related to the fields of education and librarianship. Frequently, the coursework for both children's and young adult literature are taught in education and library science curriculums. Consequently, many of the standard reference tools such as the *Education Index, Current Index to Journals in Education,* and *Library Literature* are the best sources to find critical articles related to young adult literature. Most of the major journals dealing with the field of young adult and children's literature are indexed in the above indexes.

The following list of sources will provide additional places to find critical materials, author interviews, and essays devoted to specific discussions of such issues as censorship, literary quality, and sexism.

Children's Literature: An Annotated Bibliography of the History and Criticism by Suzanne Rahn. New York: Garland Press, 1981.

Comprehensive bibliography covering aims and definitions of children's literature, the history, genres, and individual authors. Indexes chapters and essays in books as well as journal articles.

Children's Literature: A Historical and Contemporary Bibliography by Irving P. Leif. Troy, NY: Whitson, 1977.

Arranged in broad categories such as "Trends in Children's Literature" and "Treatment of Minorities in Children's Literature."

Children's Literature: A Guide to the Criticism by Linnea Hendrickson New York: G. K. Hall, 1987.

Divided into two major parts: Part A, individual authors, and Part B, subjects, themes, and genre in the criticism of children's literature. Sources cited include book chapters and essays and journal articles.

Choosing Books for Young People, Volume 2: A Guide to Criticism and Bibliography, 1976–1984 by John R. T. Ettinger and Diana L Spirit. Chicago: American Library Association, 1982.

This annotated bibliography provides a key to criticism that has appeared from 1976 to 1984 about all kinds of books for young people. Arranged alphabetically by author with a subject index.

Contemporary Literary Criticism. Detroit: Gale Research, 1973 to date.

This multivolume work is a key source for locating criticism in the field of literature. Alphabetically arranged by author with a brief biographical sketch and excerpts of critical reviews of the author's works. The cumulative index of the last volume locates information on an author.

Dictionary of Literary Biography. Detroit: Gale Research, 1978 to date.

Bio-bibliographical essays listed by author. Index of final volume of the set locates the author. Excellent references at the end of each essay. The following volumes are exclusively devoted to children's/young adult literature:

v.22: American Writers for Children, 1900–1960

v.42: American Writers for Children before 1900

v.52: American Writers for Children since 1960: Fiction

v.61: American Writers for Children since 1960: Poets, Illustrators and Nonfiction Authors.

Fantasy Literature for Children and Young Adults by Ruth Nadelman Lynn. New York: R. R. Bowker, 1989.

Annotated bibliography of 3,300 fantasy novels and story collections arranged by type of fantasy and including a brief summary and review sources. Research guide on selective authors of fantasy.

Horn Book Index 1924–1989, by Serenna F. Day. Phoenix: Oryx Press, 1990.

Although the *Horn Book,* a key journal for the field of children's/ young adult literature, is indexed in a number of standard commercial indexes, this one-volume index to the journal will provide access to over 80,000 separate references.

Index to Literary Criticism for Young Adults by Nancy E. Shields. Lanham, MD: Scarecrow Press, 1988.

An index of over 4,000 authors included in many standard reference sources brought together in this one volume. Arranged alphabetically by author with sources listed for each entry.

Only Connect: Readings on Children's Literature, edited by Shelia Egoff, G. T. Stubbs, and L. F. Ashley. New York: Oxford University Press, 1980.

This collection of pertinent essays on literary criticism, standards, changing tastes, writing and illustrating, and children's responses to literature includes articles by J.R.R. Tolkien, Pamela Travers, Rosemary Sutcliff, T. S. Eliot, and Clifton Fadiman.

Survey of Modern Fantasy Literature, edited by Frank N. Magill. Englewood Cliffs, NJ: Salem Press, 1983.

This five-volume set includes essays and critical analyses of such authors as Lewis Carroll, C. S. Lewis, J.R.R. Tolkien, and Ursula K. LeGuin.

Twayne's United States Author Series: Young Adult Authors Books.

This groundbreaking series signals the "coming of age" of young adult literature by providing the first critical studies series of young adult fiction. Each volume of the series examines the life and work of a notable young adult writer.

Presenting Judy Blume by Martann N. Weidt. New York: G. K. Hall, 1990.

Presenting Sue Ellen Bridgers by Ted Hipple. New York: G. K. Hall, 1990.

Presenting Robert Cormier by Patricia J. Campbell. New York: G. K. Hall, 2nd ed., 1989.

Presenting Rosa Guy by Jerrie Norris. New York: G. K. Hall, 1988.

Presenting S. E. Hinton by Jay Daly New York: G. K. Hall, 2nd ed., 1989.

Presenting M. E. Kerr by Alleen Pace Nilsen.New York: G. K. Hall, 1986.

Presenting Norma Klein by Allene Stuart Phy. New York: G. K. Hall, 1988.

Presenting Norma Fox Mazer by Sally Holmes Holtze. New York: G. K. Hall, 1987.

Presenting Richard Peck by Donald R. Gallo. New York: G. K. Hall, 1989.

Presenting Walter Dean Myers by Rudine Sims Bishop. New York: G. K. Hall, 1990.

Presenting Paul Zindel by Jack Jacob Forman. New York: G. K. Hall, 1988.

Book Review Sources

Knowing the various sources for book reviews enables one not only to find some critical comments about a particular book but also to help in selecting works for students to read and to study. Examining various reviews of a young adult novel may help the teacher find the most suitable novel for class or group reading. A number of indexes to journal articles in the field of education and librarianship, in addition to indexing scholarly and research articles for these fields, also index book reviews. The two most notable ones are the *Education Index* and *Library Literature,* both produced by the H. W. Wilson Company. Reviews are found listed at the end of each year's annual index volume arranged by author. Other worthwhile sources are included below.

The Best in Children's Books: The University of Chicago Guide to Children's Literature, 1979–1984 by Zena Sutherland. Chicago: University of Chicago Press, 1986.

The guide reviews children's books and is arranged alphabetically by author. Ratings are given by grade level and Developmental Value Index.

Book Review Digest. New York: H. W. Wilson, 1905 to date.

Indexes reviews published in approximately eighty-five American, Canadian and British magazines and journals. Arranged alphabetically by author of the books. Each entry includes a brief descriptive note and excerpts from reviews with references to the periodical in which it appeared. Subject and title index.

Book Review Index. Detroit: Gale Research, 1965 to date.

Index of reviews appearing in more than 200 periodicals. Reviews are arranged alphabetically by last name of the author.

Caldecott Medal Books: 1938–1957, edited by Bertha Mahony Miller and Elinor Whitney Field, 1957; *Newbery Medal Books: 1922–1955,* edited by Bertha Mahony Miller and Elinor Whitney Field, 1955; *Newbery and Caldecott Medal Books: 1956–1965,* edited by Lee Kingman, 1965; *Newbery and Caldecott Medal Books 1966–1975,* edited by Lee Kingman, 1975; *Newbery and Caldecott Medal Books: 1976-1985,* edited by Lee Kingman. Boston: Horn Book.

These volumes include the author's acceptance speech and a biographical essay. They present a good overview of the authors who have received these two distinguished awards.

Children's Book Review Index, edited by Ann Block and Carolyn Riley. Detroit: Gale Research, 1975 to date.

Annual listing of reviews of children's and young adult book reviews taken from the *Book Review Index.*

Children's Literature Review. Detroit: Gale Research, 1976 to date.

Arranged alphabetically by author and provides summaries of reviews of books for children and young adults.

High-Interest Books for Teens: A Guide to Book Review and Biographical Sources, edited by Joyce Nakamura. Detroit: Gale Research, 1988.

Review section arranged by author, each entry includes review source as well as the subject of the book. Subject-index categorizes titles by broad subject area.

Masterplots II: Juvenile and Young Adult Literature, edited by Frank N. Magill, 4 vols. Englewood Cliffs, NJ: Salem Press, 1991.

Presents an essay-review of select juvenile and young adult literature. Each entry also includes type of plot, time, locale, principal themes. The Themes and Meaning sections outline the major issues in the work from the perspective of the young adult reader. The Context section places the novel in the context of the author's work and young adult literature. Each entry concludes with a brief biographical note. Includes an author and title index as well as a subject index arranged by broad themes such as "coming of age," "sexual issues," and "job and work."

Olderr's Young Adult Fiction Index 1988, edited by Steven Olderr. Westport, CT: St. James Press, 1988.

Index of 852 works for young adults reviewed in *Publisher's Weekly, Booklist, VOYA,* and *School Library Journal.* Two major parts are the main entry section, by author, and the subject, title, and character index.

Young Adult Book Review Index, edited by Barbara Beach. Detroit: Gale Research, 1988.

Index of reviews arranged by author, includes an illustrator and title index. Reviews cited are from periodicals associated with young adult services such as the *School Library Journal* and *VOYA.* Each entry includes the title of the reviewing source, date, volume, and page number.

Bibliographies

Finding the right book for that student who has asked advice on a "good book on . . ." or selecting titles to include in a thematic unit is now fairly easy to accomplish. Recent interest in children's/young adult literature has resulted in not only numerous bibliographical sources, but very specialized ones. Bibliographies listed here range from sources that include impairment and disabilities to multicultural books. Such standard sources as NCTE's *Your Reading, Adventuring with Books,* and *Books for You* are particularly valuable. These bibliographies, using a category arrangement for listing the works, are very convenient for classroom teachers and librarians working with students to find recreational reading as well as required reading. Dreyer's *The Bookfinder,* which has been updated and expanded, is an excellent source that every teacher should have access to.

Accept Me As I Am: Best Books of Juvenile Nonfiction on Impairment and Disabilities by Joan B. Friedberg, June B. Mullins, and Adelaide W. Sukiennik. New York: R. R. Bowker, 1985.

Arranged topically including such disability topics as deafness, speech impairments, and mental retardation. Excellent annotations include a brief critical analysis at the end of each annotation.

American History for Children and Young Adults: An Annotated Bibliographic Index by Vandelia VanMeter. Englewood, CO: Libraries Unlimited, 1990.

This annotated bibliography of both fiction and nonfiction books on American history lists 2,900 titles arranged by time period and subject. Each entry includes standard bibliographic information, grade level, and a list of reviews that appeared in periodicals such as *Horn Book, School Library Journal,* and *VOYA.* Author, title, subject, and grade-level indexes provide easy access.

The Bookfinder: A Guide to Children's Literature about the Needs and Problems of Youth Aged 2–15 by Sharon Spredemann Dreyer. Circle Pines, MN: American Guidance Service, v.1: 1977; v.2: 1981; v.3: 1985; v.4: 1989.

Volumes 1 and 2 include ages 2–15 years old; volume 3 and 4, age 2 and up. Each volume has annotations of books alphabetically arranged by author and the four volumes cover books published from 1977 through 1986. The subject index is very useful and comprehensive, spanning subjects from "abandonment" to "youngest child."

Books for the Teen Age 1990. Published annually by the New York Public Library; issued by the Office on Books for Young Adults, 1990.

An annotated list of some 1,250 books. Bibliography is arranged by subject, such as "Vietnam Remembered," "AIDS," and "The Universe."

Bilingual Books in Spanish and English for Children by Doris Cruger Dale. Englewood, CO: Libraries Unlimited, 1985.

Annotated bibliography of bilingual books in Spanish and English for children published or distributed in the United States since the 1940s. Arranged by decade with various indexes to provide ample access.

Books in Spanish for Children and Young Adults: An Annotated Guide by Isabel Schon. Lanham, MD: Scarecrow Press, 1978, 1985, 1987.

This annotated series is arranged geographically and then by genre. An excellent source for identifying books in Spanish for the young adult audience.

Fantasy for Children: An Annotated Checklist by Ruth N. Lynn. New York: R. R. Bowker, 1979.

Arranged by types of fantasy, such as "Alternative Worlds and Imaginary Lands," "Time Travel," "Magical Toys, " and "Mythical Beings." Guide to more than 1,650 recommended fantasy books for children in grades 3–8. Each entry briefly annotated.

Information Sources in Children's Literature by Mary Meacham. Westport, CT: Greenwood Press, 1978.

Bibliography of bibliographies and finding tools for the field of children's/young adult literature. Useful in finding books dealing with such broad topics as American history in juvenile books, the black experience in children's/young adult books, and storytelling.

Japan through Children's Literature: An Annotated Bibliography by Yasuho Makino. Westport, CT: Greenwood Press, 1985.

With the growing importance and interest of multicultural study this bibliography is especially useful for identifying books depicting the Japanese culture and people in children's/young adult literature.

More Juniorplots: A Guide for Teachers and Librarians by John T. Gillespie. New York: R. R. Bowker, 1977.

Excellent annotations of books for young adults. Arranged by topics such as "Getting Along in the Family," "Developing Lasting Values," and "Developing a Respect for Nature and Living Things."

Newbery and Caldecott Medal and Honor Books: An Annotated Bibliography by Linda K. Perterson and Marilyn L. Solt. New York: G. K. Hall, 1982.

Essay on the history of the two most important awards for the field of children's/young adult literature. Arranged by year with extensive annotations of the books. A subject, author, illustrator, and title index are included.

New York Times Parent's Guide to the Best Books for Children by Eden R. Lipson. New York: Times Books, 1988

This annotated bibliography is arranged by broad categories such as "Story Books," "Early Reading Books," and "Middle Reading Books." Very well annotated.

Notes from a Different Drummer: A Guide to Juvenile Fiction Portraying the Handicapped by Barbara H. Baskin and Karen H. Harris. New York: R. R. Bowker, 1977.

Although somewhat dated, it is still an excellent guide to juvenile fiction portraying the handicapped.

Science & Technology in Fact and Fiction: A Guide to Children's Books by DayAnn M. Kennedy, Stella S. Spanger, and Mary Ann Vanderwerf. New York: R. R. Bowker, 1990.

A thoroughly annotated guide of 380 selected books covering subjects from "Acid Rain" to "Zeppelins." Each entry is evaluated on such criteria as literary quality, attention to detail, and accuracy and suitability for intended audiences.

Science & Technology in Fact and Fiction: A Guide to Young Adult Books by DayAnn M. Kennedy, Stella S. Spanger, and Mary Ann Vanderwerf. New York: R. R. Bowker, 1990.

This annotated bibliography is an excellent source for locating titles related to the physical and earth sciences. The book is divided into two sections, "Science" and "Technology," each again divided into "Fiction" and "Nonfiction" and organized alphabetically by author. Each entry has a summary, complete bibliographic information, age and grade levels, series, and whether the title received any rewards.

Seniorplots: A Book Talk Guide for Use with Readers Ages 15–18 by John T. Gillespie and Corinne J. Naden. New York: R. R. Bowker, 1989.

Arranged by twelve subject and genre areas such as "Growing Up," "The World Around Us," "Interpersonal Relations," and "Suspense and Mystery." Each work of fiction is annotated and sources for book reviews and bibliographical information on the author are included at the end of each annotation.

Supernatural Fiction for Teens by Cosette Kies. Englewood, CO: Libraries Unlimited, 1987.

Some annotated 500 paperbacks are included in this specialized bibliography on the supernatural. Annotations are arranged alphabetically by author with a brief summary of the book or in the case of short stories, a listing of all the stories. Titles are coded to indicate for teens, for young adults, for adults, or a classic.

Survival Themes in Fiction for Children and Young People by Binnie Tate Wilkin. Lanham, MD: Scarecrow Press, 1978.

Listing of fiction of value to children and young adults in helping them deal with issues such as sexuality, identity, self-image, peer pressure, and loneliness.

Values in Selected Children's Books of Fiction and Fantasy by Carolyn W. Field and Jacqueline S. Weiss. Hamden, CN: Library Professional Publications, 1987.

Over 700 annotations of books from preschool to eighth grade are categorized by the values they represent or reinforce. The selections demonstrate or project values that help children/young adults develop skills for decision making and problem solving.

Directories and Handbooks

These directories and handbooks can provide quick answers to questions related to terminology, characters, setting, authors and awards that may crop up in class as students are exploring a particular work of young adult fiction.

Award-Winning Books for Children and Young Adults: An Annual Guide, 1989, edited by Betty L. Criscoe. Lanham, MD: Scarecrow Press, 1990

This directory of awards is arranged A to Z by award. Complete address is given of the award sponsor; award background; winner with biographical information. A selected bibliography on the winner and winner's writings also is included. Various appendices at the end include genre and age/grade preference appendices for all the titles given awards. A title and author index also provides another access route.

Children's Literature Awards & Winners: A Directory of Prizes, Authors, and Illustrations by Delores B. Jones. New York: Neal-Schuman Publishers in association with Gale Research Company, 1983.

A comprehensive guide describing various awards for excellence in children's literature. Part I is arranged alphabetically by award name; Part II, by authors and illustrators; Part III, selected bibliography, lists, articles, book chapters, dissertations, and reports on topics germane to children's book awards.

The Oxford Companion to Children's Literature edited by Humphrey Carpenter and Mari Prichard. New York: Oxford University Press, 1984.

Dictionary arrangement of authors, illustrators, characters, and terminology related to the field of children's/young adult literature.

A Reference Guide to Historical Fiction for Children and Young Adults by Lynda G. Adamson. Westport, CT: Greenwood Press, 1987.

Dictionary covering novels written since 1940, arranged by author, title, protagonist, historical personage, and place. Appendices include listings of novels by setting, dates and locale, age level of readability, bibliography on writing historical novels, and some literary criticism.

A Reference Guide to Modern Fantasy for Children by Pat Pflieger and Helen M. Hill, advisory editors. Westport, CT: Greenwood Press, 1984.

The dictionary format of this book, with its entries on authors, books, characters, places, and magical objects, makes it rather easy to find that elusive person, place, or thing in fantasy literature for children and young adults.

Who's Who in Children's Books: A Treasury of the Familiar Characters of Childhood by Margery Fisher. New York: Holt, Rinehart and Winston, 1975.

Characters in children's books alphabetized by character name. Index of author and title.

Biographical Indexes and Dictionaries

Young adults are very curious about the people who write the books they read. They want to know what kind of person Judy Blume is or how Robert Cormier got his idea for writing *The Chocolate War.* Teachers and librarians can, of course, capitalize on this curiosity. Specialized biographical sources dedicated to the children's/young adult field have increased in the last few years enhancing information about these writers beyond what such traditional sources as *Something about the Author* can provide.

Authors and Artists for Young Adults by Miriam Hoffman and Era Samuels. Detroit: Gale Research, 1989.

Alphabetically arranged by author, this source concentrates on young adult writers. Entries are thorough and detailed with extensive references at the end of each article.

Authors of Books for Young People by Martha E. Ward and Dorothy A. Marquardt. Lanham, MD: Scarecrow Press, 3rd ed., 1990.

Dictionary arrangement by author, these brief entries provide a quick reference of basic information on children's/young adult authors.

Behind the Covers: Interviews with Authors and Illustrators for Children and Young Adults by Jim Roginski; bibliographies compiled by Muriel Brown. Englewood, CO: Libraries Unlimited, 1985.

Some authors comment on reviewers, on buyers, on bookmaking, and on the creative process. The full scheme of creating children's/young adult books is presented by a diverse group of authors. References are included.

Black Authors and Illustrators of Children's Books: A Biographical Dictionary by Barbara Rollock. New York: Garland Press, 1988.

Excellent source for biographical materials on black writers and illustrators.

British Children's Authors: Interviews at Home by Cornelia Jones and Olivia R. Way. Chicago: American Library Association, 1976.

Includes not only interviews but one- to two-page biographies of such authors as Joan Aiken and Nina Bawden. Each section concludes with an annotated listing of the works of the author. Arranged alphabetically by author.

Children's Authors and Illustrators: An Index to Biographical Dictionaries, edited by Adele Sarkissian. Detroit: Gale Research, 3rd ed., 1981.

Arranged alphabetically by author and illustrator. Sources for biographical information abbreviated in each entry and keyed to full citations in the "Key to Publication Codes."

Contemporary Authors. Detroit: Gale Research, 1962 to date.

Multivolume set, consisting of three series, contains biographical information on authors. Each entry is followed by Biographical/Critical Sources which are useful. The cumulative index for the set locates information on the author.

Index to Collective Biographies for Young Readers by Karen Breen. New York: R. R. Bowker, 4th ed. 1988.

This index provides access to biographies in collective biographies. The fourth edition indexes approximately 9,700 biographies in some 1,100 collective biographies in such fields as sports, music, education, and religion. Primary access is alphabetical by the last name of the person. There is a subject index and an alphabetical list of fields of activity and nationality. The first edition of this source in 1975 was titled *Bowker Index to Young Readers' Collective Biographies: Elementary and Junior High School Level.*

Something about the Author, edited by Anne Commire. Detroit: Gale Research, 1971.

This multivolume set is a key biographical source for the lives and works of children's/young adult authors and illustrators. Includes extensive biographical/career information as well as additional references.

Speaking for Ourselves: Autobiographical Sketches by Notable Authors of Books for Young Adults, edited by Donald R. Gallo. Urbana, IL: National Council of Teachers of English, 1990.

Organized alphabetically, the sketches are one to two pages in length, and each includes a photograph and a bibliography of the author's works (with dates).

More Books by More People by Lee Bennett Hopkins. Santa Clara: Citation Press, 1974.

The author conducted interviews with well-known children's/young adult authors. Includes photographs.

Junior Books of Authors Series. New York: H. W. Wilson. *The Junior Book of Authors,* edited by Stanley J. Kunitz and Howard Haycraft, 1951.

First in a series, following, of books which provide biographical sketches of authors and illustrators of children's/young adult books.

More Junior Authors, edited by Muriel Fuller, 1963.

Third Book of Junior Authors, edited by Doris De Montreville and Donna Hill, 1972.

Fourth Book of Junior Authors & Illustrators, edited by Doris De Montreville and Elizabeth D. Crawford, 1978.

Fifth Book of Junior Authors & Illustrators, edited by Sally Holmes Holtze, 1983.

Sixth Book of Junior Authors & Illustrators, edited by Sally Holmes Holtze, 1989

Teller of Tales by Roger L Green. Leicester, England: Edmund Ward, 1946.

Although a very dated book, the insightful biographical sketches of such notables as Lewis Carroll, Robert Louis Stevenson, and Kenneth Graham provide readable information on early children's/young adult authors. A chronological table of famous books by all the authors in the book is included.

Twentieth Century Children's Writers, edited by Tracy Chevalier. Chicago: St. James Press, 3rd ed., 1989.

A major biographical source for the field, alphabetized by author, with a list of works published. Some entries have a personal statement by the author regarding his or her writings. Includes address of where to contact the author.

Who's Who of Children's Literature, edited by Brian Doyle. New York: Schocken Books, 1968.

Alphabetical by name, listing authors and illustrators of children's books from the early nineteenth century to the 1960s. Illustrations enhance the book's appeal and bibliography.

Yesterday's Authors of Books for Children, edited by Anne Commire. Detroit: Gale Research, 1977–1978.

Excellent biographical information for authors and illustrators from early times to 1960. Alphabetized by author to include personal and career information; writings; and sidelights. Includes a photograph of the author as well as sample illustrations from some of the author's works.

Shift Out of First: Third-Person Narration Has Advantages

Elizabeth C. Schuhmann

English teachers who have used contemporary young adult novels in their literature classes probably realize that one of the literary techniques that is relied upon heavily by the authors of these novels is first-person narration. Many of the best known authors—Paul Zindel, Judy Blume, John Donovan, S. E. Hinton, Bette Greene, and Robert Newton Peck among others—use first-person narration in their books. Because of this prevalence of first-person narration in young adult novels and because of the popularity of these books, many advocates of novels written for young people have come to consider first-person narration a preferred technique for this kind of literature.

Undoubtedly there are some strong and valid reasons for using first-person narration in young adult novels. The first-person narrator provides a readily recognizable figure with whom the adolescent (who is characteristically preoccupied with finding his or her own identity) can identify. Also, first-person narration in the young adult novel generally restricts the language to the appropriate expression of an adolescent protagonist and thus achieves a readability low enough to suit a majority of adolescents.

However, the first-person narration technique is not without its natural weaknesses and limitations. A close look at novels by Hinton and Zindel can reveal some of the limitations that first-person narration can impose upon the experience of the reader. In contrast, a close look at novels by Cormier, Hamner, and Bridgers can reveal some of the extra opportunities for richness of literary experience that can be offered by third-person narration.

In several ways first-person narration can limit characterization in a young adult novel. No matter how keenly observant of

Reprinted from *The ALAN Review* 9.2, Winter 1982, pages 40–42, 48.

details the first-person narrators may be (and some first-person narrators in adolescent novels possess an observational acuity that seems extremely sophisticated for their age and experience), they can never really observe directly what goes on in the mind of any other character. So, not only are readers of the first-person novel denied direct access to the personal thoughts and attitudes that can reveal directly how a variety of characters (other than the narrator) feel about themselves and their lives, but they also are unable to view directly how a variety of characters feel about each other. How fully characters other than the narrator are developed depends on how many situations the author devises in which the narrator is able to observe the words and actions of those characters. It also must be realized that certain character information conveyed through these observations is necessarily biased by the singularity of its source and by the biases of that same source. Sometimes these limitations that first-person narration imposes on characterization can result in the reduction of some characters to mere stereotyped figures.

Characterization in S. E. Hinton's *That Was Then, This Is Now* seems in at least one important respect to be limited by first-person narration. Although the book attempts to contrast the characterization of two teenage protagonists (Bryon and Mark) the story is told from the single viewpoint of Bryon. Therefore, when Bryon develops into a responsible citizen and Mark ends up in jail, the reader understands how feelings and attitudes have matured inside of Bryon; however, the reader knows only what Bryon thinks has happened inside of Mark. Even though the reader is allowed to know certain things about Mark's attitudes and beliefs from his actions and his conversations with Bryon, he still misses an intimate view of Mark's pressures and motivations as they are perceived in Mark's own mind. Therefore, the story has to be a somewhat more reliable exposé of why Bryon avoided trouble than of why Mark did not. Because of the limitations of first-person narration, only one character is given the in-depth characterization made possible by direct access to the minds of characters.

First-person narration, besides limiting characterization in a young adult novel, also imposes limitations on the language of the novel. Because the language must be appropriate to the adolescent narrator, it can at times be denied the expanded opportunity for richness that often accompanies the expression of individuals with greater maturity and experience. Sometimes if an author does permit an adolescent narrator to use very lengthy and mature images and comparisons to articulate very mature insights, the author weakens the consistency and credibility of the narrator's character. In Paul Zindel's *Confessions of a Teenage Baboon*, Chris, the fifteen-year-old narrator, generally uses clever but relatively compressed images and metaphors to describe his impressions of isolated situations and events. Chris' typical mode of expression describes a nod between himself and sixteen-year-old Harold as "a weird nod that reminded me of the kind of expression beaten-down slaves shared in those old movies about flesh traffic from Africa" (16). When Lloyd's liquor case is raided, Chris quips, ". . . all the bottles of Wild Turkey had flown the coop" (133). This brief and cute mode of expression certainly seems to leave the reader open to surprise when the same narrator ends the book with an expanded mental soliloquy that includes a barrage of rather mature and eloquently expressed insights about the human condition. In part the soliloquy reads,

> I felt as though I was unfolding under the moonlight. I was opening up like a seed that had been thrust painfully and deeply—even ruthlessly—into the ground and given a merciless warning and command to grow. The cloud that had been hanging over me for so many years of my life on earth was suddenly lifting thanks to an anguished, tormented man who now lay lifeless on a bed not far away. And when the moon moved again from behind the cloud it seemed I felt an understanding and a compassion for the entire human race. (154)

Although most readers expect some growth in insight, and even in expression, to occur in an interesting dynamic character, an overly sudden and extreme growth, such as the one that is reflected in Chris' soliloquy, can compromise the credibility of the character. It would seem then that Zindel, in failing to conform to the limitations that his particular first-person narrator imposes on the language of his novel, has marred the effectiveness of his work.

Zindel's *Confessions of a Teenage Baboon* also can be viewed as an example of how plot development can be restricted and even weakened by first-person narration. With first-person narration events must usually be sequenced according to the movements of a single character, and sometimes the reader's view of events has to be somewhat contrived. Events in the plot of *Confessions of a Teenage Baboon* have to follow the movements of fifteen-year-old Chris, who narrates the story. When Chris's mother forces him to leave the house that is the scene of the major portion of the plot, the reader has no way of filling the gap in what goes on there before Chris returns. Also, because Chris's presence might not seem appropriate in the scene in which the character Lloyd shoots himself, the author has to invent a loose floor board in the attic for Chris and the reader to be able to observe this climactic event in the story. Undoubtedly the use of a first-person narrator seems to cause events in the plot to be somewhat incomplete and manipulated.

In contrast to the weaknesses of first-person narration and the limitations it often places on the scope of the reader's experience with characterization, language, and plot is the strength and versatility of third-person narration. Third-person novels by Cormier, Hamner, and Bridgers can serve as good examples of the extra opportunities for richness of literary experience that can be offered. It should also be noted here that, despite the fact that these third-person books focus on more than a single teenage narrator, each book does present at least one central teenage protagonist with whom the young adult reader can identify. Each book also falls well within an appropriate range of readability for the young adult audience. As a matter of fact each of the four books falls below ninth-grade readability on a Fry Readability Chart.

The Chocolate War by Robert Cormier displays the extra richness of characterization that is possible with a third-person narrator. In this novel the third-person narrator delves into the minds of not just one character, but of at least ten characters. In so doing he creates vivid individual portraits of a number of characters. Through the thoughts and feelings of Jerry, Archie, Obie, Goober, Emile Janza, Brian Cochran, and a handful of other student characters, the reader gets a strong well-rounded image of the individuals (particularly Jerry and Archie) who are primary actors in the war. Cormier also demonstrates how third-person narration can be manipulated to serve artistic purposes that require some limitation of characterization. For instance, the mystery surrounding the true source of Brother Leon's obsessively cruel behavior is one of the focal points of the book. Since Cormier seems intent on avoiding any easy answers to this question about cruelty and evil, he gracefully manipulates his third-person narration so as not to reveal any of Brother Leon's inner thoughts and feelings. Thus the versatility of the third-person omniscient narration technique enables a skillful writer to manipulate the reader's attention toward many different viewpoints that create rich characterizations, and yet only toward the viewpoints he wishes the reader to be aware of.

The Homecoming by Earl Hamner Jr. is another good example of the richness of characterization facilitated by the use of the third-person narrator. It is also a good example of how this extra richness of characterization can enhance at least one other aspect of the reader's experience with the literature. In this book, which is the basis of the popular TV series "The Waltons," Hamner takes the reader to a small Virginia community during the Depression and helps the reader develop a warm acquaintance with Clay-boy Spencer, his parents, several of his siblings, his maternal grandparents, and the old-maid Staples sisters. Although much of the action centers on Clay-boy, Hamner devises plenty of opportunity for his omniscient narrator to tell about the backgrounds, thoughts, feelings, and habits of most of his characters and also about their impression of and attitudes toward one another. The omniscient narrator even devises opportunities for Clay Sr. to reveal his feelings throughout the book despite the fact that he does not personally enter the story until the last chapter. For example, in Chapter 2, Clay-boy's thoughts of his father's intentions concerning a new house on Spencer's mountain smoothly lead into a third-person revelation of Clay Sr.'s internal feelings and desires. In this way third-person narration allows Hamner to characterize many people freely and richly, and through these characterizations to build interest and suspense in a plot that revolves around the absence of one of the characters. In this novel third-person narration enhances the reader's experience with plot as well as with characterization.

A young adult novelist whose books offer good examples of the ways in which third-person narration can enrich a reader's experience with characterization, plot, and also language is Sue Ellen Bridgers. In *Home Before Dark* this narration technique adds many dimensions to characterization by looking into the mind of Stella, the fourteen-year-old protagonist, and also into the minds of at least seven other characters. Readers get not only a very objective view of Stella by viewing her in relation to other people's thoughts as well as her own, but they also get to know Stella's mother, father, stepmother, aunt, uncle, and two boyfriends.

Plot also seems to benefit from third-person narration in *Home Before Dark.* Action involving various important characters occurs at the same time in two locations. While Stella Willis is sharing an emotional scene with her injured friend Toby in her aunt's kitchen, her father James Earl is at the store in town buying medical supplies for Toby and building his acquaintance with the old-maid storekeeper he will eventually marry. Because a third-person narrator does not have to be present for all the action, various aspects of the plot can gracefully develop simultaneously.

Third-person narration seems to provide abundant opportunity for richness of language in Bridgers's *All Together Now.* When Hazard Whitaker is introduced into the story, Bridgers uses verbs such as "crunched," "shuffled," "flailing," and "straining" (12) to create a unified image of the "kind of desperation in his movements" (12) that mirrors the anxious frustration in the fifty-two-year-old bachelor. Whereas the choice of words and the expanse of this image might seem inappropriately mature for the twelve-year-old protagonist in the story, they are effective and understandable coming from an objective third-person narrator.

It would seem possible to say in summary that third-person narration in young adult novels can sometimes enrich a reader's experience with a novel by allowing an author to be more creative, versatile, and thorough in characterization, plot development, and language than is possible when using first-person narration. Third-person narration often allows for fuller development of a larger number of characters than does first-person narration. The extra control over characterization that third-person narration provides enables authors to manipulate characterization with a versatility that can subtly enhance both plot development and theme. Finally, third-person narration also seems to release the language of the young adult novel from the limitation of an average adolescent expressive vocabulary and thus allows for more variety in modes of expression.

Novels that are enriched by third-person narration can have many practical benefits for adolescent students and their teachers. The in-depth characterization permitted by direct access to the minds of an assortment of characters provides the teenage student with many facets of the adolescent experience from which an aspect of particular personal interest might be identified. Moreover, because the many-faceted teenage protagonist can appeal to a wider range of student interests, it has a better chance of meeting teachers' instructional goals than a more limited character might. Third-person narration is also able to produce a greater variety of three dimensional characters that teachers can use to improve students' understanding (from several viewpoints) of people in different positions in life. The plot in a third-person novel can be more complex and thus more likely to hold the interest of young students who characteristically like action in their reading. Finally, the increased opportunity for richness of expression in the third-person novel can expose students to an element of the literary experience that English teachers are traditionally committed to and perennially troubled about neglecting when using young adult novels in their classes.

Certainly students' learning opportunities and teachers' assignment opportunities (in such areas as writing, discussion, role-playing, dramatics, etc.) are maximized by the extra dimensions third-person narration adds to the young adult novel. It would seem then appropriate for teachers who are concerned about offering their students a variety of young adult books from which they can get the most personal and literary benefit to include some third-person novels among their selections.

References

Bridgers, Sue Ellen. *All Together Now.* New York: Knopf, 1979.

———. *Home Before Dark.* New York: Knopf, 1976.

Cormier, Robert. *The Chocolate War.* Pantheon, 1974.

Hamner, Earl, Jr. *The Homecoming.* Avon, 1970.

Hinton, S. E. *That Was Then, This Is Now.* Dell, 1971.

Zindel, Paul. *Confessions of a Teenage Baboon.* Harper, 1977.

Part III Something about ALAN and *The ALAN Review*

A Brief History of ALAN

Ted Hipple, Executive Secretary, ALAN

When I stepped out into the bright sunlight from the darkness of the movie house, I had only two things on my mind: Paul Newman and a ride home.

With that sentence, S. E. Hinton began—and, as it happened, ended—*The Outsiders,* the 1967 novel generally credited with ushering in the modern age of adolescent literature, moving the field away from its romantic past toward its realistic present and future. Within a year or two, other novels appeared that reinforced Hinton's effort, works like *The Pigman,* by Paul Zindel, *Mr. and Mrs. Bo Jo Jones,* by Ann Head; and *The Contender,* by Robert Lipsyte. The "new" adolescent novel was alive and well and had an exciting future ahead of it.

At about that same time, changes were occurring in secondary school English classrooms. Where, before, *Silas Marner* had been an almost universal American reading experience, with virtually every high school sophomore being required to read the story of the miserly weaver, teachers now began instead to use young adult literature, accepting it for book reports and even using it for readings in common. Books by Hinton, Zindel, Robert Cormier, and Judy Blume were of such high quality, these teachers believed, that using them in English classrooms was completely justified. Also, these teachers' philosophy had changed somewhat, to a position that the "that" of teenage reading was more important than the "what." Better to produce a generation of readers nurtured on young adult literature, they thought, than to develop a hatred of reading by insisting on the classroom study of difficult classics that the students regarded as irrelevant to their own lives.

Also at about that same time, the National Council of Teachers of English adopted a new organizational structure called "assemblies." These were, in effect, special interest groups for people committed to a particular area of study, but they differed from other subgroups within NCTE in that one could be a member of an assembly without concurrently being a member of NCTE itself. Thus librarians, say, whose primary professional allegiance and dues monies might well go to the American Library Association, but who also had an interest in adolescent literature, could join an NCTE assembly devoted to the study of such literature. ALAN—the Assembly on Literature for Adolescents of the National Council of Teachers of English—was born of such a mix of K–12 level teachers, college professors of English and education, librarians, publishers, and authors.

The Founding of ALAN

It was in 1973, at the NCTE Annual Convention in Philadelphia, that ALAN began. This new NCTE structure—an assembly—had to have twenty-five people sign up and pay dues in order for it to become accepted by the parent organization. To Marguerite Archer must go much of the credit for rounding up these twenty-five folks and getting them to pay the initial dues: $1. These first twenty-five literary pioneers included some who have remained active in the organization throughout its entire twenty-four-year history, most notably people like Jerry Weiss, C. Anne Webb, Alleen Pace Nilsen, and Ken Donelson. Other early activists in the development of ALAN were Helen Painter, G. Robert Carlsen, Sheila Schwartz, Mary Sucher, Alethea Helbig, and Gerri LaRocque. They wanted an organization, open not only to NCTE members but also to others with an interest in young adult literature, that would promote that literature via a newsletter and activities that could be held in conjunction with the NCTE Annual Convention. They recognized in the works of an M. E. Kerr or a Robert Newton Peck that young adult literature was making signal leaps in quality from much of what had been published in the 1950s and 1960s. They knew, too, that it was making an impact on English classrooms in the schools.

A year later, at the NCTE Annual Convention in New Orleans, a constitution was adopted and ALAN was officially off and running in what has been a remarkably successful existence. That Convention also marked the beginnings of several activities that have continued and expanded over the years: a rotating roster of officers, a regular ALAN publication, an annual ALAN Breakfast, an annual ALAN Workshop, and an annual ALAN Award to be given to people in the field who have made outstanding contributions.

ALAN Officers

The ALAN Constitution called for an Executive Board composed of nine officers: a president, a president-elect, a past president, and nine directors, all of them elected by the membership of ALAN. Thus, the presidency is a three-year commitment, first as president-elect, then as president, then as past president; directors also serve for three years. ALAN has been fortunate in having a group of college and K–12 professors and teachers, librarians, publishers, and authors of young adult literature who have been willing to serve ALAN through their work on its Executive Board. The Executive Board meets formally each year at the NCTE Annual Convention in November and, for those able to attend it, informally at the NCTE

Spring Conference; additionally, there are mailings, e-mails, committee teleconferences, and other communications throughout the year among the board members.

As might be expected, the president assumes many of the major duties of ALAN: chairing the board meetings, assigning the committee members, and, most especially, choosing the speaker at the annual ALAN Breakfast and planning the ALAN Workshop. This last duty can be particularly daunting—the development of a two-day program of speeches, panels, and small-group sessions, though the workshop has been the beneficiary over the years of enormous cooperation from publishers willing to send YA authors to the workshop and provide books for the registrants. Following is a roster of the presidents of ALAN and the respective year of their presidency:

1973—Marguerite Archer
1974—M. Jerry Weiss
1975—Helen Painter
1976—Ted Hipple
1977—Sheila Schwartz
1978—Alleen Pace Nilsen
1979—Ken Donelson
1980—Hugh Agee
1981—Al Muller
1982—Robert C. Small, Jr.
1983—Mike Angelotti
1984—Richard Abrahamson
1985—Hazel Davis
1986—Don Gallo
1987—C. Anne Webb
1988—Barbara Samuels
1989—Patricia Kelly
1990—Betty Poe
1991—Kay Bushman
1992—Betty Carter
1993—Virginia Monseau
1994—Diana Mitchell
1995—Charlie Reed
1996—Gary Salvner
1997—Lois Stover
1998—Joan Kaywell
1999—Connie Zitlow

Virtually all of these presidents served an earlier stint on the Executive Board as a director.

In 1982, believing that ALAN needed a continuing presence to handle many of its affairs—for example, alerting officers to their responsibilities, working with the parent organization (NCTE) in the conduct of such business affairs as money management and membership recruitment and renewal, and coordinating the work of the ALAN Foundation—the Executive Board established the position of executive secretary. Since 1982, Ted Hipple has served as executive secretary.

The ALAN Review

Most members of professional organizations never get to national meetings; instead, they get their dues' worth via their association's publications. Such is the case with ALAN. For the majority of ALAN members, their principal relationship with the organization is through its journal. The history of *The ALAN Review,* as told by its former editors, follows this overview of ALAN. It is best to let them tell their stories of its genesis and changes.

The ALAN Breakfast

From 1975 onward, ALAN has invited members and friends to what has become known as the "ALAN Breakfast," held each November on the Saturday of the NCTE Award Convention. What began as a continental breakfast for about $2 has mushroomed to a full breakfast of eggs and sausage or crepes or French toast costing six to eight times that amount. What began as a gathering of the faithful, a meeting of about 100 aficionados, now regularly attracts some three or four hundred people who purchase breakfast tickets and another two or three hundred who come in after the food in order to hear the breakfast speaker. But cost and size aside, other elements of the breakfast have retained their historical roots. From the outset the breakfast was to include the installation of new officers (originally there was a formal swearing in, with candles held high and solemn oaths of office), the presentation of the ALAN Award, and the Breakfast Speaker.

This last—the speaker—is the usual reason for the large attendance; and, in fact, the speakers at the ALAN Breakfast represent a Hall of Fame listing of authors in the field of young adult literature: writers like Hinton, Zindel, and Cormier, and also Gary Paulsen, Sue Ellen Bridgers, Cynthia Voigt, Harry and Norma Fox Mazer (in a tandem performance), Chris Crutcher, and Richard Peck, among others. Occasionally, too, authors whose principal audiences were adult readers but who had large followings among adolescents addressed the assemblage: Michael Crichton and Jerzy Kozinski, for example. For many attendees at NCTE Annual Conventions, this is the one meal function they will not miss.

The ALAN Award

From its earliest times, the organization's Executive Board (its president, past president, president-elect, and nine directors) wanted to honor those who had made significant contributions to young adult literature, whether as author, publisher, librarian, teacher-scholar, or servant to the organization. The ALAN Award, presented at the annual breakfast, has been the method the Executive Board established for doing so almost twenty-five years ago. Rather than describe honorees and their considerable achievements, it may be fairest simply to provide a list of those who have received the ALAN Award; in some years the selection committee gave two awards:

1974—Stephen Judy and G. Robert Carlsen
1975—Margaret Edwards
1976—Margaret McElderry and Jerry Weiss
1977—Marguerite Archer
1978—Mary Sucher
1979—Gerri LaRocque
1980—Dwight Burton
1981—Sheila Schwartz
1982—Robert Cormier
1983—Ken Donelson
1984—Louise Rosenblatt
1985—Sue Ellen Bridgers
1986—Madeleine L'Engle
1987—Katherine Paterson and Alleen Pace Nilsen
1988—Ted Hipple
1989—Cynthia Voigt
1990—Richard Peck
1991—Gary Paulsen
1992—Don Gallo
1993—Chris Crutcher
1994—Walter Dean Myers
1995—Robert C. Small, Jr.
1996—Bill Morris
1997—Mildred Taylor
1998—S. E. Hinton

The ALAN Workshop

For decades, a major feature of any NCTE Annual Convention has been its workshops. Given calendar changes over the years at NCTE—for its first seventy years the Convention met during

Thanksgiving weekend—these workshops have either preceded or followed the Convention proper. For many conventiongoers, a principal major reason for attending the NCTE Annual Convention is a particular workshop, an extended period of one or two days devoted to a specific area—in ALAN's case, adolescent literature. Early on, the ALAN Workshops were popular, attracting some 150 or more people. Like the membership of ALAN as a whole, these two-day workshops have grown in size; now it is almost a given that each year the ALAN workshop will attract the maximum number acceptable: 300.

Each year a variety of activities at the workshop provides excitement aplenty for the participants. Usually there is a keynote speaker, often an academic focusing on trends and issues in adolescent literature (Bruce Appleby, Bob Small, Leila Christenbury, Steve Dunning, Ruth Cline, Alleen Pace Nilsen, Dwight Burton, among others), but also authors popular with adolescents have led off the workshop (S. E. Hinton, Ray Bradbury, Aidan Chambers). Other teachers and authors follow in individual talks, panels, debates, large- and small-group presentations, media-centered activities, writing sessions in which people try their own hand at adolescent fiction, presentations of research findings, and on and on. At coffee breaks and during meals, conversations sparked by the presentations give the workshop a life beyond the hotel meeting center. Rarely do participants leave unhappy.

And even if they do, they can carry along with them a bag—literally, during the past few years—of books they have been given at the workshop. It is important to note ALAN's indebtedness to publishers for their unwavering support. At their own expense, publishers send author after author to the workshop. Name someone from Arnold Adoff to Paul Zindel who writes for young adults, and the chances are good that that person has spoken at an ALAN Workshop, with his or her expenses being paid by a publisher. But beyond this valued support are the books given to ALAN each year to be distributed to participants at the workshop: the latest novel by Bette Greene, a volume of poetry by Mel Glenn, a a biography by Russell Freedman. And what is truly frosting on a rich cake, since 1981 the publishers have sponsored a wine and cheese party at the end of the first day of the workshop, at which participants can meet authors face to face and secure their autographs. It is one thing for a ninth-grade teacher from a small town in Indiana to be able to say when she returns to her classroom, "I heard Sue Ellen Bridgers speak at the ALAN Workshop." It is quite another to be able to add "and here is an autographed copy of *All Together Now.*"

The ALAN Foundation

Adolescent literature has been and will remain a field ripe for research. Before the mid-seventies, when what young adults read began to attract the attention of scholars, there was simply not much done in this field, perhaps a dissertation here or there or an occasional survey. And, certainly, until then there was little financial support for such research. In 1983, ALAN tried to expand scholarship in adolescent literature through its creation of the ALAN Foundation, monies that would go to support research in young adult literature. Each year members and nonmembers alike can submit requests for funding to the executive secretary of ALAN, who sends them on to a standing Foundation Committee made up of the five most recent past presidents. These past presidents study the merits of each request and independently say "yes" or "no," up to a level of $1,000. To date, approximately fifty proposals have been funded, representing a variety of topics: e.g., using recorded young adult literature with reluctant readers of print literature; studying the university-level young adult literature course; focusing on reader-response to adolescent novels in middle schools. Money to support the foundation comes from two sources—$1 from each member's dues (currently $15) and a portion of the royalties earned from the sale of books of young adult short stories edited by Don Gallo.

The history of ALAN, then, is really the history of books written for young adults, the authors of those books, the teachers who use them in school and college classrooms, and the librarians who stock them on their shelves. It is the history of publishers who send their authors and their authors' books to ALAN Workshops each year. It is the history of the founders of the organization, people like Marguerite Archer, C. Anne Webb, and Jerry Weiss, who had the foresight to anticipate the growth of young adult literature and to value having a vehicle—an association—both to study that growth and to help facilitate it. It is the history of the editors of *The ALAN Review,* who maintain the most direct link between the organization and its members. In some ways, too, it may be the continuing history of Ponyboy, who, in opening *The Outsiders,* unknowingly began a movement that went far beyond anything that he or his creator, S. E. Hinton, ever dreamed of, an organization known to everyone for whom young adult literature is important, an Assembly on Literature for Adolescents of the National Council of Teachers of English—ALAN.

43 The Beginnings of *The ALAN Review*

Alleen Pace Nilsen

ALAN was born at the 1973 NCTE Annual Convention in Philadelphia, in a hotel that was later to become famous not for being the birthplace of ALAN, but for being the birthplace of Legionnaires' disease. It has since been torn down, but both ALAN and Legionnaires' disease live on.

As documented elsewhere in this book, the organization grew rapidly. Marguerite Archer, founding president, sent out a two-page dittoed letter shortly after the Convention, and then in August of 1974, she sent out over 200 copies of a four-page mimeographed letter which she headed *News from ALAN* Vol. 1, No. 1. This publication was the real beginning of what is now *The ALAN Review*. It was filled with information about the upcoming Convention in New Orleans, at which ALAN had been given two program slots as well as a preconvention conference. Names sprinkled throughout the newsletter read like a who's who of scholars and writers of young adult literature. Among others they included Dorothy Briley, G. Robert Carlsen, John Conner, Thomas W. Downen, Sr. Jean Dummer, S. E. Hinton, Ted Hipple, Paul Janeczko, Norma Klein, Geraldine LaRocque, Katie Letcher Lyle, Faith Schullstrom, Sheila Schwartz, Lou Willet Stanek, and Jerry Weiss.

By the time of the business meeting in New Orleans, we had more than 200 members and were considering raising the dues. I said I would be happy to help out by doing a newsletter. At the time I had a new Ph.D. but only an adjunct position at Arizona State University, and so one of the first things I did after coming home from the Convention was go see my new friend Ken Donelson and convince him that he should be co-editor, so that we could mail the newsletter out under the bulk-rate permit of the ASU Department of English. My husband, Don, was a new faculty member in the same department, but I instinctively knew that I shouldn't tread on his privileges since he was untenured and was hired as a linguist rather than as a specialist in anything remotely related to adolescent literature. Nevertheless, a couple of years later, when Don started working with humor, Ken and I appointed him as ALAN Humor

Editor in what we clearly confessed was an "out-and-out case of nepotism."

We joked about finding a job for Ken's wife too, because one of the hardest things about editing *News from ALAN* was mailing it out, which we turned into a two-family affair. The four of us would gather around the Nilsen's dining-room table and, with the help of a bottle of wine, would collate, fold, and staple the newsletters and then glue on the labels. The catch was that to qualify for that wonderful bulk rate, we had to put everything in zip-code order. The labels were typed according to when people paid their dues, so sorting was always a major challenge, coming as it did at the end of the task when the wine was gone and our eyes were blurry. When I look back at the first few issues of *News from ALAN*, I'm truly embarrassed. It was desktop publishing in the days before photocopy machines and computers. Everything was done with a typewriter and rub-on letters—many of which were crooked—and a mimeograph machine. However, except for an overuse of the word *hopefully*, I'm not ashamed of the contents.

In 1975, after living in Arizona for two years and working at various part-time jobs, I was given a tenure-track position in the Department of Educational Technology and Library Science at Arizona State University, where I was to teach classes in literature for young readers. This was good for me, but it was even better for ALAN. My new department chair took one look at *News from ALAN*, Vol. 3, No. 1, which I thought was unusually attractive since the San Diego sailboat design from the 1975 NCTE Spring Conference announcement graced the front page. He failed to see the charm, especially when he came to a page on which a couple of the rub-on letters had fallen off and I had inked in replacements. He had seen the newsletter as part of my application materials, and the homemade look hadn't bothered him as long as the return address had been the Department of English. But now that it was the Department of Educational Technology and Library Science, he suggested I get myself downtown to the *Tempe Daily News* and see how much they would charge for professional printing. To my happy surprise, I found that if we submitted the material camera-ready and went to three issues a year instead of four, the printing costs would be affordable. My son, who was in a high school drafting class, designed the ALAN logo, changing the name to the *ALAN Newsletter*; my new department furnished a headline-making machine (at thirty-five cents per foot); a department colleague, Karen Tyler, joined Sheila Schwartz in rounding up book reviews. In these prephotocopy days, Karen had the good idea of limiting the typed reviews to the size of an index card and printing them on loose sheets so they could be clipped and filed. A local high school teacher,

Nel Ward, agreed to be our media editor, and we were off and running with what looked like an actual professional publication.

During the four years that Ken and I edited the *Newsletter,* there was always more to be published than we had room for. Preceding each workshop, we used considerable space to give a preview of what participants might expect, and then afterward we printed highlights from the various presenters. We usually gave the first page over to information about the winner of the ALAN Award.

Today, the Margaret A. Edwards Award is the most respected award in young adult literature. It is sponsored by the Young Adult Library Services Association and *School Library Journal,* and has been given to S. E. Hinton, Robert Cormier, Richard Peck, Lois Duncan, M. E. Kerr, Walter Dean Myers, and Judy Blume. But ALAN was ahead of the game. In 1975, we gave the ALAN Award to the real Margaret A. Edwards, thirteen years after her retirement from the Enoch Pratt Free Library in Baltimore, where she had established the concept of young adult librarianship. The cover and inside front page of the Winter 1975 *ALAN Newsletter* was given over to her gracious acceptance, which was delivered via the mail rather than in person because she didn't think it very practical to travel 5,000 miles to speak for five minutes. Besides, she had retired to a Maryland farm, where she was devoting herself to the breeding of Hereford cattle, and her new calves—Kojak, Bulldozer, Loverly, Bonnie, and Clyde—their fertile mothers, and her bull, Wilbur Mills, needed her.

By printing all of Edwards's speech, we were gradually edging toward the printing of articles. In that same issue, Ken and I were also brave enough to write our first critical editorial. We complained about the logistics of the ALAN Workshop in San Diego, to which more people were invited than could be accommodated as speakers and discussion leaders. We urged "those of us who had a turn on the speaker's platform in San Diego" to return next year to Chicago "and take a turn in the audience." We went on to say that "It isn't up to us to offer apologies to those people who went home this year either disappointed or offended, but at least we can offer our thanks. We did notice and we did appreciate" (Winter 1975, Vol. 3, No. 2).

With this issue, we also began printing dissertation abstracts and giving whole pages over to our media editor and our humor editor so that they could develop some sustained points rather than just make announcements. We had a "President's Page," and we reprinted "Best Book" lists, reported on censorship cases, and excerpted speeches from various meetings nationwide. In the Fall 1977 issue we got in trouble with New Yorkers because we headlined the front page with "ALAN Presents the Only Bargain in New York City." We were advertising $6 tickets to George Bernard Shaw's *St. Joan,* starring Lynn Redgrave. Jerry Weiss had arranged the special price for ALAN members. It was $3 less than the cost of the ALAN Breakfast, which at $9 we criticized as "admittedly no bargain," but we encouraged people to come anyway to hear Jerzy Kozinski speak and watch Sheila Schwartz inaugurated as president.

The last issue that Ken and I edited was Vol. 5, No. 2 (Winter 1978), in which we wrote:

> Over the last four years, we have seen the newsletter grow from a two-page ditto to sixteen pages of text plus four of reviews. We are pleased with its growth and even more pleased to be turning it over to the capable hands of Guy Ellis, who will undoubtedly take it in new directions in the course of his three-year term. (15)

And, as the cliché goes, "the rest is history."

The *ALAN Newsletter* and *The ALAN Review*, 1978–1984

W. Geiger Ellis

I think it's safe to say that my contribution to *The ALAN Review* was more entrepreneurial than intellectual. My spirit soared as I watched the growth of advertising, circulation, reviewers, and content. I was rewarded with a feeling of accomplishment and with a wealth of new and enriching professional relationships. How do I view those six years? There is no simple way to convey such an exhilarating experience, but I will offer this brief attempt, if my gender-sensitive audience will permit. I was a surrogate mother, entrusted with a healthy fetus and given a nurturing environment. I carried that living entity through various developmental stages and experienced its birth. Yes, with some difficulties and pain, but always with joy and satisfaction. I won't carry this metaphor too far, but I am certain that when I let go as editor, I felt the same sense of anticipation, anxiety, and pride as when my wife and I watched each of our four offspring venture forth from home. We knew they had had our best efforts, and we eagerly awaited news of their continued growth and accomplishment. So it has been with *The ALAN Review.*

My first involvement with our publication was writing "Clip-and-File" reviews while Alleen Nilsen and Ken Donelson were editing the newsletter. Before I knew it, Alleen expressed their desire to be relieved of the duties of producing the newsletter and asked if I had an interest in taking on that role. Having had some editorial background and fancying myself a better editor than a writer, I agreed and subsequently was installed by a vote of the ALAN Executive Board.

The immediate challenge was to maintain the quality and pedigree already established by the publication's founders. That meant, among other things, continuing some input from and about popular authors and the popular "Clip-and-File" reviews, which had been edited by Karen Tyler. I soon learned that the job also meant that publishers would be sending me more books than I had imagined were being published at the time. I had known that adolescent literature was a growing field, but that knowledge took on tangible meaning with the arrival of each case of newly published books.

The Grunt Work

Before getting too far into describing the content of our publication at that time, it is important to convey the nature of the task then set before the "editor." I use the term editor only because that was the official title; the job went far beyond what most editors of this or other NCTE publications normally have experienced. Oh, that I had only to edit, coordinate schedules, and communicate with reviewers and writers. The job at that time entailed everything from setting schedules to physically carrying the publication to the post office, not to mention arranging postal rates and sorting for mailing. Alleen and Ken had hinted at the task in their final issue, thanking others for their help with "the nitty gritty of folding, stapling, labeling, and mailing." Let's see if I can recall the various tasks in some sequence, although things never seemed to flow quite that smoothly.

Aside from working with reviewers, authors, copy, and all the correspondence entailed therein, there were the areas of production, circulation, promotion, advertising, and business management. Production included contracting a typesetting service after outgrowing the capacity of departmental secretaries. My newspaper experience and work with high school publications was invaluable throughout the processes of proofreading, layout organization, dummy pasting, and delivery to the printer. Circulation involved applying up to 2,000 labels, sorting by zip code, bundling by zip-code class, and delivering to the post office. The cases of journals were heavy and the stairs steep, I'll note. The production and mailing of ALAN election materials and conference promotions soon became part of the routine. Somewhere along the way paper stocks and fonts had to be selected, and graphic artists were led to produce an ALAN logo and our letterhead stationery.

Promotion overlapped circulation when it came to reminding members to renew and in maintaining the mailing list, which I did with Apple Post on the original Apple computer in our Mathematics Education Department. I soon had all the excuse I needed to buy two computers of my own during my tenure as editor. To expand our circulation, I secured mailing lists from other organizations and sent letters soliciting memberships/subscriptions. These lists were committed to my computer and worked to make any good mail-order business proud. Circulation expanded from approximately 400 to nearly 2,000. I attended various conferences, often with a publisher's support, to promote subscriptions among the memberships of other organizations and to generate more interest and support from publishers in the form of advertising and more books for review.

This brings me to advertising, a development necessary for the continued expansion of the journal. After establishing a rate structure, I started making a sales pitch to my contacts among the publishers. When you start talking money and advertising budgets, you have entered a new ballpark. After the first ad from Bantam in the fall of 1979, other publishers were more willing to follow their lead, as witnessed by Scott Foresman and Avon coming on board for the next issue. Soon there were many publishers, each with an advertising agency to be coordinated with our production schedule. The advent of advertising necessitated additional tasks—invoicing, collecting, bookkeeping, sending tear sheets, and negotiating the position of individual ads.

Duties More Editorial

Developing and overseeing the journal's content was stimulating. As the title new to our journal in 1979 indicates, reviews should be central to the publication. As mentioned earlier, the retention of "Clip-and-File" reviews was a must. I issued a call for volunteer reviewers and determined areas of interest for each. As books arrived from publishers, I scanned them to determine which would be reviewed. Generally, that meant including any, good or otherwise, by well-known authors and the most promising from relatively new writers. I felt that readers should either be told the good news of another book from a favorite author or be warned that the latest was not up to that author's customary standard. The best works of new writers needed to be given attention. Reviews of professional publications, such as new textbooks, were published in article format under the heading "The Bookshelf—In-Depth Reviews." Nonprint media relative to literature teaching were reviewed in article format under the heading "Beyond Books—Media for the Classroom," produced by Dan Ward.

Articles by and about authors were an important feature. Such articles had been included by my predecessors, and I made it a regular part of the journal, running from "Ten Questions to Ask about a Novel," by Richard Peck (Spring 1978), to "Writing for Adolescents: Pleasures and Problems," by Zibby Oneal (Winter 1984). Persuading authors to produce free articles was generally one of the more rewarding aspects of being editor. I must say that handling their manuscripts was quite an education. Most were so easy to work with and provided beautifully written pieces. Then there was the rarity, who gave me vastly increased respect for the editors of their novels. Occasionally there was an author interview that provided interesting and informative reading.

Professional articles about adolescent literature or its teaching were meant to be the mainstay, while reviews and author articles were viewed as features. In my first editorial, I was hungry for copy, calling for everything from abstracts and bibliographies to announcements and reports. Innocently I wrote, "Did I miss something? Send it anyway. My mailbox is large." That was to change as circulation expanded into thirteen countries and the journal grew in size. The first *ALAN Newsletter* issue (Spring 1978) of my editorship was twelve pages, including the covers. Two issues later (Winter 1979) the title had become *The ALAN Review* and ran to sixteen pages. One year later (Winter 1980) *TAR* had grown to thirty-two pages, covers not included. More important, we had instituted an Editorial Review Board, making *TAR* a refereed journal. From that issue onward, submitted articles were read and judged by members of this board, rather than that judgment being solely the editor's. My last issue (Winter 1984) ran to forty-eight pages, including eleven advertisements. It was the advertising that made possible the expansion, including a doubling of "Clip-and-File" reviews from sixteen to thirty-two, and improvements in paper stock and printing.

At each step in the expansion of the journal, Alleen Pace Nilsen was a vital supporting force, always offering encouragement and helping the ALAN Board of Directors understand the desirability of changes as they came. Closer to home, Hugh Agee provided moral support whenever my spirit sagged. The stable of reviewers consistently met deadlines with well-written reviews. In short, I was fortunate to have been where I was when I was. Opportunity was knocking; I opened the door and found a world of professional riches ready for the mining.

45 Editing *The ALAN Review*, 1984–1990: The Coming-of-Age Years

Arthea J. S. (Charlie) Reed

Ouida Sebestyen wrote the author article in the first issue of *The ALAN Review* that I edited (Vol. 11, No. 3 [Spring 1984]). In her article she expressed exactly what I was thinking and feeling as I was embarking on my new venture as editor of this young journal:

> Physically, having a book [or editing a journal] is a lot like having a baby. It looks easy until you try it. There's the same early mixture of apprehension and high hopes, the feeling of being burdened and blessed and happily scared. Later comes the struggle to share this tender new creation trustfully with the world.

The minute I finished reading the first author article I would edit (and that thought scared me to death), I penned a "love" letter to Ouida, thanking her for writing such a wonderful article and, more important, helping me put into words my feelings. It is amazing how clearly I remember those early days of my editorship—much more clearly than the latter days. I remember exactly where I was when I read Ouida's article; I know the title and author of every other article in that first issue; and I can even remember some of the books that were reviewed.

I vividly recall my own excitement and my own fears. My stomach muscles still tighten when I think of laying out that first issue and taking it to the printer. It had appeared so easy when I visited Guy Ellis in Athens, Georgia, just a few months earlier. Why was it so difficult now?

But, I also felt blessed. I was taking over a journal that was just entering its adolescence—it was only eleven years old. I would edit *The ALAN Review*, if all went well, through its middle school and high school years (Vols. 11–17). It was already a well-established and financially healthy publication; however, it was young enough that it had not become stodgy, stuck in its own traditions. It's personality was still emerging. What an opportunity! *The ALAN Review* was not mine: It belonged to ALAN and her members, an organization and people I had come respect. But, maybe, I could make the journal a vehicle that would help define literature for young adults and find a place for it among the already-established fields of adult and children's literature. This was my goal.

The same day I wrote to Ouida Sebestyen, I also wrote "The Back Door." At the end of each issue would appear my editorial column, and I'd call it "The Back Door," symbolic of where I became an inveterate reader—under the apple tree just outside the back door of my childhood home. I wanted *The ALAN Review* to have a voice—not my voice alone, but the collective voice of those of us who cared about adolescents and the books they read. I attempted to communicate these thoughts and goals in my first "Back Door" column. "I am concerned," I wrote, "that if those of us who know adolescents and their literature do not attempt to determine its value and its place, others will decide for us" (51).

As I reflect on the six years of the journal that I edited, I am most proud of the fact that *The ALAN Review* did become a forum for the ideas, issues, and concerns of teachers, librarians, professors, editors, and publishers. For the first three years of my editorship, readers, through letters sent to the "Readers React" column, both reacted to issues presented in *The ALAN Review* and brought up new issues as well. During those years, the journal was dynamic, exciting, and sometimes surprising. It was a vehicle for all the members of ALAN to discuss books, authors, curriculum, publishing, writing, reading, and common concerns. Between its covers, we examined and argued about the definition and place of adolescent literature.

Did we help define the literature and establish a place for it? Even now, I am not sure. Certainly, both the literature and the journal came of age, and growing up as an adolescent or an adolescent journal is not easy. During those years between 1984 and 1990, some of the best books ever written for adolescents were published. And in spite of the efforts of far too many censors, adolescent literature was incorporated into the curriculum, not as a distinct genre to be studied apart from other genres, but as literature to be studied along with other literatures. Literature written for young adult readers may not have found its own place but, instead, was included in the vast world of literature read by adolescents. Maybe this is where it belongs, just as the history of women needs to be included in all history courses, not just in women's history courses. But this is a philosophic argument.

Without a doubt, the membership of ALAN responded to the charge I gave them in my first column. Never once did I have too few good articles to publish or too few good books to review. The problem was selecting the best and most appropriate from the many excellent articles and books we received. Not only were the articles written by university faculty who *must* publish, they were also written by teachers, librarians, editors, publishers, authors, and even adolescents who had something important to say and could say it articulately. The books were reviewed not only by professors, teachers, and librarians, but also by parents.

In the second issue of my editorship (Vol. 12, No. 1 [Fall 1984]), the first "Readers React" column appeared. Several people responded to the concerns I had expressed about the place (or lack of place) of adolescent literature in the school and university curriculum. Others made suggestions for ways to make *The ALAN Review* more useful to classroom teachers; one requested help in finding books on a particular subject which would not be targets of censorship; still others offered congratulations. In the next issue of *The ALAN Review* (Vol. 12, No. 1 [Winter 1985]), the request for help was answered. A book was suggested, along with a positive way to avoid censorship while encouraging students to read censored books. Many readers responded to the results of a survey conducted by the National Endowment for the Humanities, reported in the previous issue, on works that should be included in a common literary heritage. The forum was active—readers were reading and responding.

By the Winter 1985 issue, we had received so many articles on Robert Cormier that it made sense to devote an entire issue (Vol. 12, No. 2) to his work and its place in the curriculum. The issue contained an article written by Cormier; several written about him; an excerpt from and a review of his then most recent book, *Beyond the Chocolate War;* two articles about Cormier's literary craft; and a discussion of how to use *After the First Death* in the classroom. The Cormier issue became the first of my editorship to be picked up by both ERIC and NCTE for distribution beyond the membership of ALAN.

More important, ALAN readers responded with enthusiasm. One even reported that her students "lined up to read those articles, finding much of interest there" (See Nugent, *The ALAN Review* 12.3 [Spring 1984]: 6). And Robert Cormier wrote of the issue:

> Although the issue focused on my writing, I think it did a service for all so-called Young Adult writers who are producing a genre that gives young people a special and relevant reading experience. (6)

In the Fall 1985 issue, a new column, edited by Ruth Cline and Elizabeth Poe, was introduced. "Now That You Asked . . ." was devoted to answering reader's questions about young adult literature. The goal of this column was to provide well-researched answers to the many readers who were writing to ask questions. I had become frustrated by the many important questions readers were writing to ask which *The ALAN Review* could not address in its present format. During the next fourteen issues, Ruth and Betty answered questions about our book selection process and review criteria; books with strong female protagonists; young adult books set in modern Europe and dealing with modern European history; realistic fiction "not entrenched . . . in personal tragedy"; humorous books; the best historic fiction; poetry appropriate for young adults; young adult literature to use in a British literature classes; and the appeal of Gary Paulsen, among other topics.

In the Winter 1986 (Vol. 13, No. 2) issue, a new organizational approach was developed. Themed issues provided the opportunity to feature numerous articles on the same genre, theme, or author. This was an organizational approach that appealed to me but did not encourage the variety that was an important goal of the journal. So, for the first time, a separate-section approach was used. ALAN Award recipient Sue Ellen Bridgers was featured (three articles) in an issue of *The ALAN Review* that included articles on many other topics. In fact, the lead author article was not by the featured author. In this case, the lead article was by gifted Canadian author Kevin Major.

As I reexamined the themed issues of *The ALAN Review,* I was reminded of a change I made that I would not make today. The final "Readers React" column appeared in Fall 1986 (Vol. 14, No. 1). I removed the column because of criticism from two influential ALAN members. These members felt that *The ALAN Review* had become too much personal opinion, including mine in "The Back Door" column, and not enough substance. This was not an unusual argument in academe. In fact, I could see their point. One of the goals of a journal such as *The ALAN Review* is to legitimatize the literature and, indeed, itself. Certainly, journals such as *The Horn Book* did this in the field of children's literature. My decision was a compromise. "Now That You Asked . . ." replaced the "Readers React" column. Its goal was to answer readers' questions, thereby providing a partial forum. I was still posing questions and concerns in "The Back Door," and contributors were responding to these in their articles. However, when I reread the original editorial I wrote in the Spring 1984 issue in preparation for this memoir, I recognized that the goal I had set for the next six years of *The ALAN Review* was to establish a forum for all members of ALAN to discuss the role and place of adolescent literature—not only in the hallowed halls of academe but also in public school classrooms, public and school libraries, in bookstores and publishing houses, and, most important, on the bookshelves of adolescent readers. Other editors could set as their goals the legitimization of the literature and *The ALAN Review.* I believe that the issues I edited after the Fall 1986 did not possess the same vitality as the earlier ones. Although some of the best articles appeared from 1987 through 1990, the readers were not as involved in the discussion of the role and place of young adult literature. I missed the forum *The ALAN Review* had begun to create—some of the voices had been silenced.

Ironically, it was in the Spring 1988 (Vol. 16, No. 3) issue that a new column, edited by M. Jerry Weiss, was introduced: "Censorship and the YA Book." In this column Jerry and other authors explored issues related to censorship of young adult books in schools and libraries. Clearly, the YA book had still not found its place. That column produced the submission of so many articles on the topic of censorship that a section of the Spring 1989 (Vol. 16, No. 3) issue was devoted to censorship and how to avoid it. In the Spring 1988 issue, the same one that introduced Jerry's column on censorship, "The Back Door" addressed the isolationism of U.S. young adult literature. Informal surveys I had conducted in Canada, Great Britain, and New Zealand led me to the realization that bookstores in other English-speaking countries stacked numerous young adult books by U.S. writers as well as their own writers, while U.S. bookstores had so few YA books by English-speaking writers from outside the U.S. that they could be counted on one hand.

As before, readers responded to this concern by submitting articles—so many, in fact, that a theme issue was developed. The Winter 1989 (Vol. 16, No. 2) issue, "Other Voices in YA Literature," featured articles about authors from other cultures, non-young adult characters in YA novels, and voices from the past.

It was through the words of Madeleine L'Engle, one of my favorite writers of all time, appearing in the Winter 1986 issue of *The ALAN Review,* that I came to understand the extent of my blessing. Listen to her words with me. And I do mean *listen.* When words are this eloquent, we must *hear* them:

> One of the more insidious forms of corruption is censorship, and I suspect that the current wave of censorship comes from a terror of leaving the old world and entering the new. Self-appointed censors are frantically and furtively trying to push books back into the old moralities of Elsie Dinsmore, where it was also possible for good Christians to keep slaves and not see any contradictions. Perhaps the pendulum has swung too far, but we must look for balance, not censorship.
>
> What an opportunity! This universe may be strange and frightening with its constantly accelerating change—the growth of technology is so rapid we can hardly keep up with it! But we are given opportunities to move with grace and vision, and we need to share this grace and this vision with the kids we teach. (3)

Censorship—resulting from the fear of rapid change—provides teachers, writers, and parents with an opportunity to influence adolescents through our positive interaction with them and our modeling of visionary behavior. Wow! Censorship may terrify us, but it allows us to teach through example—to be models of grace and vision. Certainly gifted writers of young adult books had done this. As a teacher and an editor I had had the same opportunity. Through the words of Madeleine L'Engle, I came to understand why editing *The ALAN Review* for six years was more blessed than it was burdened. My editorship of *The ALAN Review* had given voice to the shared vision of hundreds of individuals who care deeply about adolescents and the books they read. I had helped to establish a dialogue about the place and the role of literature written for adolescents. And for this opportunity, I am deeply grateful.

46 Four Years, Ten Issues, and 560 Pages: The Brief but Happy Life of an *ALAN Review* Co-editor

Leila Christenbury

With Robert Small, I served as co-editor of *The ALAN Review* from 1989 through 1992. Together, we published ten issues, beginning with Spring 1990 (Vol. 17, No. 3) and ending with Spring 1993 (Vol. 20, No. 3). Bob and I had succeeded former editor Arthea "Charlie" Reed, and after some discussion with the ALAN Board and Charlie herself, we undertook a number of significant changes in the journal and, further, as co-editors, established how we would split the duties between us.

Working Arrangements

Bob agreed to take care of the editorial office and to receive, acknowledge, and process all manuscripts. The physical typesetting, printing, and mailing of the journal would be done at his university and under his direction. I agreed to shepherd *The ALAN Review's* initial interior and cover redesign, the layout of each issue, and the soliciting, receipt of, and billing for all advertising.

Together, we decided on issue foci, acceptance or rejection of manuscripts, manuscript revisions, and together we edited and proofread all copy for each issue.

Bob believed strongly in using regular columns and column editors, and book reviews and other aspects of the profession were handled by people he had invited to work with *The ALAN Review:* Betty Poe, Ruth Cline, Karen Hartman, Don Kenney, Betty Carter, Jerry Weiss, and Kay Bushman.

Interior Redesign

Besides soliciting manuscripts and planning first issues, our first order of business was the redesign. The subject was of great importance to me, perhaps more so than might be assumed for an English teacher. My interest, however, came honestly: Before Bob and I became co-editors, I had left teaching and been a full-time writer and publications editor for some years. Although I had missed the classroom during that time away from teaching, the experience had given me an appetite for—and some ideas about—graphic design.

Tucker Conley, a graphic designer who had done work for my Virginia state teaching organization and its academic journal and newsletter, was given the task—on a highly limited budget—of transforming the look of *The ALAN Review.* Using ideas from Bob and me and his own experience with journals (among other publications, he had worked on *Infantry* magazine and *National Geographic*), Tucker did a clean sweep of *The ALAN Review,* including:

- a four-color cover which would appear every issue, with space in the center for the different article names and authors;
- a full redesign of the journal interior, including new paper stock, and, for graphics, a new typeface, column grid, footers and headers (publication information located at the bottom or top of each page), and repetition of the ALAN logo to signal the start of each article;
- a new table of contents and column design.

The Cover

For me, one of the most creative parts of *The ALAN Review* redesign was the cover. After initial conversations, what we kept returning to was a cover that would reflect YA lit and teen interests. The idea caught on: We "saw" a type of teenage collage or still life which would be snappy, fun, and colorful. But how, with virtually no money to vary a cover, could we assemble, photograph, and print such a collage issue after issue? Tucker came up with the idea of doing a four-color cover and printing a huge, multiyear supply, leaving white space in the center for the changing table of contents as well as *The ALAN Review* title, volume, number, season, and year.

Deciding what would be on the cover took some time. Bob and I talked; we consulted younger friends. Tucker and the cover photographer, Lee Brauer, then gathered the elements. The pens, cell phone, calculator, and dictionary came from Lee's desk in his studio; the Walkman® and rock music tape came from a teen friend. The copies of *The Outsiders, Bridge to Terabithia, The Chocolate War,* and *Roll of Thunder, Hear My Cry* came from my bookshelf at home. When the book covers didn't look sufficiently used, I "distressed" them on the spot. The change—pennies, quarters, and dimes—were a last-minute addition and came from Tucker's pocket. The homework "assignment" and the names and phone numbers on the sticky note were also done at the last minute. The tennis shoe was bought at a local store.

As I stood in the photographer's huge studio, in the center of which was emerging the still life of *The ALAN Review* cover, I watched Tucker study the arrangement and shift the elements, including what seemed to me to be an endless fiddling with the tennis shoe laces and the Walkman wires. The photograph had to be precise: Not only did it have to be pleasing, colorful, and representative of YA lit and teen life, and appealing to the readership of *The ALAN Review,* the photo itself needed to have enough blank space so that the type would always fit in the center. As a final complication, shadows were also needed to give the photo depth, but those shadows could not reach far into the center white space.

After three hours and numerous adjustments, changes, refinements, light checks, and test photos, the last shot was taken. The cover of *The ALAN Review,* a cover which would last for four years and ten issues, was in the can.

The Bad Stuff: Hours on the Phone and the Goofs

Once the cover was shot, the interior redesign set, and the manuscripts received and acknowledged, it was time for the work of editing and proofreading. Bob and I liked each other and had worked well together first as teacher and student and then as colleagues. But nothing could prepare us for our marathon sessions on the phone when we would—sentence by sentence, paragraph by paragraph, article by article—compare our proofreading notes from the edited copy and the galley proofs.

Thus Bob and I were the only safety nets for typos, transposed words and phrases, misinformation, incomplete references, missing words, inadvertently deleted lines, and even lost paragraphs. Sometimes, in the last stages of proofing for a single issue, we would have two conversations across two days, each of which would last between two to three hours apiece. It was tedious and difficult and, while it was important work, neither of us really enjoyed going back and forth and back and forth over the articles and the bibliographies and the details.

And, of course, there were the goofs. Every editor has a list of things that, regardless of checking and rechecking and re-rechecking, show up in the final, printed copy. Bob and I agonized over these, but my experience is that no printed piece is wholly "clean," and the two of us left behind us some indications that we were, indeed, fallible.

A flagrantly wrong return address for NCTE, printed on thousands of copies, showed up inexplicably on one issue, and the fall *ALAN Review,* which contained crucial information on the upcoming ALAN Workshop in November, always seemed to be the one issue that was printed or mailed perilously close to the deadline. One spring issue arrived in readers' mailboxes in the dead of summer: This article is not long enough to list what went wrong, went wrong repeatedly, and why that issue was not anywhere near ready to mail on time. It was Murphy's Law incarnate.

While we acknowledged our occasional errors and deadline difficulties in our "From the Editors" page, we also had a few spectacular "saves": One of our favorite and most generous authors, Norma Fox Mazer, was listed in galley proofs in two separate years for two different issues first as *Normal* Fox Mazer and then as Norma *Fax* Mazer. Mercifully, Bob and I caught both of these and could only rejoice that *Normal Fax Mazer* never saw print.

Reader Reaction

With the changes we had initiated, Bob and I knew that we needed to find out readers' reactions, so after two issues, we created, distributed, and compiled results for a readership survey. We printed readers' reactions on the back cover of the Winter 1991 issue.

One survey finding which struck us was the loyalty of *The ALAN Review* readers; one respondent, reacting to the new appearance, cautioned: "Don't let the slick look get too intimidating [so] that it would discourage teacher authors from submitting." We didn't notice any change in submissions, but the advice was important.

Layout

In my years of nonteaching life, I had done the layout of another magazine I had edited, using the now defunct method of literally cutting, arranging, and affixing waxed galley proofs to design "boards" (this process is now done mostly by computer). With *The ALAN Review,* it was the same familiar procedure, and multiple galley proofs of an issue would take about two days to cut up and place. I did this on my dining-room table and in my kitchen, and I would spend the days moving from room to room to room, making this giant adult jigsaw puzzle come out right. I also had a reviewer and teacher: Tucker Conley would go over the "spreads" (the two facing pages) and make sure that the design was logical and pleasing. If it wasn't, the pages would be redone.

Using the type for the articles, the "pullout" quotations, the article art, and the photos for ads, I would first sketch a rough map or storyboard indicating how long each article and its attendant art would be and where it would fall within the journal. Then I would wax the back of the galleys, cut them up, and place them and the appropriate photos and drawings as my storyboard plan indicated.

My acquisition of two curious kittens did not speed up this process, but they were remarkably restrained about jumping into the paper strips and the enticing piles of art. Mostly, they stayed on the steps of the hall staircase where they could peer down into the dining room and assess my progress. My aging cocker spaniel, however, loved to eat paper, and if a strip of type floated off the table onto the floor, it was a quick snack, wax and all.

Advertising

Besides reader support and subscriptions, the lifeblood of *The ALAN Review* was advertising. The publishers of young adult literature would use advertising agencies who, in turn, would request space in a specific issue and send finished art for the ads. My contact was mostly with those advertising representatives, the overwhelming majority of whom were located in New York City and who often, in our monthly phone conversations, sounded hurried and overworked. Yet they were professional, quick, and often funny on the phone; I had somewhat of a personal relationship with one rep who had moved to New York City from rural North Carolina. We traded southern accents and a few friendly conversations.

By and large the representatives were always grateful for consistent extensions of deadlines and, when one ad was sent for publication with a misspelling in the title of a Shakespearean play, the rep was enormously relieved when we held up production and waited for a corrected ad.

Content

Every editor has a private list of favorite articles (and, in addition, a store of stories which, alas, cannot be shared in print). Despite a few roll-your-eye moments, however, Bob and I were most lucky with what appeared in our years as co-editors of *The ALAN Review.* I also have a personal list of honorees:

> **Most Generous Authors:** Norma Fox Mazer and Julian Thompson shared their work quickly and without much fanfare or fuss; the then-reclusive Judy Blume allowed her interview with Lanny van Allen to be printed.
>
> **Funniest Article:** Hands down to Susan Beth Pfeffer for "Basic Rules of Teenage Life," points of which I still make with my students and points of which still make me laugh.
>
> **Most Impressive Research:** For me, it is a three-way tie among Lois Stover for her fine work on cultural diversity, Don Kenney's comprehensive reference article, and Suzanne Reid's fine essay on wood, music, and sailing in the novels of Cynthia Voigt.
>
> **Favorite Focus Issue:** I call this a tie between the one on Sue Ellen Bridgers (Bob's idea) and the one on science fiction (my idea).
>
> **Favorite Amateur Art:** The use of my beloved niece Erica's art for the Richard Peck piece is my favorite. Peck wrote "Notes for the Refrigerator Door," and Erica's drawing had been on *my* refrigerator door

for some time. I thought it might be useful for *The ALAN Review* and, in retrospect, it was a perfect match.

Articles Which Made Me Think: Margaret Mackey's "Derek's Story" presented a vivid and painful account of a young person who can read—but, like *Bartleby the Scrivener,* would prefer not to—and Rickey Cotten's excellent piece on religion is still important to my thinking.

Most Consistently Creative Act: Kay Bushman's fine quizzes on YA lit appeared in each issue, and when deadlines came, she never let us down. I loved the quizzes—and so did readers.

Favorite Guest-Edited Issue: There was only one, but it was very good. The topic was censorship, and it was submitted by John Simmons. Bob and I were proud to print it.

Best Use of the Inside Back Cover: We had no ad for the inside back cover of the censorship issue, and a quotation from John Milton's *Areopagitica* seemed appropriate. I picked a favorite passage, and Tucker Conley worked graphic magic so that Milton's words would fill the entire page handsomely.

Most Startling Moment: While I had read some of Madeleine L'Engle's work, nothing prepared me for her *ALAN Review* interview with Gary D. Schmidt. In that interview L'Engle, clearly and unmistakably, cited her belief that she could, as a child, walk above the ground. I had read the galleys numerous times, looking for the usual typos and problems, but it was only at the last proofing stage when I *really* read it, and I was stunned.

During one of our proofreading sessions, I just had to ask. The conversation, reproduced from memory, does not sound very erudite, but it's pretty much how it went:

> "Uh, Bob, just one last thing."
> "Sure. What is it?"
> "Did you actually read *that part* of the L'Engle article?"
> "What part?"
> "You know, *that part.*"
> "You mean the part where she recalls being able to walk above the ground?"
> "Yes. Wow—do you think she really means it?"
> "Yes. I think she really does."
> "Wow."

L'Engle had written that her theory was that "whatever Jesus did while he was alive we should be able to do too, but we've forgotten." Interviewer Schmidt had prompted: "You speak of this also in one of your journals, when you recall that you used to be able to float down stairs as a very young child," and L'Engle had cheerfully responded: "Oh yes,and I cannot tell you how many letters I have had that say, 'I've never dared tell anybody this before. I did it too'" (Winter 1991, Vol. 18, No. 2, pp. 13–14). Wow.

Conclusion

In 1993, I cast my eye upon another journal with many more issues per year and many more complications. I thought I might submit a proposal for the editorship and that it might be time to bow out of *The ALAN Review.* Pat Kelly, who knew adolescent literature, editing, and journals thoroughly, was willing to be co-editor. In spring 1993, I left *The ALAN Review,* and Pat Kelly joined Bob as co-editor. I was named editor of the *English Journal,* and I began plans for my next adventure.

It had been four years, ten issues, and 560 pages of edited, proofed, and printed copy of *The ALAN Review.* It had been an exciting cover and interior redesign, days of layout with waxed galley proofs, hours of advertising negotiations with people from New York City, and much time editing and proofing. It was, as they say in car racing, a great ride.

And to this day, I still wonder about Madeleine L'Engle and floating above the ground.

Index

Abby, My Love (Irwin), 140, 145
Abortion, 244
Absalom, Absalom! (Faulkner), 171, 268
Achébe, Chínua, 255
Adoff, Arnold, 158
Adolescent homophobia in novels of Bette Greene, 105–12
Adolescent novels. *See* Young adult novels
Adolescent readers, 181
  Appalachian literature and, 270–80
  complex history of, 289–95
Adolescent relationships
  friendship as first level of, 87–88
  gaining freedom of choice in, 90–91
  pairing off, as second level of, 88–90
  Paul Zindel on, 86–104
Adult midlife crisis in adolescent novels, 229–35
Adult reading, difference between teenage reading and, 223–24
After the First Death (Cormier), 3, 9, 12–13, 16, 17, 222, 340
ALAN (Assembly on Literature for Adolescents of the National Council of Teachers of English)
  founding of, 324
  history of, 323–29
  officers of, 324–26
  workshops of, 327–28
ALAN Award, 327
ALAN Breakfast, 326
ALAN Foundation, 329
ALAN Newsletter, 334–37
ALAN Review, 326, 334–37, 344–50
  advertising in, 348
  beginnings of, 330–33
  content in, 348–49
  cover of, 345–46
  editing, 338–43
  interior redesign of, 345
  layout of, 347–48
  problems with, 346–47
  reader reaction to, 347
  working arrangements in, 344
Alcott, Louisa May, 181–82, 186
All Together Now (Bridgers), 29, 30–31, 35, 43, 46–48, 47, 49, 268, 318, 328
American Library Association, 323
Ames, Cherry, 207
The Amethyst Ring (O'Dell), 219, 220
Amulets Against the Dragon Forces (Zindel), 78
Anaya, Rudolfo, 217
Anchor Man (Jackson), 246
. . . And Now Miguel (Krumgold), 217
Appalachian literature and adolescent readers, 270–80
Appel, Alfred, 171
Appleby, Bruce, 328
Archer, Marguerite, 324, 329, 330
  as recipient of ALAN Award, 327
Archetypal Patterns of Women's Fiction (Pratt), 175–76
Areo, Agbo, 250, 253
Are You in the House Alone? (Peck), 122–25
Arilla Sun Down (Hamilton), 156, 239, 240, 281, 282
Armstrong, William, 267
Arnold, Matthew, 250
Asher, Sandy, 181–98
  on advice for aspiring writers, 197
  on censorship, 197–98
  on dealing with frustration, 197
  on encouraging reading in children, 198
  on importance of attitude, 193
  influences on, 195
  and problem with realism, 188–92
  on promoting writing in young people, 194–95
  on providing of mechanical corrections, 193–94
  reasons for writing, 181–87
  on reasons for writing for young adults, 195–96
  on suggested activities for students, 194
  on writing, reading, and teaching, 193–98
  writing habits of, 194, 196
As I Lay Dying (Faulkner), 174
Assembly on Literature for Adolescents of the National Council of Teachers of English. *See* ALAN (Assembly on Literature for Adolescents of the National Council of Teachers of English)
Avon Books, 205
  Flare imprint in, 206
Award books, student complaints about, 95

B. Dalton Bookstores, 204–5, 206
Babin, Pierre, 244
Bach, Alice, 230, 231
Baldwin, James, 239
A Ballad for Hogskin Hill (Forman), 266, 272, 273–74, 275–76
Ballad of the Sad Cafe (McCullers), 267
A Band of Angels (Thompson), 207
Bantam Books, 201–3, 223
  Sweet Dreams imprint of, 206, 222, 223
Barnard, Laurel, 201–3
Beautiful Girl (Ogilvie), 223, 225, 226, 227
Because We Are (Walter), 240
A Begonia for Miss Applebaum (Zindel), 68, 77
Beloved (Morrison), 168
Bettelheim, Bruno, 191–92
Beyond The Chocolate War (Cormier), 3, 6, 340
Bibliographies, 305–9
Bibliotherapy, adolescent literature as, 237
Biographical indexes and dictionaries, 310–13
The Bird's Eye Gazette (Zindel), 56
Black English, 165–66
The Black Pearl (O'Dell), 220
Blacks, image of working, in young adult novels, 236–41

Bless Me, Ultima (Anaya), 217
Bless the Beasts and Children (Swarthout), 222
Blume, Judy, 195, 314, 323
  as recipient of Edwards award, 332
Bonham, Frank, 257
Book review sources, 303–5
Books, student complaints about award, 95
Borland, Hal, 281
Bradbury, Ray, 328
Bradford, Richard, 217–18
Brancato, Robin, 206, 257–58
Brauer, Lee, 345
The Bride Price (Emecheta), 250, 251, 252, 253–54, 255
Bridgers, Sue Ellen, 23–52, 206, 286
  advice for aspiring writers, 44
  advice to teachers of writing, 43–44
  attention to place in, 46
  on being labeled young adult author, 43
  characteristics of, as writer, 35–36
  characters in novels of, 29–30, 31–32, 33–34, 35–36, 39–40, 42
  commitment of, as writer, 33
  dilemma of, in writing about life, 32–33
  emphasis on memory, 46–48, 50
  encouragement of writing, 36–37
  family ties in books of, 41–42
  on family values, 48
  first interest of, in writing, 36
  first-person narration in books of, 314
  importance of oral tradition to, 37
  influences on, 36–37, 38
  language in books of, 48–51, 318
  literary analysis of novels of, 51
  multidimensional women in novels of, 37
  novels of, 23–28, 29–34, 45–51
  as recipient of ALAN Award, 327
  role of mothers in novels of, 37–38
  small-town rural way of life in books of, 40
  as Southern writer, 45–51, 266, 269
  subjects written about by, 23–28, 29–34
  success of, as young adult writer, 55, 326, 328, 341, 348
  third-person naration in books of, 318
  work habits of, 42–43
  on writing fiction, 35–44
A Bridge to Terabithia (Paterson), 287–88
Briley, Dorothy, 330
Bring to a Boil and Separate (Irwin), 135, 145
Brontë sisters, 168
Brooks, Bruce, 208–9
Buddy movies, 185
The Bumblebee Flies Anyway (Cormier), 9, 13–14, 16–17
Burch, Robert, 270
Burton, Dwight, 265, 328
  as recipient of ALAN Award, 327
Bushman, Kay, 344, 349
Butler, Beverly, 281

Cabell, George Branch, 168
California Girl (Quin-Harkin), 223, 227
The Captive (O'Dell), 219–20
Carlota (O'Dell), 220
Carlsen, G. Robert, 229, 270, 324, 330
  as recipient of ALAN Award, 327
Carter, Betty, 344
The Castle in the Sea (O'Dell), 218–19
The Cat Ate My Gymsuit (Danziger), 234, 256, 258
Censorship, 342–43
The Ceremony of Innocence (Forman), 244
Chambers, Aidan, 328
Characters
  in novels of Bette Greene, 96
  in novels of Paul Zindel, 84
  in novels of Robert Cormier, 3, 4, 5, 14, 17–18, 19
  in novels of S. E. Hinton, 315
  in novels of Sue Ellen Bridgers, 29–30, 31–32, 33–34, 35–36, 39–40, 42
  in novels of Virginia Hamilton, 163, 164, 167
Chekhov, Anton, 6
Childress, Alice, 222, 259
The Chocolate War (Cormier), 3, 4–6, 7, 8–9, 10, 11, 13, 16, 17, 84, 120, 222, 260, 286, 288, 317
Christenbury, Leila, 328, 344–50
Christianity in American adolescent realistic fiction, 242–49
Clark, Walter Van Tilburg, 18, 19
Classmates by Request (Colman), 246
Cleaver, Bill, 222, 266, 272, 277–78
Cleaver, Vera, 222, 266, 272, 277–78
Clifton, Lucille, 236
Cline, Ruth, 328, 340–41, 344
Cole, Brock, 209
Collaborative writing for young adults, 129–44
Colored ethnic fiction, 145–52
Confessions of a Teenage Baboon (Zindel), 79, 80, 81, 83, 85, 315–16
Conley, Tucker, 345, 347, 349
Conner, John, 330
Conrad, Pam, 209
The Contender (Lipsyte), 323
Cooder Cutlass (Frank), 210
Corky and the Brothers Cool (Petersen), 218
Cormier, Robert, 3–20, 260, 286
  autobiographical stories of, 8
  characters in novels of, 3, 4, 5, 14, 17–18, 19, 317, 326
  death as theme in novels, 10
  emotions of, 4
  extremism in novels of, 12
  hope in novels of, 9–10
  influences on, 10–11
  listing of phone number in book, 12
  literary approach of, 18
  novels of, as catharsis, 8–9
  on parental manipulation of children in novels of, 12–13
  pessimistic view of, 9, 13, 15–20
  as recipient of ALAN Award, 327
  as recipient of Edwards Award, 332
  responses to books of, 13–14
  socioliterary context of novels, 15
  struggle between individuals and institutions in novels of, 16–17
  telephone interview with, 8–14
  on writing sequels, 3–7
  as young adult writer, 14, 208, 222, 323
A Country of Strangers (Richter), 281, 282–83
Crichton, Michael, 326
Critical sources, 300–303
Crook, Beverly Courtney, 272, 274–75
The Crow's Nest (Zindel), 56
Cruisin' for a Bruisin' (Rosen), 122
Crutcher, Chris, 326
  as recipient of ALAN Award, 327

Daly, Maureen, 207
Danziger, Paula, 230, 234, 256, 257
Daughters of the Law (Asher), 183
A Day No Pigs Would Die (Peck), 212, 244
Death
  portrayal of, in relationship to Christianity, 244
  as theme in novels of Robert Cormier, 10
Deaver, Julie Reece, 210
Desk 15 (Irwin), 146
DeVoto, Bernard, 20
Dick, Philip K., 289, 290
Dickens, Charles, 123, 168, 204
Dickinson, Emily, 66
Dinky Hocker Shoots Smack, 232–33
Director! (Areo), 250, 251, 253, 255
Directories and handbooks, 309–10
The Disappearance (Guy), 239
Donelson, Ken, 16, 18, 324, 330, 334
  as recipient of ALAN Award, 327
Donovan, John, 222, 314
Don't Look and It Won't Hurt (Peck), 117–18
Downen, Thomas W., Sr., 330
The Drowning of Stephan Jones (Greene), 101, 103, 104, 105–6, 108–12
Dummer, Jean, 330
Duncan, Lois, 16, 18, 258–59
as recipient of Edwards Award, 332
Dunning, Steve, 328
Dykeman, Wilma, 28

Edgar Allan (Neufeld), 246
Edith Jackson (Guy), 239
Edwards, Margaret
  as recipient of ALAN Award, 327
  Margaret A. Edwards Award, 332
The Effect of Gamma Rays on Man-in-the-Moon Marigolds (Zindel), 55, 62, 67, 71, 72, 73, 76, 78
Eight Plus One (Cormier), 8
Ellis, Guy, 338
Ellison, Ralph, 168
Emecheta, Buchi, 250, 253–54
Everything Is Not Enough (Asher), 183

Fabiano, Ted, 102
Fair Annie of Old Mule Hollow (Crook), 272, 273, 274–75
Faith and the Adolescent (Babin), 244
Family values in Southern literature, 48
Far From the Madding Crowd (Hardy), 253
Fast Sam, Cool Clyde and Stuff (Myers), 239
Father Figure (Peck), 244
Faulkner, William, 174
  Gothic novels of, 171
  influence of, on Virginia Hamilton, 168
  as Southern author, 45, 264, 265, 266, 268
The Feathered Serpent (O'Dell), 219–20
Feiwel, Jean, 203–7
Fiction, definition of serious, 182
Fiedler, Leslie, 168
Finney, Barbara, 258
First Love books, 222
First-person narration, 314–16
Flare (imprint), 205
Flaubert, 123
Flowers for Lisa, 223
Fogarty (Neville), 245
Forman, Jack Jacob, 68
Forman, James, 266, 272, 273–74, 275–76
Forster, E. M., 252
The Fourteenth Cadillac (Jackson), 237–38
Frank, Elizabeth, 210
Freedom of choice, gaining, as level in adolescent relationship, 90–91
The Friends (Guy), 244, 260
Friendship as first level of adolescent relationship, 87–88

Gallo, Don, 329
  as recipient of ALAN Award, 327
Gide, Andre, 96
Gilman, Charlotte, 173
Girl in the Rough, 223
A Girl Named Wendy (Butler), 281, 282
The Girls of Huntington House (Elfman), 244
Gitlin, Todd, 201–3
Glenn, Mel, 328
The Goats (Cole), 209
God Tale, 155
Gone with the Wind (Mitchell), 207, 263
The Good Earth (Buck), 207
Gothic and grotesque effects in Virginia Hamilton's fiction, 168–78
Graham, Lorenz, 236, 237, 238, 239, 265
Great Expectations (Dickens), 292
Greene, Bette, 95–112
  adolescent homophobia in novels of, 105–12
  characters of, 96
  first-person narration in books of, 314
  on realness in books, 95–104
  writing habits of, 96
Greene, Graham, influence of, on Robert Cormier, 11
Greenfield, Eloise, 236
The Grounding of Group 6 (Thompson), 205
Growing Up in a Hurry (Madison), 122
Guy, Rosa, 236, 237, 260

Hadley, Lee, on collaborative writing for young adults, 129–44
Half Nelson, Full Nelson (Stone), 210
Hall, Lynn, 212–13, 214
Hamilton, Virginia, 155–78, 239
  adolescence of, 158–67
  and Black English, 165–66
  characters of, 157, 163, 164, 167
  gothic and grotesque effects in fiction of, 168–78
  on identity crises, 281
  as imagemaker, 236
  influences on, 168
  and problem of national illiteracy, 165
  reasons for writing for youth, 155
  recognition of, as young adult writer, 266
  success of, as young adult writer, 162–63
Hamner, Earl, Jr., 314, 317–18
Hard Times (Dickens), 123
Hardy, Thomas, 253
HarperCollins Junior Books, 207–8
Harry and Hortense at Hormone High (Zindel), 56–66, 76
Hartman, Karen, 344
Havighurst, Robert, 236
Hawthorne, 123
Head, Ann, 323
Heads You Win, Tails I Lose (Holland), 257, 258
The Heart Is a Lonely Hunter, 267
Heilman, Robert, 45
Heins, Ethel, 202

Helbig, Alethea, 324
Hemingway, Ernest, 96
  influence of
    on Robert Cormier, 10
    on Sue Ellen Bridgers, 38
Hentoff, Nat, 261
Here at the Scenic-Vu Motel (Wyss), 210
A Hero Ain't Nothin' But a Sandwich (Childress), 222, 259, 262
Herriott, James, 28
Hill, Robert B., 238
Hinton, S. E., 329
  characters of, 315
  first-person narration in books of, 314
  as recipient of ALAN Award, 327
  as recipient of Edwards Award, 332
  success of, as young adult writer, 208, 323, 326, 328, 330
Hipple, Ted, 326, 330
  as recipient of ALAN Award, 327
Hispanics in young adult literature, 217–20
Holland, Isabelle, 222, 257, 258
Home Before Dark (Bridgers), 29, 30, 35, 37, 40, 42, 43, 46, 244, 266, 267, 268, 286, 318
The Homecoming (Hamner), 317–18
Homophobia. *See* Adolescent homophobia
Honeybunch and Jake (Irwin), 151
The Honorable Prison (Becerra de Jenkins), 220
Hoops (Myers), 239
The Hopeful Lovers (Areo), 250, 253, 254, 255
The Horn Book, 35, 341
House Made of Dawn (Momaday), 281, 283
The House of Dies Drear (Hamilton), 166, 169–71, 176
The House of Fifers (Caudill), 245
Huckleberry Finn (Twain), 291–92
Hunter, Kristin, 238

I Am the Cheese (Cormier), 6, 8, 9, 11–12, 16, 17, 84, 222
I Be Somebody (Irwin), 133
Idealism, 20
Identity, search for, in adolescent and Native American literature, 281–88
If Beal Street Could Talk (Baldwin), 239
If I Love You Am I Trapped Forever? (Kerr), 118
I Heard the Owl Call My Name (Craven), 246
Ike, Chukwuemeka, 250
I Never Loved Your Mind (Zindel), 79, 82, 83, 90–91
Intelligent entertainment, 203
Invisible Man (Ellison), 168
Irwin, Ann, on collaborative writing for young adults, 129–44
Irwin, Hadley, 129–52
  on collaborative writing for young adults, 129–44
  as writer of colored ethnic fiction, 145–52
Is That You, Miss Blue? (Kerr), 231–32, 257
It's Not What You Expect (Klein), 234–35

Jackson, Jesse, 237–38
Jacob Have I Loved (Paterson), 244, 245
Janeczko, Paul, 330
Judy, Stephen, as recipient of ALAN Award, 327
The Jungle (Sinclair), 123
Junius Over Far (Hamilton), 162–63, 178
Justice and Her Brothers (Hamilton), 240
Just Like Jenny (Asher), 183, 186

Kate Herself, 223
Kelly, Pat, 350
Kenney, Don, 344, 348
Kermode, Frank, 250
Kerr, M. E., 118, 257
  on identity crisis, 230, 231–32, 235, 324
  as recipient of Edwards Award, 332
  success of, as young adult writer, 208, 222
Killing Mr. Griffin (Duncan), 258–59, 260
Kim/Kimi (Irwin), 133, 145
King, Stephen, 291
The King's Fifth (O'Dell), 220
Klein, Norma, 206, 230, 234–35, 330
Klevin, Jill Ross, 223
Kozinski, Jerzy, 326
Kriney, Marilyn, 207–8
Krumgold, Joseph, 217

Language
  Black English as, 165–66
  in Southern literature, 46, 48–51, 267, 318
LaRocque, Geraldine, 324, 330
LaRocque, Gerri, as recipient of ALAN Award, 327
The Late Great Me (Scoppettone), 233, 234
Laurie's Song, 223
Lawson, Lewis, 45
Lazar, Irving "Swifty," 97
The Leaving (Hall), 212–13, 214, 215
Lee, Harper, 266, 268
Lee, Mildred, 272
L'Engle, Madeleine, 342, 349, 350
  as recipient of ALAN Award, 327
Lessons in Love (West), 238
Lester, Julius, 236
Let the Circle Be Unbroken (Taylor), 237
Levinson, Daniel, 229, 230
Lewis, Matthew Gregory, 168
A Light in the Forest (Richter), 283
The Lilith Summer (Irwin), 145
Lions in the Way (Rodman), 265–66
Lipsyte, Robert, 208, 222, 323
Listen for the Fig Tree (Mathis), 239
"Listen To The Voice In Your Head" (Adoff), 158
Literary South, 264–65
A Little Love(Hamilton), 162, 163–64, 165, 178
Little Sister, 223
Little Women (Alcott), 181–82, 195
Lord of the Flies (Golding), 120
Love Is a Missing Person (Kerr), 235
Ludell and Willie (Wilkinson), 238, 245, 266
Ludell (Wilkinson), 266
Lukens, Rebecca J., 251
Lyle, Katie Letcher, 266, 330

Mackey, Margaret, 349
Madame Bovary (Flaubert), 123
Madison, Winifred, 122
Maggie (Breck), 246
The Magical Adventures of Pretty Pearl (Hamilton), 177
Major, Kevin, 341
Malin, Irving, 171

Mame, 67
Mansfield, Katherine, 289
The Man Without a Face (Holland), 222, 257–58, 258
Maria's Lovers, 67
Marked By Fire (Thomas), 205–6, 238
Mathis, Sharon Bell, 236, 239
May I Cross Your Golden River? (Dixon), 244
Mazer, Harry, 205
  success of, as young adult writer, 208, 222, 326
Mazer, Norma Fox, 205, 347, 348
  success of, as young adult writer, 208, 222, 326
M.C. Higgins the Great (Hamilton), 156, 176, 266
McCullers, Carson, as southern writer, 264, 265, 266, 267, 268
McElderry, Margaret, 135
  as recipient of ALAN Award, 327
McKay, Robert, 259
McLeod, Justin, 258
Means, 266
The Meat in the Sandwich (Bach), 231, 232
The Member of the Wedding (McCullers), 120
Memory, emphasis on, in Southern fiction, 45–48
Midnight Hour Encores (Brooks), 208, 209
Miller, Jim Wayne, 271
Milton, John, 349
Missing Pieces (Asher), 183
Moby Dick (Melville), 292
Moccasin Trail (McGray), 245
Momaday, N. Scott, 281
Moon and Me (Irwin), 135–36, 145
Morning Is a Long Time Coming (Greene), 244
Morris, Bill, as recipient of ALAN Award, 327
Morrison, Toni, 168
The Moved Outers (Means), 244, 245, 246
The Moves Make the Man (Brooks), 208
Mr. and Mrs. Bo Jo Jones (Head), 244, 323
My Darling, My Hamburger (Zindel), 79, 82, 83, 89–90, 122, 244
Myers, Walter Dean, 236, 238
  as recipient of ALAN Award, 327
  as recipient of Edwards Award, 332
The Mystery of Drear House (Hamilton), 166, 169–71

Naira Power (Emecheta), 250, 253
National Council of Teachers of English, 323
New American Gothic (Malin), 171
New Boy in Town, 223
Nigerian youth literature, 250–55
Nilsen, Alleen Pace, 18, 324, 328, 334
  as recipient of ALAN Award, 327
The Nitty Gritty (Bonham), 257
Nixon, Richard, 97
North Town (Graham), 238, 239, 246
Notes for Another Life (Bridgers), 31–32, 37, 38, 42, 48
Novels. *See also* Southern novels; Young adult novels
  questions to ask about, 120–21

O'Connor, Flannery, 168, 265, 266, 267
O'Dell, Scott, 218, 219, 220
Ogilvie, Elisabeth, 223
Oguntoye, Jide, 250
The Old Man and the Sea (Hemingway), 286
Orphans of the Wind (Haugaard), 245
The Outsiders (Hinton), 323, 329
The Ox-Bow Incident (Clark), 18, 19

P.S. I Love You, 223, 227
Painter, Helen, 324
Pairing off as level in adolescent relationship, 88–90
Palmer, Eustace, 252
Parallel culture literature, 164
Pardon Me, You're Stepping on My Eyeball (Zindel), 62, 79, 80, 81, 82- 83, 85
Paterson, Katherine
  characters of, 287–88
  as recipient of ALAN Award, 327
  as Southern writer, 266, 269
  success of, as young adult writer, 208
Paulsen, Gary, 219, 326, 341
  as recipient of ALAN Award, 327
Peck, Richard, 115–25, 348
  concern over lowering of reading level, 116
  decision to leave teaching and become writer, 115
  on directing books toward adolescents, 116–17
  first-person narration in novels of, 314
  on perfect young adult novel, 117
  on questions to ask about novel, 120–21
  as recipient of ALAN Award, 327
  as recipient of Edwards Award, 332
  success of, as young adult writer, 208, 324, 326
Peck, Robert Newton, 212, 222
The People Could Fly (Hamilton), 166
The People Therein (Lee), 267, 272, 273, 276–77
Permanent Connections (Bridgers), 36, 50–51
Pessimistic view of Robert Cormier, 15–20
Petersen, P. J., 218
Pfeffer, Susan Beth, 348
The Pigman's Legacy (Zindel), 79, 81, 83, 85
The Pigman (Zindel), 67, 68, 69–71, 72, 73, 76, 82, 83, 87, 88, 201–2, 323
Pines, Nancy, 223
The Pistachio Prescription (Danziger), 257
Place, in Southern novel, 45, 46
Plain Girl (Sorenson), 246
The Planet of Junior Brown (Hamilton), 171–78, 239
Plato, 98
Please Let Me In, 223
Plot in Southern novels, 268
Poe, Edgar Allan, 168, 175
Poe, Elizabeth, 340–41, 344
The Popularity Plan (Vernon), 223, 225
Porter, Katherine Ann, 268
Poverty South, 263–64
Power, Jane, 203
Prairie Songs (Conrad), 209
Pratt, Annis, 175–76
Price, Reynolds, 38
Pride and Prejudice (Austen), 207
Princess Amy, 223
Problem novel, 207–8
Professional reading and general sources, 298–300
Protherough, Robert, 292

Queenie Peavy? (Burch), 270–71
Quin-Harkin, Janet, 223

Radcliffe, Ann, 168
Rawls, Wilson, 266
Realism, problem with, 188–92
The Redneck Poacher's Son (Wallin), 212–13, 214–15
Red Sky at Morning (Bradford), 217–18
Reference and bibliographical sources, 297–313
Reid, Suzanne, 348
Reit, Ann, 222
Return to South Town (Graham), 237, 240
Richter, Conrad, 281
River of the Wolves (Meader), 246
The Rock and the Willow (Lee), 245
Rodman, Bella, 265–66
Roll of Thunder, Hear My Cry (Taylor), 259, 266, 267, 268
Romantic South, 263
Rosen, Winifred, 122
Rosenblatt, Louise, as recipient of ALAN Award, 327
Royster, Vermont, 224
Rubin, Louis, 45
Ruby (Guy), 237
Runaway Train, 67
Rural themes in young people's books, 211–15

Salinger, J. D., 195
Santiago (Clark), 244, 246
Sanctuary (Faulkner), 171
Sara Will (Bridgers), 36, 48–51
Saroyan, William, influence of, on Robert Cormier, 10
Say Goodnight, Gracie (Deaver), 210
The Scarlet Letter (Hawthorne), 123
Schmidt, Gary D., 349
Scholastic, Inc., 203–7, 206
  Wildfire Imprint in, 206, 222
Schools, place of young adult literature in, 67
Schullstrom, Faith, 330
Schwartz, Sheila, 229, 324, 330, 333
  as recipient of ALAN Award, 327
Scoppettone, Sandra, 230, 233
A Season of Dreams (Appel), 171
The Seasons of Man's Life (Levinson), 230
Sebestyen, Ouida, 338, 339
Sentries (Paulsen), 219
A Separate Peace (Knowles), 19
Sequels, writing, 3–7
Serenade, 223
Setting in Southern novels, 267–68
Sexual relationships, 244
Sheehy, Gail, 229, 230–31, 233–34
Shuttered Windows (Means), 265, 266
Silas Marner (Eliot), 323
Simmons, John, 349
Simon and Schuster, 223
Simpson, Lewis, 45
Sims, Rudine, 236
Sinclair, Upton, 123
The Sixties, Years of Hope, Days of Rage (Gitlin), 201–2
The Slave Dancer (Fox), 266, 267
Small, Robert, 240, 328, 344
  as recipient of ALAN Award, 327
Social protest in young adult fiction, 122–25
Something About the Author, 41
The Soul Brothers and Sister Lou (Hunter), 238, 240, 244
The Sound and the Fury (Faulkner), 171
Sounder (Armstrong), 267
Southern novels, 45–51
  concern with clash of traditional values in, 46
  family values in, 48
  language in, 46, 48–51, 267
  place in, 45, 46
  plot in, 268
  setting in, 267–68
  for young adults, 263–69
Southern Renaissance, emergence of, as literary phenomenon, 45
South Town (Graham), 245, 246, 265
The Spanish Smile (O'Dell), 218
A Spy in Williamsburg (Lawrence), 245
Stanek, Lou Willet, 330
Starfire Hardcover Books, 202–3
A Star for the Latecomer (Zindel), 79, 81, 83, 85
Steinbeck, John, influence of, on Sue Ellen Bridgers, 38
Stokely, Wilma Dykeman, 271, 274
Stolz, Mary, 207
Stone, Bruce, 210
Strawberry Girl (Lenski), 244
Stuart, Jesse, 264
Stub, a College Romance (Bro), 244
Sucher, Mary, 324
  as recipient of ALAN Award, 327
Su-Mei's Golden Year (Bro), 246
Summer of My German Soldier (Greene), 106–7
Summer Smith Begins (Asher), 183
Swarthout, Glendon, 222
Sweet Dreams (imprint), 222, 223
Sweet Valley High, 206
Sweet Whispers, Brother Rush (Hamilton), 162, 171–78

Taking Terri Mueller (Mazer), 205
Tate, Allen, 45
Taylor, Mildred, 236, 237, 259, 266, 269
  as recipient of ALAN Award, 327
Tchudi, Stephen, 202
Teacher, image of, in adolescent fiction, 256–62
Teenage Heartbreak Blues (Adoff), 158
Teenage novels. *See* Young adult novels
Teen romances, 206
  success of, 222–28
Telephone interview with Robert Cormier, 8–14
That's My Girl (Klevin), 223, 225, 226, 227
That Was Then, This Is Now (Hinton), 315
Things Are Seldom As They Seem (Asher), 184
Third-person narration, 314–19
This School Is Driving Me Crazy (Hentoff), 261
Thomas, Joyce Carol, 205–6, 238
Thompson, Julian, 205, 207, 348
Thomson, Jack, 292–93
Thoreau, Henry David, 98
The Time Ago Tales of Jahdu (Hamilton), 177
Toads for Supper (Ike), 250, 253, 254
Tolliver (Means), 246
Too Cold for Comfort (Oguntoye), 250, 251–52, 254, 255
Traditional values, concern with clash of, in Southern literature, 46
Tree of Freedom (Caudill), 245
Trial Valley (Cleaver and Cleaver), 266, 272, 277–78
The Troublemaker (McKay), 259, 261
Tunes for a Small Harmonica (Wersba), 259–60

Twain, Mark, 20
Tyler, Anne, 38
Tyler, Karen, 334

The Undertaker's Gone Bananas (Zindel), 55, 80
Up the Sand Box, 67

Vernon, Rosemary, 223
View of audience, 9
Viva, Chicano (Bonham), 219
Voigt, Cynthia, 326, 348
  as recipient of ALAN Award, 327

Waldenbooks, 205, 206
Walker, Mildred, 212–13
Wallin, Luke, 212–13, 214–15
Walpole, Horace, 168
Walter, Mildred, 240
Warren, Robert Penn, 268
We Are Mesquakie, We Are One (Irwin), 145, 146
Weaver, Gordon, 45
Webb, C. Anne, 324, 329
Webster, Jean, 207
Weinstein, Else, 68
Weiss, Jerry, 324, 329, 330, 342–43, 344
  as recipient of ALAN Award, 327
Welch, Jack, 271
Weller, Jack E., 272
Welty, Eudora, 28, 30, 38, 45, 168, 266
Wersba, Barbara, 222, 259–60
West, Tracy, 238
What About Grandma? (Irwin), 145
When the Legends Die (Borland), 281, 283
Where the Lilies Bloom (Cleaver and Cleaver), 244, 266, 272, 274, 277–78
Where the Red Ferns Grow (Rawls), 266
White, Ellen, 206
A White Romance (Hamilton), 164
Whole-class reading experiences, 286–87
Whose Town? (Graham), 239
Wilderness Bride (Johnson), 245
Wildfire (imprint), 206, 222
Wild in the World (Donovan), 222
Wilkinson, Brenda, 236, 238, 266
Willie Bea and the Time the Martians Landed (Hamilton), 162
Willow Hill (Whitney), 246
Winning (Brancato), 257–58
Winter Wheat (Walker), 212–13, 215
Wishing Star, 222
The Witch of Blackbird Pond (Speare), 244–45
Wolfe, Thomas
  influence of, on Robert Cormier, 10
  as Southern author, 264, 268
Would You Settle for Improbable? (Petersen), 218
Writers
  advice to aspiring, 197
  demands made on, 96
  problems with reality, 97
Writing
  collaborative, 129–44
  sequels, 3–7
Wyss, Thelma Hatch, 210

The Yellow Wall Paper (Gilman), 173
Yep, Laurence, 208
Yesterday's People (Weller), 272
Young adult novels
  adult midlife crisis in, 229–35
  characteristics of, 15–16
  characters in, 17–18
  Christianity in American, 242–49
  considerations in teaching, 285–88
  differences between adult reading and, 223–24
  distinguishing features of, 117–18
  evolution of, 204
  Hispanics in, 217–20
  image of teacher in, 256–62
  image of working Blacks in, 236–41
  impact on value system, 181–82
  longevity of great, 201–2
  place of, in schools, 67
  publisher's view of past 20 years of, 201–10
  purpose of, 181
  rural themes in, 211–15
  search for identity in, 281–88
  separation of, from children's books in bookstores, 204–5
  social protest in, 122–25
  South in recent, 45–51, 263–69
  successful authors in, 68, 208, 222, 323, 326, 328
  success of Paul Zindel in, 68
  touchstones in Nigerian, 250–55
Young adults
  collaborative writing for, 129–44
  reasons for reading, 181
The Young Landlords (Myers), 238

Zindel, Paul, 55–92, 201–2, 323
  adolescent relationships through eyes of, 86–104
  burden of guilt in, 81–82
  characters of, 56–57, 58–59, 84
  childhood of, 83–84
  description of inside of, 73–76
  emotional truth in novels of, 69–70
  first-person narration in novels of, 314, 315–16
  humor of, 85
  irony in, 82
  success of, as young adult writer, 68, 70–71, 74, 208, 326
  themes of, 80–82
  timeless elements in books of, 70
  writing of
    as anecdotal, 56, 57
    as senseless junk, 55

Editors

Patricia P. Kelly is professor of English education and director of the Center for Teacher Education at Virginia Tech. She is a former president of ALAN and a former co-editor of *The ALAN Review.* She has also been the director of the Southwest Virginia Writing Project since its beginning in 1979. Her publications about young adult literature frequently center on gender issues, for example "Gender Issues and the Young Adult Novel" in *Reading Their World,* "Reading from a Female Perspective" in *Adolescent Literature as a Complement to the Classics I,* and "Transitional Novels for Readers of Teen Romances" in *The ALAN Review.* Her critical analyses of works by young adult authors include those of Margaret Mahy, Joan Lowery Nixon, Sue Ellen Bridgers, Kathryn Lasky, and Rosa Guy.

Robert C. Small Jr. is dean of the College of Education and Human Development and professor of educational studies at Radford University. He has served as president of ALAN, co-editor of *The ALAN Review,* chair of the Conference on English Education, and co-editor of *The Virginia English Bulletin.* He chaired the NCTE Teacher Preparation and Certification Committee that prepared the current *Guidelines for the Preparation of Teachers of English Language Arts.* He has written about young adult literature for *English Journal, Adolescent Literature as a Complement to the Classics, Volumes I and II,* and *The ALAN Review* and has presented on literature for young readers at the conferences of NCTE, ALA, IRA, and a number of conferences of state NCTE affiliates. His works on censorship have appeared in publications of IRA, NCTE, ALA, several books, and NCTE affiliate journals.

This book was typeset in Palatino and Avant Garde
by Precision Graphics of Champaign, Illinois.
Typefaces used on the cover and spine were Garamond and Univers.
The book was printed on White 50-lb. Finch Opaque by Versa Press, Inc.